Michael Collins.

AGAINST ALL ODDS

Best wishes

Cai

AGAINST ALL ODDS

GAI WATERHOUSE:
WOMAN IN A MAN'S WORLD

Kevin Perkins

MACMILLAN

First published 1996 in Macmillan by Pan Macmillan Australia Pty Limited
St Martins Tower, 31 Market Street, Sydney

National Library of Australia
cataloguing-in-publication data:

Perkins, Kevin.
Against all odds: the Gai Waterhouse story.

ISBN 0 7329 0857 4.

1. Waterhouse, Gai. 2. Women in horse racing – Australia –
Biography. 3. Racehorse trainers – Australia – Biography.
I. Title.

798.40092

Typeset in 12/14 Caslon 540 by Post Typesetters
Printed in Australia by Griffin Paperbacks

CONTENTS

PROLOGUE		VII
ONE	Blue Ribbon Scallywag	I
TWO	The Rebel	8
THREE	The Good Times	28
FOUR	Looked the Part but . . .	43
FIVE	Foxes and Leprechauns	53
SIX	The Beautiful People	64
SEVEN	Still Known as TJ's Girl	83
EIGHT	Moment of Decision	91
NINE	Meeting Robbie Waterhouse	101
TEN	Wife, Motherhood, Career	116
ELEVEN	The Fine Cotton Farce	127
TWELVE	Triumph and Disaster	150
THIRTEEN	The Smith Family Splits	165
FOURTEEN	Sexual Assumptions	184
FIFTEEN	The Great Dilemma	198
SIXTEEN	Equal Opportunity and Below the Belt	211
SEVENTEEN	Brutality in the Court of Appeal	234
EIGHTEEN	Gai in Her Own Right	256
NINETEEN	The Waterhouse Legacy for Women	277
TWENTY	The 'Lady' Trainer	286
TWENTY-ONE	The Last Hurdle	300
TWENTY-TWO	The Eye Has It	318
TWENTY-THREE	The Breakthrough	329
TWENTY-FOUR	Those Hats, That Gear	342
TWENTY-FIVE	Pharaoh's Purse and Other Riches	356
TWENTY-SIX	Gai Time	375
TWENTY-SEVEN	Her Cup Runneth Over, Almost . . .	394
EPILOGUE		414

Gai Waterhouse gunned her blue BMW station wagon through the traffic on the Sydney Harbour Bridge on her way to Randwick in the eastern suburbs.

She wanted to be inside the committee room of the Australian Jockey Club by midday to hear a decision vital to her future.

The glamorous, articulate, heiress-daughter of legendary racehorse trainer TJ Smith, Gai was a household name in Australia following a classic struggle against the powerful Jockey Club.

As a woman in a man's world she had fought and won against their discrimination in a public brawl that lasted almost three years.

They had denied her the right to become a thoroughbred trainer because she was married to a man barred from race-courses throughout the world.

Her husband, former dashing young bookmaker Robbie Waterhouse, of the famous Waterhouse gambling dynasty, had been warned off because of his role in a notorious racing scam known as the Fine Cotton ring-in affair.

Gai had already endured the heartache of his banishment for 11 years, receiving many kicks in the teeth from racing officialdom.

Recently in a highly publicised hearing, her husband had applied to have his ban lifted. The finding was to be handed down in a few minutes.

At midday she drove into the AJC parking lot and sprinted

for the committee room inside the main building of racing's headquarters.

Gai burst into the hearing, taking in the scene quickly as she glanced around to find her husband.

She was too late. The decision had just been announced.

CHAPTER ONE

BLUE RIBBON SCALLYWAG

Le Cordon Bleu in London is not normally the haunt of struggling young actors, especially newcomers from Sydney.

After all, it represents everything that is excellent in the art of culinary experience.

Like its sister cookery schools in Paris and Tokyo, the London school is intended for chefs and cooks who wish to attain the highest level of training to create classic French cuisine.

The style, like the Eiffel Tower, is a symbol of Paris itself. It is an institution that has gradually encircled the world from the time the first Cordon Bleu cookery class opened in Paris in the Palais Royal in 1896, with the new technology of electricity installed for the occasion.

However, the tradition goes back even further.

As *aficionados* of food would know, the title comes from France's most exclusive order of knights, the *Ordre du Saint Esprit*, in the 16th century. When members met, including royals, they always wore blue ribbons called *Cordon-bleus*. The dinners following the order's ceremonial knees-up were legendary.

In the 18th century the term was extended to anyone who excelled in a particular field. Soon it was applied to fine cooks.

I

Some insist this was because final year students at Madame de Maintenon's famous school of learning at Saint Cyr wore a blue sash in the cooking class. Others say good cooks took this cue from a one-liner delivered by Louis XV to his mistress Madame du Barry, who tired of his boorish remarks that only men made great chefs.

The lady, obviously one of history's early feminists, had a female cook secretly prepare his meal and when the king asked 'who is the new man doing your cooking?' Madame du Barry coolly answered, 'It's a woman cook, Your Majesty.'

To which Louis replied, probably with an appreciative but refined belch, 'She deserves nothing less than the *Cordon-bleu*.'

Since 1895 the term has been synonymous with the pleasures of the table, when a Parisian woman, Marthe Distrel, began publishing a weekly journal of recipes and advice called *La Cuisinière Cordon-bleu*, which led a year later to the first Cordon Bleu school in Paris, affiliating in time with a similar school in London and later, in 1996, in Sydney.

The London Cordon Bleu cookery school became a state-of-the-art gourmet centre in the 1980s when it was bought by Andre Cointreau, a descendant of two French families noted for their fine tipple, the Cointreaus and Remy-Martins. Cointreau updated the school with the best equipment and teaching chefs.

But in 1975 it was still blueblood territory for aspiring chefs from around the world, a strange place indeed to find Gai Smith, a young Sydney woman then in her early 20s.

Gai couldn't cook to save her life, nor would she try. The reason she was in London was to pursue her ambition of becoming an actress. She was following the traditional route of bright young women from the Antipodes, making the grand tour of Europe before settling in London where greater opportunities supposedly beckoned.

She had joined up in London with an old school friend, Barbara Oswald, from the Rose Bay Convent of the Sacred

Heart in Sydney. Barbara, from an affluent family, was simply enjoying an extended holiday doing the sights of Europe.

Gai had just spent three months touring the United States and Europe with her mother, Valerie, and famous father, Tommy Smith, known throughout the racing world as TJ.

One of the world's wealthiest and most successful thoroughbred horse trainers, Tommy at that time was well on the way to winning a record 33 consecutive training premierships in the tough and competitive Sydney racing scene.

And if that wasn't spectacular enough, he would come back once more to make it an astonishing 34 premierships.

He had promised his only daughter he would treat her to the trip as a kind of finishing school if she graduated from the University of New South Wales.

Tommy had passionately asked Gai to complete her tertiary education. He did not want to see her struggle without an education as he had, unable to read and write except for the rudiments he taught himself by studying form guides when he battled to survive as an impoverished young stablehand in Melbourne, running SP bets to keep the wolf from the door.

Tommy's rise from penniless obscurity to legendary status was one of the most inspiring of Australian rags-to-riches sagas, a true romance of the turf.

Born into the harsh environment of the hot, red plains of south-western New South Wales, he attended a tiny bush school for only a few months. From the time he was a child he worked like a man for a boozy, cruel and demanding father.

Young Tommy left home in his early teens to seek fame and fortune as a jockey and pulled himself up to superstar status in a different field by sheer ability and determination. He was also helped by a touch of genius in his eye for a horse.

Gai was proud of his achievements and always tried to please him. As a child she loved being with Tommy around the horses at his Tulloch Lodge stables in Sydney, riding her ponies at the adjacent Randwick racecourse while he trained the thoroughbreds in the cool pre-dawn air, or dashing off to the yearling sales with him from the age of six, always asking questions.

From an early age, though, it was the stage that appealed to her.

She had a rich imagination, seeing herself as a star of the future with her name gleaming in lights. Her mother encouraged her towards the arts. Valerie Smith was a talented singer; as was her sister Belle whose son Anthony had performed at the *Lido*, the Las Vegas-style cabaret in Paris.

To prepare herself for the footlights Gai took drama lessons after school, and on finishing high school auditioned for a place in the National Institute of Dramatic Art (NIDA), Australia's leading acting school.

Her parents didn't expect her to be chosen because it was difficult for inexperienced performers to meet the entry standard, but Gai was thrilled to receive a letter of acceptance.

Valerie was pleased too but Tommy said he didn't want her going to NIDA. 'It's full of poofters and I don't want you mixing with them,' he said in his direct, laconic way. Dispirited, she wrote to NIDA expressing her regret that she could not accept.

So although not a dedicated student she went to university. But she was restless and unable to settle down to study, and wanted to leave at the end of her second year.

Tommy intervened. 'I haven't worked hard all these years to get the pack off your back and put shoes on your feet to hear you say you're not going to finish,' he declared.

Gai knuckled down and finished her arts degree, majoring in drama, which covered only a theoretical course in acting, stage building and directing.

The graduation over, they had completed the promised three months' tour, and Gai's parents had returned to Australia. Now Gai was staying on abroad hoping to begin her career.

Meanwhile as she waited hopefully for acting roles to turn up, she enrolled in London's Cordon Bleu school with her friend, Barbara Oswald.

It was all the more extraordinary because Gai had never cooked even the simplest fare. Therein lies the tale.

Gai and Barbara shared a little mews house near Harrods, minding it for a woman friend in Ireland. By arrangement Barbara did all the cooking, Gai the cleaning and washing up.

They joined the demonstration school in Marylebone Lane, sitting apart and pretending they didn't know each other.

The first dish to be cooked was eggs mimosa, basically boiled eggs topped with yellow mayonnaise and served with salad or hors d'oeuvre. The female instructor explained the recipe and asked if there were any questions.

'Yes,' said Gai brightly, 'how do you boil an egg?'

Everybody laughed, thinking she was trying to be funny. She was, but at the same time she wasn't kidding.

Two or three other recipes were demonstrated, then the students formed into several groups and cooked the dishes under supervision.

At the end of the night a limited number of dishes were to be auctioned among the students for extremely moderate amounts.

This was the moment Gai and Barbara were waiting for. Their hands shot up first with bids.

Each night as the recipes were rolled out, through chicken paprika, beef tournedos, Scottish salmon, steak Mirabeau, veal escalopes with Milaise sauce, lamb noisettes with garlic cream sauce and a whole range of delicious desserts, Gai and Barbara repeated the process—snapping up a generous share of the tasty meals before most of the other students made up their minds.

Not wishing to make it too obvious they bid for only two courses, but decided to add some of the desserts to their list. Secretly they joined forces with a friendly Canadian doing the opera circuit and, without letting on that he was talking to them, he completed their bids.

In this way they made sure they had entrees, main courses and desserts. At the end of the night they invited the Canadian to their mews and all three would sit down to enjoy the traditional tucker, talking and laughing at their cheek into the early hours.

The teachers woke up to the young Australian scallywags after a few weeks, and waved admonishing fingers at them on behalf of other students, among them toffee-nosed chefs from London hotels who had been too slow off the mark.

But Gai had fun and relished the cheap dinners while the good times lasted. And at least she learned how to boil eggs.

The idea was hers. Money was short while she waited for work and she was determined not only to survive, but to live in style, although feeling the pinch financially.

She had been shown the good things in life from an early age and wanted to continue enjoying them, despite her changed circumstances.

It also showed several other things about the young Gai Smith.

Suddenly on her own after living in the secure and comfortable environment that went with a privileged background, she was enterprising and resourceful when put to the test.

And she was determined to be her own person.

The manner of parting from her parents had brought Gai to a crossroads in her young life. She was searching deeply within herself to discover her identity and establish her future.

She loved her parents dearly, respected and admired them and normally would not think of defying their authority. But her quandary was that she wanted to act and was not receiving any encouragement from them.

Gai was exhilarated by their long tour, taking in the sights, shopping, visiting stud farms, attending some of the classic race meetings of Europe and Ireland like the English, Irish and French Derbies, meeting rich and powerful people whose friendship was opened up by the great camaraderie that racing engenders across the world.

In London Tommy Smith had introduced Gai to wealthy and influential Sourin Vanian, who stood a large number of stallions in England. Sourin also had racing interests in Paris where he lived most of the time. He said to Tommy, 'If your daughter stays in Europe, I'll look after her for you.'

Gai had hinted at wanting to stay on for a few weeks after the tour finished. But Tommy and Valerie did not treat it seriously until they were in Rome at tour's end and about to return to Australia.

'Aren't you packing, Gai?' Tommy asked in their hotel.

'No, because I'm not going back to Sydney.'

Both parents stared at her. 'Don't be silly, of course you are,' said Valerie.

'No,' said Gai, 'I'm going back to Paris. Then London.'

'If you're going to be like that I don't want anything to do with you,' said Tommy, brusquely. And zipping up his bag he walked out the door without saying goodbye.

Valerie rang from the airport before they boarded their flight.

'You have broken his heart,' she said.

Gai was unmoved. 'Of course I haven't, Mum, that's nonsense.'

Now Gai was on her own. She wasn't sure how much Tommy would be prepared to help her now, because he didn't approve, and he could be stubborn.

She sensed she needed all the singlemindedness and determination she could muster to meet the challenges ahead.

Without realising it she had already begun to show these qualities at Rose Bay Convent.

CHAPTER TWO

THE REBEL

Gai Smith was an only child. She spent more time than most children with adults and her parents. Almost every night she sat at the dinner table listening to them talk.

As a result she was more focused and confident than children who had siblings. She spoke out right from the time she was a young girl.

This combined with the fact that she did not go to school until she was seven and a half caused problems for her from the first day she went to her mother's old school, Rose Bay Convent.

Valerie simply liked having her around the home, not even sending her to pre-school to learn about routine and the rough and tumble of normal school life.

Gai didn't even know her alphabet and was forced to play catchup to try to reach the standard of other children her age.

Gai would always regard herself as being hopelessly backward in her early school years. She found it difficult to cope, didn't like the regimentation and constantly rebelled.

Former teachers and school friends say she was not a dyed-in-the-wool rebel but bucked the authority imposed on her designed to make her do something that didn't interest her. They say ironically she respected authority but was always challenging it.

Even so she was rebellious enough to run away from her junior co-educational school one day, organising 15 other children to 'escape' with her. It was not just wagging school but an executive decision at the age of eight to run away and never come back.

She left her run too late because school was too close to finishing for the day when she made her break. By that time after lunch most of those in the plot had developed cold feet and only two other pupils joined her.

Gai was to be at the front gate after school to meet Valerie's sister, Aunt Heather Mouncey, who was looking after her at the time. When none of the three rebels turned up at the gate to be picked up the nuns naturally assumed they were missing and, fearing the worst, called the police and sent out a search party.

Gai and her fellow travellers were located around nightfall, planning their next moves. The nuns were furious. Next day they gave Gai a severe tongue lashing and punished her with solitary confinement.

Aunt Heather, a kindly soul who loved Gai, was summoned to the school and told of Gai's dangerous brand of disobedience.

When Tommy and Valerie returned from abroad, he treated the incident philosophically. But then, he could hardly do otherwise. His minor flirtation with school lasted only a few months and ended forever when his cruel teacher in the little town of Goolgowi yanked him out the front of the class by the hair for being late, although little Tommy had been helping his father that morning with the horses.

A kicking and screaming match ensued between Tommy and the teacher before he was caned and shoved roughly into the corner.

Tommy walked to the window, said 'I'm off and I won't be back,' jumped out and that was that. It would be his life's regret that he never received even an elementary education.

Gai was never involved in any physical fracas with teachers although she had fights with other pupils in her early days.

Born on 2 September, 1952 at St Margaret's Hospital in Sydney, she was christened Gabriel Marie after the archangel because her mother thought she looked like an angel, a grandiose flourish due to Valerie's devout Catholic background.

Fortunately Valerie called her Gai for short and it stuck. And it was soon apparent that as she was such an extrovert with a bright personality, the abbreviation suited her.

Gai was a fragile baby who suffered many allergies as a child, such as eczema and other skin ailments from touching grasses and animals, especially horses. In her junior school days she often had to take medication.

Throughout her life she would suffer hay fever from touching horses. People said she was fastidiously clean, always washing her hands, but her main concern was to keep hay fever at bay.

For seven years Gai lived with her parents in a tall apartment block in Wylde Street, Potts Point next to Kings Cross, alternating between her Uncle Dick Smith's hotel, 'The Light Brigade' in Paddington, and her Aunt Heather's.

Tommy then built their dream house at Point Piper in the heart of the eastern suburbs money belt. Here Valerie provided the secure home life Tommy didn't have as a boy. They were a private family, and visitors were not encouraged to drop in casually.

The Potts Point apartment was always home to various creatures because Gai, in spite of her allergies, was an inveterate animal lover. A Mr Moss at the Sydney Markets, for whom Tommy trained horses, kept giving her baby animals and she always had a plentiful supply of chickens, ducks, rabbits or cats.

She was a happy child who enjoyed her own company and was well able to entertain herself. Playing make-believe was a regular pastime, including talking to imaginary friends.

In one favourite game she sat on a box full of toys and imagined she was driving around the world. An old whip of champion jockey George Moore's was the gear stick and an old tennis racquet the steering wheel. At the age of six after she had her first flight with her parents, to New Zealand, the whip became a joystick as she floated around the world up in the clouds.

In New Zealand Tommy left Valerie and Gai with friends in Auckland while he bought yearlings in Wellington. Gai was too young to realise it but the social benefits of racing contacts began to work for her from that time. Industrialist Sir Ernest Davis looked after them and while on a private boat cruise of Auckland Harbour she met beautiful Vivian Leigh, who was accompanied by a boyfriend although married to Laurence Olivier.

Gai did not have any girlfriends until she went to school. But she often played with two boy cousins, Douglas and Phillip Mouncey, the sons of Aunt Heather. She was very much a tomboy with little interest in dolls—she wanted guns. Little Miss Smith could be rough in play, hitting one of her cousins over the head one day and laying him out cold. Gentle Aunt Heather almost blew a fuse.

One interesting aspect of her childhood was that she loathed wearing dresses or having to dress up to go out, preferring matador pants or shorts. Valerie commissioned a painting of her wearing a pretty little blue dress, and Gai always hated having to dress up and sit for the artist.

But she took to wearing big hats as a child because the sun rays affected her skin allergies.

Like many other youngsters, she had trouble with her teeth. A gap between her two front teeth was so large she could squeeze a two-shilling piece between them. At night to correct the fault she had to wear 'cat whiskers', a plate with rubber bands.

Tommy and Valerie Smith regularly went out to dinner but never took Gai, leaving her with a babysitter. It was typical of Gai's nature and personality that she became closely attached to her babysitters as wonderful companions sharing an important part of her life.

The first, Mrs Dadswell, whom Gai nicknamed Dadsy, was an elderly grey-haired lady who took Gai everywhere on trams, buses, ferries and trains, proudly introducing her as 'this is Tommy Smith's daughter'. Dadsy often took her to Manly on the ferry, returning to the city without getting off.

Just before she died, Dadsy bequeathed to Gai a friend named Mrs Hayes, an outgoing redhead who was equally as warm and caring a companion as Mrs Dadswell. Gai would remain friends with Mrs Hayes until her death.

Always full of life and energy, Gai could be mischievous and annoying at home, testing her mother's patience until Valerie lost her temper. When this happened Valerie would slap Gai.

This sometimes caused a domestic dustup as in any normal family. Once at Aunt Heather's, an angry Valerie raised her hand to clout Gai and Heather stepped in, grabbed Valerie's arm and warned 'don't you touch the child.'

Naturally Valerie said 'she's my child and I'll do as I like,' and a protective Heather replied, 'no you won't, not in my home.' The fury passed with Gai escaping punishment.

Another day in the Potts Point apartment, which Valerie disliked because she thought it was no place in which to bring up a child, Gai was driving Valerie's nerves to the limit by reaching up and pulling the telephone cord while she spoke to a friend. Valerie kept saying, 'not now Gai, not now Gai.'

Finally Valerie could take it no longer. 'I'll get you when I get off this phone,' she threatened.

Gai at once rushed into the lounge room and hid in the corner out of reach under the cocktail cabinet. Valerie spent the next hour trying to winkle her out with a feather duster. The Mexican standoff ended only when calm was restored.

Gai hated vegetables and whenever Valerie wasn't looking she would chew them up, spit the remains into her milk glass and hide it somewhere in the kitchen until she could dispose of the evidence. As in all things she was definite in what she liked and disliked.

Fish caused her serious allergies as a child and being a Catholic she didn't eat meat on Fridays. It meant that on those days the fare at the Smith home was rather spartan, like tinned spaghetti and cheese on toast.

Gai and her father were close from the earliest days, enjoying each other's company so much that as a small child she even showered with him.

At the age of five the bond between them grew even closer when he began taking her to the track at Randwick in the early morning as the rest of the city still slumbered.

At the stables he sat Gai in front of him on his frisky skewbald pony, Cornflakes, and just before the sun rose they headed out into the centre of the vast track. From there Tommy shouted instructions to jockeys as 50 or 60 horses under his care galloped through their training regimen.

Then they rode over the ridge and down to Coogee Beach, where he swam some of the horses while she sat in the boat watching them enter and leave the surf.

On the way home they usually drove through Centennial Park where Tommy indulged his daughter's fantasies.

In his pocket he carried a hen egg which he usually hid in the grass near a pond, pretending there were duck eggs somewhere nearby. After she found the egg, not suspecting it came from their own refrigerator, Gai would excitedly take it home for Valerie to cook for breakfast that morning.

Her mother obliged, going along with the pretence it was indeed a duck egg. Tommy's innocent little game ended abruptly after a skylarking Gai crashed into him in the park one day, smashing the egg hidden in his pocket to a gooey mess.

Gai became a regular at the stables. The only female there, she was introduced at that tender age to the sweat, snorting and earthy language that epitomised the undiluted atmosphere of what was then totally a man's world.

She sat on the back of Tulloch, the freakish and slightly unpredictable champion her father trained, riding him at a gentle pace under the supervision of a strapper and Tommy's watchful gaze.

Whether she went to the track or not in the mornings she always waited to have breakfast with Tommy when he returned from the early gallops. Then while he slept she watched the movies on the new medium of television—rather too much, she would later recall.

Subconsciously as a young girl she became to some extent an extension of her father.

While visiting the yearling sales in New Zealand with Tommy and Valerie she caused them concern by suddenly developing a limp at Rotorua while her parents were staying on a property owned by their friends, Sir Woolf and Lady Fisher.

They took her to a doctor who could find nothing wrong and he referred her to a specialist. He, too, could find no physical reason for the limp even after an x-ray. Finally the specialist explained, 'It's psychosomatic—only in her mind.'

He had worked out that Tommy walked with a limp from an old injury when he fell from a hurdler in his early jockey days and Gai, following him around, had unconsciously developed the same limp.

It disappeared after the problem was explained to her.

That was the first time Gai met a girl called Liz Fisher on an adjoining farm. Liz, several years older than Gai, was a member of the Fisher family, of Fisher and Paykel industrial fame in New Zealand. Her uncle, Sir Woolf, raced horses and owned New Zealand's biggest stud, Ra Ora, in Auckland.

Gai and Liz became lifelong friends. Each year for at least 15 years while the yearling sales were on Gai would visit Liz on her Rotorua farm to ride horses and go water skiing.

At six Gai rode her first pony. The friendly little white horse was lent to Gai by Harry Darwon, a trainer friend of Tommy's who helped him in his struggling early days.

She rode it at the Eastern Suburbs Pony Club, quickly learning to care for her saddle and bridle and to dress her pony properly, always keeping her gear in immaculate condition.

Gai's pleasure in ponies began a long period of maternal duty for Valerie in which she drove Gai to various gymkhanas and the Royal Easter Show where she competed. Valerie, although not at all interested in the horses, waited around for Gai for hours.

She shared in the disappointments as well as the joys of Gai's pony competition days. At about 12 Gai had a smart walking pony named Trigger which she trained for a walking race at the Easter Show. To help her Tommy gave her an 18-carat gold stopwatch which one of his thoroughbred owners had presented to him.

For months Gai trained Trigger in Centennial Park every afternoon after school, clocking him over various distances to set a good pace. 'I'm going to win this, Dad,' she said on the big day.

Trigger set a merry clip as soon as the walking race began over one lap of the main arena at the Sydney Showground and looked certain to lead all the way.

But right on the line a boy drew level on the outside and just pipped her by breaking into a jog in the last second or so.

The kid should have been disqualified but wasn't. Gai had done everything right. Desperately disappointed, she complained to Valerie who said she'd just have to grin and bear it.

Valerie, too, suffered from hay fever when around horses. Gai always thought that was partly why her mother didn't really like what Tommy did for a living, preferring him to have been a doctor, solicitor or businessman.

In addition, Valerie did not like racing or racing and horsey people. From the earliest days she steered Gai away from any likely interest in racing, influencing her towards the arts. Gai learned to play the piano and guitar.

But it didn't stand in the way of Valerie giving all the time and encouragement needed to support a young girl's love of horses.

Gai hated school from the very first day.

At seven and a half she was mature for her age but being unable to read or recite the alphabet made her feel awkward and foolish.

Coming from a wealthy and successful household, she had been largely sheltered from the outside world. At the same time, her parents had encouraged her to be a free spirit.

If she'd had brothers and sisters or mixed more with children of her age, she might have learned to share and be more tolerant.

She was already independent in outlook. If she thought she was right, she would stand up and fight. Even then she had the gift of the gab to a surprising degree for one so young, and usually argued to have her own way.

Although not a trouble maker, she was noisy and disruptive in class, and always cracking jokes or working a prank. She was energetic and competitive.

The teachers at Rose Bay Convent found her hard to handle. For instance, if she knew the answer to a question she couldn't contain herself and simply yelled it out while the other students were holding up their hands. That sort of exuberant behaviour made the teachers cranky and brought her into conflict with them.

After only a few months at the school Gai was involved in a memorable fight.

Quite tall for her age, she was standing at the head of her class assembly line when a girl named Christine pushed in and took her position.

'I'm not going to have this,' Gai said, and sharply pushed the girl out of the way.

Christine retaliated and next instant they were at it, two eight-year-olds punching and kicking, knocking each other to the ground and rolling down a grassy incline as they fought.

That brought a stern rebuke from the nuns and two days in solitary detention.

The attempt to run away from school followed soon after and with Gai being behind in her class work owing to her late start in school, something had to give.

It happened in third class. She failed her exams. At the time she was staying with Aunt Heather, sitting on the settee in Heather's bedroom when she received the news.

'The teachers have decided you must repeat third class,' Heather said.

'But all my friends will be in fourth class—I won't be with them,' protested Gai, shocked.

Heather took both her hands in hers. 'It will be better for

you. You'll make new friends and you can catch up on things. It doesn't matter that you'll be the oldest child in the class.'

Gai was lucky. A lay teacher, Miss Ursula Bygott, saw potential in her and without trying to suppress her natural personality, encouraged her with patience and understanding.

It set her on the right path. Within a few months Gai improved as a student and didn't look back, although she would always remain indifferent to spelling and arithmetic which she believed, rightly or wrongly, was due to the lack of early grounding. Miss Bygott became her pin-up person.

The teacher would always be proud of the fact that she taught Gai to read and write at the age of eight.

A gentle dedicated teacher, whose PhD on the Jesuits was later published by Melbourne University Press, Miss Bygott became the author of numerous papers and publications including co-author of a history of Sydney University. After retiring she went to live for a time in Cambridge, England, from where she gave this special assessment of the young Gai Smith she knew and taught.

'I remember her as a very lively little girl, she was full of impishness, could be quite naughty at times but was always lovable.

'I had her for two years when she was eight and nine. She could always think up something amusing to set the class laughing.

'I remember when the Beatles were famous and Gai was very keen on them. She brought some Beatles' products to school, including a mask which she wore, and they were immediately confiscated.

'Rose Bay at that stage was very conservative and they didn't approve of such things. Another day Gai brought a Barbie Doll to school. The nuns considered that too revealing and it was sent home quickly.

'Children like Gai interested me and I perhaps was more tolerant of her than most other teachers, although

Sister Dorothy was also very understanding. You must realise that children have different personalities and all have to be catered for in a class.

'I appreciated Gai was an only child, dearly loved by her parents. I suppose I made allowances for her in what was a very formal school because outspoken little people like her could easily run foul of the teaching establishment.

'We had a school merits system in which pink cards were awarded every week, leading up to a blue ribbon. It was difficult for children like Gai because they continually lost their pink cards.'

Miss Bygott said her effort in bringing Gai up to scratch was one of her teaching triumphs.

'I thought Gai was a shining example of how you could easily give up on a child,' she said.

'I imagined she would have gone on into the social world but I was delighted to bump into her one day and find she was attending university and later that she obtained her degree.'

Once Gai settled in she loved school and enjoyed her friendships.

Barbara Oswald was one of several close friends in her class. She recalls Gai spoke out freely and her opinion was usually different.

She had an opinion on everything, was active, energetic and had a wonderful sense of humour.

'I think it's unfair to say she was a poor student,' says Barbara.

'She started late but caught up in high school. I'll say this: If she ever set her mind on anything, she did it.

'I remember she was very popular, and never catty. If

she was shy and sensitive about anything, she covered it up well.

'I never heard her speak against her parents, even when you might expect it. Valerie sometimes took singing lessons from Mother Wheeler upstairs in the convent and one day sitting in class we could all hear her trilling up and down her scales.

'It sounded rather melodramatic as the voice rose and fell, floating eerily down to us. We all got the giggles, especially as Gai sat there trying to look serious for once.

'Although embarrassed she wasn't about to knock her mum.

'When she was about 10 she would take us into the school's lovely gardens which she called her imaginary fairyland. She knew every garden plot and would describe what she saw there.

'Often at lunch she told us stories about people, reciting poems or parts of plays. We all knew she wanted to be an actress.

'She was an organiser. She arranged a Beatles fan club and lots of us exchanged records and other paraphernalia and spent Saturday or Sunday mornings listening to their music.

'Our school was a closed order of nuns but somehow Gai organised for us to go to another school, Xavier College, to do a play. It was *School for Scandal* in which she played a lead part. That would not have happened without her.

'Gai didn't excel at any sports, although she was a very physical person, unaware of her highly competitive spirit.

'She liked individual events like swimming and tennis. She was fond of organising others into team events and was always trying to arrange something, even games of marbles.

'Gai was a busy bee who always tried to fit too much into the time available. When she got her L-plates at 17, she drove me home eating an ice cream, talking and gesticulating all at the same time.

'Of all the girls I grew up with, Gai stands out because she always had a cause and was tenacious. She was going to succeed no matter what.

'Her whole childhood was fostered on success and she has been motivated all her life by a wish to succeed.'

Anne Dalton, another of Gai's early school friends who went on to university with her, recalls Gai's well-developed sense of justice at junior school as her most striking feature.

She would challenge unreasonable or outlandish statements and take up the cause for anyone in her group being treated unfairly.

According to Anne, Gai never stopped talking and laughing, had a strong character and was well liked.

'She was something of a thorn in the side of the nuns,' says Anne.

'All her friends knew her mother ran a tight ship and Gai had to conform, although she wanted to buck the system.

'She liked testing the rules at school. A nun's cemetery was out of bounds, but Gai often led some of us there just to talk and tell jokes to see if we could get away with it.

'Rumour had it that there was a ghost in the tower at the top of the convent. This was out of bounds too. Gai asked us to sneak up there at a particular time one day. When we did, she had already climbed the steps and was sitting there in a wheelchair with a white sheet draped over her, uttering weird sounds.

'Apart from all the laughs she was a very sensible, pragmatic sort of person, loyal to her friends and very determined.

'Never into smoking or drinking or anything like that. She always looked after her body. I thought she was a lovely person.'

Anne recalls that Gai was upset at one stage by an element of snobbery. The children of wealthy parents from privileged backgrounds or the landed gentry were commonplace in the school.

In a series of incidents several girls taunted her with a display of bitchiness when she was 13 or 14.

They all knew there was affluence in her background as distinct from just being well off and although she never flaunted money or showed any pretensions, they tried to put her down by saying her father was 'only a horse trainer, a little man'.

They were all aware she was proud of her father, that from stories in the papers he came from a childhood of poverty and had pulled himself up by the bootstraps.

The remarks hit below the belt.

The same girls tried to prick her confidence by calling her 'Bumpy Nose,' an unkind reference to the less than smooth outline of the Gai Smith olfactory organ.

Sensibly Gai never hit back at these snobbish attacks and although hurt, she kept quiet and waited for the catty aggro to pass.

At the time Gai was going through a Plain Jane period—skinny, with knobbly knees and long hair—just an average kid who was not considered good looking. She ate heartily without putting on weight.

Gai was sensitive about her mother driving her to and from school every day, especially when she turned up in Tommy's new Rolls Silver Shadow. Gai just wanted to be one of the girls and when Valerie drove the Rolls, Gai insisted on being dropped and picked up around the corner to avoid being teased.

To make matters worse, Gai was always late for school.

For years Valerie drove Gai the short distance from their home to the convent, arriving just before 9 am so she would be in class on time.

One morning the mother superior was waiting. 'Mrs Smith,' she said, 'I know you and your husband have been generous benefactors to the school but I must ask you—would you mind bringing Gai to school on time?'

Valerie bristled, 'But I do. She's here by 9 o'clock every morning.'

'Mrs Smith,' the mother superior intoned, 'Gai has been late for the past five years—school starts at ten to nine.'

Gai adored male company, perhaps because she was born into a masculine world and spent so much time with her father around his stables.

She was keen on boys and her tomboy nature always came to the surface.

At 15 while staying in Rotorua with her friend Liz, then married to John Wells, she was riding one of Liz's hunting horses around the farm when John dared her to jump a high wire fence. While following the hounds in New Zealand the Wells family and their friends jumped a lot of full wire fences.

Tommy and Valerie were following behind in a Land Rover when John dared Gai a second time. 'Go on, jump that fence,' he called out.

Tommy, looking worried, said 'She's not going to jump that, is she?'

All Valerie could do was scream, 'Tommy, Tommy.'

Gai took off on the hunter and flew over the fence with ease.

'Gee,' said Tommy, 'you can see the horse just loves it.'

After that, being a horseman and knowing the hunter could cope, he couldn't help himself in urging Gai to jump every wire fence in sight.

The following year an incident while Liz and John Wells were water skiing with Gai showed that she not only could handle the fellas but she was also a determined teenager.

John, driving the power boat on a lake near Rotorua, had on board two meat hunters, whom he described as rough diamonds. They had their eyes on Gai who at 16 was well formed.

As she stood up on her skis for a fast run she fell out of her bathing top, giving the meat hunters a glimpse of what they had been ogling through her blouse.

They cheered and yelled sexist remarks as the boat sped around the lake. She wasn't impressed but refused to let go, hanging on until the boat slowed before fixing her bathers.

The Wells were pleased to see she was well adjusted in male company.

At 16 she was allowed to have her first boyfriend, a lad named Ray Delohery who went to Waverley College. They kept company for five years and remained good friends.

At this time she and her girlfriends began going to parties with boys, but Valerie remained strict and the young tearaway was always on a tight curfew.

One night in this period she and Barbara Oswald went to a roaring 20s party and Gai wore a feather boa wrapped around her neck. Feathers flew as she threw herself into the fun but she didn't care. Friends noted that in her zest for life she had a natural and unstudied glamorous touch about her.

Her quirky sense of humour knew few bounds. Before one Mothers' Day Gai asked Valerie what she would like and she said somewhat sardonically 'a feather duster'.

Valerie wasn't impressed when she opened her elaborately wrapped gift to find exactly that inside.

Gai was coming out into the world, to the sophisticated environment of Sydney's cosmopolitan eastern suburbs. But she wasn't the little daughter who had sat on her rich daddy's knee and was spoilt. Gai was never spoilt, never handed a privileged lifestyle on a silver platter.

She had been indoctrinated with the Christian work ethic, had a sense of values and although she loved fine things and quality as an adolescent, she was beginning to understand that money had to be earned and was not meant to be squandered.

On her own initiative in the school holidays and on Saturday mornings, she took a job in the toy department of Grace Bros' Bondi Junction store to earn her own cash.

Sometimes she worked in her uncle's newsagency in the town of Griffith, wanting to be more independent.

In the second last year of high school the rebellious

helter-skelter kid who had bucked against the restraints of the nuns, received the nicest possible recognition from her peers.

They voted her captain of the school.

But Mother McGrath said no. 'I don't think you would be able to discipline the other students,' she said.

So they made her vice captain. But it really didn't matter. She was a prefect and it meant her peers not only liked and respected her, they felt she had leadership qualities.

An emotional and proud Valerie said, 'I never thought I would have a daughter who would become a blue ribbon.'

Gai obtained her leaving certificate the following year at Kincoppal school, Elizabeth Bay, a sister school which later amalgamated with Rose Bay Convent. And forfeiting her right to attend NIDA to take drama, she put her acting ambition on hold to please her father and went to the University of New South Wales.

Now in addition to her studies she began riding serious trackwork for Tommy every morning at Randwick, arriving there around 5 am, having ridden casually for him for some time. Tommy was the first to employ girl track riders in Sydney, believing they were generally more gentle with his thoroughbreds.

The only trouble was Gai did not have the physical strength to hold the powerful animals as she galloped them around the inside track. But she had remarkable energy and enthusiasm which partly made up for her slender frame. Certainly she wasn't frightened to throw herself into the gallops.

Track regulars like Kevin Langby and Bobby Pearson would range up behind her, urging her on. The course curator often grumbled to those near him, 'Here comes that bloody Smith kid again with hair flying.'

On her first holiday from university several of Gai's fellow students decided to take a back-packing tour to Singapore and Indonesia. Tommy would have said no straight off, but Gai asked Valerie who chose the right moment and said to him, 'If we don't let her go she'll think she's missed out on something.'

Gai insisted on roughing it the same as the other girls and taking the same amount of money. When she left home to go to the airport, her pack was so heavy she could hardly lift it off the lounge room floor.

Her parents thought it would be a good character builder. 'You won't be looked after like you have been at home,' Tommy cautioned.

She had flown to Singapore when aged 12 on her first international flight alone. Tommy had been seriously ill in England suffering from a nervous breakdown and Gai met her parents in Singapore and travelled back by ship with them.

Now the girls were all housed with friends in Singapore, Gai staying with racing friends of Tommy's. After that they were on their own.

Gai soon showed her organising ability. When they reached Johore in Malaysia she said to her friends, 'My father knows the Sultan. I'll give him a ring.'

She rang the Sultan's secretary who invited them all to lunch in the palace. While waiting in an outer room the girls admired superb Victorian furniture and to fill in time they played with magnificent prisms, making rainbows in the room. Later they learned the prisms were valuable gifts from Queen Victoria.

Finally they were shown into the dining room where the Sultan was ready to welcome Miss Australia and her entourage!

His secretary whose English was only passable had misunderstood the identity of her guest. The Sultan laughed to find it was really Tommy Smith's daughter from Sydney.

He gave them a nice lunch anyway.

In Indonesia Gai travelled into a mountain region to buy some batik, for which she paid $100 as a special gift for her father.

When she walked back into their Point Piper home Gai said after her experience of roughing it in the verdant Indonesian countryside, 'Gosh, this house is crowded. Look at all the stuff you have around.'

Valerie said, 'Listen, Miss Bareboards, leave my house alone. It is comfortable.'

Gai presented the batik to her father, telling him it was the best. But it was too bright even for Tommy. Valerie said she would have to redecorate the house to accommodate it.

Gai walked about with the batik wrapped around her for a few days, then washed it. The colour ran everywhere. Far from being the best, it was coloured with vegetable dye. Gai learned a valuable lesson in not to listen to the blandishments of hucksters.

Nobody at home encouraged Gai to go to the races or even talked about the possibility and it wasn't until she was well into university life that she finally attended a Randwick meeting.

Accompanying her was Valerie—not a regular racegoer then—and a friend of Gai's, Barbara Oswald.

It felt natural and comfortable to be there, because she had been on the periphery for so long. She enjoyed it but not as much as the training and preparation and planning that went on behind the scenes, the routine that was so familiar to her.

It didn't matter if she heard someone talking coarsely, she'd heard it all before in the stables, even from Tommy when things weren't going right there. Neither did it come as any surprise to see people throwing money around with abandon because she understood it was a game of gambling and tipping.

Gai was used to Tommy coming home after the races, talking about what kind of day he'd had on the punt, and putting his winnings on the sideboard.

Another day, another dollar. Sometimes big dollars.

On that first day at the races Gai went along dressed to thrill in a white mini skirt—English model Twiggy having shown the way—breaking out of her normal conservative mould.

Flashing her toothpaste smile, she entered the fashions on the field contest, and won it.

The prize was a trip for two at Surfers Paradise, staying at the Chevron Hotel. 'Great,' said Gai, 'I'm going to take this.'

Valerie wasn't too sure about that. 'Who would you go with?' she inquired.

Gai nominated Barbara Oswald, and Valerie relented. Gai had a fabulous time, amazed that her mother had relaxed her strict guidelines.

At the end of 1974 Gai finished university and obtained her arts degree. She regarded herself as just messing around at that stage, waiting to settle on something worthwhile.

Tommy had to race his horses in the Randwick autumn carnival before taking Gai on the promised three-month trip to reward her for gaining the education he never had, and while waiting Gai did a spot of modelling and took a couple of part-time jobs.

At this stage Gai had only an acting career in mind for the future. She felt that her mother thought she would just fiddle around with the idea for a few years, then settle down and marry a nice professional man—a popular ambition of mothers for their daughters in the 70s.

They embarked on the trip that would change Gai Smith's life forever in May of 1975.

The time seemed to pass quickly.

Soon her parents had departed for home, leaving her alone in Rome at her insistence.

She stood in her hotel room wondering what to do next.

CHAPTER THREE

THE GOOD TIMES

Gai had taken a certain amount of money when she left Sydney, but checking her traveller's cheques and loose cash now she suddenly realised she'd spent most of it on tour.

She knew she must spend frugally or find a job.

She'd decided to stay on without considering whether she could afford the luxury.

Reflecting on her situation she realised she had not paid enough attention to the dollars and cents to sustain her until she found some acting roles. What if she failed?

Fortunately she had her return ticket and if things went wrong she knew she could jump on a plane. Mum and Dad would be glad to see her and everything would be fine.

Except that this was something she must do.

She had to stand on her own feet and prove she was capable of achieving a goal on her own. Gai loved her father but didn't want to be known as TJ's daughter for the rest of her life.

Pouring herself an orange juice she strolled to the window and gazed on the street scene below in the centre of the Eternal City.

She felt grateful to her parents for the wonderful trip. Images of places visited and people she'd met floated through her mind.

Rome had been very much a tourist's exercise. They had not explored the city as individuals so much as taken guided tours.

Gai was interested in history and this had been a fascinating refresher course, taking in the crumbling ruins of the mother of civilisation, the centre of power which had been sacked, destroyed and rebuilt as the finest city in the ancient world, richer than Athens, Egypt or Babylon.

She knew Emperor Augustus had assembled most of the world's art treasures in Rome, still the centre of western Christianity.

These were the sorts of historical detail that had stimulated her interest. She'd looked over the galleries and museums, the Roman Forum, the vast basilica of St Peter, the Vatican and its treasures, the Colosseum without suffering from 'ruin fatigue'.

Tommy made sure they had some of that *dolce vita* for which Rome is known. They tried famous nightspots like the Cafe de Paris and Harry's Bar on the Via Veneto, checked out the shopping which was every bit as good as Paris and not as expensive.

Gai remembered the garrulous taxi driver who had given Tommy a friendly warning when dropping them off at the Vatican.

'Watch your wallet when you gaze up in wonderment and religious zeal at Michelangelo's ceiling in the Sistine Chapel— that's where the pickpockets knock your money off,' he said.

'They'll need luck on their side', Gai had laughed.

She recalled with affection the pretty young wife of Jim Keele, a friend of Tommy's whom they stayed with in the Bahamas. Susanne Keele was a ball of style and took it upon herself to give Gai some beauty tips.

Gai dressed very much as her mother did—conservatively. Susanne showed Gai how she could dress more in keeping with her youth and bubbling personality, and how to show off her figure.

Gai's figure was no longer the straight up and down shape of her teenage years but was showing curves and bulges in all the right places. Susanne also gave her pointers on makeup.

It came as a revelation to Gai. And she'd had to go to the Bahamas to find out . . .

Suddenly Gai found herself speaking out aloud, 'What am I

29

doing here in Rome? I don't know anyone. I'm really not prepared for this.'

She packed her bags and flew out to Paris that afternoon.

The only hotel she knew was the one where she had stayed with her parents. As soon as she unpacked Gai looked at the back of the door where the tariff was displayed. The price rocked her.

'Oh well,' she mused. 'Better get on the phone and ring a few people.'

The first was Alec Head, an old friend of Tommy's, and the leading trainer in Paris. His son Freddie, now a top jockey, had stayed with the Smiths in Sydney for nine months when Gai was 11.

Alec came from a famous Anglo-French racing family. In 1952 he had taken over the Aga Khan's horses previously trained in England and that year with Nuccio won for him the Prix de l'Arc de Triomphe, the world's most prestigious race.

He had a string of other classics to his name and his daughter, Criquette, was also a top trainer. Alec had his home and stables at Chantilly, the Chateau du Quesnay.

Alec's wife, Madame Ghislaine Head, took the call. 'I'm in Paris again,' said Gai.

'This is marvellous,' she said. 'When would you like to come and stay?'

'Well, I'm in Paris now.'

'So,' said Ghislaine, 'we are busy this week but we will see you on the weekend.'

It was only Tuesday. One more glance at the back of the door and she lifted the phone again.

Sourin Vanian was on the line at his luxurious home in the city limits of Paris. Gai had met Sourin, a big stud breeder, with her parents recently at the English Derby and again at the French Derby, after which they all had dinner at a casino.

As soon as he heard her say 'Sourin, this is Gai Smith,' he asked, 'Where are you?'

'The Hotel Lotte.'

'You fool. Jump in a taxi immediately and get over here to us.'

His apartment was so plush it nearly knocked Gai's eyes out. Middle Eastern in style, it was heavy with marble and gold.

He was a huge man of Arabian appearance, bald, moustached, charming and smart. He introduced Gai to his wife, Arlene, and Gai momentarily felt stunned because she was the most beautiful woman she had ever seen.

Without letting her imagination run away, Gai thought her face was so exquisite she resembled the fabled Nefertiti, wife of the Egyptian King, Akhnaton. Gay knew a sculptured head of Queen Nefertiti, one of the finest existing specimens of Egyptian art, was displayed in the Dahlem Museum in Berlin and had greatly influenced the modern European ideal of feminine beauty.

Sourin was in his 40s, Arlene was only 27. It had been an arranged marriage but they were happy enough.

Gai and Arlene hit it off at once. After a chat Gai was shown to her luxury room at the end of a long hallway.

Gai was fascinated by Sourin, who spoke 24 languages. Gai spoke French, but the Vanians spoke English to her in the apartment, Arabic between themselves and French when they went out.

Something of a mystery man, he had been an adviser to the King of Chad but had been forced to flee the central African state when the political scene there hotted up and the King was murdered. He periodically received large amounts of money from Chad.

All Gai knew was that he was a kind man and probably the most intelligent she had met.

He would later stand the sire Blazing Saddles in England after Tommy trained it in Australia, and also Rory's Jester, which would become the leading stakes-winning sire in Australia and New Zealand in the 1993–94 season.

At the weekend Gai went to stay with the Heads and when she returned Sourin said to her 'You have got to stay with us. You are good for my wife, young like she is.'

Each day Sourin would say to her, 'What are you doing today?'

When she said she didn't know he would settle it with an air of finality, 'Let's go to the races. No good you just staying here. Tomorrow we'll go to lunch.'

At the end of the first week she said to him, 'Well, thanks Sourin, I'll be on my way now.'

Gai had been busy on the phone and was heading to London to stay with Norma and Ron Hutchinson, the successful Australian jockey whom she knew and had called on with her parents. This was still in the era when English and Irish owners tapped into the brilliance of Australian riders.

'Nonsense,' said Sourin.

The amusing scene was played out week after week, with Gai's attempts to leave nonchalantly brushed aside by her generous host.

She went to the races at Chantilly, Longchamp, Saint-Cloud and elsewhere around Paris, took tours, went shopping and window shopping with Arlene and enjoyed every minute of it.

Back home in Sydney, Tommy had grown used to his girl being away. For a while, anyway.

'She'll only stay away for a few months,' he told Valerie. 'We'd better make sure she's all right and send some money.'

Nothing silly, of course. Tommy was not one to throw money about. But he wanted to make sure she comfortably had enough cash to take her on to London and tide her over for a while. He could allow his daughter to go overseas and have a bit of fun. He'd always pleased himself.

Tommy genuinely believed everyone should be free to think for themselves. He'd always done things his way. And when he thought about it he accepted Gai had that right too.

But this theatre game didn't impress him. Poofs and not much money in it either.

Tommy could not tolerate anyone who was lazy or idle.

Gai certainly wasn't either, and she'd shown she was a tidy person who kept her room and belongings in order.

Even so, Tommy took no risks that she might become a layabout.

When he came home from the morning gallops, always by 7 am, he would run up the stairs and even if she was sleeping in, call out 'where's madam?'

Valerie might say, 'She's in bed asleep. She's had a late night.' A late night being the curfew hour of midnight.

Tommy would enter Gai's bedroom and say, 'Madam, the sun's burning your eyes out, get out of bed,' and pull the sheets off.

The work ethic was never far away when Tommy was around.

Still, Gai didn't mind. Until this point when she was trying to come to grips with doing something really serious in her life alone, she considered her life had been a dream.

The weeks with the Vanians stretched into months and Gai simply had a ball, out nearly every night.

Arlene had a brother who visited and he proved a good friend to Gai. Arlene also had two cousins in Paris who showed her a good time, and the three males and Gai swam, dined in the colourful little outdoor cafes and generally did the sights.

They took her to all the main landmarks like the Eiffel Tower, Notre Dame, The Louvre, Tuileries Gardens and to atmospheric spots like the Latin Quarter between the Seine and the Luxembourg Gardens where she thought the jazz clubs were exciting.

She visited Montmartre to see the street theatre, disappointed to find this one-time mecca for artists, writers and poets did not have the charm she had read about.

She loved the Avenue des Champs Elysées, especially the end with its shady chestnut trees and pretty flower beds lining the footpaths. In and around this smart area she breathed in the fashion shops which characterised the glamorous side of Parisian life.

Overall she appreciated the elegance of Paris through its

beautiful buildings, the statues to past glories, the wide boulevards and the style of the city shown in the dress and flair of most Parisians, the quality of goods and standard of presentation in the shops.

Sourin and Arlene took her to some of the best restaurants, many of them off the tourist beat and not shown in the guides. 'We have to keep some of them unspoiled for the locals,' said Sourin.

But the touristy and expensive restaurant she enjoyed most was La Tour d'Argent, whose owner fooled the Germans in World War II by bricking up a wall and keeping his fine cellar intact until the Allies freed Paris.

She loved the pastries that were so prevalent, the croissants and little chocolate-filled pastries called *pain au chocolat*, which many preferred to normal croissants, and the brioches and crepes suzettes.

Gai could feel the change doing her good. She knew it was giving her time and space to grow up. She sent for some money and Tommy responded with the equivalent of four thousand pounds.

Every now and then she popped over to stay with Alec and Ghislaine Head and also saw Criquette Head. The Heads went every year to Deauville on the west coast of France for the yearling sales, about a three-hour drive from Paris, staying on for the season.

Gai went there with them, rode horses and spent a lot of time in the discos just letting her hair down. She loved the softness and beauty of the French countryside.

She lazed on the sands at Deauville with her Gucci beach bag.

In this period, spent mostly with Sourin and Arlene Vanian, Gai saw a good deal of Lester Piggott, the legendary maestro of the stirrups and king of English classic races who had won nine Epsom Derbies and ridden 5,000 winners.

The champion had just been awarded an OBE for services to sport, later stripped from him over tax matters.

Lester rode in races in England on Saturdays and would fly over that night to spend a few days with Sourin in his apartment, adding to the impressive list of house guests.

After a good dinner he and Sourin relaxed in the apartment until the late hours smoking huge cigars. Gai sat up later than normal, joining in the racing talk.

Lester, who stayed in the room next to Gai, had a well-earned reputation as a ladies man. It wasn't only the best of British thoroughbreds he liked to throw a legendary leg over.

Rumour had it that Lester knew his way to a lady's bedroom with as much panache as to the winning post.

His approach was always made in the most charming way. Gai wasn't interested and it was nothing she couldn't handle. But she always had to be sure to make it to her bedroom before Lester and keep the door shut. Tightly. She couldn't help liking him.

Gai and Lester may not have ignited a spark but there was a touch of romance in the air towards the end of her Parisian jaunt.

While staying with the Heads she met a suave Frenchman whom she felt she could easily fall for—and he had all the right credentials. He was a horse trainer who had spent some time working among horses in America.

His name was Jean de Roualle, he owned a training establishment on the outskirts of Paris with a beautiful home, had a nice group of friends and was well connected.

Gai went out socially with him, stayed at his property, met his parents and joined him in training sessions.

At this point Barbara Oswald linked up with her. Barbara had been studying French at a language school in Lyon and intended doing the big circuit of Europe, allowing herself one year away from home. But first she was stopping off in Paris to see Gai.

Barbara met Jean and knew instinctively he could be the one for Gai. Her intuition was confirmed when Gai said to her in her direct way, 'I could go for this bloke.'

Barbara said later, 'Gai was always happy and vivacious,

loved people, and guys fell in love with her before she realised it.

'When I saw these two together I just knew it, they were very keen on each other. This guy was absolutely besotted by her. He told me he thought she was wonderful.'

But there was one big problem—he was a trainer of trotters!

'If it hadn't been for that,' said Barbara, 'Gai would have remained in Paris.'

At the end of three months Gai had spent the most exciting time of her life. She enjoyed most of all just being herself, doing the things she wanted to without worrying about commitment, responsibility or restrictions.

She had no idea how she would start on her career, or even exactly what it would be, but she had benefited from being able to meander along and begin to sort herself out.

She felt she knew Paris backwards, but had hardly scratched the surface outside racing due to the interests of her host.

Gai had not discovered the soul of Paris or spent enough time on its history. She realised she should have improved her schoolgirl standard of French. Given the time over again she would have been more studious and less superficial.

Still, a short burst of the hedonistic lifestyle in such a romantic city had worked its charms.

And the pleasure was far from over yet.

Gai and Barbara decided to take a swing around Europe. They had been in touch with a young touring Australian, John Newton, who had raced horses in Melbourne. Gai, knowing him from the races, phoned him in London and suggested he come to Paris.

He and a mate flew over to meet the girls and they all went out to the Crazy Horse Saloon, a risque cabaret with dancing girls sporting names like Nouka Bazooka and Betty Buttocks.

The Wild West strip-tease show made sure they didn't go thirsty, with a champagne bucket stuck to each seat.

Next day Gai and her friend were off to Florence on the night train. 'Why don't you come with us?' they asked the fellas.

John's mate said he was going back to London but John said, 'Oh all right, I'll come.'

They booked three bunks and clambered aboard. The bunks were all together and Gai said to Barbara on the side, 'We don't know him that well, what do we do when we change?'

Barbara said, 'We'll send him to the loo, then change and jump into bed.' They did so and John returned and climbed into the bunk above them. Next morning when he walked down the corridor to go to the bathroom so they could change again, other passengers whistled and called out 'ooooh'.

In Florence they booked into a *pensione*, whose walls were so thin the girls hoped they would not be kept awake by amorous travellers in the next room.

They stayed in Florence for 10 days, just young people learning and having fun.

They soon realised that if you don't enjoy history and art, you won't like Florence, famous for the Renaissance.

It suited Gai because she had long wanted to run an eye over the paintings, sculptures and buildings which had been created during an explosion of ideas in the relatively short Renaissance period from about 1400 to 1550.

Since that time Renaissance Florence had changed very little except perhaps for a widening of some main streets.

Florence is one of those places where history hangs in the air.

The works and genius of Leonardo da Vinci and Michelangelo, two of the greatest sons of Florence, were there for all to see, along with the magnificent buildings, churches, museums, palaces and signs of the once-powerful Medici family which reflected all aspects of the Florentine Renaissance.

Just strolling around Gai and her companions came upon some revelation of history without searching for it.

A passerby casually pointed out to her the house where Galileo worked and the very window from which the philosopher and astronomer studied the stars more than 300 years earlier, the first to use the telescope to open up the universe and reveal a Milky Way powdered with stars.

Gai visited the main cathedrals including the Baptistry with its splendid bronze doors and the Duomo, whose dome is the centrepiece of the skyline and the symbol of Florence appearing on postcards and brochures.

Being fit and adventurous Gai climbed the 463 steps to the dome, spotting half-way up the famous stained glass windows designed by leading artists of the 15th century.

At the top she gazed out on the panorama of Florence, the brownness of its buildings relieved only by white Tuscan marble.

But the building she admired most was the Santa Croce, a beautiful Franciscan church full of tombs, works of art and monuments to famous people.

She was obliged to stop for long periods by the sheer significance of the monuments.

Michelangelo's tomb lay just inside the entrance to the right, with three figures representing Architecture, Sculpture and Painting.

Moving along she stopped at the tomb of other famous Italians including Dante and Rossini. And then the one that took her by surprise—Machiavelli, the master of intrigue.

Gai could not resist a feeling of awe at finding herself standing before the remains of the man whose name and reputation were universally synonymous with treachery.

'I dips me lid to you,' she said, not dreaming for a second she would encounter more than her fair share of Machiavellian characters in her career or that she would have cause to remember this moment.

Next she popped into the San Lorenzo church where the Medicis worshipped, to see Michelangelo's chapel memorial to the famous family and the artist's figures of Dawn and Dusk, Night and Day.

A highlight in the Accademia museum was Michelangelo's most famous sculpture, the huge David, carved from an imperfect block of marble which other artists could do nothing with.

The Uffizi art gallery held so many Medici family art riches left to the people of Florence that Gai had to go back a second time.

Naturally she did more than take in the history, looking over the leather goods, antique and clothes shops, including the one that is the Gucci brand headquarters, and dining in the cafes and bustling trattorias where music comes with the spaghetti.

The fun of Florence over, John Newton went back to London and Gai and Barbara wandered on through Italy, taking a breather in Venice.

The whole place just spelled romance. They loved the atmosphere, the sense of history, the intimacy of this unique city from where Marco Polo began his journeys in 1271.

Gai and Barbara just enjoyed themselves as tourists rather than taking in the historical side, finding pleasure in walking or catching the waterbuses.

To them Venice was more a vision, a dream than a reality. Out on the Grand Canal in a gondola gliding through the heart of the city they felt they knew it well from the familiar photos, films and music over the years. The mood music that came to Gai's mind was *The Carnival of Venice* with Harry James's brilliant trumpet.

They spent hours in the Piazza San Marco, one of the world's most beautiful and romanticised squares with its famous clock, visited landmarks like the Doges' Palace, the Rialto bridge over the Grand Canal, the Bridge of Sighs, palaces, a few of the many churches, wandered for hours among the souvenir shops, saw the famous Murano glassblowers in action and put on weight from over-indulgence.

The girls nipped into the tiny standup coffee shops which sell liqueurs and agreed, 'These places would go like a house on fire in Sydney.'

Then they took the train to Switzerland.

Gai had been on the phone again, this time to an extroverted lady named Clarissa whom she'd met in Sydney through her father's friendship with Dave 'the Dasher' Segenfield, colourful punter and raconteur.

39

Clarissa Kay had met James Mason in Australia many years before on the film set of *Age of Consent*. They became lovers and eventually married.

'Hi ya, luv,' said Clarissa, who had a colourful and amusing way of speaking. 'How you going, luv? Yes, come out and see us.'

So luv arrived, Gai the brunette and Barbara the blonde, at the charming home of the Masons on a hillside in Vevey not far from Lausanne and Lake Geneva.

Gai wasn't sure why, but she found it remarkable that whenever she phoned people, they would invariably say come and stay with us, whether for a week or longer.

The obvious catalyst was the universal nature of racing and her father's connections around the world. Tommy even went to Russia to look at the horses.

But Barbara Oswald had a different view of it.

She knew Tommy's reputation and contacts usually provided the entree, but she believed it was Gai's personality that carried her through with such ease.

Barbara, who flatted with Gai and travelled on and off with her for a year, said of the young Gai she knew then, 'She was always bright and cheerful and people were pleased to have her around.

'She was not just a taker but put into life and situations. It's the same with a plant—if you want it to grow you must water it. She did this and contributed in whatever avenue she found herself.'

After a few days with James and Clarissa Mason, Gai said to them, 'It has been very nice, thank you, Clarissa and James, now we'll be on our way.'

'Oh,' said Clarissa, 'you're not going away, luv? We've got quite a few restaurants we want to take you to.'

Every day for the next week the Masons took them out to lunch or dinner or both, sampling the best restaurants and a wide range of Swiss cuisine. In one restaurant James introduced them as young Australian friends to Charlie Chaplin.

The Swiss experience would leave a lasting impression on Gai and give her an appreciation of food she never even contemplated before. For instance she had never known fondue. James showed her how best to eat the tasty cheese dish and ordered other typical Swiss courses to please her taste buds.

Gai had never savoured such quality or seen such efficient service from waiters.

She said to James, 'I've only been used to plain food. My mother is not a natural cook, and I can't cook at all. With me it's been spaghetti on toast on Friday nights, grills most nights and corned beef the other night.'

Gai found James, the star of many first class films including *Five Fingers*, *Flying Dutchman*, *The Verdict* and *The Macintosh Man*, to be the nicest possible, mild-mannered man. He was kindly, considerate and genuine without the ego that most actors had.

When Clarissa met him he had just been through a disastrous divorce to a Californian gossip writer, his finances were depleted and his career in decline. He was hitting the singing syrup.

Clarissa, a knockabout type with a heart of gold, had his interests in mind, encouraged him to resist the booze and helped him pick up his life again. His career blossomed once more.

They were a delightful if unlikely couple. Both greenies, they had a beautiful garden and fed the birds and local small animals.

Each morning the three women sat at the breakfast table gazing out at the view below, while James read the *Herald Tribune* aloud in his cultured tones from a big church-like rostrum.

Clarissa, in the broadest of Australian accents, was highly opinionated and continually interrupted him, 'That's wrong, James, that's wrong.'

James would look up slowly from the newspaper and ask in the politest and most understanding way, 'What do you mean, my love? What are you saying?' It always took him a long time to read through the morning paper against the tide of Clarissa's comments.

Naturally Gai sought the great actor's advice.

'Look,' he asked, 'what do you want to do?'

'It's my intention to get a job and to act.'

'Well, you can't do that unless you have an Actor's Equity card.'

The great actor spent hours talking to Gai, telling her what she might expect in London and how to go about it.

Unwittingly he hit on a delicate point. 'If there's one piece of advice above all else I can give you it's this: Be on time for all your theatre and rehearsal appointments.'

None of Gai's friends could ever accuse her of being on time.

James Mason gave Gai the name of his London agent.

CHAPTER FOUR

LOOKED THE PART BUT...

Maggie was expecting her.

She was one of London's leading theatrical agents, well connected throughout the city's artistic circles with producers, directors and theatrical entrepreneurs.

Her husband had been the leading agent there when James Mason was at the peak of his career. He died and Maggie carried on the agency.

True to his word Mason had phoned Maggie ahead of Gai's arrival, said she had talent, was a friend of his and asked her to help Gai find work.

It was a dream start in the big league for a young woman whose only experience had been in a school play.

Gai looked like some bright apparition when she breezed into Maggie's tasteful offices near the Hilton Hotel, decked out in a vivid red mohair coat she'd bought in Florence and a pair of high-heeled patent leather boots well past her knees. Also from Florence.

'Oh, you look fabulous,' said Maggie, warming to her at once.

And getting straight down to business she said 'There's a job over at the BBC. They're auditioning for it now. Go and do it.'

So she caught a red London bus to the BBC studios at Shepherds Bush and joined the queue. There must have been almost 500 other young hopefuls sitting and standing around vying for a starring role in *Sweeping Plains*, an Australian entrant in what was a BBC television series on Commonwealth countries.

Being Johnny on the spot, referred by a top agent and looking as sanguine as a house on fire, she got the job.

It was only Gai's second day in London. If she had turned up one day later it would have been too late. And here she was landing the job without any experience.

Beginner's luck, but with a strong dash of the old adage it's who you know that counts.

Gai also had a little luck with the director. He was Ken Hall, a well-known Australian and one of the pioneers of the Australian film industry whom she had heard of in Sydney from his association with the Channel Nine TV channel. She found him a nice man and very helpful.

The play was only a four hander, with two girls and two boys, an inconsequential piece of drama. But it was a good start, boosting her confidence and setting her off on the right path straight away.

Gai was staying with Ron and Norma Hutchinson and their children at Reigate in Surrey. Ron, the Australian jockey, was then riding for the Duke of Norfolk, who had long been the Queen's representative at Ascot and was one of England's most enthusiastic owners and breeders.

Steeped in racing the Duke was a sound administrator of the turf, had served as a steward of the English Jockey Club and among his successes was the Ascot Gold Cup with Ragstone.

Ron was still in the era when Australian jockeys were highly desired in England and Ireland as racing fans thrilled to the artistry of riders like Ron, Bill Williamson and Garnie Bourgure and to the style of Scobie Breasley and George Moore in the Classic races.

In the 1960 Irish Oaks Australian jockeys filled the first three places and at a meeting in The Curragh near Dublin, Ron Hutchinson was one of three Australians who won five out of six races among them on the day.

Gai travelled each day to London from the Hutchinsons' home by British Rail to Victoria Station and found her way in the teeming city by tube to Shepherds Bush where the BBC play was rehearsed and taped.

The job lasted three weeks and Gai felt on top of the world. For a nobody she had received a wonderful kick start.

She was excited to be in London, which had been a happy hunting ground for Australian artists. The scene was bigger and more challenging than in Sydney and the rewards greater.

Australians were still popular from the days of the Empire, the warm feelings of family and cultural ties, the shared war experiences and the keen sporting rivalry.

Many Australian artists had made names for themselves in London and Gai knew from their experiences it was possible to win through. She could gain heart from the careers of stars like Dick Bentley and Wilfred Vaughan Thomas in radio, Peter Finch, John McCallum, Kitty Bluett and Ron Randall in theatre, Elaine Fifield and Kathy Gorham in ballet and a string of newspapermen and women who had carved enviable niches in Fleet Street. Joan Sutherland was just beginning to follow Dame Nellie Melba and thrill Covent Garden audiences.

But after her initial euphoric role, obtained with such ridiculous ease, reality began to set in for the inexperienced young woman who had nothing to recommend her in the bitchy, clannish and snobbish world of theatre except high velocity enthusiasm, determination, personality and good looks.

Her personal qualities weren't enough. She pounded London streets for audition after audition, almost wearing the heels down on her fancy black leather Florentine boots.

The acting roles simply didn't materialise.

But she was determined to make it and create opportunities.

'I'm going to learn how to be an actress properly,' she told herself as frustration began to set in.

Gai was frustrated because she was not trained in her craft. She didn't know the tricks of the trade, the automatic reactions and responses that come with every profession. She was like a racehorse that had talent and speed, but was wild and untamed—the hardest to train.

The aspiring young actress was aware of her shortcomings and this made her desperately nervous and hopelessly inadequate the whole time while auditioning.

Uncertain how to make the correct dramatic delivery, she was likely to goof badly. Fortunately she went better with comic lines.

The directors and casting executives could see that, although talented, she was untrained.

They were polite and encouraging because they saw she was keen and looked the part, but with expensive productions to fill and experienced actresses on hand, they passed over her repeatedly.

If she had gone to NIDA in Sydney she would have learned these basic skills.

To make matters worse Gai had a distinctive Australian voice. That was poison to theatre directors and television producers who only wanted to hear English-sounding voices unless the part called for it.

The only really happy aspect of this part of her stay in England was living with the Hutchinsons. It was a home away from home and she would remain with them on and off for the next six months before finding her own digs. She came and went bringing chocolates and flowers.

But Gai was never one to sit around and feel sorry for herself. With a little financial help from home, she decided to see something of England while waiting for the illusory acting roles.

Once again she teamed up with her old school pal Barbara Oswald, now finished with her French classes in Lyon and still on holiday in England, having done France and the rest of the European scene.

They hired a campervan in London, the cheapest way to see England. Touring around, they stopped at quaint little villages, noting and absorbing, stayed in the lovely Lakes district and moved on to Scotland.

In Edinburgh they went to a cinema one night and came out to find rain bucketing down. They had a spartan meal in the campervan, decided it was too miserable in its confined space and went back to the warmth of the theatre to see another movie.

Next morning they decided it was time to ring their folks back in Sydney and drove back to Edinburgh from their camping site to a hotel where they each rang from a phone booth.

Gai was asked by her mother where she was staying. In a hotel? In that case why was she ringing from a phone booth?

Gai had to own up that she and Barbara were touring by campervan. For God's sake be careful and stay together was about all Valerie could say from the other side of the world.

As they neared London after that trip, the two friends had the only argument they would ever have in a long-lasting friendship. Barbara, driving while Gai was cleaning the refrigerator prior to returning the van the following day to a London rental company, ran over some bumps and threw the back of the van into chaos. They shouted at each other and called each other names. Barbara recalled long after the event:

'It was the only cross word we ever had. She was very direct and would tell you exactly what she thought. She called me stupid first. Perhaps her directness came from growing up around men and having to speak up for herself.

'Her character was already strongly formed. She didn't have any identity crisis but was just sorting herself out and establishing her independence after being brought up by strict parents. As any fledgling must do, she had left the nest.

'If you crossed Gai then her reaction was the same as in later life. She wouldn't throw daggers at you but just wouldn't waste more time on you. She wouldn't even cut you dead, it would just be a case of not bothering with you any more.'

That night the girls had tickets for the opera and intended going, but before doing so they met up that afternoon with Arthur Hancock, one of the great characters of the American racing scene.

A wild man who would have a woman for breakfast, lunch and dinner if he could, Arthur joined them in their campervan, yodelling, singing and playing his guitar.

Gai had met him a couple of years before at the Keeneland Yearling Sales in Kentucky, when her father and a Sydney syndicate Tommy formed with Jack Ingham, Don Storey and Tris Antico successfully bid $280,000 for a colt by the champion Claiborne Farm sire, Bold Ruler.

At those sales, where the social life is always brilliant, Gai went to a party and met Arthur Hancock and Viscount Petersham, hitching a ride to her hotel in their car, slipping through the lanes of Lexington with Arthur drinking bourbon and yahooing beside her. A crazy man, she decided, but what lovely wild blue eyes.

She kept bumping into him, one of the numerous people from the top drawer in racing she would meet regularly in the next few years.

The story of the Hancocks is an integral part of the folklore of American racing. Arthur's father, AB 'Bull' Hancock, who once tried to entice Tommy Smith to Kentucky to train for him, owned the famous Claiborne Farm which had been in the Hancock family for three generations and was one of the most influential breeding establishments in the world.

Among the great sires to stand at Claiborne were English Derby winners Sir Ivor and Nijinsky, then Round Table and Buckpasser, Nasrullah, Blenheim 11, Bold Ruler and his son, the incomparable Secretariat himself and Riva Ridge, the 1972 Kentucky Derby winner.

Gai was fascinated by all this racing lore and the characters associated with it. Arthur Hancock told her no horse had ever achieved the adulation that Secretariat did in the spring of 1973 when he won the Triple Crown—the Kentucky Derby, Preakness and Belmont Stakes—breaking all three track records and winning the Belmont by a staggering 31 lengths.

In the space of one week, Hancock told her, Secretariat had appeared on the front covers of *Time*, *Newsweek* and *Sports Illustrated*, starring soon after also as the centrefold in *Vogue*.

Gai had never seen anything like the Kentucky horse farms such as Claiborne, Spendthrift and Bluegrass Farm, or seen spreads so magnificent or bloodstock so impeccable, supported or fought over by some of the richest individuals in the world.

But all was not well when Gai first met Arthur in 1973. Bull had died in 1972, leaving the most famous of all Kentucky farms in the hands of executors to be run by his two sons, Seth and Arthur. But it didn't work out, Arthur ending up rowing with his executors.

The hard-drinking Arthur who knew horses as well as girls, fast cars and country music, leased a small stone farmhouse from the estate and helped by oil-rich Nelson Bunker Hunt, then the biggest player in bloodstock breeding in the world, went on to develop a bigger farm than Claiborne, breeding and racing two Kentucky Derby winners.

Yodelling and carousing in the campervan at the end of 1975 he looked anything but the enormously successful breeder and businessman he was about to become.

Gai was enjoying doing her own thing while awaiting the next acting role, keeping busy meanwhile by popping over to Ireland with Barbara for the Irish Derby.

Ireland had a special lure.

She had been to The Curragh with her parents for the running of the Derby when a child of 12, and Bing Crosby collected the trophy on behalf of the American winner, Max Bell. Bing gave the crowd a treat by singing *When Irish Eyes are Smiling*.

Gai had seen all the old Bing Crosby films on television and was excited beyond words at the prospect of meeting him. But when her mother introduced her to the Old Groaner, her face dropped. As Bing moved away, she said, 'Mum, he's got no hair.'

Even Gai was allowed to stay up for a while that night when the party in the Gresham Hotel in Dublin, including Bing, shook the cobwebs out at a monstrous rave.

All that trilling up and down the scales at Rose Bay Convent paid off when Gai's mother sang *Fairy Tales of Ireland* and kicked on until, for her, the ungodly hour of 3 am.

Some of the Emerald Isle's appeal was due to two of Gai's forebears coming from there, the rest from England and Scotland.

William Smith, Gai's great-great-grandfather, who was born in Gloucestershire in 1819, married Ann Nesbitt of Derry, Ireland, in Melbourne in 1852 and they went to live in Castlemaine, Victoria.

Old William's son Thomas—Gai's great-grandfather—who was an itinerant worker and ran horse teams out at Ivanhoe in western New South Wales, married Joanna McColl at nearby Hay in 1884.

Her mother, Joanna Ryan, had come from Tipperary in Ireland and had married Neil McColl from the Isle of Mull in Scotland.

Gai's grandparents, Neil Alfred Smith and Mabel 'May' Spencer were married in 1914 in the southern New South Wales town of Braidwood. Both were Catholics and connected with horses.

May, a show rider, was a person of some style and refinement whose family didn't want her to marry Neil, a labourer, horse breaker and buckjump rider.

May's family had married settlers around Berridale and Cooma and their names formed part of the legend of the Snowy River mountain horsemen.

So horses and Ireland were a significant part of Gai Smith's background.

On this visit with Barbara to the Irish Derby she bumped into Robert Sangster, the wealthy English owner who was then engaged on a massive assault on the world's yearling sales, especially in Kentucky, in his bid to develop the best bloodstock team in Europe.

Gai had met him earlier while with her parents at the French Derby when he accompanied his then wife, Susan. Now in Dublin a few months later he was with Susan Peacock, whom Gai had known in Australia. As soon as she saw them together Gai knew they were having an affair. She chatted brightly to them both.

She would keep crossing paths at the races with Sangster and other big names of the turf in England, Ireland and France.

It was in this period when Gai was struggling to make ends meet that she began flatting with Barbara and they looked after a mews house near Harrods for a friend in Ireland.

She hit on the idea of dining in style by joining the Cordon Bleu cookery school and buying the best meals produced by the school at giveaway prices.

After eight months in London Gai was asked by Channel Nine if she would return to Sydney to appear on a *This is Your Life* program devoted to her father. She said to the producer, 'No, you can film me over here and send it back.'

They negotiated further with her, offering to pay her fare one way but she said, 'This is final. I won't come back unless you pay my fare to Australia and back to England.'

Without such an arrangement she could see herself being stranded back in Australia because she couldn't afford to pay her fare even one way, and she knew her parents would certainly not pay.

Eventually, her mother rang and said Channel Nine had promised to pay her fare both ways. She returned, appeared before Mike Willesee with the entire Smith clan and after 10 days flew straight back to London.

Her parents tried to persuade her to stay but she was determined to go back, explaining she still wanted to be an actress.

Gai knew she hadn't yet achieved anything with her career. She was still searching, still trying to find where she was going in life. It wasn't for identity but for career and ambition.

She wanted to see what Gai Smith could achieve. Racing was very much in the background.

She was just enjoying life and letting it wash over her.

CHAPTER FIVE

FOXES AND LEPRECHAUNS

Arriving back in London Gai realised she was even more dependent on herself than before in this big crowded city.

Her parents were unhappy at her decision to return and she felt this placed more pressure on her to show her worth and achieve something in the field she had chosen. She obviously had to be more serious about it. But she had tried.

The first thing she tackled was her accent. Her distinctive Australian voice was a dead giveaway. It was clear and resonant, perhaps the words were a little clipped but the accent made the difference. No director wanted to employ a colonial when there were plenty of talented English girls with the right accent to fill the parts.

Gai located an elocution teacher in north London and earnestly began voice and speaking lessons, reading aloud to herself in private as she practised.

Then she auditioned to enter the London Academy of Music and Dramatic Art (LAMDA). Five hundred candidates from several countries had applied for the available vacancies, and only 26 were accepted. Much to her joy Gai was one of them.

She was now retracing the steps she should have taken more

than three years before when to please her parents she declined the opportunity of learning the rudiments of acting at NIDA.

Knowing she was a long way behind, she worked hard at it. Her efforts helped her concentration and taught her to focus in a more single-minded way on the task at hand.

To support herself she took odd jobs, such as pouring drinks in a wine bar just up the road in Putney.

Her rent was £11 a week. She was sharing a room in a flat in Putney with a girl named Jennie Charleston. Gai had arrived to inspect the room at the same time as Jennie, who turned out to be from Queensland and knew mutual friends of the Smiths.

They decided to share the room to defray costs, and became the best of friends.

When Gai wasn't working and plumbed the financial depths, her parents were always kind enough to help her out. While working she could always look after herself, except when she needed extra money to fly over to France or Ireland. Yet Tommy wasn't over generous—if she enjoyed herself too much, well, she might stay.

In between jobs, she went to the races whenever possible.

Her parents intended coming to London for their annual pilgrimage to the Epsom Derby in a few months and Tommy decided to buy a spanking new Mercedes sports for Valerie in Germany. Gai agreed to pick it up.

She flew to Germany and drove it back, putting it on a ferry in France for the final leg to Dover. It was a long journey, nearly 24 hours, and she didn't quite make it back to Putney before falling asleep at Wimbledon. But she had the presence of mind to pull over first, wakened by a curious but friendly bobby.

At the races at Kempton Park one day she bumped into some people she knew and on their tips won quite a few pounds. She bought herself a push bike to pedal around her area of London.

Joe Manning, a friend from Australia who had known Gai from a child, was visiting London at the time and later told an amusing story about her and the bicycle.

He owned the property, Woodburn, at Cootamundra where Tommy Smith spelled his horses when not in training. Gai had visited Woodburn with her father from about the age of 12.

Joe saw quite a bit of Gai in London at the time she bought the bike and noted she was surrounded by a social group of people, including William Hastings-Bass, son of the late Captain Peter Robin Hood Hastings-Bass, a notable athlete from Oxford days with racing in his blood who claimed descendancy from Robin Hood of Sherwood Forest. He had trained horses at the famous Kingsclere training establishment. William, or Willie as they called him, was a little older than Gai and seeing a lot of her.

A handsome young American turned up to take Gai out to dinner. He didn't have any money, neither did she.

'I'm meeting this fellow, then we're going on to dinner,' she told Joe, mentioning the restaurant.

'That's okay, you'll be able to park the Mercedes there,' said Joe.

'Oh, I'm not taking the car,' said Gai. 'It might scare the fellow off if I arrive in a flash car.'

And she rode off up Fulham Road to meet him.

Gai returned to the flat later riding 'side saddle' on the bar of the push bike, with the American doing the pedalling.

It impressed Joe that she chose not to trot out the Merc because she didn't want to give the idea she had money or came from a wealthy family. In his view it showed she could be singleminded and level headed and had no 'side' or pretensions.

Joe's opinion was there had never been any veneer with Gai.

'What you get with Gai is Gai,' he recalled after knowing her for so long. 'She has absolutely no bullshit in her at all.'

She could be fiery but he had never heard her say anything derogatory about anyone.

'At the same time she was like her father in that she didn't tolerate negative or flippant people,' he said.

'She just didn't waste any time on negative people. There are plenty of good people around.'

Joe remembered how tenacious she was as a kid when she often came to his Cootamundra property to ride ponies or some of the hundreds of horses.

He recalled an incident when she was 14 and he went out riding with her and Gary Buchanan, a jockey who worked for him.

Gai rode a quiet two-year-old racehorse called The Godfather, named after Tommy, who was called Little Caesar or The Godfather because of his dictatorial attitude towards owners. He had raced, but slowly, and it was thought he would be a good hack for Gai.

They broke into a brisk canter and The Godfather took off, wanting to go. A slender slip of a girl, Gai couldn't hold the bolting horse and he careered on under trees and over rocks and rough terrain, Gai clinging on grimly. Neither Joe nor Buchanan could catch him, both trailing helplessly in her wake.

But Gai rode The Godfather out and when he finally stopped after showing a surprising turn of speed over about four kilometres, Joe and Gary reined their mounts in alongside.

Expecting Gai to be frightened by what must have been an unnerving experience for one so young, a concerned Joe asked tightly 'Are you all right?'

The first thing she said was 'We might have found a champion.'

She wasn't worried, although puffing from the exertion, her cheeks red, her arms aching from trying to hold in the bolter.

As soon as they reached the homestead, Gai rang her father and repeated that they might have found another champion.

'Gee,' said Tommy, 'I might win the St Leger with him.'

And that's exactly what happened, Tommy Smith being part owner when The Godfather won an Australian St Leger.

Gai wasn't too good on mustering, though.

Joe sent her out on her pony, Trigger, when she was a school girl to help two Woodburn hands muster 3,000 sheep on a neighbouring property, Woodlands. One hand was a battling Cootamundra trainer named John Shaw, later to win an Epsom Handicap with Nick's Joy. It was a fiercely hot day and they

56

came in yelling for water, with only half the sheep. Joe sent them back for the rest of the mob.

Joe remembered her in those days as always asking questions about horses. 'Why Dad, why do you like this horse?' she would say. 'Why are you doing that?'

He felt she was storing knowledge on horses from the time she was a young girl.

When not working at odd jobs or studying drama at the London academy, Gai was busy networking in racing by using her father's contacts or her new friends.

For the first time in her life she was doing things entirely on her own.

She developed a group of young friends, guys and girls, and went places with them. Not afraid to go without a partner or in a group, she would also just turn up on her own and meet people there.

Always the enthusiast she made it her business if not working to be out and doing things. If she had the money between jobs, she would travel.

Among the delightful people she met while at the races in Paris with her parents had been the Earl of Stanhope, Lord Bill Harrington and his charming wife, Lady Silla. Much younger than her husband, Silla was his third wife. They were said to have a glorious estate in Ireland.

The connection had begun a few years before when Lord Harrington's son, The Hon Stephen Stanhope, had come to work in Tommy Smith's Tulloch Lodge stables in Sydney after finishing at Eton.

Gai happened to mention to Bill Harrington on that occasion in Paris that she might be staying on in England for a few weeks and he said, 'Oh, we will look after you.'

It could have been a casual remark, dropped in to make up the pleasantries with people met fleetingly. But when Gai bumped into them again at Ascot while living in Putney, they invited her over to Ireland to go fox hunting.

Now, Gai was the sort of person who should never be invited anywhere—because she always turned up!

She arranged the visit and prepared herself for the foxhunt deep in the green heart of southern Ireland.

For many years the passionate followers of this sport had hunted over the steep banks and ditches of Limerick county not far from Tipperary and the Shannon estuary, which was the fox hunt territory of the great landholder of the area, the Earl of Stanhope.

Gai had never been on a fox hunt, knew nothing of the rules of the hunt which was originally a royal and aristocratic sport, but it sounded exciting and she was prepared to give it a go.

Before leaving London she priced the gear one should have for the hunt, and of course it was too expensive and she couldn't afford the several hundred pounds necessary. So she bought herself a pair of high rubber boots, jodhpurs and a shirt. She didn't have a cravat or the proper coat but made do with a black substitute.

She duly arrived at the estate, Greenmount Stud at Patrickswell in County Limerick and Bill Harrington took one look at her gear and said to his wife, 'Oh Silla, go and get her outfitted. You look the same size.'

Only then, as Lady Silla fitted her out and chatted to her, did Gai realise she had offended a great tradition by being regimentally undressed.

It was necessary for the fashionable fox hunter to have the perfect London-tailored red coat or swallow tails, white breeches so tight the rider would be grateful she breathed through her mouth, making it impossible to remount in the field unless she stood her horse in a ditch, the outfit completed by wearing mahogany-topped boots that were fashionably so close fitting that only silk stockings could be worn under them. Some would wear black coats but all would have on bowlers.

'Thank goodness things are more relaxed today,' said Gai after the Harringtons explained how the traditions of the hunt and the sartorial turnout had changed over the years.

In the 1800s, they said, the Hunt Club became the hub of social life in numerous towns. In York and Shrewsbury, for instance, the clubs organised suppers and dances, the origin of the Hunt Ball, and distinctive dress coats were designed for these formal occasions.

The red coat with its characteristic collar and club buttons was intended for the dining room rather than the hunting field. Some of the great houses of England had their own uniforms based on their liveries.

Exclusivity in hunting dress was often designed to make outsiders feel uncomfortable. The red coat did not become standard until the 1850s. Before that fox hunters went out into the fields in long, loose coats and a variety of boots, breeches and hats.

Masters and hunt servants wore hunting caps, while the rest of the field came out in top hats. Prince Albert once offended the purists by donning trousers and jackboots on the hunt, causing his 'essential Englishness' to be questioned.

In earlier days enthusiastic fox hunters of limited means were separated from the rich and the fashionable hunts because they could not afford the smart gear and the pricey horses.

But the 'democracy' of fox hunting was maintained by allowing foot followers, sometimes whole villages, to trail the hounds at a respectful distance, provided they didn't make a nuisance of themselves.

Gai had no idea fox hunting was once the common activity of the English countryside, requiring skilled huntsmen, highly bred hounds and fast, durable horses.

Indeed, it spawned a minor economy, establishing social conventions, enabling some to hunt for social status, others merely to treat it as a means of exploring the peace and tranquillity of the English countryside.

'Here we just do it for fun and as a test of horsemanship,' said Silla Harrington.

After receiving this slice of background on the strange English pastime, Gai set off on her first hunt.

The meet gathered in the early morning before the sun had a chance to burn up the scent of their quarry.

Riding up front was PP (Patrick) Hogan, regarded as one of the greatest riders to hounds in all Ireland. For years he had been fieldmaster for the great Irish fox hunt known as the Black and Tans.

A legendary bloodstock agent and buyer of foals, he was one of Robert Sangster's key advisers who at this time was credited with having advised Sangster to buy more than 200 winners.

Sangster respected the little Irishman so much he always took him to the Kentucky sales with him for an independent opinion before investing millions.

Lord Daresbury was there, and also the Earl of Stanhope's son, Lord Petersham. He was a glamorous and handsome man whom Gai had warmed to as soon as they met.

Petersham and his wife, Ginny, had flown in from Monaco specially for the hunt. Gai would later meet Lord Petersham and Ginny at quite a few race meetings in Ireland and England. They would be present at any social gathering of the elite.

Gai, placed at the back of the pack, was feeling out of it. She wanted to be up front in the thick of the action.

She didn't realise there was protocol, a strict procedure to be adhered to as well as a general strategy. The master by tradition and practice had the right to discipline the field and rebuke mavericks who threatened to ride over his valuable hounds, or by carelessly straying apart were likely to head the fox off in the wrong direction.

Spurring her horse on, Gai galloped to the front to be near Patrick Hogan. As she did so, she heard a woman's voice call out in tones of pained dismay, 'Who is that abominable person?'

It was Lord Daresbury's lady friend, Mary, riding side saddle.

The Hon Alan Lillingston, whose mother-in-law the Marchioness of Abergavenny was lady-in-waiting to the Queen for a forthcoming tour of Australia, was one of the huntsmen. He quickly explained to her that she was not observing protocol.

'You must stay behind—you could ruin the hunt by straying

the hounds and sending the fox off in a direction where he can't be scented,' he said.

Chastened, she fell back.

The hounds mostly stayed together, sniffing all around to pick up a scent or flush a fox out of wooded patches or the undergrowth.

Lord Harrington had explained that his hounds were bred specially for the hunt, the ones who would not follow a weak scent being weeded out in favour of those who would pursue it all day.

He said it cost him more than £100,000 a year to maintain a strong pack, all bred from the highest pedigree.

Gai was not disappointed. After riding for about three hours, a fox was sighted ahead in the clear, the huntsman sounded his horn and tally ho, the chase was on.

The more daring in their party kept up the pace in hot pursuit, leaping over fences and fallen timber, while the less adventurous went through gates and fell behind as the hounds bayed.

This is where Patrick Hogan was seen to live up to his reputation, with a courageous, almost reckless brand of horsemanship.

Gai knew now why he had set records as an amateur jockey, riding for all the great Irish trainers, including Vincent O'Brien. He rode five winners and a second from six rides one day at the Punchestown track.

Now Gai was up near the front runners, unable to contain her exuberance at the thrill of it all, which she was told later was referred to as the 'ecstasy of pace'.

With the hounds stopping and sniffing and, trying to keep protocol in mind, she had hardly stretched into full gallop before the fox was finally cornered. Two more were sighted and hunted before it was time to turn for home.

After the hunt a grand dinner was held and Gai had the time of her life. She would be invited back and went at least three times a year to Ireland for the hunt or to visit other people.

There were always parties and good times in Ireland.

She noted there was no feeling among them that this was a cruel sport. Rather they were ridding the area of a noxious vermin and local farmers were in agreement with the whole concept.

The way the Harringtons approached it, the hunt was the sharp end of a splendid social occasion.

The vision of Patrick Hogan in full flight after a fox stayed with Gai for some time. He could ride a horse as if he were glued on.

One day, while she rode down a path with him, he wanted to ride into the next field. Instead of going through a gate, he casually stood his horse stock still, took three or four steps and jumped it over a fence at least six feet high.

But as a person he was a little too eccentric for Gai's liking. On one visit to his house with a girl he was keen on, Gai saw a pig run out the front door. Fowls and other game ran around. To him it was all perfectly natural. His eccentricity was accepted as only the Irish can, and she had to concede that the small man with the big smile had all the charm of a leprechaun.

It seemed they found her something of a trick and good fun, and her directness and enthusiasm made her a welcome guest.

The socialising gave Gai an insight into the lifestyles of the rich and influential. They knew how to enjoy themselves. The fact that they accepted her for herself, and not that she was somebody's daughter, gave her enormous confidence.

In Ireland if she wasn't in Limerick or Tipperary she was in Dublin where a wealthy owner, Mrs Meg Mullion, took a shine to her and invited her to be her house guest whenever she could get away from London.

Mrs Mullion, who had about 60 or 70 horses in training and operated a stud in County Kildare, was elderly but quite an identity, a woman of character and style with a sharp intellect. Her husband was a retired European shipping magnate.

Gai met her through her trainer Paddy 'Darkie' Prendergast, a leading Irish trainer for whom Australians Jack Thompson and Ron Hutchinson had ridden.

For some reason that Gai could not define, Meg Mullion befriended her and whenever Gai crossed the Irish Sea to stay with her, she staged magnificent dinners for 14 or 16 people.

Through Mrs Mullion Gai would meet many of the outstanding names in Irish racing and breeding.

The friendship would have an unfortunate aftermath.

Mrs Mullion had a horse called Galway Bay which she bred on her stud farm. He had lost form when Gai saw him and Mrs Mullion was considering putting him to stud.

Gai suggested she might like to send him to her father to train in Australia where she thought Galway Bay could find form again in the warmer conditions. Later Tommy Smith spoke to Meg Mullion about it and she sent the horse to him.

Galway Bay struck form in the spring of 1977 by winning the Craven A Stakes and the George Adams Handicap, but his form petered out again. Meg Mullion agreed to sell the horse to Smith, he resold him to a syndicate, there was a dispute, she sued him and came twice to Sydney with all the obstinacy of the Irish to press her claim and the matter was settled out of court.

None of those dealings had anything to do with Gai, who would always remember Meg Mullion for her kindness, independent spirit and generous hospitality.

Meanwhile, in between the races and mixing with the elite of the international horsey set, Gai was still trying to make it as an actress.

CHAPTER SIX

THE BEAUTIFUL PEOPLE

Always the realist, Gai had felt embarrassed for some time over her agent.

Maggie had a reputation that commanded respect not only among the glitterati of London but also where it counted, among the professionals. She had hundreds of actors on her books, all of them experienced and many of them stars.

Gai was just an amateur. But with the imprimatur of Maggie's name behind her, they expected her to be trained. She could see the disappointment on their faces.

Maggie had accepted her at face value only because of James Mason. She was simply too big for her, and the jobs weren't coming through.

Gai went to Maggie and told her plainly she didn't think she could live up to having her backing as she was still learning the business and perhaps it might be better to engage a smaller agent.

Maggie understood and was happy to release her.

Gai found another agent and it was almost a case of 'have I got a job for you.'

They were auditioning at that very moment for the role of a bright young thing at a theatre in the Haymarket, someone to partner Patrick Cargill as the juvenile lead in an uproarious romp called *Two and Two Makes Sex*.

Once again Gai was first cab off the rank. And as usual, if she was first to apply for a role or a job, she would score.

Another Australian, Peter Whitting, was auditioning at the same time. He did the same reading as Gai and both obtained roles, Gai as the girl whom the leading man was entangled with and Whitting as her psychoanalytical boy friend.

The play was a six hander, a bright and breezy farce with loads of double entendres built around its ageing star, Patrick Cargill, of *Father, Dear Father* fame. He was also director.

Others in the cast were the elegant Ursula Howells, Margo Johns and Anthony Howard. The slick script was written by Richard Harris and Leslie Darbon.

With Cargill the play had run for a year in the West End three years previously before touring the provinces, Canada and Australia. Now it was being revived mainly for a touring season.

Briefly the plot was ageing businessman suffering virility crisis meets 20-year-old girl, his wife finds out, she gets involved with the girl's other male companion, and all become entwined in deceptions and confusions of an hilarious nature.

The first difficulty arose while the cast was going over the script in the Haymarket. As Gai read her lines, Patrick Cargill said to her, 'There is something terribly annoying about your inflections, Gai.'

'What do you mean, Patrick?'

'At the end of all your sentences, your voice goes up.'

He paused, then said, 'The only time I have ever heard that is in Australia.'

Gai knew it was true. Many Australians had developed the habit of raising their voices at the end of sentences as if every statement was a question. She was obviously doing the same thing.

'When were you in Australia?' she asked.

'About two years ago. In Sydney.'

'Oh, isn't that great,' she replied enthusiastically. 'I'm from Sydney.'

Cargill looked at her in a peculiar way. 'What do you mean, you are from Sydney?'

'I'm an Australian. That's where I come from.'

'That's what it is,' he said, raising his voice. 'I should have known. What a fool I am to have been tricked like this . . .'

He was suddenly angry, employing an Australian instead of an English girl.

Many Australians worked in English theatre at the time and there was a feeling they should not be allowed to take any more work from their English counterparts. Some people even went to the trouble of placing obstacles in the path of Australians.

Gai had worked hard on her voice, trying to iron out the accent, travelling twice a week across London to an elocution teacher. To give herself every chance, she had also studied tap dancing and singing to broaden her stage capabilities.

Meanwhile no job was too menial for her. She even took a cleaning job in a boys' house which included cleaning the dunnies.

It was heavy, demanding toil. She stuck it out for two days then told the manager, 'I think you need a cleaning firm here, not me.'

Gai tried working as a hat check girl in a gambling club but lasted only one night. She quit after sexual demands were made on her, knowing it would happen again.

Now the director and star of *Two and Two Makes Sex*, after she had been in the wilderness for months, looked like sacking her because of a minor inflection in her voice.

She could tell he wanted to get rid of her but when nothing happened quickly she realised Cargill thought it was too late to move—the show was already into its second week of rehearsal.

But in deciding to take a gamble on her he then insisted she go to a speech therapist for a quick fix.

Patrick Cargill seemed to go out of his way to find fault with her after that. One incident, due to Gai's lack of experience, caused a minor crisis.

She had never used a telephone before on stage. When her part called for her to do so, she spoke normally into it instead of dropping the mouthpiece down towards her Adam's apple or to one side so her voice would carry directly to the audience

This little hiccup just about drove Patrick mad. He ranted and raved and belittled her as if murder had been committed on stage.

Another blemish on Gai's part in the rehearsals almost caused Patrick to blow a gasket.

He referred to 'the rake' which in theatre jargon means the angle or slope of the stage. Gai asked 'what rake?' and began looking around the stage for a rake, common garden variety. Well, Patrick almost went into orbit. As distinct from Herbert.

As Gai told her friends, 'Patrick is just an old queer.'
Tommy was right.

She felt he hated women. Particularly incompetent women. And unfortunately Gai fell into that category with him.

These were only minor points, but admittedly they were an essential part of an actor's *modus operandi* that any qualified player should have known.

She tried desperately to please, but his attitude made her feel nervous and insecure.

Each night she went over her lines and each morning took a deep breath before entering the theatre for rehearsal.

Patrick's scorching criticism had undermined her confidence. She kept getting her lines wrong, or at least not delivering them up to his required standard, and he kept abusing her.

'You stupid bitch—get on with it, for Christ's sake,' he bellowed at her. He was extremely blunt and rude, repeatedly using the word bitch.

A strict stage disciplinarian, he pulled her up one morning and shouted, 'You still can't get the inflections right. I've told you half a dozen times. Obviously you haven't been working on it at all.'

She burst into tears when she arrived home that night, recovered, then went over her lines with great care.

She was also upset because it created a poor impression of her in the minds of her fellow actors and this caused a strained atmosphere. She sensed she could not change this impression and worried about it, although they did not refer to it in any way.

But although embarrassed at having her deficiencies shown up in such brutal fashion, Gai was too determined to let it put her off her goal for long. She told herself she was going to succeed and would keep on trying.

She consoled herself with the view that although this popular star was not a nice man, and certainly no gentleman to her, he was a brilliant comedian with wonderful timing and she was lucky to work with him and learn something positive about stagecraft.

Things eventually settled down, the problems faded into the background, the show had a successful short run in London and Gai's performance was well received. Cargill was superb.

While it was running Gai's parents came to London on their annual racing sojourn and saw her on stage a couple of times.

They stayed back after the show and went out with her to meet some of her theatre friends, but it wasn't Tommy's scene.

He said to Gai, 'I think it's a waste of time. There's no money in it. You'd be better off coming into the family business rather than staying here and battling for parts.'

His views hadn't changed on actors, either. *Poofs*.

'It's still my ambition to be an actress, Dad,' Gai told him, knowing it was not what he wanted to hear.

In this period while *Sex* was in London, Gai's domestic arrangements suddenly became difficult.

She was still in the same flat but the circumstances had changed. Her girlfriend Jenny had gone, leaving her alone in the bedroom they once shared. Now the flat, consisting of five bedrooms, had six people living there.

Two of the girls she shared the address with were Julia and Bianca. Julia was a pain in the neck. Her boyfriend had just left his wife and moved in with her. The couple made Gai's life a misery by being unpleasant to her.

They abused her with unseemly language because she took a bath at midnight, although she explained it was the time she came home from the theatre and her hours were unavoidable.

When their abuse didn't succeed in driving her out, they began turning the other girls in the flat against her. Their intention was obvious—they wanted her larger room.

But she told them bluntly, 'You can try as hard as you like, I'm not leaving. You will leave before I do. I have no intention of moving.'

She found no pleasure in the arguments but had nowhere else to go. Besides, it was a lovely place and she wanted to stay put.

Eventually the situation resolved itself when Julia and her boyfriend moved out. Gai once more enjoyed a good relationship with the other girls and one, Jane, later bought the unit.

After its London season, *Sex* went on tour for three months in the southern towns of Brighton, Bournemouth and Eastbourne, then Windsor.

Critics praised her performance, describing her as 'spirited and attractive', 'glamorous', agreeing that 'this newly arrived Australian has a future in theatre'.

John Butler in the *Bournemouth Times* thought she was a vivacious charmer who made her role of temptress believable.

Robert Wells went a little further in the *Eastbourne Herald*. He thought her 'shapely' as well.

She celebrated her 22nd birthday in the Bournemouth Playhouse with the cast and company giving her an Edna Everage party. The stage hands sent gladioli, each flower with one of their names on it.

Gai enjoyed the provincial theatre audiences and the experience generally. It did a lot for her acting skills to be on stage with the masterly Cargill but it also taught her about people, giving her a new understanding of the English character and life.

On tour she flatted with strangers, and sharing digs with

them and having to consider their needs taught her to be more tolerant.

It was part of her growing up process and a strong development period for her.

She was a working girl living away from home, trying to make it on her own. It wasn't easy considering she was an only child who came from a totally different background, where security and comfort were never in question, but she was willing to learn.

Gai would never be known as a modest person. Humility, though, was something she was beginning to understand.

The one aspect of English life Gai felt at home with was horse racing and mixing with racing people.

Perhaps it was due to spending all those early years as a young girl around the stables with her father while he trained. But now, in a foreign environment, for the first time in her life she could feel herself being drawn to the sport.

And being able to enjoy it without any pressure or suggestion that racing was something she should not be actively involved in, she began to develop a passion for it.

At no stage did she see herself as having any future in racing, regarding it as a means of fun and excitement and a wonderful social atmosphere, where all the best and most interesting people could meet on equal terms.

However, she did have a secret wish. She thought she would like to become an amateur jockey.

Loving horses, she contemplated how pleasant a lifestyle it could be in England. But she didn't approach anybody or follow up on the idea.

She went to race meetings at every opportunity. While performing in the theatre in Brighton she made sure she went to every meeting at Goodwood, which wasn't far away.

At other times Gai also went to Kempton Park, Royal Ascot, the Derby at Epsom, Newbury and Sandown Park.

One of the main advantages of this growing interest was

meeting such a cross section of people from around the world, Americans, French, Italians, Irish and English. To a young woman seeking experience it was not only interesting but fascinating.

Quite literally her true character was developed in this period when a love of racing came bubbling to the surface. She enjoyed it so much she didn't stop to think how much she had missed the racing atmosphere that surrounded her in Australia.

To see racing in all its facets in another part of the world, without conditions or directions being imposed on her, enabled her to absorb different training, feeding and breeding methods in her own good time.

Barbara Oswald, who went with Gai on one of her trips to Ireland, where among other things they went to Goffs' sales ring to see the Irish thoroughbreds sold, observed that it was Gai's love of horses that interested her most, more than the fun or meeting the big names of racing.

She saw Gai watch foals being born, feel their legs and comment on their shape and the breeding. It seemed to come naturally to her and was in her blood.

Gai was developing a feeling for the bloodstock industry through racing identities like Willie Hastings-Bass of Bass breweries fame, his good friend the bloodstock agent James Wigan, and Willie's brother-in-law, the top trainer Ian Balding.

Willie, a distant cousin of the Queen, would later become Lord Huntington. He had just obtained his own stables at Newmarket and Gai often went there and stayed with him.

He had worked as assistant to the great English trainer Noel Murless and studied in Australia and the United States before setting up at Newmarket.

Friends said there was no emotional or sexual relationship between them, they were just good friends with a mutual interest in racing.

On his last visit to London Tommy Smith had bought a horse, Budding Star, which he left for Gai to keep an eye on and Willie Hastings to train.

A neat chestnut filly, Budding Star was a half sister to several winners. Gai went with Willie for the filly's maiden race at Newmarket where she went out short-priced favourite on a miserable day with the track a quagmire almost up to her fetlocks.

After challenging for the lead most of the way the filly finished a miserable and remote sixth.

The Queen gave Willie several of her horses to train and he would eventually have 100 in training for influential owners.

Gai often popped up to Newmarket for a day or two to watch Budding Star in training, stay overnight and return to London.

The Queen was due to come to lunch one day within a few hours of her leaving, so Gai rose early to make everything nice for the Royal visit, thinking this would please Willie.

She made the beds, cleaned and tidied the house, then took a closer look at the kitchen where she drew his attention to cracked crockery.

'Willie,' she admonished, 'this is atrocious, this cutlery and crockery is just terrible.'

'Oh,' he said, 'it doesn't make any difference.'

Gai nagged him. 'I think it *would* make a difference. Can't your mum bring over something decent?'

But he would not hear of it. She couldn't believe he was about to entertain the Queen when his place was so rough and ready and, until she busied herself, in need of a good clean.

Willie's relaxed manner was in stark contrast to another friend of hers, Patrick Hogan (no relation to the fox hunter), when the Queen visited his Cambridge stud in New Zealand.

For six months he groomed the lawns and prepared the place so thoroughly it was immaculate when Her Majesty walked in— not a horse dropping to be seen for miles.

But the poor chap was in such a nervous state that as soon as he saw her and the various functionaries he blurted out the greeting 'Ma'am, would you like to go to the toilet?' She looked a bit startled. He told Gai it was his worst faux pas.

Gai found this casual air of blue bloods like Willie in England hard to understand at first. She reasoned it was because they felt they had the title, the breeding, and nothing to prove. They didn't have to dress up and display their wealth like the middle classes, who were trying to prove they were somebodies.

The aristocrats dressed well, but so many of the blue bloods she met dressed down, even showing holes in their sleeves. That was the trendy thing to do. If they had to buy clothes they might do so at Marks and Spencer but not Harrods or Savile Row.

It was as if they were saying we don't have anything to prove, we are the upper classes, it is vulgar to show your wealth.

Many, of course, didn't have any wealth to display but they still had the perceived status to go with the pedigree.

Gai knew of one member of the literary elite in London, a titled person, who went to work looking as if he had just climbed out of bed, untidy, his hair uncombed. He looked fey and acted vaguely, yet his mind was razor sharp.

He had the confidence of his class that told him he didn't have to try. So why bother dressing up or putting on a show?

The whole class syndrome seemed to be based not on how you dressed but how you spoke, the references you made. By your manner of speaking others judged whether you were working, middle or upper class.

Gai came to understand that if you walked into a shop or restaurant and were incredibly confident, it usually didn't matter how you looked. But it was the way you spoke, the way you treated people that enabled others to place you.

One titled gent cynically summed it up to Gai, 'We can always tell the upper from the lower-middle classes when we go to a wedding, for instance. The middle and lower classes are the ones in the new suits. They have hired out their clothes and you can see they are not accustomed to wearing them. The people of upper class rank are the ones in the old clothes, perhaps with buttons missing. Their gear is well worn. They are not out to impress anybody.'

For all that, Gai had some nice friends among the 'haves' who dressed and looked the part, just as she always did.

She went out with Will Bailey, whose father was prominent in racing in South Africa and had made a fortune from diamonds. Will was studying at Britain's National Stud at Newmarket where many Classical winners were bred and she often visited him there.

Gai also went out for a time with Alec Wildestein, son of Daniel Wildestein, the international art dealer and historian. They went to the races together in Paris and London.

They were regarded as the number one art dealers in the world through their operations in Paris and New York. Strongly into racing, they trained their horses mainly in France. Gai was present in Longchamp in 1974 when the Wildesteins' star filly, Allez France, won the Prix de l'Arc de Triomphe.

After that win Daniel Wildestein quickly became the leading owner in Britain, training his horses there instead of France.

Gai saw many of the best horses of the time in action at Epsom and Ascot taking out classic races like the Queen Elizabeth Stakes, giving her an appreciation of European thoroughbreds.

Through Willie Hastings she met the outstanding trainer Ian Balding, married to Willie's sister, Emma. Although not in Gai's age group, Ian and Emma became close friends and showed enormous kindness to her, inviting her to regularly stay the weekend at their famous training establishment, Kingsclere, not far from Newbury.

Their house was always full of lively young people, artists, writers and other interesting folk. Gai rode out on the gallops with Ian, good naturedly teased by other guests as they set off.

Among the famous people she met at Kingsclere was Paul Mellon, one of the wealthiest owners in America. Paul owned Mill Reef, which Ian Balding trained to win the 1971 English Derby, as well as the Eclipse Stakes, King George VI and Queen Elizabeth Stakes and the Prix de l'Arc de Triomphe.

Ian also trained for the Queen at Kingsclere, some of her best horses there being Example, Escorial and Magna Carta.

All this contact with eminent people made Gai insatiable to

learn as much as she could around their stables. She was having a ball and learning at the same time. Ian Balding said to her one day, 'Gai, I wish you'd shut up sometimes. You never stop asking questions.'

This period was a critical and essential part of her education, although she didn't look at it in that light at the time. She didn't think it had any significance beyond taking a normal healthy interest.

Without realising it she was beginning to slip into the racing game in a way not possible in Australia because of the strong feelings of her parents that she should not be directly involved.

The struggle she had to achieve any measure of success in acting was also a bonus in this process.

The fact that, untrained and not being a natural, she had to battle so hard, sharpened her mind generally in other directions.

And after a while she was able to rationalise that she should not be discouraged by failure to obtain roles. Trying harder was the answer.

Meeting the Sangster set at various places also gave Gai the confidence to move among high calibre people and celebrities, without regarding them as remote and unapproachable.

She was thrilled to meet them because she knew they were people who would go down in racing history.

She met most of the bloodstock specialists Sangster assembled in Ireland for his assault on the Keeneland sales in Kentucky beginning in 1975, buying the best bred yearlings money could buy and eventually sending prices through the roof.

It would end only after yearling prices reached such dizzying heights that some of the biggest players in the world of bloodstock breeding would go bust and Sangster's place at the top of the totem pole was taken by the fabulously oil-rich Sheikhs of Dubai, the Maktoum brothers, especially Sheikh Mahammed.

But not before Sangster and his team would marshall the greatest bloodstock empire the world had seen, one that would cost the Sheikhs something approaching $1 billion before they could gain supremacy.

The Sangster phenomenon originated in Limerick and Tipperary near where Gai rode to the hunt with Sangster adviser, Patrick Hogan. When she first went to Limerick, Robert Sangster was carefully putting his plans and talented team together, using his fortune from Vernons Pools as the base.

Gai knew most of them and would continue to bump into them.

The operation was centred on the Ballydoyle stud and training spread in Tipperary, where the master was the great trainer Vincent O'Brien. Gai had first met him as a girl of 12 with her parents, visited his stud and continued to meet him at the races, always looking up to him as one of the truly great trainers.

A young Irishman named John Magnier, whose family had a long history of stud breeding, managed the Ballydoyle operation which became the strongest breeding group in Ireland.

Gai met Magnier and his wife at various parties and at the races.

Then there was Richard 'Galloping' Galpin, the Newmarket bloodstock agent who seemed to bob up everywhere in the racing social scene Gai frequented. Even if he wasn't invited to parties he somehow turned up. Robert Sangster always told terrible jokes about him.

Billy McDonald, a wild boozy Irishman, was the court jester in Sangster's group. Gai met him at the races in Dublin when she saw Susan Peacock there, and he kept floating in and out of her life, either at the races or yearling sales.

Charles St George, one of England's biggest racehorse owners who played a financial role in the Sangster operation, befriended Gai. She met him and his glamorous wife Christine through family connections, stayed briefly with them at their lovely Newmarket home, dined with Charles in London and watched his track gallops.

Gai many times met Sangster's English trainer, Barry Hills, who took over Manton, Sangster's training establishment in England.

She was lucky enough to visit Manton and be shown around

by Hills. Even before joining Sangster, Hills had an international reputation, winning the Arc de Triomphe with Rheingold in 1969 and a host of top English races, including two Classics.

The group embracing Robert Sangster and his new wife Susan Peacock—Vincent O'Brien, the Hancocks of Kentucky, the Magniers—just travelled around the world from Kentucky to Ireland, London and Deauville.

Whenever Gai was at the 'right' race meeting she always bumped into these people. Some of them ribbed her because she was the only actress they knew who was always reading the *Sporting Life* and *Sporting Globe*.

Gai's performance in *Two and Two Make Sex,* despite all the internal problems with Patrick Cargill, boosted her chances when young new roles were in the offing.

It took a while but her new agent landed her a role that was keenly sought after by the battalions of young actresses available in London.

This was to play the part of Trevor Howard's mistress in a serious drama called *The Scenario*, by Jean Anouilh, one of the world's foremost playwrights.

Gai was excited at the prospect of playing opposite such a famous performer, the star of stage and screen, who portrayed the essentially decent Englishman in so many fine films, among them *Brief Encounter*, *The Third Man*, and *Gandhi*. In this play he was an anti hero.

One of her co-actors was the Australian John Bluthal, with whom she immediately formed a good working relationship.

This was a more demanding role but by now she had brushed up on her professional skills and was looking forward to the challenge.

Rehearsals went off more or less without a hitch and then the cast headed for the north of England to polish its presentation before a scheduled tour of Canada.

The action was set in 1939 in a ramshackle hotel in the forest of Fontainbleau where two writers are struggling to create a film script. One is young, ambitious and idealistic. The other, played by Howard, is old, cynical and alcoholic, a shambling slob and shadow of his former self. His wife the Countess suffers everything with tolerance and good grace, including her husband's affair with the servant girl (Gai, playing Jeanette, a barmaid and whore).

They played in Billingham, a dreary, grey, cheerless working class town near Newcastle which to the outsider had little or nothing to recommend it.

The weather was bitingly cold, the people looked beaten and poor, and until this moment Gai had not realised just how monotonous some lives could be.

It rained constantly, the scene was totally bleak and it came as an eye opener to her to see how sombre another part of England could be, all concrete and greyness. She had lived in Putney amid all the excitement and colour of London and this was a shock. The sunshine and vivid colours of Australia were a universe away.

Billingham had been bombed in the war and things didn't seem to have changed all that much. An ideal setting as Grottesville. The actors called their hotel The Colditz.

To make matters worse the play was a disaster there. For a start, nobody could pronounce the word *Scenario*. But the Billingham Civic Centre subsidised the losses, the only reason anyone would play there.

This grim setting had the unusual effect of causing Gai to feel depressed, the first time in her life she knew such an emotion.

For the first time since coming to England she began questioning her actions. 'What the devil am I doing over here in this gloomy place?' she asked herself.

She felt homesick, too. Her only relief came when she went riding in Northumberland.

After three weeks they returned to London for a week's rest, then flew to Toronto for a scheduled three-month season.

As soon as she reached Canada the feeling of depression lifted and she was back to her normal bouncy self.

Gai had enjoyed working opposite Trevor Howard who was extremely pleasant to her all the time they were in England. He behaved in an entirely professional manner. They were together for about two and a half hours on stage each night and it was a nice change to be on friendly terms with the star.

But from the time they boarded the plane for Canada, Trevor was in the grip of the grape.

He took his role so literally he hit the bottle the whole time and was as pissed as a parrot every night on stage.

Trevor was elderly then and his marital situation unhappy. It didn't help the tension that his wife was also in the play.

But even allowing for that his drinking made Gai angry. Here was this most distinguished actor whom people were flocking to see, here was this aspiring young actress wanting to make an impression as his mistress, and he was treating the whole thing as a booze-up.

Late one afternoon it was snowing heavily when Gai arrived at the stage door of the Royal Alexandra Theatre in Toronto to prepare for the night's performance.

Two people were lying on the ground, partly covered with snow.

'My God, these dreadful derelicts,' she said, mentioning it to several members of the cast when she reached the dressing rooms.

John Bluthal took a look and who should the 'derelicts' be but Trevor and a drunk he'd picked up with somewhere.

John and some of the cast had to pick him up, brush the snow off and help him to his dressing room—not long before the show. Gai was certain he couldn't stand, let alone act.

She could see the irony of it all considering his role as a drunk, but this was too much.

The management thought so too.

They already had the wisdom of former phenomena to rely on with Trevor's boozing, and asked an official of Actors' Equity to specially monitor his performance that night.

The judge's verdict: What a brilliant actor!

79

The other actors were upset because it was affecting their performances. Gai was angry enough but luckily she didn't have any long dialogue scenes with him.

Trevor didn't just miss a few lines, on a bad night he literally missed pages of text and this threw them right off balance.

Gai could laugh about it later but at the time she thought it a nightmare. Through it all, Trevor remained pleasant to her.

It proved one thing: Trevor Howard was a real pro. Even if he didn't give cues to his fellow actors.

Apart from these infuriating little irritations, the play was highly successful. The famous old theatre was packed out for the three months. Gai's mother came across from Sydney to spend Christmas with her in Toronto.

Gai was elated that she was doing something worthwhile in her own right. She made a lot of friends on tour and enjoyed the travelling. The troupe visited Niagara Falls.

John Bluthal, a Shakespearian actor who would become well-known to Australian television viewers as The Boss in the *Oils Aint Oils* ad, was asked by this writer at the end of 1995 for his impressions of Gai Smith in Billingham and Toronto.

He took time off from his stage appearance with Diana Rigg in *Mother Courage* at London's National Theatre to record these comments:

'I can only tell you she was one of the most delightful people I have ever worked with,' he said without reservation. 'She was just a gorgeous girl, just a joyous member of the company.

'Nothing was too much trouble for her. She was a treat to be with and was regarded by us all as the company mascot. And she was so attractive. We all loved her.

'Gai joined in everything as a kind of blithe spirit. It was 24 degrees below freezing in Toronto, the snow ploughs were out all the time. We had a heated swimming pool on the rooftop of our hotel but only half was covered in. I remember Gai swimming out to the weather side laughing at the snow falling on her face. It was so exhilarating.

'Gai was so friendly and well mannered. There was good breeding in her background. Must have gone to a good school. You could see from her behaviour as a young adult that she was well brought up. She had talent too.

'Acting can be pretty tough and ruthless, a precarious profession.

'People read magazines about the rich and famous and go into acting because they think it's glamorous. It's not. I know there was money in Gai's family and I think she showed courage in giving it a go. Please give her my love.'

Back in London Gai worked as a model and sales person for a prêt-à-porter house, a manufacturer of ready-to-wear clothes in Earls Court. Her specialty was coats which she modelled and sold to the rag trade.

She simply fronted up to the firm one day when in need of a job and stayed with them for a year. She was so successful at it that many people in the trade thought she was a member of the Jewish family that owned the business.

The family was so pleased with her work that they sent her to Copenhagen to demonstrate and sell the whole range. She automatically slipped into the role of seller.

Gai missed out on many of the modelling jobs she applied for because she was not tall enough, but usually managed to get through the door anyway as an extra.

A non-smoker, she was asked when applying for a cigarette advertisement, 'Do you smoke?'

'Oh yes.'

'Are you a heavy smoker?'

'Oh yes.'

After the interview she bought a packet of cigarettes and went home to practise, frantically puffing on the dreaded weed before the audition. She missed out.

Gai turned down the female lead role in *Stand Up, Virgin Soldiers* after it was offered to her because it required her to appear in a nude scene. 'I want it,' she told her agent, 'but if I take my clothes off I won't get a part unless I do it every time.'

Actress Pamela Stephenson, a New Zealander who had lived in Sydney and married Scottish comedian Billy Connolly, stripped for the show.

Gai's acting career took a turn for the better when she landed a role in a BBC film directed by Ken Hannan of *Sunday Too Far Away* fame.

Then she capped it off with a major part in the BBC series *Dr Who* with Tom Baker.

On the night it opened on television, Gai invited all the cast to her flat for a party. It went with a swing but Gai still had little idea of cooking or quantities—she prepared so much spaghetti she didn't know what to do with it.

The show ran for 13 weeks.

Gai had been away from home for two and a half years. She hadn't met the great love of her life among the beautiful people. And she hadn't scored that blockbuster role that would put her name up in glimmering lights.

She was living in rented premises, which didn't please her, but she was not unhappy over any part of her life. There was just the question of whether she would achieve anything more by staying on.

In her heart of hearts she felt she had been away long enough.

It was December, 1977. She told everyone she was going home for Christmas.

Throwing a huge farewell party in her Putney flat, she made a weekend shopping run to Paris before flying out.

She honestly kidded herself she would be returning to London.

CHAPTER SEVEN

STILL KNOWN AS TJ'S GIRL

Valerie and Tommy Smith had no doubt their daughter was home for good, welcoming her with open arms.

Indeed, when she said she was coming home they naturally took it to be permanent.

They were frankly surprised at her success in London. They didn't think she would obtain any worthwhile roles, and although they still had serious doubts about acting as a profession, they were prepared to go along with it if it made her happy.

As Gai explained to them, her real reason for leaving London was hopefully to break into the local acting scene through the full-length feature films now being produced in Australia.

Films funded by the Australian Government as part of its new arts policy were beginning to make an impact abroad.

She knew that not being known at home for her acting except through the media, she might have to start all over again.

The newspapers, hailing the return of TJ's prodigal girl, painted glowing pictures of her acting career.

But Gai knew the truth. She was lucky to have landed the roles she did and although she had blossomed as an actress, those roles had been few and far between.

She could not have survived in London on acting alone.

Sydney, she believed, could not possibly be as difficult a scene in which to find work.

In her first newspaper interview just after Christmas, 1978, her picture with the brilliant, confident smile appeared above the caption, 'Gai Smith . . . successful? That's an understatement!'

After listing her acting credits the *Daily Mirror* writer said, rather naively, 'All that was required for her instant acting career was a large amount of confidence, a reasonable degree of talent, an attractive appearance, a good voice and good friends.'

To justify her return Gai mentioned her ambition to break into the booming film industry in Australia, pointing out that few films in comparison were being made in England.

She even put in a good word for Australians, saying they were more open than the English and more expansive in their actions because of the greater time spent outdoors.

That was the public persona, the big smile and vivacious personality, looking forward to a bright future as an actress.

Now 24, she had developed into a beautiful young woman. Her brown hair bounced with vitality, her blue-grey eyes were fetching, her smile winsome yet caring.

The slim brunette with the fashion model figure, lovely face and stylish clothes, was totally composed and self-assured. But the happy public exterior hid her inner feelings. She felt unsettled, as if floating in a time warp.

Gai had changed dramatically, but those around her were not showing any differences.

She had returned from nearly three years away after having a fabulous time meeting influential and important people, being invited to some of the most palatial homes and estates in England, Ireland and France, and treated as if she were an equal.

Sure, many of the connections were due to her father's status as an outstanding trainer of thoroughbreds, opening doors in all stratas of society. But she had also made her own friends, created her own opportunities and had been accepted as a reasonable, civilised and sought-after person in her own right.

She had gone to the races of her own choosing because she wanted to and it was a link with home, not because it was her father's business as had been the case in Sydney.

Gai had been her own boss, done what she wanted to and as a result had felt independent.

She had changed and become more worldly, but it seemed that everyone she met in Australia now was standing still and in the same spot as three years before.

It was like a newspaperman who has worked for several years abroad and returns home to his favourite watering hole. His old mates are still grumbling and arguing about the same things, and in no time at all he or she feels they have never been away.

Gai was no longer thinking along the same lines as her old friends and others near to her. And she felt the men she was meeting were, well, boring.

With men she had that feeling of *deja vu*—the unmistakable illusory feeling of a situation being tediously familiar.

Her feelings were no different to any other young person who experiences travel and a wide spectrum of life at an impressionable stage of their development, crowding knowledge and myriad images into a short time span. Comparisons with home inevitably keep surfacing.

The change was normal, but Gai couldn't come to grips with it and felt desperately unhappy.

'What am I doing here?' she asked herself.

Trying to shake off her despondency, she rang around various contacts trying to find acting work. The message was pretty much the same, 'You sound like a Pom. You can't expect an Australian part if you sound like a Pommy.'

Deliberately stifling the thought of going off to an elocution teacher again, this time to reverse the accent, she decided to take singing lessons once more. She might find a part in a musical.

She told her parents of her feelings. They were not about to be generous again and send her back to London. She knew that if she had the money to pay for her fare, she would have left on the next plane. But it was out of the question.

Gai was aware she needed time to regain her balance and let things settle down.

One immediate and pressing problem was living at home again with her parents in their Point Piper home.

She had always enjoyed the best possible relations with her parents, a situation engendered by her respect for them and her willingness to conform to their lifestyle.

But her new-won independence made this no longer a tenable arrangement. Through unavoidable differences of opinion Gai and her mother fought like alley cats. There were shouting matches.

Gai had gone away as Valerie's daughter and returned her own person. Valerie could not cope with that.

Valerie still wanted to tell Gai what to do and perhaps worst of all, impose a form of curfew on her as had existed before she left for England. If Gai brought friends home and sat up talking and drinking coffee, Valerie was likely to enter the lounge room and say, 'This is disgraceful Gai—it's 2 am.'

'But mum, people do this all the time,' Gai would protest.

If Gai was going out, her mother was likely to sit on her bed while she dressed and ask what time she might be home.

In Toronto Gai recalled her mother saying she didn't know how Gai could cope with an actor's life, working until 11 o'clock in the theatre, then going out with the rest of the cast until all hours, in heavy snow at that.

Gai wanted to live her own life, sleeping in on Sunday mornings after a late night if she wished, not feeling obliged to have a sleep on Sunday afternoons as her parents normally did.

It was the normal case of youth growing into manhood or womanhood and the generation gap not bridging the differences.

Will Shakespeare had a phrase for it, 'Crabbed age and youth cannot live together.'

Three months before Gai returned home a death had occurred in the Smith family, the effect of which was still being felt.

Her Uncle Dick had been with Tommy since the days just

after the war when Tommy started out as a battling trainer with one horse, a buckjumper and brumby named Bragger.

Dick was Tommy's only strapper. They did their entertaining in the feed room next to Bragger, using an old kerosene tin with a block of ice to cool the beer.

Their other brother, Ernie, had been with Tommy too from soon after the war, acting as stable manager.

The brothers and sisters of Tommy Smith were a large and close-knit family thrown together by adversity after their parents died early within a year or so of each other, leaving the eldest girl, Gladys, to become mother to the four younger Smith children.

Loyalty to one another was considered an essential part of their lives. Dick and his wife ran the Light Brigade Hotel in Paddington but each morning Dick went to the track at Randwick to clock the horses for Tommy. Liked by everybody, Dick was the peacemaker in any disputes within the Smith racing scene.

Tommy was shocked by Dick's sudden death, due to a clotting abnormality.

Three months after she came home, Tommy invited Gai to fill the vacancy as clocker in the stable, occupying about three hours every morning.

Not one to be idle Gai began rising at 3.30 five mornings a week, riding to the Tulloch Lodge stables near Randwick with Tommy in his Rolls and clocking up to 60 horses as they galloped around the inside track. Some would be winners in the next few days or weeks.

Her timing had to be spot on. Nothing less would satisfy The Little Master, as many called Smith. Gai referred to herself as The Golden Thumb.

She felt very much at ease in the scene, fitting in naturally just as she had on those early morning visits with friends to some of the tracks in England, Ireland and France.

She loved the pre-dawn atmosphere of Randwick, a peaceful time of day with little else happening and nothing to distract her, when the temperature was cool: sometimes chilly but never hot.

And she loved working with the animals, seeing the steam rise off them from their exertions just as the sun came up and shifted the patterns on the grass and skyline.

She liked the stable lads, enjoyed the jockeys' banter and above all, enjoyed working with her dad.

The footlights still beckoned but the jobs weren't coming.

TJ recognised her ambition. He and Valerie still didn't like the idea of her becoming an actress but they did not suggest any alternative.

Tommy knew from the time she was about 16 that she had ambitions to do something outside the norm.

He told his longtime secretary, Pauline Blanche, 'She'll never be content to be a housewife. I don't think she's the type to be happy with just a domestic situation. She won't rush in and get married early and have kids.'

He also understood her feeling of independence and was first to go along with the idea that Gai should leave home, although to begin with he pushed it to one side.

Being an astute property dealer who built up a considerable fortune through investments from his training and betting activities, Tommy had bought an apartment from a deceased estate two doors away in Point Piper. The Smith family company, in which Gai was a shareholder, bought it.

Gai suggested she move in there on her own but her parents said no, not just yet. Valerie, a strong willed person, could think of many reasons why it was not a good idea.

Finally after three months Tommy said to Valerie, 'Look, you and Gai won't get on under the same roof. Madam has been away too long now. For God's sake let her move into her own place.'

She did.

Gai's name began appearing in magazines and newspapers alluding to her acting aspirations with expected racing connotations—'TJ's top filly', 'Tommy's star filly', 'TJ's best looking filly'.

Her first break came not in acting but the media.

Max Presnell, a racing writer on the *Sydney Sun* and radio commentator on the sport, phoned her to ask if she was interested in doing a spot as track reporter on the Sydney Channel Seven current affairs program, *Eleven AM*.

'I've told them you're back, you've done acting, know about racing and might like to do it,' he said.

'Love to,' said Gai, enthusiastic as ever.

She began right away, interviewing racing people for the show.

Then she was asked if she would like to be a glamour tipster for the *Daily Telegraph* in Sydney. Absolutely.

So she picked up a press pass, wrote a few thoughts on likely winners for the newspaper's readers, and as a bonus went to the track and interviewed racing people like jockeys and trainers for Ian Craig's racing segment in the Channel Seven news on Friday nights.

She was still clocking, and just so the grass didn't grow under her dancing feet, she rejoined the fight to have women admitted as full members of the Sydney Turf Club. She pitched in by campaigning with friends Julie Ritchie and Gail Selwood and the victory was sealed in May, 1978, when she was one of the first 26 women to become members. Her mother was also among them.

Gai took the headlines on the issue on page one of the *Daily Mirror* with 'Gai's a winner—like dad!' and 'It's about time, says TJ's Girl.'

In the story she drew on her experience abroad by saying Sydney racing 'finally has both feet in the 20th century', and had been 'dragging one leg through the Middle Ages as far as women are concerned'.

Warming to the subject, she drew the comparison that in England 'everyone from the aristocracy down' was amazed that women in Australia were not allowed full rights as members.

She had never been afraid to say exactly what she thought.

Gai could also behave exuberantly in public and show her emotions whenever the mood dictated.

While still a university student before going overseas she had a minor brush with racing authorities one day, drawing headlines and putting her individual stamp on the situation.

Sydney businessman Len Plasto, who owned the horse Oncidon, trained by Tommy Smith, decided to sell it for a pittance when it repeatedly broke down through lameness.

He sold it for a princely $2 to Gai and her friend, Averil Sykes, daughter of the leading veterinarian, Dr Percy Sykes. The girls intended using it as a show horse.

But when it showed improvement, Smith decided to put it back in work. Oncidon went out favourite in the $10,000 Villiers Stakes in 1973 and donkey-licked the field.

The two young owners, all dressed up for the occasion, could hardly suppress their joy and Gai couldn't wait to congratulate the winning jockey, Neville Voigt.

Under the rules of racing nobody except a steward should touch a jockey until he weighs in. Gai risked having Oncidon disqualified when she rushed forward in the birdcage to throw her arms around the jockey and plant kisses on his cheeks. A steward moved in quickly to stop the 'Gai time' but did not take disciplinary action.

Members of the Smith family had been known to hurl hats, cheer lustily and shake hands all around, but this was the first time one had hugged a jockey—and ahead of time.

In her quest to establish a career Gai continued to win favourable publicity but there was always the TJ tag to it.

It didn't worry her at this time but she realised in coming back to Australia she carried the baggage of being her father's daughter.

CHAPTER EIGHT

MOMENT OF DECISION

Six months went by without Gai gaining so much as a sniff of a film role, in spite of all her efforts.

Then, as if from the clouds, a role dropped into her lap. Not the type she had been hoping for, but a nice start. She felt things were on the move for her at last.

The Reg Grundy organisation offered her a prominent part in the *Young Doctors* soap series on TV.

The role was that of a high-powered dress designer, Natalie French, who became a patient in the hospital drama.

The magazines and newspaper TV sections played the same old lines: 'Gai Smith, actress daughter of famous Sydney horse trainer Tommy Smith.' 'Gai's sire, leading racehorse trainer TJ Smith . . . '

Gai told reporters that although she loved the part and was glad to have it, she wasn't a bit like Natalie French.

'Natalie is quite aggressive and bitchy,' she said. 'She's got sex appeal but she's too formidable for most men. She's overpowering, bossy and thinks only of herself.

'I'm a fun-loving person and my friends and family are very important to me. The only thing we have in common is our love for fashion.'

These comments tripped easily off the tongue but Gai's friends knew she wasn't spouting pap. She was sincere.

Many people knew she could relate to the fashion angle.

She had nearly as many hats as her father, whose celebrated collection of lids was a talking point among racegoers.

The fashion pages were pointing to Gai's flair for bright and stylish clothes, noting that she had them made up from designs she either created herself or saw in the glossies. She was too much the individual to allow anyone to dress her.

In her honest, direct way Gai told writers how things had been pretty quiet since her return, that she expected the work situation for actresses to have been easier.

She was asked about being the daughter of a famous man. Yes, she said, it was a stroke of good fortune. It was helping her career and she knew the publicity she was receiving at that moment was because of her father's name. James Mason had helped her through knowing her father.

'Having contacts helps,' she said, 'but you still have to knock on doors and audition. You still have to prove you can act, so knowing the right people isn't everything.'

So far, pretty straightforward stuff.

Then she touched lightly on the topic that was really at the back of her mind.

'There's a disadvantage in being the daughter of a well-known and extremely successful man,' she told *TV Week*.

'People tend to look at you as a little rich girl sitting on her daddy's knee and playing at acting. I take myself seriously and I take my career seriously. I get offended when other people don't take me seriously.'

That was the woman of the future talking.

But it was early days yet.

After eight episodes of *Young Doctors* in which her pretty face was seen in homes all around the nation and in many other countries, Gai was set to tread the boards again for the first time since Toronto.

She landed the role of Alice, Duchess of Gloucester, in *Crown Matrimonial*, a play based on Edward VIII's abdication set for a long run in Sydney before going on tour, with June Salter the star.

It opened at the Seymour Centre to an appreciative audience, some patrons so enthused they jumped on the stage when the curtain came down to hug June Salter.

Gai's father made one of his rare visits to the theatre on opening night still trying to see what all this acting business was about. No mention of poofs this time but he was quite adamant the part wasn't big enough.

'All that time spent in rehearsal, I spend two hours in the theatre and you're only on stage for ten minutes,' he said.

'Well Dad, it was a good cameo part,' she said. Gai didn't care that the part wasn't so big, pleased that once again she was in good company.

To take the part Gai relinquished the chance of an overseas trip with her parents.

She enjoyed acting so much she didn't regard it as work, confessing to people she sometimes felt an attack of the 'guilts'.

Her personal ambition at that time, widely stated, was simple: 'I want to be good at whatever I do. Yes, I desperately want to be a good actress and I'd also like to be more involved in racing.'

Anyone who knew Gai was aware of her desire for success and the truth of what she was now saying low key in the papers—she had never been prepared to be mediocre, always wanting to be good or exceptional at whatever she touched.

That was the first time, in August, 1978, she had expressed such a desire about racing. It had not sprung from any family discussion, just a thought spontaneously aired to a newspaper interviewer who asked a question.

Gai was already becoming a little more involved in racing with her father, not in any hands-on way, but more or less as a growing interest on the side.

Apart from the practical aspect of clocking, this interest had increased since her return. She had become a kind of human sponge, soaking up information on racing generally, and constantly asking questions of her father.

She had gone into partnership with him in breeding horses in England. They had one brood mare there and were hoping to have more.

Gai also had a brood mare, Classic Connection, at the Derby King Ranch in the Widden Valley in the Hunter district of New South Wales.

Earlier in the year at the Trentham Yearling Sales in New Zealand Tommy allowed her to have a test run to try out her 'eye' for a horse. He said he'd let her pick out a yearling and he would pay for it—but she would have to pay him back after finding an owner to buy the horse.

Gai made her choice and bid for it.

'You did well,' said the old maestro of the sale ring, whose business depended on buying good yearlings and selling them to prospective owners. 'If I hadn't approved I would never have let you catch the auctioneer's eye.'

She chose a chestnut colt by Balkan Knight out of Sarafan, from the Priongia Stud, in Te Awamato. She called it 'Sneezy' because it gave her hay fever.

The Smith girl could not have had a better teacher, although it all seemed a pretty academic exercise at the time.

Still, she was absorbing the mysterious knowledge of bloodstock that came only from long experience and insight, and even then it was a most inexact science. Instinct played a big part.

Even after all the known factors were taken into account, there was still the big element of luck.

She had observed Tommy examine yearlings hundreds, probably thousands, of times before buying them, running his hands around their legs. Onlookers thought he was feeling for muscle quality but he was searching for joint or sesamoid weaknesses which might mean disaster.

Tommy would then run his hands around the neck and windpipe looking for goitre, a possible sign of wind troubles.

And he would sometimes surprise a horse by 'grunting' it—frightening it with a sudden movement. He could tell from the squealing sound made under pressure if it was likely to have breathing problems. A good square jaw also indicated if a horse could breathe freely.

He didn't like piggish or 'cunning' eyes, believing the intelligence of a horse and its will to win could be detected in the eye.

Gai had seen him take in the conformation of a horse at a glance, noting that the head, neck and shoulder had to fit properly if the horse was to show good balance.

He liked the legs straight and the knees well set and always tried to see them led in to check their walking style, preferring horses with sloping shoulders who walked with a relaxed gait.

But it wasn't a priority to see them walk if all else was right.

He could point to great sprinters like Todman who were poor walkers. He took the breeding into account but in the end it came down to instinct.

And who could argue with that?

At the Trentham sales in New Zealand in 1956 nobody was interested in a small dark bay colt with a sway back out of Florida by Khorarassan, a smart galloper that had been raced in England by George VI but was really only a moderate sire. With an unobtrusive flick of his catalogue, Smith bought him for a bargain-basement 750 guineas.

The colt turned out to be Tulloch, probably the greatest champion ever seen in Australia, after whom Tommy named his stables.

In one interview in 1978 Gai was asked the sixty four dollar question: 'Would you like to follow in your father's footsteps?'

She answered thoughtfully.

'Yes, in a way. I've ridden track work, helped a little in the office, raced horses, clocked them, but I have no aspirations to train. It's very hard to follow a genius.'

The word 'genius' was questioned, but she had thought that one out too.

'Anyone like Dad who has been the country's leading trainer for 26 years has to be a genius. Besides, I'm very proud of him.'

Tommy had long since passed the world record for winning a major training premiership, taking it for the 26th consecutive time with 156 winners for the season. He'd also passed $1 million in prizemoney for the fourth year, confidently expecting to be the first trainer to pass the $2 million mark.

Also, on May 13 of the previous year, 1977, he'd reached another record by training six winners and two seconds on the eight-race program at Sydney's Warwick Farm.

Nobody had been better than TJ in taking advantage of the press to promote his own interests, but now Gai was becoming a celebrity in her own right.

Her life was running at a hectic pace. After working late at the Seymour Centre in *Crown Matrimonial*, she still rose early several mornings a week to arrive at the stables before dawn.

She usually spent some time in the office each day, chauffeuring her father to and from the races, researching material for her TV appearances and recording her Channel Seven program.

She did commercials, voice overs and anything else her chase for work turned up.

She also turned her attention to fighting the Australian Jockey Club in the struggle to have women admitted as full members as she had with the Sydney Turf Club.

One of 16 women in the crusade, she went public. 'These women are not only keen racegoers,' she told the Sydney *Sun*, 'they put a lot of money into the sport. This is what makes me so annoyed.

'The AJC is prepared to take our money but won't fully accept us. Australia is the only country in the world where this happens.

'A provision to give us associate membership with no voting rights holds no interest to us.'

In between, she found time to play, enjoying a busy social life.

The question of marriage came up in the tabloids.

'I think of blokes but not marriage,' she said. Nice one.

Yes, she said, it would be good to be married and have kids, but when she was married, she would be married for long enough.

Gai had more boyfriends than the Sydney punters had certainties.

But there was always the feeling that they had to fit in with her arrangements, that her work—acting, TV and helping her father—was the most important thing in her life.

Joe Manning, the man from down Cootamundra way on whose property Tommy spelled his horses, recalled an amusing incident which showed Gai's independence when it came to male suitors.

She had returned from England and was acting in *Young Doctors* at the time.

'Gai had lots of boyfriends and often brought them down to the farm,' said Joe. 'We were going to the Griffith races this day and a boyfriend was staying with us for two or three days.

'If he wanted to see anything of Gai he had to watch the horses because she spent all her time with me looking at them.

'Griffith was about a hundred miles away, it was a hot day with the temperature around the century mark, and I had a little Alfa Romeo sports car with a dickie seat at the back. I had to take a jockey and the car could only seat three.

'So I said to Gai, "I only have room for three."

'Without a pause she said, "the boyfriend will just have to stay at home, won't he?" She didn't worry much about him, she wanted to go to the races.'

Joe said he thought Gai had always had it in mind to do something in her life with horses.

'I used to go to the New Zealand sales with them and right from the time she was young she would rather look at the yearlings than go out with her friends,' he said.

'Every horse you looked at she'd look at too, wanting to know everything about them.'

Joe made the point that he was impressed with Gai's manners and friendly nature from the time she was a girl.

'She had a nice style about her, a very human side to her and treated everyone the same,' he recalled.
'She always remembered every member of the staff. We had one old chap named Frank Moore on the property, he was about 80 at the time, and she would always seek him out and have a yarn with him.'

Gai's parents had noted her recent passion for racing, although she was still only on the periphery of the sport.

She was on a kind of roller coaster, always trying to fit more into a life that was already crowded, although nothing dominated.

They now both seriously doubted she had a future in the theatre.

Tommy convinced Valerie of that. And at this time there did not appear to be any suitable prospect in sight for marriage, which might have solved the problem, although Gai didn't seem concerned about her future at all.

Gai's parents talked about her situation. Tommy was one of the wealthiest trainers in the world, had developed the most powerful stables in the land, and while he had no thought of retiring—'they'll carry me out in a box first'—the time would come when he could use some assistance in the stables.

They thought the time was right to broach the subject.

Tommy realised that Gai had been working for him part time and there was a role somewhere in the business for her to play. But he didn't give too much thought to what that should be.

He knew she was a hard worker as well as being gregarious and vivacious, and she was wasting her time in the theatre world.

The last thing Valerie wanted to see was Gai becoming too involved in racing but she could see there was sense in what Tommy was saying, and supported him.

Gai was in the process of deciding whether to go on tour with the *Crown Matrimonial* play and, in discussing this with Valerie, gave her mother the opportunity of talking to her about the future.

Valerie said, 'The role isn't big enough and the money isn't good enough. Acting is a very precarious profession—you'll only work for six months of the year.

'You should be thinking seriously about learning your father's business. It's your heritage, you know.'

The advice set Gai thinking. It meant if she followed it she would have to give up the ambition she had cherished from childhood in the apartment at Potts Point, from her days at the Sacred Heart Convent at Rose Bay when she featured in *The Pirates of Penzance* and other productions.

She still loved the stage but had to admit to herself it was hard to make a living from it.

On the other hand she was thrilled by her small role in television and thought she could use her acting skills to enhance that.

In the end, after turning it over many times, the practical side of her nature came to the fore.

She was on the way to Randwick at 3.30 am with Tommy in his burgundy-coloured Rolls when she told him. Gai simply said she had decided she would like to learn the family business.

Tommy would convince himself in the years ahead that Gai had mentioned in that conversation she would like to become a trainer.

Gai was sure she didn't mention the word, only that she would like to join the stables on a more permanent basis in place of her acting career.

Certainly Tommy was pleased with her decision but mentioned what a tough game it could be, pointing out some of the difficulties in running a big stables and obtaining good horses.

The truth is Gai did not have being a trainer in mind at that stage. Tommy had no intention of retiring and there was no scope for such a role at Tulloch Lodge.

Besides, it was a man's world.

CHAPTER NINE

MEETING ROBBIE WATERHOUSE

Gai's life was now headed in a different direction. That in itself created a problem.

She was never told in which direction to go.

Gai turned up in the office of Tulloch Lodge, the nerve centre of a big thoroughbred training establishment, expecting to have her role spelled out.

She had been around the stables casually for years and that had been fun. Now coming in for several hours every day on a permanent basis, she expected to have certain duties and to be taken seriously. Instead, nothing seemed to have changed.

It would have been better for all concerned if Tommy had said to the senior personnel in the stables, particularly his brother Ernie, 'Look, Gai is going to work so many hours in the office, she will come to the track and clock the horses and I will train her to eventually take over from me.'

But to Gai's knowledge nothing like that was ever said. As a result, the situation just drifted along.

Ernie Smith, the stable manager, had played a leading role in organising the horses for training and when Tommy was away on his normal long holidays or interstate preparing his runners for the big races, Ernie made the decisions and ran the stables.

They were a successful team, partly because Ernie did things the way his brother, The Little Dictator, wanted it. When Tommy was on the spot, Ernie was under his influence and went along with him. When Tommy was away, he did things differently.

Being brothers and associated for such a long time they understood each other so well there was little need for conversation.

The office and all TJ's personal business was run by his loyal and efficient secretary, Pauline Blanche, who had been with him since 1962. She did things her way and had her own system.

In this situation Ernie and Gai, and Tommy himself, would no doubt have found it much easier if Gai's role had been defined.

This may have ruffled feathers and Tommy hated confrontation, even in minor matters, preferring to walk away than be involved. It was often hard to obtain an answer from him.

The stable was run on easy lines that had existed for years, and Tommy didn't want to upset the status quo by signalling any change. And really, there *was* no change. He was the boss and everyone took their cue from him.

The notion went around the stables that although Gai was obviously there to learn more of the ropes, even Tommy thought she was just dabbling in spending more time there.

She was still fiddling around with television work and there was the feeling that she was in the stables only because she was the boss's daughter and should not be taken seriously.

How could she? She was just a girl and this was a man's business.

So Gai would drift into the office, then drift into the yard but soon realised she was not welcome there. It was Ernie's territory and nobody wanted to take any notice of her there anyway.

She mainly confined herself to the office where there was a great deal to learn on such subjects as race nominations and acceptances, assigning of jockeys, who to contact among owners or other persons when certain things happened or went wrong, and generally how the system functioned, especially the keeping of records and their daily updating.

Gai settled into a public relations role, liaising with clients and the media, soon showing she was a good communicator.

She worked hard at learning the system, wanting to do more and take more responsibility, but nobody wanted her to have it.

Her enthusiasm kept her going, driving her to achieve something.

She was on the spot with her father every afternoon when the master vet Percy Sykes came to examine the horses, and she discussed every aspect with them.

She took more notice of the practical side of the stable operation without interfering in the yard, quietly studying the bloodstock magazines, other literature on horses and videos of races.

Nobody was going to offer this intruder in a male-dominated world anything or go out of their way to help her, and she had to be a brain picker, making sure she talked carefully to people to obtain their opinions. Being a good talker and listener, she learned quickly.

But in trying to turn her secondary role into something more significant, Gai trod on the toes of Pauline Blanche.

Gai was clearly a driven person, highly focused with tunnel vision, and to tell her something could not be done, or certainly not the way she suggested, was to provide her with a challenge and make her determined to prove her point.

Pauline found her very thrusting. 'Oh my God,' she told herself, 'is it always going to be like this?'

Pauline had seen Gai grow from a child and was extremely fond of her, but like some others in the stables she hoped Gai might just quietly find another interest.

In her enthusiasm to learn, Gai tended to do Pauline's work as well as her own, and this led to friction. Pauline tried to understand and put it down to her keenness, that in doing this Gai was trying to teach herself. But it was hard to take.

Pauline even tolerated being told to do certain things with

her work when she well knew what to do and had been doing it for years.

But she bucked about the notes.

Gai adopted the habit of leaving notes for Pauline asking why this or that had not been done, why was the key left in the door?

Pauline could have cheerfully choked Gai about the little stickers she left on her desk telling her to clean up her drawer. Gai did not even say 'Pauline' on the note, just a curt 'Clean up this drawer'.

To Pauline it was just a working drawer. She thought Gai's attitude was over the top and took it personally, not realising that to Gai it was nothing more than an untidy drawer.

Gai was fastidious and tidy to the point of being punctilious. If a wall picture was off centre, she would be compelled to straighten it.

While standing at a desk and talking animatedly about a horse, she would be tidying everything on the desk. If anything was out of place, it had to be rectified at once.

The boss's daughter was hyperactive, a characteristic which showed out in this new period of her life. She was a Bossy Boots, a bit abrasive to those who did not understand her.

Gai and Pauline finally blew up with each other due to a misunderstanding over the nomination of a horse. Pauline, herself a woman of strong character, walked out.

Tommy and Gai exchanged strong words. 'How could you do this?' he demanded. Pauline returned and good relations were established.

They were saying at the stables if only Gai would find herself a husband . . .

Gai wasn't keeping regular company with anyone at this time, just going out with various guys.

Soon after attending the stables fulltime she arranged a new television show with John Singleton of Channel Ten called *Racing's New Faces*. It was a half-hour show, a comedy with various racing identities to raise money for charity.

Sitting with her producers one morning, she suggested they ask a bookmaker to go on the panel. Good idea. 'I only know one bookmaker, that's Bill Waterhouse,' she said. Okay, go ahead.

She rang Bill. 'Dear, I'm not going to be in Sydney, I'm flying out to America tomorrow,' he said. 'But I've got a good looking son, a bookmaker, who's also in the cosmetics business . . . '

She rang Robbie Waterhouse. 'I'm Gai Smith. Would you like to appear on *Racing's New Faces*?'

'Oh yes,' he said, 'thanks very much.'

Next day she went to the studio, told them who she had and they said, 'Who the devil is Rob Waterhouse?'

'Bill Waterhouse's son.'

'No, no, we don't want him.' They settled for Joe Hasham, of the *Number 96* show.

Robbie Waterhouse had not yet been elevated to the rails ring at Randwick and was still fielding at provincial meetings. But as the son of 'Big Bill', Australia's biggest and most colourful bookmaker, he was on the rise.

She rang him next day and said, 'Look, I'm really sorry, it's so embarrassing but they don't want you.'

'That's all right. Why don't we go out to dinner instead?'

'Sounds great,' said Gai, and they set the date.

When the day arrived the following week, she rang him and said, 'I can't go to dinner with you tonight, I'm having a nervous breakdown. This show is driving me to distraction. Going out would be too much. I have to cancel.'

He was sure she was giving him the runaround, but said okay.

Then Gai said, 'Aren't you going to ask me out another night?'

He was surprised by her direct manner. They arranged it for the following week.

In the interim they saw each other at a Black and White Ball at the Wentworth Hotel. He was with a pretty girl who won the best dressed competition that night and she was with the son of Jim Bell, Chairman of the Australian Jockey Club.

On their date at the Burton Restaurant in Darlinghurst, he bought a bottle of wine and sipped half a glass. She sipped half a glass. The rest remained untouched.

'Why did you buy that bottle of wine?' she asked.

'Don't you drink?' he replied.

'Not really. Do you?'

'No.'

'Then,' said Gai, 'why did you buy it?'

Trying to be amusing Robbie said a silly thing, 'I find it gets the girls going.'

'Well, you've pulled the wrong rein here.'

She would tell her friends he tried to get her drunk.

He dropped her home and received a polite kiss on the cheek.

Next day Gai's mother asked her what she thought of him.

'He's very nice but I don't think he's my type. I must say, though, he's an intelligent person and I enjoyed his company very much.'

Robbie didn't think he would ask her out again. She was attractive and bright but had not given him any hint she liked him.

About two weeks later Gai had two tickets for a turgid play, *Metamorphous*, at the Nimrod Theatre and went through her list of beaus to see who would be best to accompany her . . . no, not this bloke, not that bloke, then she thought of Robbie Waterhouse.

She rang and asked him if he'd like to go to the show with her. Again he was surprised. It was the first time a girl had rung him and asked him out.

Of course Gai was late and the tickets were sold, so they had to sit on the stairway.

They went to dinner after the show, to dinner a few more times and each time found they were more attracted to each other.

Robbie fell in love with her very quickly. After about three weeks he said to her over dinner, 'You and I should get married.'

Dismissing this as the talk of some mad person, she rejected him completely. 'That's ridiculous. It's out of the question.'

But they began seeing each other every day.

Valerie did not like it at all. She could see the attraction Gai felt for the young bookmaker, she knew he posed a threat and she did not want to lose her daughter.

She began a campaign against him, continually finding fault.

Valerie had seen Robbie picking Gai up in his gold Mercedes convertible and she said, 'He drives that lairy car. What's the matter with him? And he wears those lairy clothes.'

Robbie took Gai to nightclubs, dancing and staying out late and Valerie hated it, trying to maintain a curfew on Gai although she lived two doors away.

After a couple of months Gai invited Robbie to her parents' home to meet them. Valerie was rather icy although good manners dictated that she made him welcome on the surface, but Tommy liked him right away. He said to Gai, 'This is the first bloke you've brought into the house who is in any way a sensible man.'

Tommy and Valerie had never approved of any of Gai's boyfriends. When discussing Robbie with some of her friends Valerie said, 'Gai met a lovely lot of men in England. One was Lord Huntington. Why couldn't she have married him?'

Gai thought her mother hated Robbie, but that was not the problem. It was the fact he was involved in racing that she hated. If he had been a doctor or a politician it would not have mattered.

She didn't want another racing person in the family, especially a bookmaker. It didn't help, either, when gossipy snippets about their relationship appeared in the papers.

In one item in the *Daily Mirror*'s Inside column, Gordon MacGregor said under the heading 'Clocker Gai is no two-timer: Gai Smith, the talented actress daughter of top trainer, TJ, has been trotting around with dashing bookmaker Robbie Waterhouse, son of Big Bill. But she tells us there's nothing in it . . . '

It was almost a case of history repeating itself.

Valerie's mother, who came from a social background in the ritzy eastern suburbs of Sydney, had opposed Tommy when he pursued Valerie, showering her with flowers and attention.

Valerie herself had not been too keen when she first met Tommy in the vestibule of a hotel, saying to her mother, 'Did you see that horsey little man had his eye on me?'

Tommy would arrive at Valerie's door with a floral bouquet almost as tall as himself. Valerie's mother did not think there could be any future in the relationship—he was a playboy and, well, a horse trainer.

She put distance between them by taking Valerie on an extended world tour.

It took six years before Valerie's mother finally relented, saying 'change what you can and live with what you can't.'

Even after all this time Valerie still could not remove from her mind the stigma on racing people.

As a member of Lloyds, Robbie had to go to England and asked Gai if she would accompany him. She said no, her parents could not accept that situation.

Then Gai came up with a suggestion, 'Why don't you come with me to Joe Manning's place at Cootamundra for three or four days?'

They drove to Cootamundra to stay with Joe and next thing, out of the blue, Tommy turned up.

Valerie had sent him down to keep an eye on the situation. After momentary embarrassment, they all acted normally.

Joe said later, 'Whenever Gai brought her boyfriends down, I noticed they all had to toe the mark. Gai was always in charge.

'When I saw Gai and Robbie together for the first time, I could tell she really got on well with this fellow. There was a good feeling between them and it looked like something special.'

Another incident occurred early in the relationship which severely rattled the portals of young love.

Tommy said to Gai, 'We're all going to New Zealand for the yearling sales. Why don't you try to get Rob to come?'

To avoid a confrontation with her mother, Gai said nothing about it but suddenly produced him at the sales in Wellington with the cheery introduction, 'Guess who's over here at the moment?'

Valerie reportedly went berserk. Well, perhaps not quite, but she made her feelings felt in the strongest way, saying she was not going to put up with this sort of thing and threatening to go home. She told Gai she had embarrassed the family.

Gai, by now feeling her independence, said, 'I don't care what people think. It's none of their business.'

A few months later Tommy wanted to go to Honolulu for a holiday and suggested to Gai she might like to ask Robbie along.

She did and at once Valerie rang Robbie and did everything possible to separate them, giving reasons why she thought them unsuited. She made it absolutely clear she did not want any more racing people in the family.

Robbie went on the trip to Honolulu and all went well until some friends of Valerie's showed up from Sydney. Gai had to keep Robbie out of sight, dodging about in the Pink Palace on Waikiki as if they were taking part in a stage farce.

It was a battle all the way for Gai over Robbie. She could not understand why Valerie felt so strongly about racing people when she loved Tommy so much, was so loyal to him and their marriage had endured so successfully.

She would always remember her mother's devotion being demonstrated on the day when Gai, aged 18, returned from her backpacking tour of Indonesia and Malaysia, and a friend of Valerie's picked her up at the airport.

Gai said on reaching home, 'You weren't at the airport to meet me, Mum?'

'No,' said Valerie, 'At 7 am your father is the most important person in my life.'

They had many frank discussions on the subject of Robbie. She even said to Valerie, 'Why do you want to bite the hand that feeds you, Mum? It's your life being married to a trainer and this has given you the lifestyle you enjoy.'

Still working in the office at the stables, Gai wanted to extend her television work.

For a time she became the face of Grace Bros for a series of advertisements, before Deborah Hutton assumed the role.

After doing her Channel Seven interviews for about a year, she came up with a new concept for a television show.

Her idea was *Track Time*, an hour of racing news and interviews planned to go to air on Saturday mornings, competing directly with radio stations in the mushrooming field of racing preview.

She put together a portfolio of shots with the help of cameraman Tom Wilson, walked into the office of Seven boss Ted Thomas and said, 'Look, Mr Thomas, I have this idea . . . '

She walked out with his approval to do 13 episodes.

Gai felt she needed a co-anchor. Robbie suggested Don Scott, a professional gambler who initiated a punting group called the Legal Eagles and reputedly won a fortune.

Apart from Sydney, the show covered two other States, with Wayne Wilson in Brisbane and Bill Collins in Melbourne.

It set out to de-mystify racing, giving punters up-to-date information and inside knowledge on race days. It was an expensive show at $5,000 a time, funded entirely from the channel's own resources.

Gai wanted to buy the air time and obtain her own sponsors but the channel was reluctant to do that.

The show was so popular it ran for a year and a half and really launched Gai as a TV personality, leading to her being invited to do national commentaries on Melbourne Cup Day.

It would end only after an unfortunate skirmish with a new man brought in to head the channel's news section, Vincent Smith.

He didn't like some aspects of the show and took Gai's name off the credits.

She went to him and said, 'Look, I don't understand this. I put the show together, I do the interviews and I edit it and you have the audacity to take my name off and leave Don's there. All Don does is turn up on Saturday mornings. I want the credit.'

Smith said, 'We're not putting your name on it. If you don't like it, you can leave.'

'I'm not leaving,' she said, 'but I'm not happy about it.'

Smith cancelled her contract and the popular show finished on the spot after he paid out her contract.

But while it ran Gai's popularity as a racing personality increased greatly and her photo kept appearing in magazines and the social pages—'Gai Smith in a close-fitting sequined gown'; 'Gai Smith wore a tweed ensemble in autumn tonings and a matching felt hat with feathers to one side'; 'Gai Smith of the famous racing family in tiny hat, jacket and skirt, a symphony in varying shades of plum . . . '

By now Gai had added skiing on international slopes to her water skiing skills. In the Christmas–New Year holiday of 1980 she skied for three weeks in Aspen, Colorado, then stopped off in New Zealand on the way home to attend the yearling sales, where Tommy spent $500,000.

Before going to America she had arranged with five young friends to pool $18,000 to buy a yearling. At the Wellington races she saw two-year-old Vintage Ash win and was impressed.

She phoned several of her friends to obtain the go-ahead to buy Vintage Ash instead of a yearling. One of her partners was Robbie Waterhouse.

A few months later an incident occurred which gave Gai a 'break' in more ways than one.

At trackwork at Randwick early one morning a two-year-old colt, Bello, ridden by Malcolm Johnston became fractious and when Tommy moved in to lead it out the colt kicked Tommy on his left side. Gai was first on the scene and on taking him to hospital she found him to have a fractured hip, his first injury since he fell as a hurdle jockey 40 years before.

He was expected to be out of action for several months, getting about painfully on crutches after three weeks for short periods each day.

Suddenly Gai was thrust into the limelight at the sharp end.

From working in the office and learning the menial administrative chores such as the banking, which she really didn't like, she found herself running Tulloch Lodge with Ernie Smith.

She and Ernie shared the responsibility but Gai received all the publicity.

Twice each day she went to St Vincent's Hospital to see Tommy and obtain his instructions on what to do at the stables.

Among other things, Tommy worked out his runners and advised her of the jockeys he wanted.

She made the *Daily Telegraph* sports backpage, leading the offending horse Bello out to exercise, with an upbeat story telling how running a million-dollar racing stable was more hectic than being an actress, starting at 4.30 am and finishing at 9 pm after going without lunch.

The mass circulation *Sun-Herald* followed on page one with a glamorous picture of her resplendent in fur coat, describing how she had landed a winning treble in the absence of her injured father.

From being the office girl, albeit the boss's daughter, and doing the clocking, she suddenly found herself out on the track every morning along with Ernie, actually involved in the training of horses.

Inside the office, too, she embarked on a new learning curve. She took part in the process of nominating horses for particular races, something she had never had the chance to do before.

Those around her could see that suddenly Gai Smith was developing a taste for the business of training horses, a business that was her true heritage.

They could see she loved it. She positively glowed with excitement as she began to feel that sense of power that came from acting as the boss.

The seeds of the future were sown in that fateful moment when TJ was laid low by a kicking horse which he part owned.

*

Gai's romance with Robbie Waterhouse was still under a cloud.

Valerie had not softened her opposition. She would berate him over his relationship with Gai, they would have long talks in which he would nod his head sagely, then go on as before.

After keeping company for more than two years, he asked Gai again if she would go to England with him. This time she agreed.

They were away for a month, going to races from one end of England to the other. Gai renewed a lot of old acquaintances.

Robbie had asked her two or three times if she would marry him and she said, 'No, I'm not ready. I don't want to rush into it. I'm just not sure yet.'

When they returned from England Gai thought about it for two weeks and said 'I'm sure. I'm ready. Let's get married.'

Gai decided to marry him because she felt he was the first person she'd met who did not have any faults, who would listen to her and was interested in what she was doing. He was kind and she found his company exciting.

She told her girlfriends she had met lots of nice blokes in Sydney who had been charming and full of fun, but none who moved her so much as to make her feel she wanted to spend the rest of her life with him. Robbie was the only person who affected her that way.

Robbie, on the other hand, told Gai she was the only woman he'd met who did not annoy him in some way.

At dinner the following Sunday night at the home of Gai's parents Robbie said to Tommy in Valerie's presence, 'Tommy, Gai and I are thinking of getting married, what do you think?'

Tommy thought it was a good idea, but Valerie said nothing.

However, from that point she came to accept it and offered no further objections.

She did say to Gai she hated her marrying into the racing world because it was such a hard tough business.

Gai said, 'Mum, I was born into it. You married into it and that's the difference. I've grown up with racing and I'm aware of the pitfalls.'

When Gai decided to do something, she did it.

She didn't want a long engagement, and needed only a few months to organise the guest list and the dress.

Gai knew exactly what she wanted for the dress, having seen a Valentino model in a magazine. But she felt she couldn't afford a Valentino which would have cost $7,000, so she asked designer Mel Clifford to make her a similar design.

She took Valerie's advice but wasn't one of those brides who needed to be wheeled around by her mother.

Robbie told Gai he was happy to remain a Protestant but asked her if she wanted him to become a Catholic. She said no, stay the way you are. He didn't convert, but promised to accompany her to church and have the children christened as Catholics.

After a three month engagement, they were married on 14 December, 1980, in the racing wedding of the year, uniting the two wealthiest and most powerful racing families in Australia.

Naturally it was Sunday, a non-race day.

The service, a 50-minute nuptial mass, was at St Edmund's Chapel at The Swifts, Darling Point. Tommy, in his first public outing since the horse kicking, threw away his crutches to give the bride away.

Father and daughter shed a tear as they embraced and Gai thanked him for everything, as a proud Valerie, Big Bill and Suzanne Waterhouse and about 50 guests looked on. Valerie read a couple of her poems.

Later the champagne flowed at a reception at the Smiths' Point Piper home a short distance away.

The bride and groom had a nice early wedding present the previous day when Vintage Ash, the colt Gai bought in New Zealand which they raced with four friends, led all the way to win the sixth race at Rosehill.

They could spare only three days for a honeymoon, spent at Gosford on the New South Wales central coast.

Later in January they went to Honolulu, with Gai, a great

family person, insisting that Tommy and Valerie stay with them at the Pink Palace—the Royal Hawaiian.

To go on holiday together was a ritual they would follow every year.

CHAPTER TEN

WIFE, MOTHERHOOD, CAREER

The newlyweds went to live in a unit on Balmoral Beach on Sydney's north side, one of the city's most delightful residential areas.

Most Balmoral homes look over a tranquil scene of bushy headlands to the Harbour, Manly and the twin headlands marking the entrance to Sydney Harbour, The Heads.

Their unit was down on The Esplanade just metres away from the promenade skirting the beach. The block had been built by Bill and Jack Waterhouse, a unit was vacant and as they had nowhere else in mind, they were glad to accept the opportunity.

As they settled down to married life they found their mutual interest in racing gave them a good feeling of compatibility. They were as happy as any young couple could be.

Robbie was accepted as a bookmaker on the rails at Randwick, where the big bets were laid, and he was seen as the young glamour bookie who would eventually take over the mantle worn by Big Bill for many years as King of the ring.

Gai still wanted to pursue her career at Tulloch Lodge and continued to go to the stables each day. Nothing much changed in their lives except that now they could share a common interest.

They were seen as a glamorous, privileged and celebrated young couple. Gai became the tipster for another newspaper, her photo appearing on the front page under the heading 'Gai Joins *The Mirror*!'

Photos of them together at various functions appeared regularly in the newspapers. Gai's views were sought on numerous subjects, for instance on marriage in the *Sun-Herald*: 'I think it's a very good institution and it suits me. Just living together is all right for some, but nothing would have upset my parents more than if we had lived together.'

Gai was still doing her *Track Time* program on TV and Melbourne Cup coverages.

As with all young married couples, a settling down period was necessary in their private lives.

Robbie found Gai hard to handle. She was direct and honest but uncompromising. She fought to get her own way and in the beginning was quick to anger and would become annoyed if she didn't have her way.

He put this down to the fact that she was an only child. He appreciated they were special people in many ways, like the early American astronauts who were only-children members of their families. But such people want to continue having things their way throughout life and have not learned to conform, share or compromise in the interests of politeness and general harmony.

In some ways Gai reminded Robbie of Peter Sellers in the film *Being There*, in which he played the role of a person who had been sheltered from the world living in a rich old lady's home, and when she died and he was forced to go out in the world he made all sorts of mistakes but things worked out fine for him, even to the extent of thinking he could walk on water, which the movie allowed him to do.

The comparison was exaggerated, of course, but he saw her in a somewhat similar vein, a person who viewed life in black and white terms, who said exactly what she thought and moved confidently into situations without realising the pitfalls of life.

Gai had a definite approach and was set in her ways. If she thought something was right, it was right.

Robbie was sure people sometimes stood back, looked at Gai and said to themselves, are you for real?

Gai would be quite unaware of the impact she might have made. In this respect her approach was an advantage, not a handicap, because she would just plough on regardless.

It took him some time to learn how to handle her. In the event of an argument, he would take her two steps back and try to be logical, asking, 'Gai, what is it you are trying to achieve?'

She did not fight to get her way in a domineering or aggressive manner but was prepared to listen to reason—if you made your point quickly and could gain her attention.

He found her kind and considerate with a genuine interest in people. Tommy would not give anyone the time of day unless it suited him, but Gai would always stop and talk to people, no matter how busy she might be.

But he blanched many times early in their marriage at Gai's directness.

He invited a female friend to a party at their home and she came with her boyfriend. Robbie introduced them to Gai who immediately said to the boyfriend with obvious indignation, 'Where's that two dollars I loaned you?'

It related to an incident at university about 10 years before when he had not repaid her small loan.

There were punters who owed Robbie thousands of dollars at the time, but he would not dream of asking and embarrassing them in front of other people.

It wasn't the $2 Gai wanted, but she was meticulous with money and if he had offered it to her she would have thanked him and put it in her purse. She wanted to point out to him he had done the wrong thing and had treated her as a mug.

In another incident a friend of Robbie's who looked like going into bankruptcy asked if he could leave a few flower pots at his home. Robbie didn't really want to but reluctantly agreed.

Some time later he returned and asked if he could have the pots back. Robbie said fine, but Gai said, 'No. You didn't want them. They're mine now.' The impasse was resolved only when Robbie reasoned with her that they had only been on loan.

Gai was a pragmatist who didn't always see life from other people's points of view.

Her father was a big factor in her life. His independent attitude had helped him succeed and Gai's approach was much the same.

Her mind was uncluttered, her attitude to life simple and direct, and she always put her best foot forward.

Gai continued her public relations work at the stables but was beginning to feel frustrated. Nobody took her seriously.

Tommy noticed her attempts to become more involved but seemed to regard her efforts as a bit of an intrusion.

At first he reacted in a humorous way, grinning and saying 'Gai is really getting involved,' as though it was the last thing he expected.

He did not seem to entertain even slightly the prospect that Gai would go on to become a trainer. Clearly he did not see the potential he had in his own daughter.

'You know,' Gai told a friend, 'if I was horseflesh he may be able to see it better.'

And right from the start when she moved into the office Gai and Ernie did not agree.

Ernie didn't appear to worry at first, but as Gai's interest increased and her ambitions became more noticeable, he took her presence in the stables personally, thinking she might be a threat after all.

Gai kept telling Robbie how frustrated she felt, that her talents were not being used. She could see things that should be changed at the stables but there was no way she could make any headway.

Robbie was the first one to suggest to Gai that perhaps she should take out a trainer's licence. She knew it didn't matter to him what she did, and if she chose to stop going to the stables and stay at home as a housewife, that was fine with him.

He felt it was the natural thing for her to do rather than just being an employee of her parents. As he envisaged it, Gai could be a trainer with about half a dozen horses in her own name working with her father, enough to give her a worthwhile interest.

About a year after they were married Robbie and Gai and her parents were in Ireland on their annual holiday when Gai said to him, 'Why don't you mention it to Dad? I can't say anything to him. Will you do it?'

Robbie did so and Tommy was cold on the idea.

He just said 'No, no,' without giving any reason. Nothing could be further from his mind at that stage than to give Gai a horse to train. It was as though he had been asked to retire.

Gai felt that people were still too aware that she was Tommy Smith's daughter and did not take her seriously as an individual because of that.

Her frustration was highlighted soon afterwards when she clashed with an assistant of Ernie Smith's in the stables, Tom Barker, who had been with her father for 25 years.

She was out in the yard trying to be involved with the horses when Tom spoke sharply to her in the presence of other employees. She believed he had been rude.

That night at home she felt like crying. Full of emotion, her throat as tight as rope, she decided she had to do something.

She rang Tom Barker and said, 'Tom, don't you ever speak to me like that again in front of other people or at any time.'

'Who do you think you are?' demanded Tom.

'I'll tell you who I am. At present I just work with you, but I won't be doing that in the future.

'I will be running the place and you will have to get used to the idea, because I assure you I will be here long after you have gone.'

And the winner is...Gai Waterhouse. The famous 'tonsil shot' as the young future trainer displays all the emotions of the winner's circle in cheering to victory Star Watch in the 1988 Golden Slipper. Gai picked out the colt in the New Zealand sales ring. (*Fairfax*)

Above left: Who's the kid with the short hair making friends with a Gimcrack Stakes favourite? Why it's Gai Smith, aged four, getting off to an early start around the stables.

Above right: An animal lover from a toddler, Gai Smith plays up for her friend, Toy Toy. She was about seven.

Above: Can you pick the kid who would talk to horses in this shot of fifth and sixth forms from Rose Bay Convent? (Try the one with pigtails, fourth from left, centre row.)

Above: Schoolgirl Gai competes in yet another show, Sydney's 'Royal' at Easter. Always with horse, of course. *(Alan D. Arnold)*

Below: A young Gai puts Faux Tirage through his paces in the Brookvale (Sydney) Show. Mother Valerie dutifully accompanied her to all the gymkhanas and horsey meets around the place.

Left: Teenager Gai at Rotorua, New Zealand. She loved jumping fences on hunting horses.

Middle left: A slim, attractive young teenager relaxes at home in Sydney's ritzy Darling Point, just after leaving school.

Below left: Waiter, champagne! About 18, coming out into the world, tasting the good life.

Below right: About 20, taking in the Melbourne Cup.

Above: Family snap on Gai's mother's side: with her grandparents the Finlaysons. From left, Uncle Neville Finlayson, Gai's mother-to-be Valerie, Aunt Heather and (extreme right) Aunt Belle.

Below left: The best of pals. Always liked to be around horses.

Below right: As a uni student, Gai rode regular trackwork at Randwick.

Above: The young Randwick track rider, with Smooch. Who's that man beside her? (*Fairfax*)

Right: The young student and old master, out in the centre at Randwick.

Above: An early winning smile. Gai, about 20 and friend Averil Sykes celebrate Oncidon's victory in the Villiers Stakes with their trainer. The girls bought the horse for a song—as a hack!

Right: A beaming TJ Smith joins his daughter on her graduation from the University of NSW, proud she has received the education he never had.

Above: Valerie and Tommy Smith, delighted at Gai's arts degree.

Centre: Portfolio shot of the young actress looking for work in London as a member of British Equity. Her vital statistics: 34, 24, 34. Inches, that is.

Below right: The sensuous face of the actress in her early London days, aged 23.

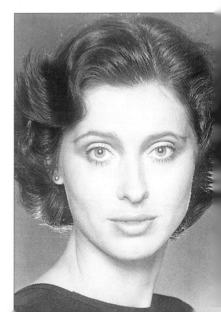

Left: Gai almost left her heart in Paris with this suave Frenchman, Jan De Roualle. Naturally he was a horsey type.

Below: Wealthy Irish breeder, Mrs Meg Mullion, who befriended Gai in her London acting days. To the right is renowned Irish trainer Paddy 'Darkie' Prendergast, another friend to the young Gai.

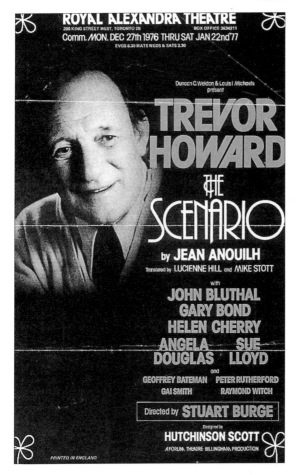

Left: The cast for the play *The Scenario* starring at the Royal Alexandra Theatre, Toronto.

Below: Gai in her role as Trevor Howard's mistress in *The Scenario* in Toronto.

Above: On stage in *The Scenario* in Toronto. (From left), Geoffrey Batemen, Sue Lloyd, Gai, Helen Cherry (Trevor Howard's real wife), John Bluthal (the man in today's oils ain't oils ads), Angela Douglas (previously married to Kenneth Moore), Gary Bond and Trevor Howard.

Left: Back home after her London acting stint, TV reporter Gai chats up a likely chap at Randwick for her TV racing show.

Left: As an assistant in Tommy Smith's Tulloch Lodge stables, Gai learns the tricks of the sales ring from an old pro in Wellington, New Zealand. (*NZ Women's Weekly*)

Below: Becoming more involved in her father's operation, Gai leads in TJ-trained Brewery Boy after he won the VRC Victoria Derby.

Above: Gai celebrates Combat's Canberra Cup win with fellow owners (from left), Chris Wilson, Robert Oyada, Ron Lloyd and Louise 'Snowy' Leddingham.

Centre: New man on the scene Robbie Waterhouse hams it up with Gai in Honolulu.

Right: Gosh, looks like it might be serious after all. Gai and Robbie Waterhouse, inseparable at a Sydney ball. (*Fairfax*)

Above: Love wins the day for Gai and Robbie as two famous racing families unite. Joining in, proud parents Suzanne and Bill, Valerie and Tommy.

Left: Newlywed Gai has the bloom of youth in her cheeks as she cuts a glamorous figure on a cool day at Randwick. (*Fairfax*)

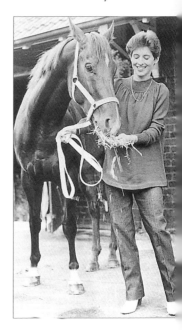

Right: Working girl, soon to be a mum, pauses momentarily at the TJ Smith stables for a photo opportunity. Get on to the 'working' boots.

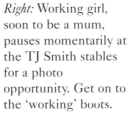

Above left: Here he is, young Tom with his brand new mum.

Above right: And again, with Gai combining motherhood and career.

Left: Big Bill Waterhouse, giantkiller among that rare species of fearless Australian bookmakers, never gave such head starts as this.

Left: Tom wants out, ungrateful lad, despite two admiring grandmothers, Suzanne and Valerie.

Below: Now Kate joins Tom as Gai and Robbie's second child.

Below: After rising at 3 am and working at the stables, Gai gets home in time to see the children off to school. Meanwhile, she challenges the AJC's refusal to allow her to train.

Above: Happy family scene as Gai and Robbie relax at their Clifton Gardens home in Sydney with Tom and Kate, giving no hint of the serious problems besetting them. But the worries are with them constantly—the AJC refuses to grant her a trainer's licence because of her marriage to Robbie, warned off over Fine Cotton.

It was a big step for her at the time, opening herself up to ridicule and possible reaction within the stables.

But she knew she had to take a stand. In later years she and Tom would become the best of mates.

Finally, two years into her marriage, Gai was forced to spell out her feelings to her father. She wanted more responsibility.

'Why don't you just stay doing the PR?' was Tommy's reaction.

She was furious.

'Look, Dad,' she said, 'I can do the PR with my eyes closed. I want something more demanding and more stimulating.'

The upshot was that Tommy made her co-foreman with Ernie, making her a licensed person with the Australian Jockey Club for the first time.

It gave her equal status with Ernie and for some time every year when her father and Uncle Ernie were away, she would be in charge of the stables.

It would give her more hands-on control out in the yard where all the action took place, but it also created new problems for her.

Ernie was one of those convinced she was still a flash in the pan, that she was just a girl having a fling.

After all, racing was still a male domain, dominated by men in every way.

The rewards were theirs, men were still considered to be the repository of knowledge and wisdom. They had received all the plaudits of the past, all the benefits. Men had overshadowed women in the industry down the years and it was just as difficult for women to gain an international reputation in this field as in most others.

Whatever anyone might argue, there had not been much of a place for women in racing in Australia.

A few women trainers were beginning to show through. Women were jockeys, track riders and strappers and were welcomed as owners but that was about all.

The differences between men and women were often

equated by males to be similar to the differences between colts and fillies.

Colts are up front and aggressive but fillies are usually demure by comparison. And no matter how the feminists might deny it, there are extraordinary differences between men and women.

Women complain there are glass ceilings that inhibit them in various industries, but there are no glass ceilings in punting or gambling. Yet there are hardly any professional women punters.

The truth appeared to be at least that racing attracted males more and it appealed more to male spirits and personalities than to females.

None of that carried any weight with Gai.

But the arrival of her first child was expected to make a difference to her ambitions. Then she'd find her place was in the home, some people around the stables said with obvious relish.

Gai enjoyed a strong commonality with her husband and they both looked forward to having a family.

She felt she had met someone who was her equal in life, whom she found stimulating mentally and physically. They could speak on the same plane and his interest in racing was as keen if not keener than hers. She also knew he admired her for her skills and strengths and would listen to her point of view.

She worked right up to the time the first child arrived. The day before the baby was born she was at the track at 5 am leading horses around and legging strappers up—all physical work— then she clocked them and worked in the office that morning.

Feeling the time was near she booked into St Margaret's Hospital that afternoon and had the child at 4 pm the following afternoon.

Thomas was born on 11 June, 1982, named after her father and Thomas Waterhouse, one of the forebears of the Waterhouse gambling dynasty.

She shared the experience with another new mother in the adjoining room, Lea Stracey, wife of solicitor Bruce Stracey.

Lea had a daughter, Madeleine, within half an hour, with both babies being induced. They would become the closest of friends.

As a girl staying with her grandmother in Todman Avenue, Randwick, Lea would be wakened by the clip clop of Tommy Smith's horses on the way to trackwork, watching them from her window in the soft light, beginning a love affair with horses.

She grew up in the same area, knew the same people and her brother took out Robbie's sister Louise, but she and Gai were not to meet until maternity classes.

Lea found Gai refreshingly unspoiled and down to earth, with the knack of encouraging people to immediately like her.

Lea was thrilled with the flowers she received on the birth of her first child, but by comparison Gai's room looked like a florist's shop. She supplied the whole hospital floor with flowers.

Nurses had to remove them at night because they activated her sinus trouble.

Lea's lasting memory of Gai from that week in hospital was of a slender person with incredible energy, refusing to rest until all her 'domestic' jobs were done, cleaning her room to a spotless state.

The *Daily Mirror* brought out a poster: 'Gai Smith And New Baby. First Photo.'

There was a whiff of celebrity status about the young parents, akin to being the Di and Charles of Australia.

Even the *Women's Weekly* cashed in on Gai's celebrity standing with a cover on her in colour—'winner in a man's world'.

Gai gave herself three months for bonding with the baby at home, then was back at the stables with young Tom underarm.

Most people didn't appreciate her taking him to the stables, especially as photos were published of her with Tom on one arm and a stopwatch in her other hand clocking the barrier trials.

She could see their point but had not organised any domestic help at that stage. She would pop Tom in the office and duck down to the yard to check on the horses.

By the time their second child, Kate, had arrived, Gai had

arranged help in the house. By then, too, they had moved to a large house at nearby Clifton Gardens, with views to the inner Harbour. They needed a mortgage to buy it.

Gai was a dedicated mother, who refused to allow her children to start off with the same disadvantage as she had in not being able to read or write at the same time as their peers. She and Robbie adopted the theories of the American Dr Glen Doman, who believed children should be taught to read while very young.

Combining this with the Japanese belief that a child's brain is most fertile very when young, they taught their children Japanese at an early age, labelling household items in Japanese and English and writing out flash cards for everything.

They prepared hundreds of flash cards with words like chair and hat, showed their children the cards and pointed to the items.

Gai and Robbie employed live-in Japanese girls to help in the process, and both children learned to speak Japanese. This unusual method of teaching young Tom was written up in the *Daily Telegraph* under the heading of 'Racing Dynasty Super Kid'.

Gai concentrated on the programme for about six years and it worked well.

She spent a great deal of time with the children, taking them to places and trying to stimulate their awareness.

She simply enjoyed being a mum, bathing and feeding them, blowing on their tummies at night before bed.

Gai tried to give them the opportunity of being all rounders so that wherever they went they would be able to pick up a tennis racquet, ride a horse, play cricket in the case of Tom and be normal kids with a chance to compete and enjoy life. Kate learned piano.

Her devotion as a mother helped her survive the period when she felt strongly she was being held back at the stables.

People kept annoying her by saying 'Oh now you have the children, you should concentrate on being a mother and stay home to look after them.'

Valerie and Tommy in particular felt she should stay home and be a wife and mother. Clients at the stables also said it.

The more they said it the more determined she was *not* to be a housewife but a working woman, a mother and wife.

She believed their attitude was wrong in a period when so many women were working mothers.

Gai was not a feminist and was not part of the feminist movement. She was not a political person at all, had no strong feelings on politics and believed there were more interesting things to be involved in than politics.

She simply believed a woman should be treated equally, with equal work for equal pay. If you weren't doing the same work you should not expect to be paid as much, but if you were more capable than a man, you should damned well be paid more.

Gai took the view that she could balance the role of wife, mother and stable co-foreman without her children or home life suffering.

At this stage Gai's ambition was still not clear cut but she continued to thirst for knowledge, wanting to master her efforts aimed at eventually running the stables.

Tommy was still leading the trainers' premiership and it would not have entered his head to allow her to take over the business.

She felt certain he could not accept that a woman could run the business as well or completely as he could. But she constantly tried to test the parameters with remarks like 'Look, this is ridiculous. You are not giving me enough responsibility.'

By now Gai was even mentioning the word 'trainer' but only in a general sense, and it certainly did not register with Tommy that she was seriously suggesting she should replace him.

But he had accepted the fact that she was ambitious.

To show how serious she was in proving she was as good as a man, she took to carrying a saddle from the weighing room to the stalls to saddle up their runners at the races.

Tommy criticised her zeal, 'You shouldn't be doing that, it doesn't look like you,' he said.

'Why ever not? If I'm going to be a trainer one day, why the devil shouldn't I? I know I don't have to do it but I can't bear this preconceived idea that I shouldn't be doing it just because people think that way.'

Tommy didn't think it was a woman's work. If she had been a man, he wouldn't have thought twice about it.

Life was sweet and sour, happy at home, frustrated at work.

Gai felt it was important to her to do her job at the stables rather than just being restricted to the home. She needed the mental stimulation.

She saw so many of her married friends doing nothing other than being housewives, which she conceded could be a fulltime job. But when their husbands came home they could talk to them about little else except their daily chores. From her point of view doing house work all day and minding the children had its limitations.

She had worked all her life, mostly in a man's world, and she had found all the human contact involved to be highly interesting.

Robbie had told her not to worry about a career and to stay home with the children if that would make her happy

But she didn't want that. She wanted her career.

Not only was it her heritage but at the end of each day, although she and Robbie were pursuing different paths in racing, they each had something interesting to contribute to the subject that fascinated them both.

That was about to change dramatically.

CHAPTER ELEVEN

THE FINE COTTON FARCE

They were driving to Hay in south-western New South Wales on Sunday, 19 August, 1984, when they caught up with the news.

Robbie was driving. Also in the car were Gai, Aunt Heather and Peter McCoy, a bookmaker friend of Robbie's from Canberra.

Robbie and McCoy owned a property called Burrabogie at Hay and were travelling there on one of their periodic visits.

They stopped for petrol at a roadside station and Robbie bought the Sunday papers. He glanced at them, stopped to study one particular story that took his interest, and drew McCoy's attention to it before passing the papers on to the others.

The *Sun-Herald* and the *Sunday Telegraph* carried prominent stories about police investigations into a ring-in at Eagle Farm, Brisbane the day before when a horse called Bold Personality had been substituted for another horse called Fine Cotton. There had been a sensational betting plunge throughout Australia.

Gai read the reports and said 'This looks like a newspaper beatup. Wonder what will happen here?'

'I don't know,' said Robbie, 'but the allegations are serious. Peter and I both had bets on the horse.' A brief general discussion followed based on the newspaper reports.

It was a quiet, uneventful start to what would be portrayed as the most sensational racing rort in Australia's history, one that would turn their lives inside out and upside down.

Nothing more was said about it for the rest of their trip.

But the story picked up momentum, mentioned on radio and TV news bulletins and in the papers next day.

When they returned home to Sydney on Monday night, numerous phone calls came in and Gai could hear Robbie talking about it. She asked him what it was all about.

'I could have a problem here because I had some bets,' he said. 'But don't worry, I'm sure it will be sorted out.'

Gai could see from the newspaper coverage that it was not going to go away but knowing how people in racing gossiped she still thought it sounded a bit exaggerated.

Rumour mongers were busy. Wherever she went racing people were full of innuendo about the ring-in.

New developments appeared in the press every day. Police were looking for Fine Cotton's trainer, New Zealander Hayden Haitana.

Although the police couldn't find him he turned up on *Sixty Minutes* to tell a lurid tale, naming 'the guy behind it'.

The name was bleeped out but as events would quickly show, he was referring to 'Bob Waterhouse'.

Then, 12 days after Fine Cotton's race, Queensland Independent MP Lindsay Hartwig named Robbie Waterhouse in Parliament, asking 'Is he the Mr Big in the scandal?' Robbie denied it on TV.

Gai, who had put a lot of it down to rumour, was now concerned. She asked Robbie for the truth.

He told her he had placed some bets on the horse but was not involved in the ring-in. He said he had not financed or organised it, and there shouldn't be anything to worry about.

'I wasn't involved in the actual ring-in and I can't see how I can be put in the position where I'll be subjected to any punishment,' he said.

Gai believed him implicitly. He had never lied to her and it had never entered her mind that he would tell her a lie.

They were totally open with each other.

She told close friends, 'It's not the way Rob is and not the way we are that he would lie to me.'

Robbie still didn't take it all that seriously and thought the matter would just blow away, but it kept on snowballing.

In a normal course of action inquiries were being held by the Queensland Turf Club in Brisbane where the ring-in occurred.

But newspapers in Sydney kept screaming for heads. They wanted the 'Mr Bigs' involved brought to justice.

After three weeks the Australian Jockey Club in Sydney announced they would hold an inquiry into the betting on Fine Cotton that had taken place at their Warwick Farm course.

Details of a huge betting coup all over Australia and in New Guinea and Fiji were revealed daily, and it was obvious the ring-in had been the worst kept secret in Australian racing this century.

The first shock Gai had to contend with was the knowledge that Robbie would be called to give evidence before the AJC Stewards' inquiry. Bill Waterhouse also was called.

About 70 witnesses were questioned on their Fine Cotton betting in Sydney, and it was amusing to hear some of their tall tales and untrue—nobody wanted to be accused of knowing there was a ring-in going on and rather than admit they were given the tip they all claimed they just 'followed the money' in the betting ring.

Robbie denied he was involved in the Fine Cotton betting.

Every day headlines rolled off the presses.

None of the 70 witnesses were accused of having prior knowledge of a ring-in, except the friends and associates of Robbie Waterhouse. They were the only ones accused of telling lies. Presumably all the others just 'followed the money'.

Nine persons, including Robbie and his father Bill, were

served with notices calling on them to show cause why they should not be warned off for allegedly having prior knowledge of a ring-in.

The others were big punter Ian Murray, the Catholic priest Father O'Dwyer, Peter McCoy, punters John Gough and Garry Clarke, his wife Glenis Clarke and bookmaker's clerk Bobby Hines.

It was a difficult and unnerving time for Gai. In racing circles people were whispering that Robbie was behind it all. Fine Cotton seemed on everyone's lips.

She and Robbie discussed it repeatedly because she was surrounded by it wherever she went. He reiterated to her that he had not taken part in the ring-in.

The hearings before the AJC Committee went ahead in a blaze of publicity.

Ian Murray's evidence was that he had invested $57,400 on Fine Cotton around the Warwick Farm ring on his own behalf. He said he sought a bet of $40,000 to $2,800 with Bill Waterhouse but the bookie reduced the bet, accepting only $14,000 to $1,000.

Robbie denied any prior knowledge of the ring-in.

Most of the racing world and the Waterhouse legal advisers were stunned when the AJC gave its verdict: Guilty of having prior knowledge that the race was a ring-in.

They warned off the Waterhouses and the seven other persons on circumstantial grounds. There was no direct evidence that the Waterhouses knew it was a ring-in.

It was, they said, a conspiracy with Robbie at the centre. All had connived at the substitution of the horse and had committed a 'dishonorable action in connection with racing'.

Neither Gai nor Robbie would ever forget the scene as he emerged from the AJC offices at Randwick after the Committee gave its decision.

Reporters clamoured for pictures and interviews and, shaken, Robbie walked out the back hoping to minimise the media feeding frenzy.

Gai, who did not attend the hearing, had parked in the AJC

car park while carrying out stable business and was driving from the course proper when Robbie emerged.

He spotted her and flagged her down.

'Darling, I've been warned off,' he said.

She couldn't believe it. With cameras turned on them to record the touching scene, she kissed him and cried.

Nothing more was said. Words were meaningless.

Gai was shocked by the headlines:

'Ring-in: Bookies Outed.'

'The End of Australia's Top Gambling Dynasty.'

The reaction was immediate.

She and Robbie lived in a conservative suburb where people generally were holier than thou and conscious of their status. She found it difficult to cope with their reaction.

When she went to shop in class-conscious Mosman she felt many people looked at her as if she were a criminal.

The difference in their attitude overnight was astounding. Gai was naturally warm and friendly towards others and she found it embarrassing and difficult to be suddenly treated as a leper.

Worse was to come.

The Waterhouses appealed to the newly-formed Racing Appeals Tribunal, presided over by retired Judge Alf Goran.

Ian Murray, unofficially promised an early return to the track if he gave evidence against the Waterhouses, turned informer and claimed he had really put the money on for Robbie Waterhouse on behalf of a friend of Robbie's. It sealed their fate.

Judge Goran confirmed the AJC warnings-off except in the case of John Gough, whose appeal he upheld. Gai's husband and father-in-law were banned from racing worldwide at the AJC's pleasure.

The words in Goran's judgment read like some forbidding lament from the Old Bailey in Dickens's time:

'While I have found that the present appellants were not the main perpetrators of the substitution, nevertheless their participation in the fruits of the fraud, with the knowledge of the fraud, by agreement, some with others, some with all, carries a deep taint of fraudulent conduct with it. Each appellant remains marked as a cheat.'

Again, there was no hard evidence that her husband knew it was a ring-in. Nor that Bill Waterhouse knew, or any of the others. The judge's finding was marked by inconsistencies.

He accepted Murray's evidence, that he had bet for Robbie, in order to convict Robbie of allegedly having prior knowledge, yet he ignored Murray's evidence that his bet with Bill Waterhouse was genuine. If he was consistent, he would have upheld Bill Waterhouse's appeal.

The judge had hob-nobbed with the AJC at Randwick on race days. His situation did not live up to the tenet of justice being seen to be done.

From Gai's knowledge of what she had been told about Fine Cotton, she thought the remarks by Judge Goran that Robbie and Bill were marked down forever as cheats was unfair.

Her private view was that he was just being a silly old codger on the side of the AJC, not wishing to fall out with them.

But here was a senior judge declaring these things and people were saying it must be right, that Robbie is a cheat. She could not say to people it was wrong.

Straight away, in the wake of the Judge's remarks, her image along with her husband's was tarnished.

Everywhere they moved people were talking about it. And it took up every moment of their time together. It was, in a phrase, all consuming and Gai could now appreciate how other people felt when caught up in sudden, enormous difficulties.

What hurt her most was the way people at the races overnight became so incredibly rude to her, without thought of her innocence.

Men, and women too, would see her approaching and

immediately go into a huddle talking about her. These were well respected people whom she had known for years.

[There were many unsatisfactory aspects of the AJC's inquiries into the Fine Cotton affair.

For instance, it is mandatory under British justice for criminal charges and investigations to take priority over quasi-judicial bodies like the AJC. That's how the QTC did it in Queensland, suspending its inquiry while the police laid criminal charges against the perpetrators of the fraud and gained convictions.

Then they warned off those who were implicated and convicted of the affair.

But the AJC did the reverse.

Before criminal proceedings began in Queensland and even before the police there finished their inquiries at the source of the fraud, they held inquiries by their stewards and the Committee, and Judge Goran heard appeals against their warnings-off.

The AJC took action using their more flexible rules of evidence. Only after the AJC warned off the Waterhouses did the police move in to lay criminal charges.

There were powerful anti-Waterhouse forces at work in the background deliberately feeding allegations with one aim in mind—to gain convictions against the Waterhouses. In both New South Wales and Queensland there was a kind of lynch-mob mentality at work against them.

The story of the Waterhouse role in Fine Cotton was told in detail in my book *The Gambling Man*, published at the end of 1990.

In that book I risked contempt of court by pointing out at an early stage before he went to trial that Robbie Waterhouse had lied in denying he placed bets on Fine Cotton.

But in my conclusions I cleared him of any suggestion that he was involved in financing or organising the ring-in.]

Gai found the gossip surrounding them so intense they had to be careful even of those regarded as friends.

The superficial ones who betrayed them were always going to be that way. Gai's staunch friends like Lea and Bruce Stracey, Louise Ledingham of Moree and other school friends, remained stoically loyal.

Some, who professed to be true friends, met them or went to dinner with them and drew them out by saying 'isn't it terrible?' then put stories around on how distressed and worried they were over the Fine Cotton charges.

Constantly under the microscope, they had to think twice before opening their mouths.

Until Fine Cotton, Gai's life had run a smooth course.

This was her first crisis.

She had faced many problems before like trying to make a living overseas and marrying Robbie against her mother's wishes, but this was a desperate crisis.

This one incident could be the downfall of all that was important in her life, her work, marriage, her persona, the future, everything.

Most people would never be called upon to face such a challenge in their lives. The details were fascinating to read about as long as they were happening to someone else.

They were the talk of the town because they were successful, colourful and privileged, the darlings of the racing industry. How the mighty had fallen! Australians love to see a tall poppy receive a kick in the arse, and this was vintage stuff.

Gai found her new circumstances excruciating. She felt insecure and unhappy and blamed Robbie that their lives were thrown under such pressure and exposure.

But she believed him, that he had not taken part in the ring-in or done anything criminal, and she was prepared to support him and remain loyal.

He was paramount in her life and she would not let him down.

If on the other hand she found he was lying, such a revelation would spell disaster for their relationship. Gai could never forgive him on a subject so vital to their well being and future.

It added to her stress that this crisis came at a most inopportune time in her life when she was busy with the children and just getting off the ground at the stables, trying to cope with her difficulties and frustrations there.

She really didn't have time for this sudden burden, or the emotional capacity for the extra responsibility.

Her father was enormously important to her, too. They were working together every day and Robbie's warning off created an unusual and tense situation for her in this relationship.

She was worried that it would cause a backlash against Tommy's reputation. He had struggled hard to reach his preeminent position, and she didn't want to see him damaged by Robbie's warning-off or by all the talk of likely police charges against him.

Tommy was an icon-like figure, now being damaged by association. The questioning of his reputation was the last thing she wanted to see.

Gai was upset too that her mother felt so embarrassed by it all.

Valerie had come from a vastly different background to Tommy and was conscious of her social position and what people might say about her. She was proud of her marriage to Tommy and his achievements from a humble start, and the fall-out from Fine Cotton cut deeply.

For the first time Valerie's associates had something to criticise her on and some never lost an opportunity through barbed remarks to remind her of Robbie's fall from grace.

She had regularly played cards with friends and associates but the games dropped away under the criticism.

The turmoil came too just when Valerie began going to the races regularly for the first time in her life, and to her surprise, enjoying it. She would lose some friends over it all. But with difficulty she held her head up in public.

She said to Robbie soon after Fine Cotton erupted, 'This is awful. I've never had to go through anything like this in my life.'

On the face of it she had been right in not wanting Gai to

marry him. After a year or so of Fine Cotton she said to Robbie, 'My God, we never want to go through anything like this again. We've always protected Gai from ugly things.'

The significance of her remark was not lost on Robbie.

He apologised a couple of times to Tommy, who was philosophical, 'What can you do?' He chickened out on apologising to Valerie, fearing the scorching nature of the reply.

Luckily for Gai, the children were too young for the situation to make much difference to them at that time.

But she was concerned about the long-term effect it might have on Tom and Kate, anxious for them to have a fair go, be treated normally and be given every opportunity in life.

Gai began to feel angry and frustrated with Robbie because she was the one taking all the blows, facing the public every day, going to the races and having to put up with their reaction to each new allegation and rumour.

She found it wearying. It took all her determination and stamina to keep fronting up.

She said to a friend, 'I'm damned if I won't go to the races. If I don't turn up people will say he's guilty because she's obviously embarrassed by it.'

As a result she was always positive in what she said and did at the races. Like Valerie, she too held her head up in the face of her detractors. When the criticism was shovelled out to her, as it was repeatedly, she had to be ready to stand up to it.

The son of a prominent owner in the Tulloch Lodge stables attacked her one day in the mounting enclosure at Randwick, yelling at her in the presence of others, 'You should stay home and look after your family. Why are you at the races? Your husband is a warned-off person.'

'It's none of your business what I do with my husband and family, you should mind your own Ps and Qs,' she said.

The same person attacked her a second time along similar lines when his father's horse did not run as well as expected. She turned at once to the owner, a wealthy and prominent businessman, and said, 'You should have more control over your son. He has no right to say these things to me. Tell him to mind his own business.'

The prominent owner himself figured in another incident.

In the early days following his warning-off, Robbie sometimes went to the stables on Sundays and poured drinks at the weekly social gathering when owners could view their horses.

The owner told the Committee how embarrassing it was to go to Tommy Smith's stables and have a warned-off person serve him drinks. Later the AJC asked him to be a witness against Waterhouse by describing how 'offended' he had been.

He intended to do so but quickly changed his mind after another prominent owner warned him he could be chopped up in cross examination. After that incident the AJC changed the rules to prevent warned-off persons visiting racing stables or offices, even on social occasions.

Gai regarded it as effrontery for friends of her father to pass derogatory remarks about Robbie in her presence.

But the most critical time for Gai in her relationship with Robbie came a few months after he was warned off.

Robbie had always been the breadwinner, going to the races several days a week. After his warning off, this suddenly ceased.

He was trying to sort himself out and find a new way of making a living. Robbie had rights to family assets but no income.

A gambling empire in which he and Bill had a turnover of $60 million a year had suddenly gone down the drain. A cloud hung over the future of the multi-million-dollar Waterhouse business conglomerate, with Bill at the head of its varied interests in hotel, real estate, property development, betting shops and a third interest in the Australian franchise of Faberge cosmetics.

Gai was accustomed to seeing her handsome husband, an ex-Shore boy described in the papers as a millionaire, leaving for the office at about 8 am before he went on to the races, always wearing a suit.

With nothing to do he slipped into the habit of not leaving until about 9.30 am. Instead of driving, he walked to the office, in runners. And he came home early and was underfoot.

To add to the impression his life was one big party, Robbie wore casual clothes all the time, including jogging shoes. His suits hung in the wardrobe gathering dust as monuments to a busier lifestyle.

He too was going through a period of frustration trying to adjust.

Gai suddenly demanded, 'How can you spend an hour walking to the office? Why have you got that much time to spare?'

The pressure had thrown her off balance. She thought of the big mortgage they had on their house with Robbie taking it easy, not earning, and she began to panic. She told him he wasn't pulling his weight financially or giving support generally in the house.

Robbie defended himself, saying this wasn't true, he was still paying the bills and was working on a new means of income and he believed all would be well.

'I'm sure Fine Cotton will be behind us in a year and I'll be back at the races,' he said.

In this uncertain period they had strong arguments over the situation and heated words were often exchanged.

These scenes finally reached boiling point one day while Robbie was driving Gai from the property at Hay to Melbourne for a race meeting. He could see she was cranky and all her emotions over their difficult situation came tumbling out.

She told Robbie she was fed up because she was the only one going out to work while he took life casually and looked as if he was in retirement. He had put them into this position because of his stupidity, he should have been more careful.

Robbie realised her anger, which had been building up for several months, posed a real threat to their marriage. He went to great pains to reach an understanding with her.

He told her he could see why she was thinking like that, but regrettably that was how their lives were at the moment.

'If you think I'm a lazy person who's forgetting how to work, please don't, because I'm working quite hard in a different direction,' he said.

'If we're to go through this together and survive it, we'll both need to be extremely tolerant.

'It's all very well saying these things to me, but there's nothing I can do about it now. If we are to stay together, unfortunately that's the way it is.'

Gradually Gai, whom he regarded as a sensible and realistic person when she understood a situation, saw the logic of what he was saying and finally accepted the position.

Through all the Fine Cotton drama, her only public reaction would be total support for her husband.

Meanwhile, the perpetrators of the Fine Cotton ring-in were brought to justice in Queensland.

In September, 1985, four men were charged with conspiring to defraud the public over the ring-in but two were acquitted. The other two, layabout conman Hayden Haitana, 39, and Robert North, 35, were each sentenced to a year's imprisonment.

The following year John Gillespie, 46, a self-styled bloodstock agent and conman with an impressive list of convictions to his name, was sentenced to four years jail after pleading guilty to being the mastermind behind it.

A number of persons were warned off the racetracks in Queensland, including colourful punter John Mort 'The Butterfly' Green, for allegedly having prior knowledge of the sting. He was sent out for 10 months, a penalty he considered outrageous.

The details that came out at the Brisbane trials showed what a farce the whole ring-in affair had been, bungled by a team of larrikins and hopeless amateurs. The horses were even a different colour. Bold Personality had to be hastily dyed at the last minute with women's hair dye in order to take him on to the track under the noses of the stewards looking something like Fine Cotton.

Both horses had four legs. The resemblance ended there.

Evidence was produced indicating that Robbie Waterhouse was to put money on for them, but no direct contact had been made with him and none of the ring-in organisers had ever met him.

All of them put Bill Waterhouse totally in the clear. The trainer Hayden Haitana apologised to him for causing all the trouble, and the mastermind Gillespie apologised to them in court for having them blamed for the ring-in.

However, the impression had been created that the Waterhouses were behind it, organising and financing it, although no such charges were laid against them or evidence produced in spite of the most exhaustive police and turf club inquiries.

Some of Gai's close friends in this period found she developed a sense of anger, confusion, sympathy and outrage over what had happened to her husband.

They admired her because under enormous public pressure and strain she stood by him. In their eyes, her loyalty never wavered.

A lesser person might have cracked up under the strain and indeed, many marriages had broken up on less justifiable grounds.

She felt it so acutely because as she often told her friends, her family meant everything to her. She drew on them for love and support.

In the first instance she confided to friends she was shocked to think Robbie might have been involved in the substitution.

Then she was angry that the AJC had listened to rumours and whispers and had gone after him personally instead of taking more note of what investigations had revealed on those involved in Queensland. Some people associated with the AJC appeared to be more interested in the agenda of 'let's get the Waterhouses'.

Some of her confusion was caused by the attitude of people who blamed her for doing something wrong or terrible. She was not connected with the affair in any way, but some were condemning her by association.

Yet at no stage did she say to her friends, 'What have I done? Why are they going after me?'

She remained positive and supportive of Robbie throughout, not once suggesting to her friends he should take the blame for her discomfort. What she said privately to him was another matter.

But in all the furore there was sympathy for her too.

People she didn't even know were overheard at the races passing remarks like, 'Isn't it awful she has to suffer because of her husband? You wouldn't blame her if she gave him the flick.'

It was a form of admiration for her sticking qualities.

Lea Stracey, in touch with her every day, knew her moods, fears and range of emotions. She regarded Gai as considerate, kind, sensitive and caring to everybody—her family, even her dog and pet canary.

Gai had insisted on caring for her Aunt Heather when she was in failing health although Heather had a family of her own.

She invited elderly friends of the family around for a meal every Sunday when it could be argued she was really too busy for these small kindnesses. To her they were important.

'I saw my role as a back stop, a sounding board, as a good ear every time she needed it,' Lea explained.

'I was amazed at her resilience and toughness, and her determination to beat this and not let it get her down. She had poise as well as pride.

'But I was also surprised at her naivety. Gai can make people feel they have known her always and that they count. Naturally she expects to be liked back.

'In the wake of Fine Cotton she couldn't believe all the nastiness and bitterness that came out.

'She couldn't understand why people didn't like her or Robbie any more, and she referred to them stabbing her and Robbie in the back. I remember thinking at the time that Gai should have been more philosophical and realised that some people are quick to be vicious and hurtful and love to pull you down.

'But Gai is a fighter all the way and she said to me there was no way she was going to let it get her down. She would hold her head high and do her best to rescue the situation.

'This won her a lot of public support. But it was more the human side of her that appealed to most people, the fact that she was standing by her husband, despite all this unpleasantness coming out through no fault of her own.

'I thought this was a great example for women and for couples to stick it out in this way. You know, you don't just give up on the first hiccup.'

It would have been easy for Gai to opt out because she would be independently wealthy one day and it didn't matter to whom she was married, she had security to fall back on.

Apart from her personal qualities, her high profile was all the more reason why she was determined not to be pulled down.

Lea knew Gai outside her public image to be a very private person, which made it hard for her to express her true feelings.

But she knew Gai was hurting. Convinced Robbie had not committed any criminal act, she was annoyed so many people wanted to believe otherwise.

Lea saw racegoers shun Gai and talk about her behind her back. People would look away as she approached, their heads would move together when she passed and gossip poured out.

If Gai stopped to talk to a client, Lea would remain several steps behind and observe heads turning and tongues wagging. Gai did not let it faze her, she got through it by ignoring anyone. At the same time she did not go out of her way to speak to any-one just to create a conversation.

She did not engage in any unnecessary or prolonged greetings.

Conversations were inclined to be short and, in spite of Gai trying to appear perfectly normal, Lea felt that at best there was unnatural tension in the air.

Among the worst aspects of Fine Cotton they were forced to contend with were rumours about their marriage and sex lives.

Almost every week for several years fresh rumours circulated that Gai was having an affair with someone. If she wasn't, then Robbie was allegedly having it off with someone else.

Reports that their marriage was on the rocks confidently went the rounds. People, probably through sheer jealousy or bitchiness, were looking for their marriage to crumble.

Reports of their infidelity were described as fact, not rumour.

One of the most consistent 'facts' that kept surfacing for almost two years involved Ian Craig, the race caller on Sydney's 2KY racing station. He and Gai were supposed to be a hot item.

Gai had worked with Ian on a Channel Seven TV show on Friday nights a few years earlier and this fuelled speculation and lent credibility to the tale.

Gai tried to ignore these sex rumours but they were so persistent she approached Ian Craig at the races one day and said, 'Look, I don't know if you've heard these rumours about us, Ian . . . '

'Oh yes, Gai, I have.'

'Well,' said Gai, who was a blonde at that stage, 'I don't know if you've got a blonde girlfriend or not, but you ought to stop it.'

It is not known what Gai expected Ian to do, except perhaps go into retreat in a monastery, but he reportedly stammered in surprise, 'Yes, Gai, yes of course.'

Ian was apparently a little embarrassed to be approached in this way from a fired-up Gai tackling the rumour head on.

One prominent businessman and executive in the racing industry, a man who took himself seriously, pulled her aside at Randwick and said in a well meaning, confidential way that he'd like to have a little talk to her.

She couldn't believe her ears when he said, 'There's nothing wrong with playing up. Everyone does it. But you mustn't play up in your own backyard.'

It incensed her to realise that responsible people were taking these rumours seriously.

Gai and Robbie attended Shane Dye's wedding at the Intercontinental Hotel in Sydney and a couple of weeks later the rumour gained currency that she was having an affair with another jockey, Mick Dittman.

Robbie discussed it with her and they tried to piece the story together. Gai had bumped into Mick, one of the guests, outside the hotel and walked in beside him. They had also chatted briefly at the function. From this Gai and Mick were supposedly having an affair.

They were the wrong two people for such a suggestion because Gai was having trouble at the time inducing Mick to ride trackwork and their conversations were strained.

But if the name of Malcolm Johnstone had been mentioned, Robbie might well have been suspicious.

Gai often told Robbie what a magnificent physique Malcolm had and what a great personality he was. It would be too much to suggest that Robbie was jealous, but he was certainly aware that Gai felt some sort of physical attraction towards Malcolm.

The rumour mongers were almost as active against Robbie. He was supposed to have two girlfriends at the same time as all these problems were going on around him.

Calls were made to newspapers, 'Robbie is going out with other women, you know.'

One night when he went to a live show with Gai at the Hilton Hotel, the story went around that he had been drugged to the eyeballs on cocaine. It was confidentially fed to newspaper columnists. On that particular night he did not even have a glass of wine, sipping only iced water.

A friend of theirs, retired bookie Jock Rorrison, had the best answer when told they were going for a divorce. Jock would say, 'Really? Well, these things do happen in a modern society. But if so, they must have only decided in the past three or four hours because I saw them this morning and they seemed pretty good mates.'

The fact they were forced to be apart so much in public helped spark the rumours.

Robbie often caused embarrassment by accompanying Gai to functions. After Tommy won the Golden Slipper with Bounding Away in 1986, the Sydney Turf Club hosted a function for him at Cassims Restaurant in the city. Tommy asked STC chairman Jim Fleming if Robbie could accompany Gai and, to his credit, Jim said certainly.

Prime Minister Bob Hawke chatted to Robbie for 10 minutes, as did Federal Tourism Minister John Brown, but vicious anti-Waterhouse stirrers reported to their tame cats in the newspapers that some of the guests resented his presence, and adverse reports appeared.

The same thing happened at various balls attended by breeders and racehorse owners. Gai liked him to be with her. After all, it wasn't on a racecourse. But still they complained. Robbie found no pleasure in going where he wasn't welcome, although he wanted to be with his wife. This antagonism rubbed off on Gai, too.

She said to one of her friends, 'If we can get through this we can get through anything.'

They realised they needed to depend on each other and nearly every day reassured the other that tomorrow would be sunny.

Life wasn't without its lighter moments, though.

At one stage Gai said to her husband, 'Rob, I want to mention something to you. In the last few weeks I've been having lunch at the races with this young vet . . .

'I want you to know that people are talking. They've seen us together. I think he's got the hots for me but I can assure you I'm not in the slightest bit infatuated with him.

'He's very nice but there's nothing to it. I wanted you to hear it from me first just in case.'

A few weeks later Gai came home and said, 'That young vet I told you about is a strange person. He's just invited me to his wedding!'

They knew they would not get through the ordeal unless

they gained strength from each other. It was, they found, emotionally draining to try to appear normal, having to turn the other cheek repeatedly as each hammer blow fell.

Gai could see that Robbie realised the situation might jeopardise their relationship and she believed the experience made him more considerate and a nicer person. He was now not too embarrassed to say he was sorry if he did anything to upset her.

Her assessment after watching him go through this character-forming time was that although he had quickly become a brilliant bookmaker, he did not possess the maturity to go with it.

He had obviously been naive and silly over the Fine Cotton incident. Anyone looking at it seriously would have said this is crazy, and moved away from it and not put his own money on as well as a commission for someone else.

She could see he was now more perceptive. In the months that dragged on after Fine Cotton he had been forced to work hard to ensure his wife and children stayed happy.

The first thing Robbie did as a means of livelihood after his income was cut by Fine Cotton was to do the race form thoroughly, using computers.

Not long before Fine Cotton, he had gone to the expense of programming a computer system in the Waterhouse office to do form more accurately and quickly, replacing the old cards system.

He was lucky enough to have a neighbour who was a computer expert and he quickly became switched on in this field.

As Gai left early each morning for the track Robbie rose and sat at his home computer six days a week to do his form work.

While studying form as a bookmaker he tried to find horses which others had overlooked, like those coming off fast-pace races last time to slow-paced races this time. In not going to the races now he could concentrate on analysing form properly.

At first he sold a betting market to a couple of friends.

Then he began betting on trifectas and by the middle of

1985 he had employed two people to go to the races and bet for him on various meetings.

It was always an early start in the Waterhouse hacienda.

Gai rose at 3 am, set the breakfast table for the children, and before leaving for the track gallops at about 3.45 gave Robbie a hot lemon drink with honey—good for the complexion, she said.

Robbie would rise then and do a couple of hours on the computer before jogging around the quiet, salubrious streets of Clifton Gardens before seeing the children off to school and awaiting Gai's return from Randwick.

Soon he was doing form for more races, country included, than anyone else in Australia, refining his method as he went.

To increase his knowledge he began studying bloodlines as part of an overview of the thoroughbred industry. He based his research on financial returns if he bought certain types of yearlings such as horses by first season sires, full brothers, just good horses or champions.

This research, which he stored in his computer, took a long time to develop but it gave him a working knowledge of what situations to avoid and what bloodline areas were worth looking at for yearlings.

He did not regard the knowledge he gained as exceptional but at least he had a good data base on various sires and their attributes which he found useful as a background for horse racing at all times.

If he had been working as a bookie still he would never have had the time to devote to this research. It gave him more depth of understanding of the industry, even helping him in the elusive business of picking winners.

Then he developed a factoring business with his computer friend, as a kind of last resort lender.

They saw an opportunity where banks refused to lend funds to any business which needed cash to keep going.

Banks once advanced money to businesses to tide them over a cash problem, but the excesses of the 80s and the likes of the

Bonds and Skases and other corporate cowboys changed all that. Now by and large they wanted security like real estate.

Robbie and his partner found a niche in the finance market where nobody else operated and their clients were grateful because they couldn't raise the urgent funds anywhere else to stay in business.

Many people with basically good businesses are forced to go into liquidation because large firms owe them money but they can't get their hands on it. They need cash to keep going and can't meet their own bills in the meantime.

What Robbie and his partner said to a profitable business was something along these lines, 'We'll buy your invoices from you. If you have an invoice worth $10,000 due to be paid to you in two months time, we'll give you say $6,900 today and when the bill is actually paid we'll give you $2,500 and keep $600 as our profit—six per cent.

'Unless you can make use of the $6,900 to make more money than it costs you to use us, there's no point in doing it.'

They were taking a risk, but not much. They always checked with the firm that owed the money and paid on the assurance of their accounts department, notifying them that they were factoring the account. If that firm didn't pay the account when it was due, they were liable. Whenever Robbie and his partner took a big firm to arbitration for non-payment to their clients, they won hands down.

Many people mistakenly thought Waterhouse had become a debt collector but he wasn't hassling anyone. He felt proud of what he was doing because this last-ditch help saved a lot of businesses from going belly up.

They had to be alert for conmen. Several hustlers out on day release from Long Bay Jail tried to set them up but were weeded out by normal checking.

In one bizarre incident Robbie's partner was approached by a man who had read of the factoring business in a newspaper advertisement, not knowing who ran it or was associated with it. He wanted funds to start a business by exporting horses to India.

The partner, without even referring it to Robbie, declined the business on his own decision because he wanted the people buying the horses to be reputable and to give him a firm order. Of course the man did not have an order and was selling on spec.

The bold personality behind this scheme was none other than John Gillespie, the Fine Cotton mastermind.

The fallout from that old Fine Cotton nag hadn't ended yet.

Robbie's confident prediction it would be over in a year was a long way out.

CHAPTER TWELVE

TRIUMPH AND DISASTER

After Fine Cotton Gai still received favourable publicity, due entirely to her charisma and personal popularity.

The media made the most of the scandal, but gave her sympathetic treatment for having her name dragged through the mud, praising her for having the guts to stick it out.

Ita Buttrose wrote a page on her in the *Sun* delving into the problem of how love could survive scandal, public speculation, notoriety and humiliation. With a smile, she declared.

Under the heading 'Will Gai follow in Tommy Smith's footsteps?' the *Woman's Day* ran a favourable feature on the young heiress with the unconventional ideas on child rearing, complete with intimate shots of Valerie and Tommy and the children inside her parents' home. Notorious Robbie was nowhere in sight.

Normally the Smiths didn't let the press inside their home.

Tommy even touched on the delicate subject of Gai's future.

'She's really taken the business seriously,' he said. 'She's got natural talent with horses and I think she'll make a good trainer.'

He quickly added he didn't intend retiring or handing over responsibility for quite a while. So there.

Gai had already had plenty to say in defence of Robbie,

going on Channel Ten to declare it a farce to see his livelihood being whisked away when the ring-in trainer was walking around like a free man and ring-in mastermind John Gillespie was planning to sell Fine Cotton for $150,000 as a celebrity.

But as she came to grips with the situation she grew more cautious.

She told the *Women's Weekly* it was tempting to have her say but 'I don't want to give people the chance to point and say "look at those bloody Waterhouses, they can't keep their mouths shut."'

The magazine highlighted Gai's once privileged position in society. Writer Susan Duncan said 'When they married, it was like the beginning of a new dynasty. In those halcyon days, the prince and princess of the horse world could do no wrong. They were feted, written about, envied and admired.'

Now in order to cope Gai was learning to take life one day at a time.

First she had to relinquish her string of 13 part-owned horses, including Vintage Ash, Triple Strike and her favourite, Combat. The racing rules made it taboo for the spouse of a disqualified person to race them.

Speculation was rife that she may not be able to continue as a foreman in her father's stables, but that was eventually cleared.

One of the hardest new experiences to accept was having to live under the constant tension of court cases surrounding Robbie in the aftermath of Fine Cotton.

Simmering too in the background was an Equity Court matter involving the Waterhouse family in which the wife and children of Charles Waterhouse, deceased brother of Bill and Jack Waterhouse, were suing the brothers over the handling of the estate. Publicity was surfacing on what promised to be a donnybrook.

After a great deal of worry, Robbie finally went before Sydney's St James Court in the middle of June, 1986, charged on 97 counts arising from his Fine Cotton betting. These ranged from conspiracy to false pretences, cheating and defrauding.

The case lasted about two weeks and Gai felt it her duty to be there in support, although she couldn't be present all the time.

Robbie was acquitted on all charges except conspiracy, on which he was to stand trial.

The dust had hardly settled from that when a public Exocet missile was fired on the Waterhouse family equity dispute in the form of a *Four Corners* program. There were extraordinary allegations, alleging infamies ranging from dog doping to illegal casinos and presenting a one-sided version of the family dispute.

It touched off daily headlines and a fresh round of litigation, including Bill and Robbie Waterhouse suing the Australian Broadcasting Corporation for defamation and Bill succeeding in having two ABC journalists committed for trial for criminal libel, an unprecedented action which the then Liberal Government prevented from going to trial by overturning the legislation.

Due to delaying tactics and other factors the defamation action against the ABC had still not come to trial 10 years later.

Just as there was no relief in the courts, neither was there any at the stables.

Gai and Ernie Smith were still at loggerheads.

They simply did not like each other although Gai tried to hide her feelings from the outside world. She just went home each night and told Robbie how frustrated and wretched she felt.

Gai did not feel overshadowed by Tommy, but with Ernie she felt she was working under a cloud. She knew the strappers and stable hands were laughing behind her back and treating her as a joke and she couldn't do a thing about it. Tommy walked the tightrope between the two and did not want to upset Ernie.

But while Gai was trying to increase the substance of her role at Tulloch Lodge, she was worrying over her father.

For the first time in 30 years he was under pressure as the premier trainer. The old ways of the industry were changing, and new ingredients were being introduced.

Although Tommy refused to acknowledge it, he was growing old.

He had slowed down considerably by 1983, needing another hip operation which kept him away from the track for several months.

He still loved the training aspect but the buying of horses was causing him concern. Unless he could maintain his old energy and enthusiasm, he feared he would be left with unsold yearlings in an increasingly competitive market.

From 1983 the pundits were tipping his decline.

It had to happen some time and it did at the last meeting of the 1986 season when King Tommy was pipped for the training premiership after 33 consecutive wins.

Sangster's millions had beaten him.

After changing the face of racing in Britain, America and Europe in the 1970s and 1980s by buying the world's best thoroughbreds and making a lucrative business out of stallion syndication, Robert Sangster had turned his attention to Australia.

The trend which Gai had seen in Kentucky and around Ireland and Europe while bumping into Sangster and his team had now come to Australia and was affecting Gai where it mattered.

A syndicate headed by Sangster and the Australian Racing and Breeding Stables (ARABS) fired first shot in buying the huge, modern Nebo Lodge stables at Rosehill in Sydney in 1984.

Sangster's partner was Bob Lapointe, a livewire Canadian, big horse owner and wealthy businessman in Australia.

They retained as their trainer a young man named Brian Mayfield-Smith, who like Tommy came from the bush. Lapointe ran Nebo Lodge like a giant factory with 90 horses in training, backed up by more at other locations ready to take the place of those who didn't measure up.

Sangster talked the AJC into staging Group races in Sydney to help the breeders, and his operation, with better prizemoney.

TJ, who had pioneered the concept of big stables in Australia run by one man, lost his crown to the corporation.

By doing it his way, Smith had enjoyed more success than any other trainer in the world, allowing him a luxurious lifestyle and a fortune estimated by business magazines to be worth $45 million.

How could he, an uneducated boy from the scrub and near the end of his career, fit into this new financial whirlpool that was racing, bristling with lawyers and accountants investing in big thoroughbred deals that called for partnerships, syndicates and tax shelters?

He pondered on how to remain a winner in this rapidly changing world and found the answer in a new venture after being approached by merchant banker and racehorse owner Brian Yuill, a corporate whiz with a reputation for pulling off breathtaking deals.

Unaccustomed to doing business at this boardroom level, TJ asked commercial lawyer Bruce Stracey to advise him.

The upshot was that in February 1987, Smith announced his Tulloch Lodge stables would launch as the world's first public float of a horse-training establishment.

True to style Tommy, MBE, AM, announced it with crystal champagne flute in hand amid the straw, hay and aroma of horse manure at Tulloch Lodge in the very box that once housed his greatest champion, Tulloch, and long before that the immortal Phar Lap.

Smith, to receive a salary of $150,000 plus bonuses, was to train the horses. He would lease his stables to the public company, Tulloch Lodge Ltd, for five years and sell his goodwill for $2.24 million, payable over five years.

Based on Smith's reputation, the public quickly invested the $15 million capital required, principally to enable the champion trainer to carry out the company's aim of stocking up with a big team of good yearlings and concentrating on the rich Group races.

It seemed the right move for the times in a buoyant market

but it was also a risk for Tommy, who was in unfamiliar territory and, for once, not in full control of his operation.

In this atmosphere Gai became even more of the dutiful daughter, doing everything to make him feel at ease in a difficult period, wishing to protect him.

Tommy was joint managing director and Gai, seeing this new project as her future, would have liked to have been on the board too.

But Brian Yuill would not have a bar of her because of her connection with Robbie. Indeed, he wanted to squeeze her out altogether.

Gai felt deeply hurt by his attitude, the irony of which would soon be apparent.

She busied herself in the work, talking the new management into sprucing up the stables. As co-foreman responsible also for PR, she worked long hours and believed she was worth her $50,000 a year salary, a figure she also negotiated for Ernie on the basis they were regarded as equals.

TJ had an open chequebook to buy yearlings and with Gai beside him, he showed his renowned skill in the first year by buying the two that would finish first and second in the next year's Golden Slipper—Star Watch and Comely Girl.

Gai picked out Star Watch as the one Tommy should buy.

At that 1988 Slipper win a stunning photo was taken of Gai that would be used over and over again, with her victory fist held high while she gave a whoop of joy. The tonsil shot, they called it.

Tulloch Lodge survived the 1987 world stock market crash and earned $4 million in prizemoney in the 1987–88 season.

Just in case Gai was beginning to think all was right with the world, Robbie then came before Judge Smyth in the District Court to face trial on the Fine Cotton conspiracy charge.

Since his last court appearance, eight new charges had been added by the Director of Public Prosecutions.

Waterhouse now faced joint charges with Garry Clarke and Father O'Dwyer of attempting to obtain a financial advantage by deception, and with Father O'Dwyer of conspiracy to defraud; and he also faced six separate accounts of attempting to obtain a financial advantage by deception.

Gai was delighted when Judge Smyth quashed and permanently stayed all the charges against him and the other persons, and the Crown did not appeal.

The judge said the charges did not disclose any criminality.

Feeling a deep sense of relief, Gai hoped that would be the end of it, with no more pursuit of her husband and no more heavy legal expenses.

The world *was* looking sunny again.

TJ was having a second golden period with plenty of horses to draw upon, Gai was working closer than ever with him and the future looked sound.

And Gai's PR skills were making headway for the stables despite Brian Yuill's attempt to keep her in the background.

Then, disaster.

Tommy and Gai sniffed there may be a problem when Yuill reneged on one of his periodic goodwill payments to TJ.

Tommy called Bruce Stracey, seeking the lawyer's help.

Within days the cat was partly let out of the bag howling when *Four Corners* went to air with a story about Alan Bond and a big property deal in Rome involving Brian Yuill and some of his companies.

The Australian Stock Exchange and National Securities Commission queried the deal in which Tulloch Lodge Ltd made a $10 million loan to Kitool Pty Ltd, a $2 Canberra-registered company. The funds, it was alleged, were to be used by Kitool to help acquire the Rome property owned by Bond Corp.

With thunderous echoes Brian Yuill's giant Spedley Group, the major shareholder in Tulloch Lodge, then collapsed in April, 1989 with debts of $1.2 billion, leaving the Tulloch Lodge public company in an embarrassing debt situation.

Tulloch Lodge Ltd had lent $3.2 million to Spedley Securities and had no chance of getting it back.

Yuill had no option but to resign.

TJ had broken a golden rule and made the biggest mistake

of his life by agreeing to let Yuill handle the finances while he looked after the horses.

Phones ran hot and everyone was shocked. Gai was in there like a terrier helping her father. Stracey, Gai and Tommy went to the offices of Spedley, demanding the records of Tulloch Lodge Ltd.

Gai jumped in and enlisted the aid of astute businessman Keith Moremon to go on the board in an effort to save Tulloch Lodge from bankruptcy. She became a substitute director and either accompanied Tommy or went herself to all shareholders' meetings to watch his interests, speaking up vigorously when necessary.

It was the worst thing that had ever happened to the great Tommy Smith. His reputation verged on ruin.

Angry scenes dominated shareholders' meetings with bitter claims hurled at the board, as plans and more plans were drawn up to save the company.

Some headlines put the debt at $11 million. 'Friends' of Tulloch Lodge were reportedly going to help out, mystery bids were cited but it was all speculation.

What concerned Gai most was that she had accompanied Tommy a few months earlier when he bought 109 yearlings in New Zealand and Australia for $9 million.

Bloodstock agents were demanding payment and now she and Tommy knew the company could not meet those payments.

Indeed, Tulloch Lodge was millions short of meeting its debts even after selling shares in Star Watch for $2.4 million in order to keep the operation afloat.

Yuill had assured Smith before he bought the yearlings that the funds were available for that purpose. But the cupboard was bare.

Some shareholders were saying Smith should bail the company out due to his personal wealth, claiming he was morally and legally bound to pay the $9 million. But he was a paid employee and possessed written proof that he was buying yearlings not for himself but on behalf of Tulloch Lodge Ltd.

In the midst of this crisis an incredible thing happened, running jauntily, almost bizarrely against the tide of depression—TJ Smith, after being in the wilderness for three years to Brian Mayfield-Smith, did a Lazarus and recaptured the Sydney trainers' premiership for the 34th time.

Euphoric as it was for Gai and TJ, it served little more than to heighten the sharp division and mixed emotions of the situation.

The big problem remained.

In desperation Smith flew to London to approach rich horsey types. There he tried to sell the horses to Kerry Packer and Kerry's friend, Melbourne businessman and casino operator Lloyd Williams. They weren't interested, nor was takeover king Robert Holmes à Court.

There was nothing else for it now but a firesale. Unfortunately it would be a slaughter because most of the yearlings had not yet shown up as gallopers, the market was depressed and everyone would be looking for and demanding bargains.

This fight was one he couldn't win. He would just have to take it on the chin and start again in a humble way.

It would be no consolation to learn that after an inquiry into the Spedley group, Brian Yuill—the man who wanted to keep Gai out of sight because of her husband's problem—would be charged with various breaches of the Companies Code.

Yuill would lose everything, even his luxury home, convicted of dishonesty as a director and sentenced to serve a minimum prison term of six years for illegally using $2.8 million of Spedley Securities money for private purposes.

Gai and Robbie were on holiday with a disconsolate Smith in London when he failed to spark any interest with Kerry Packer.

She felt sad for him and realised how it would hurt him if Tulloch Lodge Ltd went bankrupt. This was on the brink of happening now that he could not sell the horses.

Many shareholders were blaming him. His name would be mud.

Gai worried about it constantly. The sales were on in Kentucky at that very moment and all the big dealers would be there. Suddenly she had an idea, suggesting they call there on the way back to Australia.

Tommy wouldn't hear of it. If the people he'd just spoken to weren't interested, nobody would be. A waste of time and money.

'All right, Rob and I will go,' said Gai.

As they flew out of London Gai said to Robbie, 'All I want to do is help Dad. We've got to find a buyer. It would hurt me to the quick if his name remains smeared because of this.'

They finally reached the Bluegrass country and spent five days at the Keeneland sales complex. She spoke to every contact she could rustle up, including old friends like yodelling Arthur Hancock.

He and all his friends only wanted to sell horses, not buy. To others, a good deal in Australia seemed a million miles away and Kentucky was where the action was taking place.

Sipping coffee with Robbie at the sales centre, she was just telling him how she hated the thought of giving up when she spotted Billy McDonald strolling past.

She leapt up, grabbed him and sat him down. 'Billy, I've got a deal for you. You should get working on it right away.'

Billy was the funny man in the Sangster team, the wild boozing Irishman who had made his name as a Rolls Royce salesman in San Francisco and about whom there were outrageous stories, all of them true, and even then probably watered down. Gai had seen him last at the races in Ireland at The Curragh near Dublin.

They caught up on old times and she told him the details. Yes, he was meeting his best client that coming weekend and might be able to do something. Be in touch.

Billy was playing it close to his chest, refusing to name his client. Still, it was better than nothing and Gai decided to wait to see what happened.

True to his word when it came to making a buck, Billy sat

down with his client on the Sunday and casually mentioned the prospective sale.

The other man said nothing. Billy asked if there was something wrong.

'No,' he said, 'but you know, Billy, I never discuss a business deal when I have a drink and the other man doesn't.'

'But I'm on the wagon. Haven't had a drink for five years.'

No dice. Billy pushed his mineral water aside and signalled the waiter. 'Double vodka and tomato juice!'

Next day when Gai telephoned Billy he said he thought it was a goer, but he still couldn't tell her the name of his client.

Staying on alone in Kentucky for the next 10 days, Gai faxed to Tulloch Lodge in Sydney for specific details of the 105 horses and three properties at Cootamundra that were part of the deal.

Gai was annoyed to find that mostly what she received in feedback from home was criticism. 'Why is she doing this? What would she know? Why is she sending us all these papers? How would she be able to sell this deal?'

She said to Robbie on the telephone, 'It's a lot harder doing this for someone else than for yourself. In some ways it's easier to build your own castle.'

When it came to selling, Gai had the gift of the gab. She was a good operator on the telephone and had already found quite a few new owners for her father by relating well to people and communicating effectively.

She gave Billy the hard sell, 'Now, let me tell you. This will make your client the number one owner in Australia. The real estate is prime. The package has older horses and young ones, trained by my father, Australia's leading trainer.

'If this man enjoys racing, he'll enjoy this and it won't cost a great deal of money by your standards.'

Negotiations continued. She was introduced to Michael Bramwell, manager for Billy's client who had poached him from Britain's National Stud at Newmarket where Gai had visited a boyfriend in her acting days.

The three flew to Australia to view the bloodstock. Only

then did they reveal their principal was John Warner Kluge, estimated to be worth $7 billion and the richest man in the United States.

Kluge, who had only recently taken an interest in bloodstock by signing a $3 million agreement with Robert Sangster on a London hotel table napkin, had arrived in America at the age of seven with his penniless German immigrant family.

He paid his way through Columbia University from poker winnings and later made a fortune in the communications business.

His only previous link with Australia was in 1985 when Rupert Murdoch bought his Metromedia group for $US3 billion, some of those assets forming the base for Murdoch's Fox global network.

Kluge had lashed out as a big spender when he married the leggy English brunette Patricia Rose, a former belly dancer in Baghdad and a Soho stripper and soft porn queen.

Patricia, 34 years his junior, had posed naked for the raunchy *Knave* magazine and written a regular magazine column giving erotic boudoir advice.

As a shopper in Paris, Rome and elsewhere, Patricia made Jackie Onassis look like a down-and-out on Skid Row.

The Kluges lived in a $500 million Georgian estate in Virginia with a live-in staff of 120, such knick-knacks as a golf course designed by Arnold Palmer, helicopter pad, Arab stud and carriage museum. Kluge also had a log cabin as a 'thinking room'.

Oh, and they had a Gothic-style chapel with a ceiling mural of the Kluges strolling off into the ether to meet the Virgin Mary.

The vulgarity of Patricia's $2 million party for her Big O (40th) birthday at the Waldorf Astoria riled even the snobbiest of New York socialites, the very people she sought to impress. It made the extravagant Marie Antoinette look like a pauper.

In one of the little diversions at the party the 400 guests were invited to fish in a lake of beluga caviar for ice sculptures containing bottles of the finest Russian vodka.

As for the flower displays, it took about 40 florists 12 hours to arrange them.

In another little diversion, the Kluges had a three-storey Manhattan penthouse with cascading waterfall and walls that rose silently at the touch of a button.

But nothing would have thrilled the social-climbing former belly dancer more than to meet the Queen.

Patricia prevailed upon old John while he had his cheque-book handy one day to pick up a quick snap, a $14.5 million Scottish estate with 28,000 hectares of deer forest near the Salmon-rich Dee River and just a short Rolls ride down the road from the Royal retreat at Balmoral.

Of course, to give royalty a run for their money, no estate could be in the top drawer without an authentic English 'shoot'.

So an Irish baronet was brought in as gamekeeper to stock up the place with thousands of pheasants, ducks and other game.

Naturally with Patricia's tastes, Klugey needed a few winners.

Then 75, Kluge might have had deep pockets but his agents proved to be tough horse traders and drove a very hard bargain. They did it on nothing stronger than mineral water, too.

Bramwell was an acknowledged bloodstock expert and McDonald, wild man or not, was no dummy. In the mid-1970s he had bought a yearling colt for Sangster for $US175,000 which would race in the name of Alleged.

Young actress Gai was present in Paris the day in 1977 when the brilliant Alleged with Lester Piggott up, in the best run in Europe that year, summarily dismissed the field to win the Prix de l'Arc de Triomphe, with Australian horse Balmerino finishing second.

Alleged won it again the following year, retiring to stud in Kentucky valued at $US16 million.

Bramwell and McDonald made their Tulloch Lodge offer just in the nick of time.

Tommy Smith, having exhausted all avenues, had already announced he would probably sell the yearlings at public auction to try to raise the millions owed to the bloodstock agencies. 'Tulloch Lodge can't pay for them and I'm not going to pay,' he said.

The crisis had arisen after the company prepared a $9.1 million syndication package named TJ 89 Syndicate, offering shares at $91,000 each with tax benefits. It then bought yearlings for $5.3 million at the William Inglis and Sons sales in Sydney and $3.8 million of horseflesh at the New Zealand sales.

Soon after came the Spedley crash.

Smith and everyone else knew the sale of those horses at auction would send Tulloch Lodge Ltd into liquidation because they would not raise anywhere near the amount needed. But it would greatly reduce the extent of the bankruptcy. He was due to meet Tulloch Lodge directors two days later to make the final decision.

After that meeting, said the *Sydney Morning Herald*, Tulloch Lodge Ltd was expected to be dead and buried.

In making his announcement of the intended firesale, Smith told reporters he would scale down his training and operate solely out of his Tulloch Lodge stables (which he'd only leased to the company), and his brother Ernie would be his right hand man.

He was reported as saying he would give other stables he owned to Gai and his nephew Sterling, son of Ernie. Gai would be given Bounding Away Lodge and Sterling, Travel Boy Lodge.

Both would have to apply for training permits from the Australian Jockey Club.

But just before that decision was made, the Kluge men put their deal on the table. They knew they were in a buyer's market.

In the previous few days they had inspected the horses and properties with Gai on hand to make the pitch.

After that they examined veterinary reports on each horse and only then were they ready to talk to Tulloch Lodge accountants.

Their bid was rejected and they appeared ready to call it off.

Tommy took the negotiators to the Regent Hotel for champagne to ease the tension. Meanwhile, Gai harangued the accountants, telling them they were crazy not to accept the offer. Nobody else would pick up the package and if they didn't move, it was curtains.

Gai's efforts helped turn them around, and when Kluge's men made an amended offer of $7.5 million for the horses and a Cootamundra property, it was as good as sealed.

The contracts were drawn up in early August, 1989. It remained a mere formality for shareholders to either accept it or go bust. It was the only deal on offer, their only hope of staying alive.

Shareholders accepted it at an extraordinary general meeting, but not without some heated debate. One stirrer who held only proxy votes claimed the board had not obtained enough evaluations and to him a hatless, angry Smith said 'bullshit'.

Michael Bramwell said on behalf of John Kluge that Tommy's track record was a key ingredient in the decision to buy the stock.

Tulloch Lodge Ltd was in business again, with a balance sheet surplus of $240,000.

Gai, by plucking a deal out of the air and making it happen, had saved Tulloch Lodge from going under.

She also saved her father's reputation. He was back in business with a big string of horses training for America's richest man with the opportunity for a second new lease of life.

In spite of all the negative vibes around her, Gai had proved herself a top business executive, wheeler dealer and diplomat.

She was on a high, bursting with enthusiasm at her incredible feat.

While in this mood, destiny beckoned.

CHAPTER THIRTEEN

The Smith Family Splits

Even before Kluge's men left Australia on 6 August, 1989, Gai was planning to apply to the Australian Jockey Club for her licence.

She was confident the deal would go through and saw this as the moment to move and seize her destiny.

She considered she'd served her apprenticeship. Taking into account the years when she rode trackwork as a university student and going to the track early nearly every morning, she had worked for her father for 15 years.

She'd gone to the sales, studied how to pick the yearlings and covered every aspect of the operation. Now she wanted nothing more than to be a trainer in her own right.

This was the inheritance that should naturally be hers. She'd earned it and *knew* she would succeed at it.

Tommy had been such an exacting taskmaster she could not have contemplated taking it on unless she felt she would be good.

Failure was not in his rule book. To take on the vocation so close to his heart and fail would be the worst thing she could ever do in her life.

Gai knew she had the Bounding Away stables at 168

Doncaster Avenue, Randwick, just around the corner from Tulloch Lodge in Bowral Street. Tommy had said so himself in the newspapers.

He had bought the stables through the family company about two years before and refurbished them. Once owned by trainer Fil Allotta, the historic boxes had been home to such great horses as Peter Pan, Amounis, Baguette and Cabochon.

The frustration of trying to work with Ernie was a major factor in her decision. Here was the chance to end this graceless, hopeless situation.

She was so worked up about it she felt like a boil ready to burst.

Gai was already used to giving orders in her husky staccato tones. Her bouncy manner had upset quite a few in the stables, ever since she was seen to enjoy the power of being the boss when Tommy was in hospital recovering from the horse kick.

Before that she was still just TJ's girl in people's eyes.

They were saying Tommy had earned the right to be bouncy, Gai had merely inherited it.

She was known in the stables as Bonaparte in Skirts, although she seldom wore a skirt there. She regarded this as an attempt to put her down because she was a woman.

She blamed Ernie for a lot of this stirring of the pot, the jokes in the background at her expense.

Gai knew that if she had been born a boy, it wouldn't have mattered. Everyone would have looked upon her differently. She would have been TJ's *son*, the obvious one to take over from him.

It didn't seem to mean anything that she had cleaned her saddle and bridle from a little girl, loved horses and tried to learn the business. She was seen as a girl in a man's world.

All this had made her more determined to succeed, to beat the atmosphere of male domination, causing her to be even more passionate about what she was doing. She bustled, she strived, every minute precious.

But she had no power as co-foreman unless both Tommy and

Ernie were away. Normally she could not hire or fire or dictate training procedures.

She felt she was the foreman of nothing. Everything was fine as long as she stayed a PR girl talking to the clients on the telephone.

She was so often annoyed at the irritations she felt at the stables while she and Ernie were in conflict that Robbie found her hard to live with as she unburdened herself to him night after night.

She kept saying to her husband, 'Rob, I've got to get out and do something about it. It's driving me insane.

'The only way I can see is to be a trainer. But I don't want to work against Dad. I want to work with him and have his help. However, I just can't see how to do it.'

There were numerous tales of Gai giving instructions to the staff and Ernie countermanding them, of Ernie working the horses early before Gai could have any input.

She felt this caused a poor reaction among the staff.

Gossip in the stables often pointed to trouble between them at the track in the mornings.

Ernie liked to punt and, in an attempt to keep the galloping performances to himself, would sometimes work the horses virtually in the dark before Clocker Gai could get into position on the track, and this infuriated her.

She felt it was a kind of game that was noticed, breeding an atmosphere of tension between Ernie and her in the stables.

She believed if she expressed an opinion on a horse, Ernie would take the opposite viewpoint, so she became cagey on what she said about a horse.

She didn't like Ernie's training methods, either.

Insiders at the stables believed it was nothing more than a clash of personality between the two and they hoped it would be resolved.

Ernie, it was said, appealed to women and they found him agreeable company, but there was also the opinion that he tended to be a chauvinist at times, an attitude not unusual among men of his era.

Some observers at the stables thought Tommy was in a no-win situation. His ambitious only daughter was showing an enormous interest and wanted to take over while his brother, with whom he had enjoyed a long and successful association, acted as his right hand. And the end of an era was coming.

Tommy knew the two were at war but did nothing.

The pity of it all, they believed, was that Ernie could not see it would end in confrontation, forcing Tommy to take sides. If that happened, there could be only one winner. Ernie couldn't bring himself to accept that he had to learn to work with Gai.

In the office Gai adopted her usual positive attitude, suppressing her personal feelings, making no comments on the subject and getting on with whatever she could. Ernie was her uncle, after all.

To complicate the situation, Ernie was anxious for his son to become a trainer. Sterling had worked in Tulloch Lodge and gained experience in other parts of the world.

At one stage it was thought Sterling would have a role in the scheme of things at Tulloch Lodge.

Having at last formulated her strategy, Gai made sure she bumped into several officials at the races.

She did not say a word to Tommy or to Valerie, because she knew what they would say, 'You really don't want to do this because you have a comfortable life, a husband and two children to think about.'

On her own initiative she approached AJC Chairman Jim Bell and asked him what he would think if she took out a trainer's licence. Bell confidently said, 'If you applied today, Gai, you would have the licence tomorrow.'

She then saw Jim Comans, the Committeeman in charge of licensing matters, and he agreed with Bell's remarks, adding that he couldn't see any problems whatsoever.

To cover all points, she then called on Doug McKay, the club's head of licensed persons. He couldn't see any hitches either, advising her on the procedures and saying if she filled in the forms her application could go before the next Committee meeting for approval. He gave her an application form.

Pleased with her progress Gai took the six-page form with her that night when she and Robbie had dinner with Tommy and Valerie at the Al Corso Italian restaurant in Double Bay.

Chatting amiably, they were half way through the meal when she produced the forms and said, 'I picked these up today, Dad. I'm going to apply for my licence.'

'What do you mean?' asked Tommy, squinting at her.

'You know, my trainer's licence.'

Tommy blew up.

'How dare you go to the AJC behind my back,' he said.

They raised their voices and argued fiercely.

'Why wouldn't I go to the AJC?' she shouted. 'I've been working for you for 15 years, I've got all the background knowledge anyone could need. I don't consider I went behind your back.'

Robbie tried to calm them. 'Look, cool down you two, you're both too fiery.'

She was angry that after all these years, Tommy did not consider this was what she wanted to do.

Tommy maintained she had no right to do this without talking to him about it first. He told her he didn't want to upset Ernie.

'How can you think of being a trainer with two children and a husband?' he said. 'You are my right hand girl and that's how I want to keep it.'

She burst into tears, rushed out of the restaurant and drove home.

Robbie stayed behind. When he came home she berated him for not supporting her and he said it would only have been worse if he too had left.

Next day Gai and Tommy discussed it in a calmer atmosphere.

She stuck to her guns and when he saw there was no way of dissuading her, he slowly began warming to the idea.

Then, in typical fashion, as a man who always liked the best for himself, he said, 'If you're going to go for this lousy licence, don't insult me by asking for a number two licence. Ask for a number one.' It carried more privileges and prestige.

To check on things, Tommy asked Committeeman Comans if he saw any problem and Comans repeated exactly what he had told Gai, encouraging her to apply and assuring she would be accepted.

Gai filled out her forms, for both number one and two licences, ran around and arranged an impressive list of references from trainers, thoroughbred consultants and owners, some of whom already promised horses for her to train, and submitted them to the AJC on 8 August, 1989.

Those who supported her application were Harry Lawton, Mal Barnes, Mark Wilson of Evergreen Lodge, Murray Bell, VRC Committeeman Bruce Gadsden, Stan Dumbrell, PR Gallagher, Neville Begg, Boris Ganke, John L Muir, Peter Vela and TJ Smith, who sent in a ringing two-page endorsement.

Tommy praised Gai's long association with horses, her great 'eye' for horseflesh, her knowledge of feeds, training, ability to judge a horse's potential and her office work. He pointed out she would have the best stables at Randwick.

As if that wasn't enough, the master of Tulloch Lodge added that for seven years when he and Ernie were away, she had sole control of his stables for periods of up to a month and did everything required just as he would have done it.

Gai didn't say anything about it but news of her application leaked out quickly and the press wrote it up.

It was mostly good PR material along the lines that as she had saved Tulloch Lodge, would she now be heiress to the throne?

But two journalists subtly introduced the subject of Robbie Waterhouse into their stories, implying it could be a problem.

She deftly parried their questions.

Nearly a month went by. She received a hand-delivered letter from the AJC signed by the Secretary/General Manager, RB Alexander.

She tore it open and couldn't believe her eyes.

'Dear Mrs Waterhouse,' it began. 'Reference is made to your recent application to this Club for a Trainer's Licence.

'I am directed to advise you that this matter was considered by the Committee at its meeting today, Thursday, 7th September, 1989, and the Committee decided to refuse your application.'

That was it. Virtually a one liner. No explanation.

She told friends it 'took the gas' out of her. She felt someone had given her the greatest punch in the gut she could possibly have received in her life.

Licking her wounds that night over dinner, she reacted to her husband and three or four close friends including Lea and Bruce Stracey in these words, 'Why didn't they tell me there could be a problem? Why the devil did they tell me I would get the licence when they didn't give it to me?

'If they'd told me there was a problem, I'd never have gone ahead with it.

'Instead, they looked me in the eye and said there is no problem at all, go for your licence and you'll get it tomorrow. It's just so unprincipled.'

She wondered what could be behind it.

Gai knew forces had been at work behind the scenes to cause mischief. Attempts were made to discredit her with racing journalists. She knew this could have no substance and didn't worry about it. Why should she when she had the assurances of three important AJC officials, one of whom repeated it all to her father?

Catherine Hale, Gai's close friend at whose home the dinner was held that night, remembered the occasion clearly. She would refer to it as 'the sad night'.

Catherine, wife of lawyer Tim Hale, saw the private Gai as distinct from the public racing figure.

'In public she's always so full of strength and puts on a wonderful face for everyone,' said Catherine. 'She entertains her clients and the media brightly and pleases the public in general.

'In private she's very kind to her friends but she does have a vulnerability. I saw it that night. I think this fragile quality is what makes her a very human person.

'She'd been dealt a huge blow but not once did she show any bitterness or feel sorry for herself. She just sat down, took it on the chin and decided how to march on from there, rather than saying "I'm not going to take this and I'm coming out fighting."

'She was hurt. Not depressed or bitter, but you could see she was hurt deeply after being attacked on such a personal level.

'Gai was extremely intelligent about it, in thinking how best to go on from there. And that really impressed me.'

It wasn't the only shocking news for Gai that day.

An hour or so before receiving that jolt she was told by Robbie the police had just served a summons on him charging him with perjury.

It related to his evidence before the Racing Appeals Tribunal on his Fine Cotton betting going back to 1984—five years before!

This latest move had a particularly nasty edge to it because perjury had been considered at the time under the Racing Tribunal Legislation but not proceeded with.

It carried only the minor penalty of a fine there. But they didn't take action in the statutory time and after six months it was no longer possible to lay a charge under that law.

Now, right out of the blue, he was being charged under the Crimes Act by the Director of Public Prosecutions (DPP). The sting was he could go to jail for seven years if convicted.

To add to the dark mystery, the detective handing over the summons told him there was no new evidence or fresh witnesses from five years before when it was first considered.

This new charge was deliberately leaked to the press.

Just minutes before Gai received the AJC letter a TV crew appeared on their doorstep to question Robbie about it. 'No comment,' he said.

That night Channel Nine splashed the story, a double whammy and scoop by reporter Steve Barratt—warned-off Robbie was facing new perjury charges arising from his betting on Fine Cotton, and Gai's licence was refused after the daughter of legendary trainer Tommy Smith received 'a slap in the face' from the AJC.

File pictures of them filled the screen, also of Tommy and Valerie, plus a re-run of old Fine Cotton's notorious race.

For good measure the bulletin also referred to the Supreme Court evidence that day in the family feud of the famous Waterhouse dynasty over the will of the late Charles Waterhouse, a case that had just started and would last for a year with titillating headlines almost daily.

The channel ran pictures of Bill Waterhouse entering court, plus headings on the court proceedings from newspapers. A real family affair on A *Current Affair*.

Gai and Robbie knew instinctively the timing of his being charged and her application being considered was no coincidence.

To say otherwise would be to believe in Santa Claus, Little Red Riding Hood and Goldilocks and the Three Bears—and then some.

The AJC Committee was told of the pending perjury charge before they sat down to consider her application.

Urgent attempts had been made to serve the summons on him on Wednesday, the day before Gai's application was heard, but he wasn't available to receive it until the following day.

If he had accepted it on the Wednesday, it would probably have been on TV that night and in the papers the next morning, the day the AJC was officially due to deliberate on her licence.

So, on a matter that had been dead for five years, someone was busy in the background bent on causing harm with impeccable timing.

Also, by an odd quirk, Robbie some time before had made one of his several applications to be readmitted as a bookmaker in the wake of Fine Cotton, and this was to be considered on the same day.

It, too, was knocked back, but the AJC did not release this information and the papers missed it.

For Gai, it all came together in one crushing disappointment.

The press quickly focused on her drama.

First report after the TV coverage was by Keith Robbins next morning in the *Daily Telegraph* quoting Tommy as shouting a loud 'no' when asked if Gai had received her licence. He was reportedly too upset to say anything more.

The *Daily Mirror* followed under the heading 'Gai Shocked by Licence Knockback', quoting Robbie that she was very angry and had been offered no explanation 'and that's what hurts'.

The *Sydney Morning Herald* summed it all up with a double-barrelled 'Gai Hides Her Hurt Behind a Big Smile' and 'Perjury Charge for Robbie Waterhouse'.

Then the papers began analysing it, saying there was little doubt the AJC had discriminated against her.

One newspaper comment hit it amidships: 'For nearly five years the AJC has allowed her to work as a paid employee for her father while living with a warned-off person, yet when she wants to earn her living as a trainer in her own right, her relationship with her husband apparently suddenly becomes beyond the pale and an impediment to her furthering her legitimate career aspirations.'

Not only was she a paid employee, she was also a licensed person as co-foreman.

The wife of a warned off person couldn't own a racehorse but there was nothing to say she couldn't train one. The ownership rule had been around since Phar Lap was a foal but racing officials did not have women in mind as trainers then. Good heavens, women would have been flat out getting into the members' enclosures.

Tommy was flabbergasted by it all. He went to several AJC Committeemen and demanded, 'How could you make such a fool of the girl? We wouldn't have gone ahead if we'd known.' They were noncommittal.

Gai told the papers she had no idea why she had been refused. She described how she had the stables and the qualifications. It was all such a surprise, she said.

Privately her friends saw she was deflated, even devastated.

To those close to her like Lea Stracey, she wasn't walking as straight and there was an unusual edginess to her manner.

Any more pressure and Gai could crack, Lea thought. Her face was strained and she looked tired. Her tread, no longer light and quick, had become more purposeful and dogged.

Gai was searching deep within herself to find some answers. What more could she do to prove herself? Should she fight them?

Tommy was dead against it—you never fought the AJC.

Still unable to believe it, she clung momentarily to the illusion that the AJC would change its mind and give her the licence.

Then she said to Lea, 'Do you think I should keep going?' Gai didn't have any doubts, but just wanted someone to agree with her that she should fight.

While out to dinner at the home of the Hales after receiving the news that day, she had taken the opportunity of asking Bruce Stracey if he would help her.

Bruce had stayed out of the Fine Cotton matter with Robbie, feeling it would be too difficult to be friend and lawyer at the same time, and he felt the same way now.

He told her he was a commercial lawyer anyway, but she seemed so vulnerable he agreed to advise her.

'It's almost impossible to beat the AJC and overturn a ruling of theirs because they're a law unto themselves, and they don't have to give reasons,' he said. 'But first of all, we should try to get a reason.'

She sent a courteous letter to the Supervisor of Licensed Persons expressing her disappointment and dismay at their decision and saying how hurt she was by the nature of media publicity (that it was due to Robbie), following their decision.

'It would help me in considering my position if you would be good enough to tell me why I was not granted this licence,' she wrote, low key.

Meanwhile, drama broke out afresh at Tulloch Lodge.

The board, now wanting to run a tighter ship due to the Kluge association and the close call with liquidation, decided to trim some senior staff. Two foremen doing the same job was an obvious area. Negotiations were held and Ernie decided he would take a settlement and finish up.

Ernie took his settlement figure but when Tommy heard about it he told him to come back. Just when Gai thought her troubles with Ernie were over, he turned up the next day as normal.

Gai confronted Tommy who said, 'Oh, we can't do without him.'

Angered, she gave her father an ultimatum.

'All right, Dad,' she said, 'this is the final straw. You either work with your daughter and you support me, and I support you, or it's the finish. I'm not working with Ernie any longer. Either they pay me out and I leave, or Ernie does.'

In an attempt to find a compromise, Tommy came to an understanding with Gai that she could work out of the Bounding Away stables.

This flowed from an earlier discussion in which Gai had asked Kluge's manager, Michael Bramwell, before he left Sydney if she could train a few of Kluge's 105 horses in Sydney at Bounding Away. It had been her way of trying to start out on her own as a trainer and still work closely with her father.

But Bramwell had been adamant, 'No, Mr Kluge's trainer must be TJ Smith.'

With her licence application rejected, Gai and Tommy now agreed to an interim plan. Tommy would give her eight or 10 horses to *manage* at Bounding Away.

He would still officially be trainer and supervise things but she would do everything required such as nominations and acceptances and be trainer except in name. It would prepare her for the time in the near future when the AJC granted her the licence.

On the first morning she turned up at Bounding Away to manage the horses in the boxes she found Ernie out of the blocks and there already. Somehow he'd got wind of it. And he was seething.

As soon as they saw each other a blazing row erupted.

Various private reports of the argument have been discussed but the following exchange is believed to be the substance of their encounter, which took place in the presence of stable hands.

Ernie: 'Who do you think you are? How dare you upset the apple cart.'

Gai: 'I'm not upsetting the apple cart, Ernie, I'm just getting on with my life.'

Ernie: 'What role is there for a woman in racing if she can't work the horses?'

Gai: 'Don't give me that. You haven't given much thought to that, yet you've had all these girls riding for you.

'Look at this poor girl, a strapper, having to carry this huge bale of straw . . .'

The argument degenerated into a shouting match about the merits of women in racing in which personal remarks were hurled.

At one point Gai was heard to shout, 'You don't scare me.'

There had been many skirmishes between them over the past few years but as far as Gai was concerned this was the first and only full-on heated argument they ever had.

Ernie told Tommy he was quitting, and he went public.

Tommy was so angry over the tense situation and remonstrated with her so strongly that Gai thought he would disown her.

Next day the three Sydney morning papers carried the sensational story. Only then would the racing public learn the depth of feeling that had been simmering for years in the most famous stables in Australia.

Max Presnell ran the story in the *Sydney Morning Herald* under the heading 'It's over: TJ, Ernie split.'

'My name is Smith, not Waterhouse,' he quoted an emotional Ernie as saying when asked why.

The paper went on to say Ernie was irate because of Smith's support of Gai in her attempt to get a licence to train horses at Randwick and there was no doubt Ernie didn't appreciate the role his niece had been playing in the stable in recent years.

'Tommy's got horses under Gai's care down the road at Bounding Away Lodge, and I can't cop it any longer,' said Ernie. 'I came here with nothing 40 years ago and I'm going to leave the same way.'

The paper referred to friction between Gai and Ernie, adding 'Like her father, Gai is a forceful personality. She has the Smith drive but in her enthusiasm can stand on toes, and obviously this applies to Ernie's.'

The *Daily Telegraph* used the story over six columns with the heading: 'Smith Family Feud: TJ, Ernie Split Up.'

It quoted Ernie, wiping back tears, as saying 'That's it. I'm definitely finished with Tulloch Lodge. It's a tragedy, a terrible, terrible tragedy. This is the end of a wonderful association. I've never been so disappointed in my life.'

The writer referred to disagreements in the stable, how Gai and Ernie simply did not get on, that this had been coming for a while.

Ernie said, 'My relationship has always been with Tommy. I don't work with Gai. I have no relationship with her and refuse to work with her.

'I just couldn't bear going to the races and seeing Gai Waterhouse saddling up horses trained out of Bounding Away Lodge.

'I think Tommy's made a terrible mistake giving her the stables to train out of.'

Ernie went even further with Chris Dowd in the *Daily Mirror* that afternoon with full front page treatment.

The heading across the top said 'Australia's Most Famous Racing Family,' then in bold type, 'Why TJ, Ernie Split', with a quote from Ernie underneath, 'I believe in Tom, I love him. He's a wonderful bloke.'

Ernie's quotes:

'I just can't work with Gai—there isn't room for the two of us. I don't think a woman can run a racing stable.

'When she missed out on her trainer's licence it meant she would just get further in the way of me and Tommy—and that just wasn't good enough.

'Tommy is a wonderful bloke, I love him. I believe in Tom. We have had a tremendous relationship, never any arguments.

'But Gai has been the problem—she doesn't have the right to be there . . . It was never intended she have that much power.

'She is out of place. Once people get a sniff of power it tends to go to their head.'

Tommy, apart from saying he hoped Ernie could come back, declared it was a family matter and offered no other comment.

The paper referred to Ernie's son intending to apply for a licence when he returned soon from New York and it paid tribute to Ernie for his work at Tulloch Lodge.

Still the papers played up the split. Next day, Saturday, 16 September, Keith Robbins had a lash in the *Daily Telegraph* under the heading 'End of Dynamic Duo' which was a paean of praise for Ernie. He had good friends in the media.

The story backgrounded Ernie's 40 years as Tommy's right arm, and offered the opinion that without Ernie it was doubtful if Tommy would have reached the pinnacles he had since starting out with one horse in the 1940s.

Robbins outlined how Ernie could not work with Gai but had let bygones be bygones for the sake of family harmony.

However, he said, the straw that broke the camel's back had come two days before on Thursday morning (the day of their confrontation in Bounding Away stables).

Gai, he said, had given an order to Ernie on Randwick race-course during the trackwork session, and 'Ernie saw red' and stormed off after angry words were exchanged.

Not letting go of this yarn with its big names and all the trappings of a good dirt fight that had the public agog, other papers and then the magazines took up the chase.

Most of the comments and opinions did not reflect the bigger battle Gai was fighting—a woman's right to a fair go and a career for which she was qualified. They saw it mainly in terms of a family feud.

She was portrayed as the stereotype of a woman in a male retreat, an attitude that still needed to be broken down considerably in Australia before women could gain equality.

The *Sunday Age* in Melbourne went deeper into the affair, remarking that the moral of the story spread far beyond Tommy and Ernie's lifetime of sharing trophies, that going into business with family was like igniting a time bomb—the stronger the bonds the bloodier the fallout.

The writer, a woman no less, questioned why Gai, wife, mother, PR woman and media performer, was so determined to succeed as a trainer. 'It is not clear why Gai is pushing so hard,' she said.

The newspaper went on:

'It is said that the disgrace that has befallen the Waterhouse family has made her all the more determined to take over the reins at Tulloch Lodge.'

Not a word about Gai believing it was her right, that she had spent so many years preparing herself for the role she was born into, that as a woman she felt she was just as entitled as a man to become a trainer.

No, she was doing this to clear the Waterhouse name!

Sydney businessman and racehorse owner Les Walters, an oldtimer who knew Tommy and worked with him in the Riverina area of New South Wales in the early days, was quoted next.

'Gai's a very nice person,' said Les, 'but she talks a bit much. Tommy should have put her in her place from the beginning and made sure she left Ernie alone when she handed out the orders. She shouldn't have been pushing him too much.

'It's been a damned kick in the teeth for Ernie the way Tommy has been pressuring so hard for Gai all the time, I wouldn't have copped it as long as Ernie did.'

Les, who owned Caulfield Cup winner Hayai, had a bit more to say touching on the role of women.

'I'll get killed for saying this and there are women trainers in Sydney who have done very well, but Tommy's operation is a big one and I don't think a woman could handle it.'

Champion jockey Roy 'The Professor' Higgins had a few thoughts quoted too:

'I haven't found Gai to be tough, I've found her very feminine but you must remember that she's been trained by TJ Smith, as Ernie has.

'It surprised me when she really threw herself into the training at the start because *she's a very good PR woman.*' [Author's italics.]

The article ended on the note:

'It was said that the Fine Cotton scandal broke Tommy Smith's heart because only two things, in the eyes of the public, ever really seemed to touch the champion trainer—his daughter Gai and his most famous filly, Bounding Away.

'TJ named his racing lodge after the horse and has, since the Waterhouse affair, become almost defiant in his support of his daughter, insisting, to his brother's chagrin, that he intends to give it all to Gai if she is granted a licence.

'TJ's fall from the top of the Sydney trainers' tree and his disastrous fling with the money market have been well documented but this latest setback is said to be just as serious. And it has come at a time when Tommy Smith needs all the friends he can get.'

Tommy and Ernie held peace talks over the weekend and on Monday Ernie announced things were looking better. He said he and Tommy missed each other, he'd wanted out at the time, he had to consider his five-year contract with Tulloch Lodge Ltd and he and Tommy would be talking again.

But it didn't work out. The feelings ran too deeply.

[Six years later when I approached Ernie and asked him if he wished to put his side to the story for this book, he declined to comment beyond saying, 'I just can't stand the woman.']

Ernie decided to go with his son Sterling, 25, who would soon apply to the AJC for a licence to train and was granted it.

Tommy gave Ernie a set of stables to train out of in Kensington Road, Kensington. Tommy's other stables apart from Tulloch Lodge, Travel Boy Lodge, would be turned into a block of units.

While Gai was in rejection, Sterling would make a flying start as trainer for the Emirates Stables, becoming a major yearling buyer for His Excellency Nasser Abdullah Hussein Lootah, of Dubai.

On behalf of their clients, Ernie bought the outstanding filly Bold Promise and Sterling trained it to win the Magic Millions races for both fillies and colts, winning $1.7 million and becoming the highest two-year-old earner in the world at that time.

Everyone seemed to be saying Sterling would be a splendid trainer while Gai would not.

Gai sued the *Mirror* and *New Idea* for defamation for using Ernie's comments implying she was not competent to be a trainer.

It had been a struggle to overcome all the family difficulties and manoeuvre herself into a position of applying for her licence, only to see the AJC whip the rug out from under her at the last minute in circumstances that were not only humiliating but also unfair and unacceptable in a modern world where women were striving for equality.

But the real battle was only just beginning.

CHAPTER FOURTEEN

SEXUAL ASSUMPTIONS

It took only a few days to decide.

Gai wanted to know her legal rights and the chance of mounting a successful challenge. She didn't know quite what to do but needed to chat to friends, her lawyer, husband and parents.

She asked herself, 'Do I really want this licence?'

When she received the AJC's letter of rejection, she had telephoned Tommy and, although a person who rarely swore, said, 'You won't believe this but the bastards have knocked me back.'

Tommy was astonished and angry then, but now when Gai asked him his opinion he said, 'Forget it. Don't waste your money.'

Robbie told her it was a matter for her. If she wanted to go on with it, he would give her all the emotional support he could. He appreciated she was the one who had to face everybody.

The initial confusion had eased, and Gai was now seeing things much more clearly. She still felt angry at what had happened, not expecting such treatment from people she considered friends.

It would have been so easy for them to have said, 'Look, Gai, there's a problem, please forget about it.'

She distinctly recalled saying to Chairman Jim Bell when asking about her licence application, 'Do you think there will be a problem because of Rob's situation?' But she felt they had not treated her with respect in being prepared to say 'the real reason is your husband.' She knew it had nothing to do with her capability.

And these people acted as good loyal friends of her father. But when the chips were down, they did not display the characteristics she expected.

She expected that Jim Bell would have pulled her aside later and said he hadn't realised there was a problem when he spoke to her. She would have understood and copped it.

All she expected was that they treat her like a human being and not just a number. She always believed there was something more to her relationship with Jim Bell than meriting that kind of treatment. She had known him since childhood, stayed at his home nearly every year and gone out with his son.

Gai believed what they had done was wrong. And the only reason they treated her like that was because she was a woman. She was not a feminist but felt certain the fact she was a woman prompted their decision. And no matter what happened, she would go to her grave thinking it.

It was obvious women weren't being treated equally in the racing industry and here was proof.

Gai knew the attitudes, knew what was being said about her situation: 'Oh well, she doesn't have to earn an income, hers is only the secondary income. Gai Smith is the daughter of a wealthy man. What does she have to work for? She goes and plays in the morning and clocks the horses. Why should we worry about her, she only thinks she wants to be a trainer. And she may not be any good, anyway.'

She said to Robbie, 'If I was the one accused of Fine Cotton and you were applying for a trainer's licence, they wouldn't think twice about giving it to you. It's disgraceful.'

The more she thought about it the more convinced she became that this had happened because she was a woman.

Gai wanted to be judged for herself, by what she had done, not because of her husband. She was then 36, had spent most of her life associated with racing, and it was ridiculous being treated like this.

She thought some of the officials opposing her had become blase about the rights of little people.

Gai considered accepting the situation and applying again in a year or 18 months. It was tempting to hang back and believe she would be successful next time. But they had already done her in the eye after telling her up front she would get her licence. How could they be believed again?

It was a big point of principle with her. If she was not comfortable with the thought that things might be different next year or the year after, then she had to go and fight for her licence. She would not get it any other way.

The AJC had the reputation of playing it boots and all in litigation. And they were so financially resourceful anyone taking them on had to think twice about it.

There was the added concern that anyone, especially a licensed person, had to work in harmony for the rest of their working lives with these powerful people who ran racing in the State. So it was a crucial decision.

Nobody told her what she should do. The injustice of it all was what decided her, even after Bruce Stracey advised her a legal challenge had only a minor chance of succeeding, not even 50/50, more like 30/70.

She took the decision alone. Fight them on all fronts.

While Gai was coming to grips with those problems, she also had the distressing matter of Robbie's perjury charge on her mind.

He came before the Downing Street Local Court in Sydney two weeks after her licence refusal.

His solicitor, Bruce Miles, went on the attack, alleging he was the victim of a vicious conspiracy to prevent him regaining his bookmaker's licence.

Mr Miles made the point that he had been charged in the

same week that the Waterhouse family had a case in the Supreme Court.

It was also the same week Waterhouse had applied to regain his bookmaker's licence and the same week his wife had unsuccessfully applied for a trainer's licence.

'It is a conspiracy imposed by someone who is abusing the powers of the Director of Public Prosecutions (DPP) for their own use,' he said.

Mr Miles said that although the DPP's office allegedly had evidence five years ago, they waited until the very day that Robbie Waterhouse was trying to get back on his feet again and earn a living before they issued the summons.

First Gai's lawyers had to decide on a strategy to attack the AJC decision. A round of legal conferences began.

Bruce Stracey retained a young Sydney barrister, Bret Walker, as counsel. He had a brilliant reputation as an advocate in technical aspects of law.

From his firm of Speed and Stracey, Bruce brought in an assistant, Hugh Scott, to help him. They knew it would be tough.

Gai had numerous well meaning friends advising her. She was aware of the reasonably new anti-discrimination legislation because barrister Doug Staff had mentioned it to her before.

Another friend, respected criminal lawyer Bruce Miles, joined in the talks and was keen to have it heard quickly through the Local Court, calling Gai and Robbie as witnesses and attacking the AJC head-on for their injustice. In his view they would be embarrassed by the publicity and Gai's popularity.

Other opinions were expressed that they should go straight to the Equity Court for denial of natural justice. Stracey himself favoured this route at first rather than the anti-discrimination law, but there were pros and cons for each strategy considered.

Ideas were bounced around in brain storming sessions before they made green light decisions.

Stracey was working long hours. The case was incredibly time consuming. He knew that legal matters like divorce where personal concern and emotion were involved took longer to reach the nitty gritty.

Gai was going through a major crisis in her life and needed to be taken slowly. Also, without having a reason for the AJC action, they were treading in virgin territory.

Basically they hammered out three ways to go.

One, the Equity Court: Certainly this course would antagonise the AJC who were already a sufficiently unpleasant monolith. And it would enable them to do it right the next time around because to win a natural justice argument it was necessary to identify the shortcoming in their decision.

The Equity Court, unable to decide the issue itself, could only send the case back to the AJC for decision on reasonable grounds. It would not gain Gai her licence and the AJC could remedy any defects the second time around.

It would really be a quick gain for an eventual loss.

Legally it seemed clear they had denied her natural justice because they disposed of her application without giving her an opportunity to respond.

Attacking it that way in the Equity Court would probably see the judge setting aside the AJC's decision, a quick and fairly spectacular result. But the big risk was in the end it would be only a Pyrrhic victory.

Two, the Anti-Discrimination Act: Even without reasons from the AJC, Gai's lawyers could argue that her marriage to Robbie must have been relevant.

Naturally the AJC would say trainers were an important part of racing. No personal reflection on Gai, but realistically her husband's warning off was enough to refuse her.

Gai could argue Robbie was Tommy's son-in-law and that could not be a problem, so where was the problem if Gai was a trainer?

Also, she was discriminated against because the AJC believed married persons were not individuals enough in their own right to have the qualifications and integrity capable of being judged on their merits.

At least there was a chance this way the AJC could be forced to do the right thing and she could pick up a $40,000 damages claim if she won.

Three, accept the decision: But as she wasn't confident after making inquiries that the committee would take any different view in the future, she might as well challenge them now.

They began to lean towards the Anti-Discrimination Act, but meanwhile they needed a reason from the AJC. Without it, they could be up that well-known creek in a wire netting canoe.

Walker and Stracey encouraged everyone to keep beavering away, but to be exceedingly polite—the AJC might loosen up to courteous inquiries.

Gai began talks with Steve Mark, president of the Anti-Discrimination Board. He thought she had a case.

On 20 September Gai lodged a complaint with the Anti-Discrimination Board, saying if media speculation was right that her licence was rejected because her husband was a warned off person, then it constituted discrimination against her because of her marital status.

She included her impressive seven-page CV sent to the AJC in which she described in detail her experience in the buying, pre-training and full work of horses and her administrative skills.

Gai outlined her considerable background in monitoring the cash flows and financing a business with 40 employees which had large prizemoney and outgoings. In short, there was nothing in her father's business she had not done or could not do.

Suddenly the press, sniffing a good story, zeroed in on Gai's dilemma.

Murray Bell, writing in *Thoroughbred News*, gave the AJC a solid kick in the arse by saying AJC Committeemen had caused anguish and embarrassment to Gai by giving verbal assurances 'to either Tommy Smith or Gai herself' that her application would be successful.

An unnamed committeeman who broke ranks was quoted as saying the rejection affair had stuck in his throat.

Murray Bell revealed to the public for the first time that the AJC's licensing sub-committee had recommended in favour of Gai's application, and it would be one year before she could re-apply.

'It's obvious there are several committeemen who didn't have the backbone to look Gai in the eye and tell it like it is,' said the newspaper.

Well, in one hit Murray's potential invitation to be duchessed in the AJC inner sanctum feasting on Bollinger and lobster mornay was just put back to around the year 3,000 AD.

The full-page story finished up with a biting comment from Peter Tonkes, 'If the AJC Committee believes a wife is guilty of her husband's wrong doings, we're fortunate they didn't have any representation on the Victorian Police Force. They might have hunted down and killed Ned Kelly's wife!'

Even before Gai's case really hit the headlines, people were talking about it as a major conflict-of-interest marriage of the 1980s, highlighting the issue facing many career women—the sexist obsession with pillow talk.

Assumptions were widespread that women's careers in particular were vulnerable to the dangers of pillow talk.

Women were seen to jeopardise their husband's professional integrity, and the woman, still looked upon as an intruder in the working world, was not trusted on how to conduct herself.

She, for instance, could not keep confidences.

Men, on the other hand, were assumed to know how to behave properly, separating personal relationships from their working lives.

Traditionally the legal view was that the interests of a married couple were exactly the same and the woman was incapable of acting independently of her husband.

But women were questioning whether it was right to single out marital relationships for discrimination.

Why was pillow talk between spouses seen to be a greater risk than loose tongues between blokes in a pub, or between friends and lovers?

Gai's complaint against the AJC loomed as a challenge to this common perception and in particular to the view that women could be corrupted by their husbands, while husbands were immune.

One person who took a close interest in this pending clash of tradition and changing views was Carmel Niland. As the first women's adviser to the New South Wales Government, Counsellor of Equal Opportunity and a former president of the Anti-Discrimination Board, she knew more than most about the idea that women would let their hearts rule their heads.

As a girl she lived at Randwick near the racecourse and was accustomed to seeing and hearing racehorses in her street. At Brigidine Convent at Randwick she was in the same class as three jockeys' daughters—Jenny Ward, Carol Munro and June Cook. Racing was often talked about and became an interest.

The three girls from racing families were often asked if they would follow their famous jockey fathers—Arthur Ward, Darby Munro and Billy Cook.

All were interested but no, in the 1950s that avenue was closed to them. Only boys could become jockeys.

Carmel always remembered that and other examples of discrimination from the period on how men and women had to separate to spend their leisure time on Saturday afternoons.

Women watched men, but men didn't watch women.

Also men and women didn't play together, a situation made clear when she went to the races in the 1960s.

As a child Carmel often went into the flat enclosure at Randwick with her grandparents. They put two bob each way on a horse called Brother Arthur for her one day and she won 10 shillings.

She didn't go for some years until, as a young woman, a man she knew obtained two tickets for women and gave her one.

Carmel saw how women were restricted in their movements, limited to particular areas, and she felt offended by it.

Indeed, there was a yellow line in the members' enclosure beyond which women could not venture. The line cut off women from going into the Men Only section.

The rule was strongly policed by the then chairman, Sir Alan Potter, who hated the thought of women being allowed into the inner circle.

The first woman officially allowed into this forbidden area was Queen Elizabeth when she visited Sydney in 1954.

This circumscribing meant that women tended to congregate, encouraged to take an interest in things more frivolous than those the men were doing.

They were cut out of the serious discussions on horses, betting and business lobbying that went on.

Later Carmel learned the idea of men receiving two tickets, introduced for members in the 1880s, was to enable an honourable gentleman to give one to his wife and the other to his mistress.

The second ticket was 'silent'—you didn't let on you had it. The same sort of practice existed with the Sydney Cricket Ground in the early days.

The clear message was that this was very much a male domain in which women were tolerated as frivolous accessories, more or less as appendages.

Of course, women entered into the spirit of this game by wearing flippant hats and gear that expressed fun. It smacked of women in their plumage popping along to the races as an attachment to men who were engaged in the serious business of owning and judging the horseflesh, gambling, drinking and taking part in the management and structure of the AJC or the STC. Women were deliberately kept out of the serious side of the business.

It was a tough fight for women to become full members of these clubs in the late 1970s and early 1980s, a struggle in which

Gai Smith played a leading role. It takes courage to fight people in authority if they are your friends because it can undermine your friendship networks and lead to you being ostracised.

In another area of discrimination, women in Australia could not go into a hotel bar until the 1960s. They had to drink in the ladies saloon, alone if necessary.

Women of today take this simple right for granted, without a casual fleeting thought for the females of Australia who went before them, unable to share a drink publicly with men in equal surroundings for almost 200 years. How dull, barren and lacking in social intercourse must Australian pubs have been.

The general breakthrough for women came in the early 1980s when the Anti-Discrimination Act began working and they became full members of various clubs—bowling, tennis, RSL, football, league and golf.

Carmel Niland was active in bringing about that sort of change. She took a keen interest in the Gai Waterhouse matter because of her early flirtation with racing, her love of animals and her memory of three young jockeys' daughters prevented by convention from following in their renowned fathers' footsteps.

Married to Professor John Niland who would later become Vice-Chancellor of the University of New South Wales after Carmel was Deputy Chancellor, she had flame-coloured hair but a gentle manner that belied her formidable record as a combatant in some of the most acrimonious battles for women in Australia.

In a changing social scene she regarded the AJC as still one of the most powerful bodies in the State, dealing with a web of people from the euphemistic 'well-known racing identities' to the most powerful and influential people in the community—judges, politicians and captains of industry—whilst maintaining fantastic land areas that were sacrosanct from normal zoning and regulations.

With this web of influence, operating under its own set of laws, it was at the centre of the strongest 'old boy' network in Sydney and the heart of the establishment.

As such it was perceived as a kind of secret organisation that by law did not have to give reasons for its actions.

For about 150 years its decisions were binding. The AJC was its own investigator, prosecutor, judge, jury and appeal body.

In the context of the action that Gai was now taking, the old assumptions and conditioning still applied to how girls were supposed to behave.

They were expected to be ladylike, polite, not outspoken and to remain above anything remotely like shady dealings. They must not be seen to be 'bold', in spirit or action. That sort of thing was suitable only for the stage where it could be regarded as farcical.

Those who were assertive and spoke out were guilty of 'common' behaviour, carrying with it a whiff of suspicion almost of prostitution or sleazy conduct at least.

Women had not entered the work force on anywhere near equal terms. Generally they were still expected to operate inside the home sphere, where they made the decisions. Outside was the sphere of men who made the decisions on politics and business.

That was pretty much how things operated right through the 1950s, 60s and even the early 70s until change began to set in.

The scene changed for a while in World War II while tens of thousands of men were overseas and women took prominent roles and made public decisions. But when the men returned so did the status quo—women were pushed out of the work force and back to the home in their traditional supportive role.

The AJC, when Gai challenged them, still reflected those post-war values.

Some of the people the AJC attracted to its board, in age and financial status, could well afford to have wives who were not working and could be more pliable to their husband's wishes. Without independent means, what else could they do?

Until Gai's challenge, women had not had much opportunity to show courage in public life. Those who did were generally considered a bit brazen or bold.

Women's courage is still something to be shown in private. In pain they give birth to children and in loneliness they help other people in times of sickness. They make critical life and death decisions about the family, all without an audience to admire their deeds.

In contrast, the bravery of men is acknowledged publicly through various badges of honour like war medals and parades, a symbolism not much different in principle today from the customs of the past, such as those of the Seneca, a warlike tribe of North American Indians in what is now western New York State. Before leaving their longhouse villages for their annual hunt or to wreak havoc on other groups, the men publicly showed their courage, donning war paint and dancing in groups before leaving the women and children.

Women don't usually score in public rituals. They're not encouraged to be adventurous and generally are not interested in risky behaviour. It doesn't mean women are cowardly, only that they're reluctant to do things likely to cause serious physical injury.

Any woman who shows great moral courage in public usually achieves heroine status. But she has to run the gauntlet of the old stereotypical assumptions.

To do so takes strong qualities of character. If she acts publicly she has to put up with all sorts of innuendoes, the most basic being who is the man standing by her? Who is bonking her?

These are the penalties a woman must pay if she comes out of the crowd, sticks her neck out and demands her rights.

This phenomenon goes back to famous women of history. Elizabeth I of England is one of the best examples of how men have taken the plaudits women deserved. As Commander-in-Chief she built up the navy which destroyed the Spanish Armada in 1588, with a little help from the storm. But history awards the honours to the blatant pirate Sir Francis Drake.

Joan of Arc, the visionary daughter of a ploughman who became the greatest national heroine of France after leading the resistance to the English and Burgundians in the last part of the Hundred Years' War, was declared a witch after her exceptional valour drove the English from town after town.

They burned her at the stake in 1431 as a heretic because she insisted she was guided by angelic voices from on high. Justice ground exceeding slow because she wasn't canonised until 1920.

The message from Joan of Arc is still significant: A woman who steps outside her role into male activities, dresses as a man and decides the outcome of wars, can meet a sticky end. In her case she not only lost her skin but also her immortal soul.

The injustice Gai fought was the stereotyped assumption of a woman's particular role in marriage. The assumption was that when women are involved in a sexual relationship, they share all, even down to the characteristics of their male partners.

Carmel Niland believed this thinking was based on men's assumptions on sexual activity rather than women's.

The stories are legion how many of the spies unleashed on the enemy in the Cold War and World War II were females, attractive women using their sexual wiles to induce the men to spill their guts while indulging in a bit of frivolity. Men spilled, not women.

'I just don't believe these assumptions about women,' Carmel says.

'I don't believe that women necessarily mix business with pleasure in that way and even if true, it is absurd to discriminate on the ground of marital status without exploring the other forms of sexual liaisons people get involved with through affairs. You really can't make generalisations about it.'

In Gai's case she was a woman wanting to move into a non-traditional role where the written rules were obscure, but the unwritten and persuasive rules questioned whether this was socially acceptable.

She was taking on a large and powerful male organisation linked to politics, money and tradition in a web of influence.

Also, she was taking on something that related to people's leisure time which had particular taboos because it was connected to social behaviour.

Gai was also challenging powerful people on the committee whom she had known socially as friends, a more difficult task than with strangers.

In effect, she was setting out to break the stereotyped mould and saying this is not something that only men can do.

Carmel Niland's interpretation of what she was about to embark on is this:

'Gai was not only pursuing what she wanted, but doing it in a way that protected her husband.

'She was saying you can't treat us that way. He can't fight for himself, so I'm going out and fighting for him indirectly.

'Gai was making a statement. She was saying whatever you say about his character, you can't impugn that to mine.

'She was making the point that there was something wholesome in her action, different to what was being assumed.

'In many ways she was no doubt saying you have got one Waterhouse but you are not going to get another. We are together and I'm going to fight you on this.

'In doing so she enhanced his public reputation which had been greatly damaged. She showed both private and public courage.'

Gai didn't think of it in those terms at the time. She also didn't see the enormity of what lay ahead.

CHAPTER FIFTEEN

THE GREAT DILEMMA

At last the AJC replied to Gai's letter of 14 September, 1989, in which she sought a reason for her licence rejection.

'The Committee does not publish reasons for rejecting an application,' it said, dated 4 October.

It advised her of Local Rule 54A of the Rules of Racing which prevented her from further applying for a year, adding 'the Committee may in its discretion reduce the said period.'

The letter came as no surprise.

Gai and her advisers determined to keep writing nice we-don't-understand letters, in the hope of flushing them out. Without a reason they realised they didn't really have a feather to fly with.

Next, President Steve Mark of the Anti-Discrimination Board entered the trenches, with Gai's lawyers still on guard duty.

In his letter to Chairman Bell on 24 November, Mark said he had received a complaint from Mrs Waterhouse alleging she had been discriminated against on the ground of her marital status.

After setting out the alleged facts he said she could only conclude she had been denied the licence because she was married to a warned-off person.

Mrs Waterhouse, he said, was further supported in her

opinion by media speculation that this could be the only reason.

Steve Mark tossed in some technical details about sections 39 and 44 of the NSW Anti-Discrimination Act which made it unlawful to discriminate on the basis of marital status, popping these in the post to Mr Bell 'for your information'.

Then casually dropping in that this may have to go to the Equal Opportunity Tribunal for a hearing, Mr Mark sought Mr Bell's kind assistance for information to help him in his inquiries.

He asked several innocuous questions, also for a copy of the minutes of the AJC sub-committee's meeting and for any other information which Mr Bell considered could assist him.

He even gave Chairman Bell the name of his senior conciliation officer, Leigh Baker, to kindly contact if he wished to discuss it with her before putting his response in writing. And co-operation appreciated.

Jim Bell replied on 7 December with a dead straight bat, stiff upper lip—and probably a cutlass beside him.

The Committee had considered all the matters raised under the heading 'Mrs Waterhouse's allegations'.

The Committee was not required by law to publish reasons. He drew attention to Rule of Racing 182(2)(a), which he quoted in all its blinding clarity:

> *So long as a person remains disqualified by the Stewards or Committee of a Principal Club:*
> *No horse shall be permitted to race which is wholly or partly owned or leased by such disqualified person or such person's spouse, or in the winnings of which such disqualified person or such person's spouse has an interest.*

It appeared they were relying on this rule.

Her solicitors thought long and hard about it. If she could avoid breaching it, she just might squeak through. It would mean she could not take the normal trainer's 10 per cent of winnings.

Then again, they could be wrong.

The anti-discrimination people continued to negotiate with the AJC by telephone, trying to obtain further details. At this point Gai's solicitors became concerned.

If the AJC said they refused her licence because she was associated or connected with a rogue rather than *married* to a rogue (Robbie for his warning off), they knew they could be in trouble.

Gai would be whistling in the dark under the anti-discrimination law unless the AJC said the *marriage* was the test, rather than Robbie.

But they batted on. The Anti-Discrimination Board wrote to Chairman Bell again on 28 February, 1990, applying pressure this time. Steve Mark pointed out that Mrs Waterhouse's solicitors had expressed the view that their rule of racing was not an anti-discrimination defence.

Further, the AJC had indicated by telephone that while it relied on the rules of racing, this was not necessarily the reason or the only reason for denying the licence.

Mr Mark wrote:

'You indicated to Ms Baker on the 30th of January that while the AJC relied on the rules, the Committee may have been prepared to discuss the reasons in a confidential setting and that you would canvass the possibility of having a confidential meeting in order to discuss these matters.

'Numerous attempts to set up such a meeting to discuss the issues and the possibility of conciliating the complaint have been made, but have failed, with the cancellation of the meeting set down for Wednesday the 28th of February, at 4.30 pm.'

He ended by saying unless Mr Bell contacted him by 5 pm on 2 March with a realistic proposal for conciliation, he would have no choice but to refer it to the Equal Opportunity Tribunal for a hearing.

Nothing was heard by 2 March. On 7 March, Gai's solicitors

wrote offering a compromise, hoping to keep the door open: If rule 182 was the problem, Gai would not take the normal trainer's 10 per cent fee but would charge a flat fee for service.

Then a letter arrived from Chairman Bell dated 9 March.

In it he wrote to Steve Mark, 'Mrs Waterhouse was not refused a trainer's licence because she is a married person but because she is married to a person who has been warned off every racecourse in Australia and elsewhere.'

Bingo!

The AJC was so sure of its rights and power that it gave the reason. Gai's lawyers now had a reason to work on. *The marriage.*

Bell gave them another clue. The facts fell squarely within the Boehringer Ingelheim Pty Ltd versus Reddrop case.

They all knew it well. Mrs Robyn Reddrop applied to Boehringer, a chemical pharmaceutical firm, for a job in 1984, and succeeded. However, before she took up the appointment it was found her husband worked for a rival company and the employment offer was withdrawn.

She went to the Equal Opportunity Tribunal on the basis of marital status discrimination, won her claim there but lost the case when the company appealed to the NSW Court of Appeal.

The court decided 'marital status' was not broad enough to cover the identity of a person's spouse. It was argued Mrs Reddrop's husband could have inadvertently learned the company's secrets from her or they would share them in bed. Therefore, 'marital status' alone did not determine the result.

Most of the staff at the Anti-Discrimination Board were disheartened on receiving Bell's letter. The Reddrop case had stood in the way of a lot of worthy anti-discrimination claims, allowing people to treat women less well than others simply because they were married to somebody—the identity of the 'somebody' letting them get away with discrimination.

They felt Gai was bound by the Reddrop decision and it was not discriminatory to refuse her licence because she was married to a warned off person.

But her lawyers felt they had a fighting chance.

In discriminating against women, people seemed to worry only about the fact they were married—the pillow talk—not about their friends, fathers or other relatives.

Gai's barrister, Bret Walker, believed the marital status of Mrs Reddrop was not the point. The woman in the case could have been in any relationship with the man to justify fears of a leakage of information. There could have been an inadvertent breach of confidential information rather than deliberate corruption.

They kicked around every possible scenario. Could the AJC, for instance, refuse Robbie's sister if she wanted a licence?

Yes, if she was close to him and influenced by him, but not if she hated him and was not under his influence.

Fortunately the AJC letter did not say the refusal was due to Gai being *associated* with Robbie. To be sure of winning, that's what they should have said. It would have sunk Gai's application.

The AJC said it was due to her being *married* to him. Marriage was the determining factor. They did not inquire about her competence when refusing the licence.

Her lawyers reasoned the AJC wasn't really relying on the Reddrop case at all. They refused her licence because she was *married* to Robbie.

A sister of Robbie Waterhouse could distance herself from him and get a licence. Gai could not. In the eyes of the AJC she was married to him, and that was the end of it. Therefore, Gai's lawyers thought she was being discriminated against.

That was their case. The AJC would obviously have to claim Gai was a wife who would be dominated by her husband.

If they were subtle, they would claim that in spite of Gai's own sturdy independence and rights as an individual, the risk that she would be influenced was too great.

Only time would tell what arguments the AJC would unleash.

As these matters were refined, Robbie's perjury charge progressed through the courts, with every detail reported in the papers.

His new counsel, Ken Horler QC, argued that he could not be charged because the Racing Tribunal was not a judicial body.

But the magistrate, Mr Hyde, ruled against this and ordered a seven-day committal trial. After this evidence was heard, Robbie was committed in April to stand trial.

While Gai's case was being prepared, the press had a field day over her licence issue. Most of the media appeared to be on her side but for once she had to get used to saying 'no comment'.

Her lawyers found it hard to keep the lid on. They repeatedly told her she must not fan the fire because arguing her case through the media could only harden the courts against her.

Winning the battle in the newspapers would not gain her licence. For such a popular personality always available to the press it was hard to stay quiet, but she mostly kept her lip buttoned.

The Anti-Discrimination Board personnel, except for Steve Mark, were still not convinced she had a case. But they were prepared to hear her submission for referral to the Equal Opportunity Tribunal.

Gai's lawyers gave the Board her submission in May, 1990, saying they still believed the AJC's refusal was discriminatory.

Although unconvinced, the Board referred it to the Tribunal.

Meanwhile, Bret Walker gave a written opinion on the case to Bruce Stracey summing up what most of the community seemed to think about it all.

'The assumptions underlying the conduct of the AJC's Committee in our client's case are somewhat extraordinary in this day and age,' he wrote.

'They amount to an assertion, wholly unsubstantiated, that our client's integrity as a racehorse trainer may be compromised by the mere fact she is married, as it happens, to Mr Robbie Waterhouse.

'If she were, by way of bizarre example, his aunt or

mistress, the rule referred to (182(2)(a)) could not have been invoked against her.

'The AJC appears to have proceeded upon the notion, which is by now surely exploded in today's society, that a wife is so subject to the domination or influence of her husband that she may not be judged upon her own merits in relation to her own advancement in her own chosen career.

'It may be, indeed, that this case raises questions of sex discrimination as well as discrimination on the ground of marital status.

'I have therefore advised our client that she should sue the AJC to force it to consider her application for a trainer's licence on the merit of her case, which would appear to be irresistible.

'On my instructions, indeed, as the decision presently stands, there must be serious questions raised about the administration by the AJC of its statutory powers to regulate the entry at this level into the racing industry of people, like our client, who are qualified and eager to train racehorses.'

Walker sounded confident, but in fact he was not confident of winning at the first level. He always felt he would have to go to the Court of Appeal, due to the difficulty of persuading a tribunal to overturn the Reddrop decision. The argument would ultimately have to be settled at a more rarefied level than a tribunal.

The Equal Opportunity Tribunal took up the claim referred to them on May 21 and the battle was joined.

A call-over was held in July to hammer out the structure of the hearing—and the first hint of dirty tricks emerged.

The AJC counsel, Robert Stitt QC, dropped a broad hint to Walker that Gai was running a risk taking on the AJC—if she wasn't careful, there was a chance the AJC might cancel her foreman's licence!

Gai's lawyers decided if the AJC did anything like that, they would immediately subpoena the AJC officer who gave her the foreman's badge to force him to admit she was fit to have it.

If they resorted to that low tactic, the lawyers would move to show them up for malice.

So much pressure was being applied Gai wondered if she was doing the right thing in fighting the AJC.

The worst aspect was so many people saying 'you can't win'.

People naturally assumed she had the support of the two people she admired and loved very much, her parents. In this maelstrom of emotions, pulled this way and that as she wrestled with what might come out in the hearing, it appeared to outsiders she must have had their emotional support.

Gai did not.

Tommy and Valerie were telling her she should withdraw because she couldn't win and it would cost so much money.

Jim Bell spoke to her father, knowing she would be talking to him every day.

'You are wrong to let her do this,' said the Chairman. 'She can't win the case. Why is she wasting her money? Tell her to concentrate on being a housewife.'

Jack Ingham, the Deputy Chairman, rang Tommy or spoke to him at the races, saying, 'She's a great PR girl. Keep her as a PR girl. She can't win this, you know.'

As the trial neared the pressure reached such a crescendo Gai had to tick Tommy off. 'Mind your own business, Dad,' she said. 'You're not paying the court bills, I am.'

Jim Bell didn't let up on Tommy, and Tommy never believed she could win. Gai had to remind him repeatedly, 'You're not fighting for your licence, Dad. I'm fighting for mine.'

The pressure came from so many quarters she would probably have thrown in the towel at that stage if it wasn't for the support she received at home.

Every night at dinner she talked it over with Robbie and her two children. Mature beyond their years, the kids said, 'You believe in this Mum. You should keep going.'

Gai had so many well-meaning people wanting to help and offering advice that they irritated her lawyers almost to the last minute.

They told her she was going about things the wrong way and she asked the lawyers to hear what they had to say.

People from the Department of Status for Women and other groups offered to take up the cudgels for her.

It made it difficult for the lawyers to run her case effectively. They felt none of these outside proposals would do anything constructive for her.

At this stage the long-running Waterhouse family feud attracted a fresh volley of publicity as it reached the summing up point.

In a case that had been described in headlines as the Waterhouses at War, the judge had appealed to the family factions to settle their differences in a 'less destructive' way.

Francis Douglas QC, one of the eminent counsel in the marathon hearing, likened it to the old Norwegian and Icelandic family blood sagas of the Middle Ages which went on for generations.

He said the case contained much of the colour and personal antagonism from the pages of the ancient scribes of that period.

Gai's points of claim were filed soon after at the Equal Opportunity Tribunal in August and the AJC filed its defence.

As expected, the AJC targeted Robbie Waterhouse, reciting in detail his warning off nearly six years before on 30 November, 1984, and the reasons for it. It also detailed why the Racing Appeals Tribunal dismissed his appeal in January, 1985. And, leaving no stone unturned, it went to great lengths on the findings in the Fine Cotton affair.

The AJC defence said Robert William Waterhouse was a deceitful and dishonest person, and because of that and his influence over Gai there was a risk he could utilise her position as a trainer for dishonourable and devious purposes.

By reason of that, the AJC claimed it was entitled to

consider those items, including the characteristics and proclivities of her spouse, when declining Gai's application. It denied discrimination.

On reading it, Gai was extremely despondent. She desperately wanted her licence. But she didn't wish to harm Robbie.

After all, he was hoping and doing his best to get back into the racing industry and if the whole notorious saga of Fine Cotton was dragged out again and the bones picked over with relish at a public hearing under the glare of the media, it would certainly not do his application to get back any good at all.

Already enough adverse publicity had been caused by the Waterhouse family feud in the Equity Court, still running after almost a year and making the papers daily. Robbie was preoccupied with that and the legal fees were overwhelming, running into millions.

The Waterhouse family fortune was on the line.

What had been a quandary now became a great dilemma.

She pleaded with her legal advisers to see if they could leave Robbie out of it. 'I don't want him harmed, I don't want to play the AJC's game,' she said.

Gai respected Bret Walker and had great faith in Bruce Stracey. He wanted to win her her licence but he knew by now their friendship would almost certainly be stretched in the process.

Patiently they tried to explain to Gai there was no way they could keep her husband out of it.

Walker worried about his inability to convince Gai that the question of Robbie's record on Fine Cotton as the AJC intended to play it was a non-issue.

He admired her loyalty to Robbie but at the time did not find it an endearing or impressive legalistic quality in the circumstances.

It caused strain and difficulty and he wished he could have got on top of her insistence that Robbie not be harmed at that early stage.

He just found it incredibly inconvenient and time wasting

and a problem that constantly threatened to blow up in his face. Walker saw his job as telling her the facts as they appeared to him, but she really didn't want to hear.

'I'll tell you why the raising of Robbie's record is a non-issue,' he said. 'He's been found by the Racing Tribunal to have been implicated in the Fine Cotton scandal, and according to them, in a pretty serious way morally.

'There's no way we can seek from any tribunal a finding contrary to the Racing Tribunal's finding. We're stuck with it. So in that sense it's a non-issue.

'We know they're going to make a point of it, but we must keep our eye on the ball—you've been discriminated against through the marriage instead of being considered on your own merits.'

Gai asked, 'What's the point of going ahead if it's going to damage Rob? He expects to get back in a year or so.'

'It's a matter of whether you want your licence. This is the only way to go. If we fight them on the issue of Robbie's record, it will only make it worse.'

Gai's obstinacy on this point gave Walker and Stracey serious doubts whether they should call her as a witness.

She believed it essential she get in the box.

They kept drumming into her that Robbie's record was not relevant, fearing that in evidence she might be tempted to vehemently dissent from the expected criticism of him.

They thought the AJC might encourage or cause her to say the Racing Tribunal was wrong, that Robbie had been framed or treated unfairly. If she did that forcefully enough or in detail, they could lose control, forced to depart from their plan and there would be the danger of another ground or justification for their decision to refuse her the licence—namely, that she was incapable of accepting the decisions of the body charged with the control of racing.

On the other hand, it was normal to want to show off an

aggrieved person in the witness box. Not for any sordid reason did they think it necessary, but in order that the Tribunal members could experience the human spark and feeling that here was a real person with a genuine grievance. These decisions were not made on cold rationality alone.

The lawyers were expressing a conservative legal view but they were dealing with an incredibly strong and determined woman who fought for her own viewpoint.

Normally it would be unthinkable not to call her but Walker in particular was worried about what he considered her apparent impetuous willingness to forget that Robbie was not the main issue.

The situation was ironic because their case turned on the fact that loyal wives should not have ascribed to them the reputed wrongdoing of their husbands—and behind the scenes they were having trouble because Gai was so incredibly loyal.

To resolve it Walker used sharp language. He told her it would be extremely unwise for her to attempt to defend Robbie because the AJC, one of Australian racing's main regulative bodies, could try to turn it to their advantage.

If she defended him and the AJC drew attention to her loyalty, it could be twisted against her and cause the Tribunal to suspect that either she had been influenced by her husband—which would vindicate the AJC's approach—or it could be a sufficiently good reason on its own to keep her out.

The risk of setting Robbie back was not Gai's only problem.

She felt vastly swinging emotions, wanting her licence, but not wanting to hurt other people.

Her father had been the most successful trainer in Australian turf history. He had a friendly and respected relationship with the AJC and dealt with them in his own individual way.

The question that kept confronting her was should she fight these people? She had to live with them every day. If she fought, it was a poor way to start on her quest for recognition as a trainer.

Tommy was concerned about that, and Gai was concerned not to do anything that would impact adversely on him.

She repeated the fears many times, expressing her inner turmoil. But her lawyers came to admire her for taking the hard decisions when necessary. At no time did she waver under pressure.

'All right,' she said finally, after a testy conference just before the hearing. 'Let's all agree we're going to get on one another's nerves from time to time. Go for it.'

CHAPTER SIXTEEN

EQUAL OPPORTUNITY AND BELOW THE BELT

The press turned up in droves when Gai appeared for the hearing at the Equal Opportunity Tribunal's building in Redfern on 21 November, 1990.

Gai's solicitor and barrister were not over impressed at having to go to Redfern, a rough area on the edge of Sydney's CBD. They were accustomed to operating in the big end of town near the Supreme Court, in the heart of the city's legal and financial centre.

Neither was the AJC contingent too impressed.

The Redfern building was rather garish, not the sober setting one would prefer for a legal battle for women's rights on a rarefied level.

As Gai arrived with her legal representatives she was immediately surrounded on the footpath by a horde of reporters and photographers, with a forest of cameras, sound guns and tape recorders thrust only centimetres from her face.

She smiled, gave them the quick grab they needed—'I hope I win so I can get on with my life'—and moved inside.

Most reporters were clearly on her side. Unusual for cynical scribes, some wished her luck and said 'all the best' and a couple even asked 'you OK?' with genuine concern.

Up close they saw that this woman with the feisty reputation was surprisingly petite and slender with a vulnerability about her, and they were supportive.

Gai was trailed at a discreet distance by Robbie's sister, Louise, there to lend moral support in the absence of Robbie. The lawyers asked her, too, not to come. She was a Waterhouse and they wanted Gai to be the focus. But Louise insisted.

Gai's smile hid her apprehension. The outcome was so important to her. She expected some criticism of Robbie but had no idea to what extent.

Bret Walker and Bruce Stracey had a better idea on Robbie but neither had any conception of how difficult the day would become.

Stracey had represented Bill Waterhouse before the AJC Committee five years before when Bill was warned off along with Robbie and he'd seen the arrogance and brute power the men of the Australian Jockey Club exercised.

They expected the AJC through its counsel, Bob Stitt QC, to use tactics that were typically hard, old-fashioned Sydney-style advocacy. Robust but not below the belt.

They had worked out their strategy in great detail. The AJC was expected to run its case on the marriage but it was a brave lawyer who would predict how the ebb and flow would run. They, too, were apprehensive.

The lawyers expected the AJC to dredge up the old stuff on Robbie again, to say this lady is married to this person and that is why we refused her. She could be influenced by him. If she wasn't married to him it would be different.

They planned to ignore this and concentrate on Gai's own merits as the main issue. Gai had instructed them to go in to bat for her licence but not to do anything that would damage Robbie. They thought this a difficult task.

But in the argument to establish their facts, they would try to subtly make the point that in the 1990s it was not really acceptable to assume a woman was subservient because she was married.

That notion was not in keeping with the way people now ran their lives. Fifty years ago wives might have done what they were told but it was wrong to suggest a married woman was susceptible to influence and could not be independent.

The hearing room was small and crowded. Several AJC officials were seated in the crowd, looking grim and uncomfortable as if they'd rather be somewhere else. Anywhere.

Gai sat behind Bret Walker who was next to Bob Stitt at the small Bar table. Bruce Stracey was between Gai and Louise. The press spilled out on top of them all.

Right on time the three Tribunal members filed in, chairman Mr Alan Cameron who although only a solicitor was known as the judicial member, Mr John Nothdurft and Mr Warren Burford.

The barristers rose and announced their appearances, Walker for the complainant, Stitt the respondent.

Already the atmosphere was tense.

Walker opened quietly, tendering various documents. He said he knew the AJC would want to go into the Fine Cotton incident in great detail, Robbie Waterhouse's warning off and his 'proclivities', to use his learned friend Mr Stitt's word.

He would not be arguing against any of that, except when it came to the stinging words 'deceitful character and fraudulent conduct' as alleged against Waterhouse.

Walker said he did not admit this and preferred the actual words that had been used in the transcript of evidence.

The stinging phrase hung in the air, a little like a smoke signal.

In paraphrasing what the AJC and Judge Goran had said at the time of warning off, the AJC had hardened up its description of Waterhouse's behaviour.

Walker said he would not argue against this evidence in relation to Robert Waterhouse because however damning the conclusions recorded in relation to him, it did not matter.

That raised a few eyebrows. Gai shifted uneasily in her seat.

But, he went on, to have decided in the fashion that the AJC had done on Mrs Waterhouse's application was a breach of the Anti-Discrimination Act and an affront to civilised values.

That seemed to stir Stitt who was on his feet in a hurry, demanding precision on the case being put.

Legal argument continued as Walker read through Gai's various points of claim setting out discrimination on the ground of marital status. It was all pretty straightforward stuff as he led the Tribunal through the background to the claim, details of Gai's application form, the correspondence on the matter, letters proving that Gai had often substituted for her father on race days, and the Reddrop case.

Among his points were that the AJC had treated Mrs Waterhouse less favourably than if she were married to someone else.

If she had been related to Robbie Waterhouse other than by marriage, the rule invoked by the AJC to refuse her licence could not have been used.

He also claimed she had been treated less favourably than they would have treated a man.

As a result, said Walker, his client had been unable to pursue a career in race training, an occupation for which her life and career had naturally fitted her.

He accused the AJC of making the 'vulgar assumption' in its finding that 'married persons infect each other with their individual proclivities in relation to matters as personal as ethics and honesty'.

After he tendered his documents and made further points, there was sudden movement and a rustle of excitement as he called Gabriel Marie Waterhouse to the witness box.

Gai hardly had time to open her mouth when Stitt objected to her counsel tendering a 30-page statement she had made, basically setting out her qualifications.

Stitt claimed the statement was not relevant to the central issue—the basis on which her licence was refused.

Long legal argument followed. The Tribunal chairman tried to mediate by saying they would be happy to assume Gai was eminently qualified to be a trainer.

But Walker wasn't happy with that, sticking to his guns with long passages of argument to wear Stitt and the chairman down.

Part of his strategy was to place on record in considerable detail the facts of the case in order to show it was different to Reddrop.

Assuming this would have to go to the Court of Appeal for final decision, he was laying the groundwork with sufficient information on the record so he could persuade the Court of Appeal to distinguish, or divide, it from Reddrop.

Momentum picked up. The voices were harder, firmer now, each side more determined to have their way.

Stitt maintained his objection to Gai giving evidence and she withdrew from the stand looking disappointed and a little bewildered. She wanted to say why she deserved her licence!

The luncheon adjournment was taken so Stitt and Walker could confer on their differences.

In the break nearly everyone involved in the case went to a little corner pub nearby for a light lunch. Gai and Louise sat at a table next to the AJC contingent, including the Chairman Jim Bell and Committeeman and Treasurer Peter Capelin, a Queen's Counsel.

They chatted to Gai in the friendliest possible way, as if they were all meeting at a jolly and lively social function.

Back in the Tribunal after lunch Walker announced that he and Stitt had agreed on a statement of assumed facts in place of Gai's evidence. Stitt appeared to have won the point.

The assumed facts, replacing the 30 pages, ran to only five paragraphs. Walker read them on to the Tribunal record.

Basically he said that TJ Smith and not Robbie Waterhouse was responsible for introducing Gai to training and the racing industry.

Smith had held a number one trainer's licence for 40 years and had won the Sydney premiership more often than anyone else; Gai Waterhouse and her father and their spouses were personally close and often mixed socially and travelled together, talking about the racing industry; Smith was very friendly with Robbie; and in considering her application the AJC did not touch on her marriage or relationship with her husband other than a question about her ability to work the hours in light of her having two small children.

Percival James Bell was called to the stand.

A countryman with a bluff manner, Bell outlined his background and described racing as the State's third largest industry employing 250,000 people. The AJC did not discriminate against women in any way and of the 2,220 thoroughbred trainers in New South Wales, 290 were women.

Robert Stitt quickly led him on to Fine Cotton.

'In all my experience of racing it was the worst thing that ever happened,' Bell said. 'The people that were corrupted in this conspiracy were sent around the country to back the horse and it was really a very damaging thing to the industry.'

Stitt asked Bell if he had formed an opinion as to the role of Robbie Waterhouse 'in that conspiracy'.

Walker objected on the ground that one person's opinion was not relevant and he sought to refer the Tribunal to the collective AJC opinion as expressed in their findings, but the question was allowed.

Bell said, 'Oh yes, it was made quite clear that he was the man . . . he was the one that did the job. He corrupted all those young people—well, not young some of them, but there was no question about it.'

It was obvious now the AJC intended to besmirch Waterhouse's character and reputation yet again in front of the Tribunal, trying to show him up as the worst thing that ever happened to racing.

At this point Gai was upset. She moved closer to Bruce Stracey and told him she wanted Bret Walker to object again. He shook his head, and whispered that nothing could be done about it.

They were freely using the word 'conspiracy' and getting away with it, although a Supreme Court judge had already cleared him of conspiracy, ordering a permanent stay against the charge.

Robbie had only ever been charged by the AJC with having had 'prior knowledge' of a ring-in, the organisers of the ring-in had been jailed in Queensland, yet he was now getting the full blame.

Bell said he was sure those who had been warned off did not tell the truth. Asked why in his opinion they had not told the truth, he said he believed they were under pressure from Robbie Waterhouse.

Louise Waterhouse now spoke to Stracey, saying it was wrong for Robbie to be under attack like this.

Stitt then focused on Gai's licence refusal.
Q: Would you tell the tribunal the basis for that
decision?
A: Because Robbie Waterhouse is a warned off person
and we believe he would be an influence on his wife.
Bell said he thought Robbie was a 'pretty influential fellow' who would have a fair bit to say in the running of Gai's horses.
Asked if he had formed an impression as to Robbie's plausibility and persuadability, he said 'no, he's always been very nice. He's a very nice sort of a person.'
And yes, he thought he would be able to persuade or influence Gai.

To say that Robbie would influence Gai in the running of her horses was to imply he would influence her to do something dishonest.

All her friends knew she was her own person, that it simply was not in her makeup to be dishonest. From Gai's point of view, she knew Robbie cared for her too much to try to persuade her to do something wrong.

Gai's friends knew he couldn't even influence her to wear a particular pair of shoes unless she felt like it. Tommy Smith said to various

*people, after this evidence came out, that it was easier to influence a
wild horse than Gai.*

Robbie could not even influence Gai to be on time.

Stitt, pressing on, introduced the question of public interest
in refusing Gai's licence.

Q: What was the view that you had?

A: Well, the racing depends a lot on the public image
and the integrity of the racing and what we're trying to
protect . . . and we try to keep the crooks out of racing.

Q: And how did you perceive Robbie Waterhouse?

A: Well, he'd done a very bad thing and as far as we
were concerned he was a crook.

The word, dropped with brutal force and clarity, created a
sensation in the Tribunal. The atmosphere was electric.

*Gai could not believe that Jim Bell had called her husband a crook.
To say that he was 'the man' in the Fine Cotton ring-in which implied
some form of dishonesty, was one thing. But to say he was a crook was
too much. Robbie had only bet on the horse, and it was never officially
suggested he had organised or financed it, and she regarded this reaction
was out of all proportion.*

*Jim had always been pleasant and courteous to her, she had stayed
at his home every Christmas for about five years, kept company with his
son, knew the Bell family well and he knew her family backwards.*

*She knew he had not worried about mixing socially with Robbie
before Fine Cotton, and if the ring-in had made so much difference, she
would rather he had come out and said it to her face than drop this
bombshell in a tribunal where it was privileged and he knew he could
get away with it.*

*Gai never said so but she could easily have spat in Jim Bell's eyes
at that point.*

*She felt anger and sadness that Robbie was being tarred and feath-
ered and key-holed all over again. She was supposed to be the person
under fire, but her husband was being put on trial in this public forum
and nobody was lifting a hand to defend him.*

She told Bruce Stracey she wanted the case stopped. 'This is too much, it has got to stop, I can't stand by and see this damage being done to Rob,' she said.

Suddenly under pressure, Stracey said he couldn't stop it and there was no way they could avoid it. Louise, on his other side, also demanded that they defend Robbie.

Bret Walker could hear this going on behind him, but just looked ahead.

This was worse than what both lawyers had expected. The AJC was being aggressive, abrasive and difficult in the way they were handling their submissions. Nothing was straightforward or helpful. It was boots and all.

Their counsel would return to the word 'crook', rubbing everyone's noses in it. He would also describe Robbie as the 'Typhoid Mary' of the racing industry, a reference to a notorious carrier of the deadly typhoid fever in New York early this century.

In that incident Mary Mallon, a cook, worked under various assumed names, moving from one household to another until finally detained 31 years after being recognised as a carrier.

Before she died in 1938 she caused at least 10 outbreaks of typhoid fever, involving more than 50 cases and three deaths.

Stitt was relentless.

Q: You said he was a crook. Did you have any regard to the position of Gai Waterhouse insofar as you would perceive Robbie was a crook?

A: Well, he was warned off, he's a warned off person and you don't get that for nothing.

Q: How did you take that factor into account when considering her application for the trainer's licence?

A: That's why we didn't give it to her because she was married to him.

A short break was called. Unusually a team of photographers and cameramen were milling around on the same floor outside the hearing room and Gai and her group had to push their way through to find a quiet spot in a corridor to hold an urgent conference.

Gai told Bret Walker and Bruce Stracey, 'You're not following my instructions. I want you to defend Robbie.'

Stracey said to her *'You're* our client, Gai. We can only look
after your interests, not Robbie's.'

'No, no, no, my interests ARE Robbie's interests and I want
you to protect him from this sort of attack.'

The hearing resumed and Bell was then cross-examined by
Bret Walker.

The barrister used a polite, gentle approach, asking the
chairman about the role of the AJC, its stewards and committee,
what a loss of confidence might cause in the industry.

*Walker really wanted to obtain from Bell a gold-plated endorse-
ment of Gai's personal qualities and he was settling the chairman down
before coming to the point.*

*He was taking a punt here that his line of questioning with Bell
would be safe. Walker had gone to the exclusive private Kings School in
Sydney and he knew that at least one of Bell's sons had gone there.*

*He knew Jim Bell only by reputation but assumed he would be an
old-school rural gentleman who would not bag a lady publicly, especially when he had been so friendly to Gai and members of her family.
He assumed it was only a small risk to expect the chairman to be chival-
rous in regard to Gai.*

*His plan was to obtain the endorsement in order to make it difficult
for Bell to turn around and suggest the licence refusal had anything to
do with her, that she didn't have any weakness or vulnerability to pre-
clude her from being licensed. If Bell did so later, he would lose
credibility.*

After softening up the chairman, without disagreeing with
his conclusions on Robbie, Walker suddenly introduced Gai.

Q: You've described Robbie Waterhouse, my client's
husband, as in your opinion a crook in relation to racing?

A: Yes. That's right.

Q: I take it you don't describe my client in that way?

A: No. Not a bit.

He then questioned Bell about his remarks that Robbie had corrupted the other warned off persons and the circumstances, still not challenging him and again he brought Gai into it.

Q: You don't regard my client as corrupt, do you, Mr Bell?

A: Not a bit, no.

Q: And you say that with some confidence?

A: Yes.

Q: You sit there as a gentleman and say . . .

A: Yes.

Q: . . . that Gai Waterhouse is not corrupt to the best of your knowledge?

A: Yes, most certainly.

Bell gave a similar endorsement of Tommy Smith, Indeed, he was the reverse of being corrupt.

Walker moved on to the refusal, and Bell confirmed the reason—Gai was married to a warned off person who happened to be Robbie Waterhouse, he was likely to influence his wife and that was the basis of it.

Bell said that the committee had not needed any information from the AJC's licensing sub-committee before deciding because Robbie Waterhouse 'was a warned off person and our belief is that the spouse of a warned off person cannot have a licence'.

Walker needed determination to get his points across but he finished his cross-examination feeling satisfied his plan had worked and he had established the essential facts—the reason, and that there was nothing wrong with Gai herself.

He was happy that if he could not persuade the Tribunal, he had created a transcript of facts for the Court of Appeal.

For Gai it was a traumatic day, having her husband publicly declared a crook, which she regarded seriously.

Rising to leave she caught sight of several antagonists of Robbie's, smiling smugly. It must have been music to their ears. They turned up like bad odours at every occasion on which his name was mentioned.

As she left the hearing room the press surrounded her in a

scrummage, poking microphones almost up her nostrils, following her to the lift.

As she pushed clear to enter the lift one newsman, Harry Potter of Channel Ten, put his hand in to stop the doors from closing, saying 'sorry about this, Gai.' His cameraman kept shooting close up shots of Gai, trapped in the corner.

She did not complain, politely declining to comment except to say once again she hoped to win the case.

Radio, television and the newspapers played up Bell's comment that Robbie was a crook. One paper would lead off its story next morning on the line that Gai's husband was a 'crook' who had masterminded the Fine Cotton ring-in.

The heading as well was unfair and inaccurate. It said: 'No Licence for Wife of "Crook".' No decision had yet been made.

The newspaper claim of masterminding Fine Cotton was untrue, but it was a reasonable interpretation of what Jim Bell had said. Gai was angry it had been allowed to go unchallenged by her lawyers.

Back in Bret Walker's city chambers that afternoon, Gai and her lawyers, with Louise present, had a strained conference.

Gai made it plain she was beginning to lose confidence in them because of their refusal to counter the heavy criticism of Robbie.

They knew she had gone close to terminating proceedings when Bell was in the box. They were looking at it in a cold legalistic way but her emotions were involved and she was considering matters in a very personal way.

Louise supported Gai and used strong language to tell them she thought their tactics were wrong. They stuck to their attitude that they were not there to defend Robbie.

'But surely you can minimise it and stop him from being the sacrificial lamb—it's simply unfair they should get away with it,' said Gai. 'The poor bloke has gone through a hard enough time already. He's trying to get his bookmaking licence back and they're making him out to be the most dreadful man.

'He's not Typhoid Mary, he's not the nasty person influencing me like they're saying. If he is, then I must be a fool to live with him and just as bad.'

Louise's main complaint was the AJC having a free kick at Robbie and being allowed to get away with it without any attempt to curb them.

'This is madness,' she fumed. 'All we're doing is to let Rob get a few more kicks.' It was unacceptable to her to let the AJC say what they liked about Robbie and do nothing about it.

The lawyers were uneasy about it. They knew if the AJC could persuade the Tribunal that Robbie was a crook, part of their argument was established. It was an effective hook to hang their argument on.

On the other hand, they suspected it was being deliberately done to provoke them into a heated response, which might serve to heighten the impression and divert attention from the discrimination angle. The lawyers agreed they should not fall for it.

That night Gai and Robbie sat over dinner at home and discussed it fully in the presence of Tom and Kate.

Still distressed, Gai was annoyed that she hadn't been allowed to give evidence. She felt her hands were tied behind her back.

She just knew that from the way the case was being conducted, she would lose.

The weight of criticism against Robbie was just too much and they weren't hitting back, making it look as if they accepted every word of it. The AJC was playing it hard and tough and winning.

'There goes my chance of ever getting back to the races,' Robbie said as they assessed the damage done.

Robbie knew he would be criticised and had been prepared for that to enable Gai to realise her ambitions. But he didn't expect to be branded a crook, or that Bell would not be called upon to justify it.

'I don't know if this is worth going on with,' said Gai. 'It's achieving the opposite result to what I expected and I know I'll lose—I can just feel it from the way things are going.'

Next morning Bruce Stracey received a call from Tommy Smith.

'Isn't there another way?' he asked. He wanted to protect Gai from the hurtful publicity rolling in the wake of the 'crook' comments.

'No, Tom,' said Stracey. 'There's no other way. We're going according to plan.'

'Okay, fair enough.' He was prepared to stick with it if there was no better way of going about it.

On the second day media interest was if anything even more intense as the Tribunal moved straight into gear.

First witness called was Peter Richard Capelin QC, Committeeman and Treasurer of the AJC and a director of the New South Wales TAB.

He and Bell would be the only witnesses for the AJC. They were the ones on the committee most opposed to Robbie Waterhouse because of Fine Cotton.

As far as Gai was concerned her lawyers had felt fairly safe with Bell, notwithstanding his rough treatment of Robbie.

They were not so sure of Capelin. They did not know what he and the dogged Robert Stitt might have up their sleeves. For Gai to succeed, there must be no criticism of her, no reflection on her morals or actions.

This could be a worrying morning.

Once more there was a feeling of tension in the air. The impression created from the AJC side was that far more conviction and animosity were involved in this case than one would normally see in an ordinary disinterested professional legal exercise.

After leading Capelin through his background, Stitt moved quickly on to the Fine Cotton findings and Waterhouse's role.

When he asked Capelin for his opinion, Walker objected on the same basis he had with Bell, that they should rely on the collective committee view, but the objection cut no ice.

Capelin gave this opinion of Fine Cotton, 'It was the most disgraceful attempt at undermining the integrity and attempting to manipulate the operation of thoroughbred racing. Done in Queensland and supported by way of betting throughout probably the whole of Australia but certainly throughout some of the States of Australia and overseas.'

And Robbie Waterhouse's role? 'It was my view that Robbie Waterhouse was the axle on which the huge wheel of betting operated in the Fine Cotton affair.'

That was not really a fair comment. Waterhouse was responsible for only some of the betting. Thousands of punters totally unconnected with him plunged on Fine Cotton all over Australia.

The word 'conspiracy' was tossed in again and used with impunity.

Asked what matters he took into account in refusing the licence, he said:

'The first thing was the character of Robbie Waterhouse. I considered he was a deceitful man with a commanding personality with the capacity to influence others. And I couldn't get out of my mind how he'd sat there before the committee day in day out, week in week out and continued to deceive us and to influence the other parties in the proceedings . . .

'The second thing was I thought that the racing public would think that the AJC were a joke if they gave a licence to Gai Waterhouse in circumstances where Robbie Waterhouse's character was as it is and has proven to be and where he was in a position to manipulate her, influence her, as he had done to all the other people who were involved in the 1984 affair.'

Asked if he had anything in mind about Gai's relationship with her husband and the races, Capelin said she had given evidence to the AJC that she and Robbie had a close relationship and talked racing generally.

Capelin said:

'The other thing that influenced me was that prior to the Fine Cotton affair Gai Waterhouse was frequently seen to walk or run from the birdcage area after the horses had left. Yes, I saw this, I saw this, yes, and went to her husband who was operating as a rails bookmaker and had conversations with him.'

Q: Why were each of those pieces of evidence in your mind important in refusing the application?

A: Well, it showed that Robbie Waterhouse had an effect, a relevant effect, a relevant interest and if you like some control over the racecourse or racing activities of his spouse.

This was a bolt from the blue, an obvious point of concern to Gai and her solicitors because it was alleging there was something wrong with Gai to make her unfit for a licence.

Anyone listening in that tight atmosphere could hardly avoid the image of a woman under the spell of her husband, dutifully running to deliver some sort of useful information.

Stitt moved in to elicit every detail.

Capelin explained the birdcage was the enclosure where the horses were paraded and the jockeys mounted before going out on to the track.

He said there was great public interest in how the horses and jockeys looked, in who was talking to who and after the horses left the people observing this scene left to go about their business 'and then it's at that time when Gai Waterhouse was seen to be going to her husband and talking to him.'

Q: What is the significance of that?

A: You could readily draw the inference that perhaps she was passing on to him her opinion of how the horse is, how a horse looked or how a horse didn't look or what somebody may have said in the birdcage enclosure about a horse's chances and that sort of thing. In other words he had an obvious interest in her activities in and around the racecourse.

Q: But it was in your mind relevant when the application for the trainer's licence came up?

A: Absolutely.

Q: Why was that?

A: Because I had seen myself the close relationship which existed between them and knowing what a dominating, domineering type of person Robbie Waterhouse was, it was obvious that anything he had to do with in relation to racing or horses or training would be passed on to Gai and anything she did would be passed on to him . . .

A short adjournment was held. Gai was furious about these allegations, telling her lawyers they were untrue.

After the break Stitt rounded off his points with Capelin, the only interesting piece being that Gai represented no risk as a foreman in TJ Smith's stables because he ran his own race and would not be influenced by anybody, even Robbie Waterhouse.

Bret Walker began cross-examining Capelin and it was pretty tame stuff about the qualities needed for licensed persons, rules of racing, punishment for improper practices, the need for racing to be free from the taint of corruption, the roles of foremen and strappers . . .

Observers might well wonder where it was leading. What about the birdcage incident! Walker was putting that at the back of his examination, establishing that the AJC would not licence anyone if there was any doubt of corruption, a way of proving Gai's fitness.

Finally he came to the birdcage incident and mentioned it casually, as if it was quite unimportant.

Q: You've told the Tribunal today that your recollection
of having seen my client run from birdcage to bookie's
stand played a part in the conclusion you formed as part
of the decision to refuse the licence, is that right?
A: Yes it was a factor . . . yes it was a minor—but it was a
factor that I had in my mind.

Capelin said this had happened in 1984 at Randwick and
Rosehill. He agreed it was entirely legitimate for bookmakers
and punters to concern themselves with the appearance of horses
in the birdcage. But when asked if he agreed it was legitimate to
share this information with others on a racecourse he said:

'It didn't look too good for the foreman of TJ Smith, who had
a runner in the race, coming from the enclosure and then going
to her husband, bookmaker, and appearing to whisper as in the
last eight minutes of betting, it just didn't look too good and it
indicated to me that there was some influence there.'

*Capelin had added another ingredient, a conspiratorial note—Gai
was whispering!*

Q: These matters that you assume were whispered were
I take it observations of the horses in the birdcage, is
that right?
A: Well, I don't know.
Q: That's what you assumed?
A: It could have been some conversation said, you know
I assumed it was something to do with the upcoming
race. I didn't know it was its fitness or whatever. Horses
sweat up. Jockeys say things. Owners say things. I don't
know.

Walker asked Capelin if in his married life he and his wife
regularly asked each other to do things, and the chairman ruled
it out because it was 'unnecessarily intrusive'.

*The ruling seemed unnecessarily sensitive. The AJC had been putting
in the boot for two days.*

Walker switched his focus to spouses generally, friends, parents and children, and Capelin agreed each case would have to be looked at to see if one person had power over another.

Seizing on the point, Walker suggested that as a committeeman he'd said he treated each case on its merits but before refusing her licence he had not obtained her response to the allegation that she was under the sinister influence of her husband.

The chairman intervened to ask the question screaming out to be asked: What did Capelin do about Gai's 'whisperings'?

Q: Did you ever raise that with Mr (TJ) Smith?

A: No, I didn't raise it with Mr Smith, I raised it with Mr Ray Alexander which is what I would normally do in the circumstances, the secretary. It wasn't for me to approach a trainer but I raised it with Mr Alexander.

Q: Do you know whether, or did Mr Alexander ever tell you, he'd raised it with Mr Smith?

A: My recollection about that is hazy . . . yeah, it is hazy . . .

There was more, but the steam had run out of it by now. Capelin, who had gilded the lily, had condemned himself.

If he had genuinely had those suspicions, he should have gone to the stewards and done something definite about it. Because he didn't, that part of his evidence could not be taken seriously.

But it made all the sensational headlines.

One paper used it over a full page, with a five-column picture of Gai looking feminine in tortoiseshell glasses, bright skirt and tasteful blouse, under the banner headlines: 'QC Attacks Gai's "Whispers" messages run to husband—court told.'

Gai was angered and upset by Capelin's sneak attack. It made her look a weak person, easily influenced. If he really thought there was something nefarious going on, why didn't he have her and Robbie questioned by the stewards or have it suggested they should stop talking to each other in these circumstances?

She knew she didn't pass information to her husband. And she didn't whisper at any stage.

To whisper she would have had to reach right up close to his ear while he was high on his stand. She was not a conspiratorial type of person and this never happened. She spoke in a normal voice and her only purpose was to come up and say hello, and usually to have a bet.

She would ask Robbie what he thought of her father's horse, if she had just saddled one up, or another horse, and take $20 or $50 out of her purse and have a bet. He would give her good odds. She would have a chat to him or anyone else around his stand, crack a joke and move on.

The fact that she was never approached over the matter showed that the stewards, or indeed, anyone else, had no concern over the alleged 'whisperings' at all.

Gai considered it absurd to suggest there was any skulduggery going on.

In addition, racing people are notoriously suspicious and extremely observant. The whole time Robbie Waterhouse was bookmaking, there was never any suggestion of him laying or backing one of Gai's horses in a way that invited attention.

Gai knew that when he laid a Smith horse, he always put it in the right place in his market according to his estimation of its form.

Everybody on the track was aware of Gai's association with Robbie but not one suspicious rumour had ever been raised. He was conscious of their relationship and anxious not to create the slightest suspicion.

The implication of running information from the birdcage could only have been along the lines that Gai might have said she'd told the jockey not to win, Robbie could reach for the horse in the market and extend its price on his betting board, get all the money from duped punters and become a rich man.

If he had ever done anything like that with a Smith horse, the rumour of skulduggery would have been all over the racecourse quicker than the knowledge that Fine Cotton was a certainty.

Following Capelin's evidence, the case was adjourned to the third day so the Tribunal could consider its finding.

Once again the hearing room was packed when chairman Alan Cameron read out his ruling.

Gai had appeared each day almost defiantly dressed in a series of vibrantly coloured suits, vivid lipsticks and shoes in matching shades. And always with a brilliant smile.

Watchers noticed that occasionally she held her mini-pager a little tightly or fidgeted with a tissue, but not once had she let her composure slip.

After some introductory remarks the chairman came to the crunch, 'The complaint of Mrs Waterhouse must, as a matter of law, be dismissed by the Tribunal.'

Gai wept silently as he finished his ruling. The emotion and turmoil of the past two days, the pressure of recent weeks, had taken their toll.

Having knocked Gai's application back, the chairman proceeded to pass some remarks which made observers think he surely must have found in her favour.

Pointing out the Tribunal was bound by the Reddrop decision and could not overrule the AJC's decision, he said:

'Nevertheless, it remains unlawful to discriminate against a person in various ways because they are married, single or divorced.

'This decision only deals with discrimination based on the identity of the spouse, not whether somebody is married.

'The Tribunal rejects any notion that it is safe or appropriate to make assumptions about people's likely behaviour based on the fact that they are married.

'To assume that a wife is or will be under the influence of a husband without making any inquiry or receiving any evidence, is the kind of stereotyping which the Anti-Discrimination Act seeks to eliminate.'

On that basis the Tribunal's decision showed little courage.

He adjourned the matter until December 18 to give formal reasons for their decision.

Outside the Tribunal Gai hit out at the AJC tactics.

'Racing is my life,' she told reporters. 'It has really hurt. The criticism of Robbie has been very hard and I think the AJC has played below the belt tactics.'

Asked what she intended to do, she said, 'I will continue my fight to become a horse trainer, which is what I have been trained to do. I've been fighting pretty hard and I will just keep on going. I will take the matter to the Court of Appeal.'

When one reporter asked what it meant to her future, she said, 'Everything. My father's been growing older. It's disappointing for him.'

At the mention of his name Gai's eyes filled with tears behind the tortoiseshell cat's eye glasses that were as much a trade mark as her father's pork pie hats.

The first thing she did on leaving the reporters was to telephone her mother and father to give them the result.

Tommy said, 'Is it worth carrying on? Maybe it's time to give up.'

'No,' she said. 'I knew it would be a long battle. It's far from lost yet.'

The young woman who had entered racing under the shadow of TJ Smith as a stablehand, won her foreman's badge and shown promise as a future trainer, was still regarded by many as Tommy Smith's daughter but in addition she was now saddled as Robbie's wife.

Some refused to budge from the narrow view that she was an upstart in the racing world, who enjoyed her position only because of her father's help, not taking into account her qualifications which she had earned through hard work and application.

She had endured the slings and arrows from the Fine Cotton

fallout, the nudges and winks, the hurtful sight of people parting at the races as she approached, then regrouping in her wake to gossip and point.

It was an uphill battle all the way for recognition as a person in her own right. But she had myriad supporters.

One prominent Sydney racing lawyer described the decision as an outrageous travesty, adding the comment 'The AJC and the Tribunal have been sitting like a bloody family law court. They say this woman cannot pursue the career that she is superbly fitted for and be married to her husband at the same time. It's disgraceful.'

Ken Callander, the *Telegraph*'s racing columnist, lashed the AJC for the whispering allegations, writing that he had also seen Prime Minister Bob Hawke walk to the betting ring after talking to trainers in the birdcage.

Asking what was the big deal, he said he'd also seen this done by pressmen, trainers, owners, stable foremen and race club committeemen. If it was so important, it should have been brought up at the time, not several years later.

'I don't know how many points Gai would get out of 10 as a budding horse trainer,' said Callander, 'but she would get 10 out of 10 for loyalty to her father and her husband in what has been a very trying time.'

Gai's lawyers lodged an immediate appeal.

CHAPTER SEVENTEEN

BRUTALITY IN THE COURT OF APPEAL

The publicity from her court appearance catapulted Gai into the national limelight.

Suddenly women saw her struggle as vital to women's rights.

Almost overnight, the case became a *cause célèbre* with women in all States.

Wherever women gathered, in shopping malls, clubs, on golf courses or beaches, they talked about this denial of a woman's rights. It was a hot topic with the everyday person.

They admired her for standing up and having a go in an area that touched the lives of so many women.

Generally they were offended by the suggestion that a wife could be infected by her husband's characteristics and was so weak she could not be relied on to have her own ethics and principles.

They knew it was only about 50 years since the law actually said a husband owned his wife and her chattels. Times had changed but the sound waves still echoed.

The inherent assumption still existed that in a marriage the wife owed a particular kind of loyalty to her husband and would spill her guts while her head rested on the matrimonial pillow.

Women resented that, also this new assumption that she would automatically take on any bad habits he might have.

Gai emerged as a public champion of the ordinary woman to challenge these entrenched practices and beliefs.

She was looked upon as an attractive, vivacious and intelligent woman who had made a name for herself in the television soapies, was well educated and switched on to the community around her.

Her acting experience had given her poise and she was well equipped to successfully handle the media.

By coming from a racing family, it was thought she had the kind of background to enable her to stand up to the AJC.

Another part of her image was that she was the product of a public family, her father being a strong and well respected figure and she was something of a chip off the old block with many of Tommy Smith's fighting qualities.

An important part of her new status with women was her ability to articulate her case, with a show of public confidence that she intended to win.

What really fascinated women, too, was that her marriage appeared to be holding up in spite of enormous pressures placed on it. Women in the late 1980s were saying they could not be married and successful at the same time.

Women who chose a public career, especially in politics and professional fields, usually found they did so at the expense of their marriage.

That was and remains the perception and any woman who appears on the scene and runs contrary to that view creates a great deal of curiosity.

Carmel Niland, based on her wide professional experience in discrimination matters, believed that apart from its historical overtones the attempt of the AJC to prevent Gai from obtaining her licence was the result of a pretext.

She believed to some extent the AJC, as a bastion of male chauvinism, tried to stop her becoming a trainer because of fear—the fear of change.

They never questioned her high qualifications. They realised that coming from Australia's most successful racing stable and backed by the great Tommy Smith, she would be a success. And she would be a big, rather than a small, trainer.

Gai would have known more about horse riding, the training of horses and horseflesh generally than probably the whole of the AJC Committee put together.

They would have to talk seriously to her, a woman, about horses, and women were accepted only as wives, daughters or dates.

They had women fixed in certain images and to license the confident, aggressive Gai would mean they would have to treat her as an equal on horseflesh.

She's a good PR girl. Why don't you keep her as a PR girl? She has a family to look after.

The excuse for knocking her back was her marriage to a warned off bookmaker who was likely to corrupt her.

Yet they admitted she was a person of good character and they didn't even inquire to see if she had weaknesses. The licensing sub-committee recommended her licence without a hitch.

Mrs Niland's experience was when a woman set out to achieve, people looked for the puppeteer. Who was the man behind her?

The truth was any woman who achieved would probably say with conviction the person behind her was a good baby sitter.

The penalty successful women faced was there had to be a man behind them, a general assumption that in the first instance made it easy for the AJC to blame Gai's husband.

Usually this assumption was seen in sexual terms. Men even joked that behind every man was a woman without clothes.

'Men are very curious about relationships, especially with successful women,' says Mrs Niland. 'When they're uncomfortable about it they turn it into humour, and often the humour is a form of ridicule. Like, "who wears the pants in your house"? and "you're under petticoat government". Those are the simplest remarks, but they can be a lot cruder and rougher than that.

'Any married woman who puts her hand up to follow a career faces these kinds of accusations. She has to face stories about her sexual affairs with other men, or that her husband is having affairs with other women—as happened in Gai's case.

'This is typical behaviour where women are successful.

'The assumption is that if a woman gets to the top, she has got there on her back with her legs apart.

'If it was that easy to get to the top on your back, the board rooms of Sydney and other cities would be stuffed with women. We would be running everything if that is the way to do it.

'Naturally the situation exists where women progress through sexual favours, but it goes on so little compared to the general belief.

'But when it does it's the subject of tantalising speculation, and often the basis of a movie script.

'People seeing it in movies think it's the norm. It's not, but these situations are rarely looked at logically. Where it happens there are penalties for both the man and woman.

'Essentially it's the men who don't want to change.

'They don't want confusion about traditional roles. They want to be quite clear on how they have to behave and they don't want to come to terms with relating to women in another kind of way.

'I think there was an element of that in the AJC's decision on Gai. They didn't want to change the way things were done in order to modify their behaviour.'

Some observers had other ideas after noting how bloody-minded the AJC behaved against the weight of public opinion.

There can be no doubt the AJC regarded it as an important power play.

The mere suggestion they could be told what to do by the Waterhouses or the Smiths was offensive to them.

The idea that some new and remote body like the Anti-Discrimination Board or the Equal Opportunity Tribunal should be enlisted to tell this ancient self-righteous body, imbued with its own sense of importance, what to do was even more offensive.

How outrageous to an elitist group of men so convinced of their centrality in the universe!

It was unlikely to occur to them that many people in the community regarded it as inappropriate for an amateur body to run a multi-billion dollar industry, especially when they were so out of touch on public feelings with such an inherently simple matter as this licence issue.

As she waited for her appeal to come on, Gai found it a vicarious feeling facing up to the racing public.

She enjoyed enormous support, but was also treated as a leper.

The big change was with ordinary people at the races. They were behind her and made their feelings plain with shouts and words of encouragement whenever she appeared at the track.

People she didn't know approached her and passed the nicest possible remarks like 'hang in there, Gai' and 'we're with you all the way, Gai'.

Some squeezed her hand, others kissed her on the cheek. Some ventured to discuss the case with her, asking why should she have to pay for something her husband might or might not have done? Friends who met her at the races found it heart warming to observe the genuine support she had.

With comments in the papers and magazine articles all her way, it was a case of the masses cheering for the underdog.

Everyone she spoke to believed she had been treated unjustly. They thought it was either something personal or the AJC was just being vindictive towards Robbie.

A typical example occurred at Sydney's Canterbury track a week after the Tribunal rebuffed her. A man approached her and with a sorrowful expression befitting a double death in the family, laid a hand gently on an arm and inquired in sepulchral tones, 'How are you, my dear?'

She patted his hand, returned it to him and said in her bubbly, disarming way, 'I'm well. Really well. How are you? Good? Super day, isn't it?' She smiled, waved him a cheery farewell and moved off. He watched her go, still looking sorrowful.

As she moved about at her normal brisk pace between stables, saddling enclosure and members' stand, her supporters came from all directions.

Strappers, jockeys, gatekeepers, owners, punters and even a few trainers all said 'hello Gai' and told her how sorry they were and for her to keep on fighting. 'It's a bit of a nuisance, but we'll wear them down,' she said.

She did not dwell on morbid sympathy or awkward condolences, turning these aside easily with a smile and a bright word or two.

Gai even momentarily put behind her the rough treatment that had been dished out to her at the Equal Opportunity Tribunal and thought the AJC would listen to the crowds, but she soon realised it was a forlorn hope. The Committee stood firm, deaf to the growing swell of resentment against them in the community.

But the pressure remained on her the whole time.

Some Committeemen were still telling Tommy she should be pulled into line. 'What the devil is she up to, Tom?' they asked. 'Talk to her!'

Most of the Committee rebuffed her as if she didn't exist, and some of their wives gave her filthy looks.

Gai might as well have been a prostitute who had slept with their husbands the previous night.

The looks were enough to cut her to the quick. To those who tried that tactic she looked straight through them, telling herself it had been their husbands, not her, who caused the problem.

The Committee could easily have avoided it by deferring her application, telling her she should wait until her husband's matter was cleared up. It may not have been palatable to her, but it would have avoided the outright conflict.

But Bell and Capelin were determined on the issue and the Committee did not back down.

Gai thought Jim Bell's dogmatism on the issue was one of the most outlandish and bizarre things she had known in her life.

Some people gave her lip service and told her what they thought she would like to hear.

She received hundreds of letters from various parts of Australia, urging her to keep up the good work. Several people sent her poems which they had dedicated to her.

Tears sometimes glistened in her eyes when battlers came up, wished her well, handed her some small change and said, 'I want you to give that to young Tom.'

Gai did not need the few dollars and would have liked to decline but these were genuine people who meant it and gave her hope.

They were the heart and soul of racing who kept the game going and cared about her. It touched her deeply.

She was always gracious in accepting any words of encouragement and found time to talk to everybody who wanted a chat, no matter how much of a hurry she might be in.

That was the good side.

But there were the toadies, hangers-on and free loaders who fawned on the Committeemen and officials, waiting around Micawber-like for a free lunch, drinks or tickets to turn up. These insincere types tut-tutted and declared for the benefit of their self-important patrons what a terrible thing it was for Gai Waterhouse to be doing this to the Australian Jockey Club.

One old fuddy-duddy, an owner for whom Tommy trained, said to Gai, 'You're not Robinson Crusoe. Prince Charles is in a similar situation to you.'

'But Prince Charles,' she replied, 'hasn't been denied the right to do his own thing and marry Di. I'm being denied my rights because of the man I'm married to, and nothing else.'

She heard a lot of barbed, back-stabbing remarks from men but just tried to ride through it.

Her approach was to keep on smiling, refusing to give the

knockers the satisfaction of seeing her down. Some people were just plain jealous and loved to see her fail.

Rumours went around that she intended divorcing Robbie to get her licence. Those who said it didn't know her very well. She told reporters who questioned her on that point, 'I didn't marry Rob to divorce him. I married him to be my partner in life. I'm not going to change my mind just because Robbie is having hard times.'

Almost everyone had an opinion on the merits of her actions.

Some detractors were quoted anonymously in magazines as saying that at the stables she was obsessive, impatient and tended to kick arse.

Strangely, those qualities would easily have been tolerated in a man and probably not even commented upon, but not in a woman, especially one who was attractive, dressed fashionably and had a famous father. Once more, her ability was not taken into account.

Gai's reaction was not to fret and agonise but to work even harder and most nights she was asleep when her head hit the pillow.

Tommy Smith advised her repeatedly to drop out. He and Valerie were worried about what would happen to the children because of all this. They wanted her to give up and make life easier for herself and her family.

Just as she was battling the AJC, Gai also was waging a draining battle with her parents.

'Gai,' they said, 'it's too much trouble, it's costing too much money and you're making yourself look stupid.'

Gai said to Tommy, 'I don't care how stupid I look, Dad, but I'm going to fight this to the end.'

It took a long time to convince them, but once they could see she was determined they stopped applying pressure and gave her moral and emotional support.

Tommy was saddened by the whole episode. He had contributed so much to the industry, was winding down, loved his daughter and was fond of her husband, and felt it was such an unreasonable denial. In spite of his training horses for some Committeemen and enjoying personal friendships with them, he was powerless to help.

For Gai it was gut-wrenching, up one day, down the next as legal opinions changed or new rumours surfaced, draining her stamina.

Gai grew tired of being made feel she had two left feet or some other impediment which made her abnormal.

Her father-in-law, Bill Waterhouse, told her that sitting in the Supreme Court one day he heard two solicitors discussing her case. One, who seemed to be associated with the AJC, said, 'She's got no chance. We've got the Reddrop case.'

She referred this to her solicitor who said, 'We think every-one else has misinterpreted the Reddrop case. We believe our view will be proved right.'

The legal position was so obscure she often felt confused, wondering if it was right to press on. Very few appeals to the Court of Appeal seemed to succeed.

But her friends noted that in spite of all the hits against her, she remained resilient. Lea Stracey likened her to the image of a sand-weighted clown in a fun parlour who kept bouncing back.

That was the image.

Not even her best friends saw the publicly gutsy woman, who kept up face at the races, only to return home and burst into tears.

She could see that Robbie was heartbroken for causing this pressure on her. Often she felt she'd had enough of facing the slights, innuendoes and intrusions into their lives and would not speak about it at home, taking an extra interest in the children and their school work to try to take her mind off the subject.

Gai proved herself a strong family person by keeping the Smiths and Waterhouses together in these difficult times.

Tommy Smith and Bill Waterhouse hardly ever spoke before Gai's wedding, and it was through her efforts that they met more often and became firm friends. She organised the family meet-ings for birthdays and parties.

She tried to maintain a strong Christian ethic in her home.

Gai was no bible banger but tried to live a Christian life, attending church irregularly because of the odd hours she worked, including Sunday mornings. When she did go to church, Robbie usually accompanied her. She didn't think ill of people, tried to help others and do charitable works as much as she could, hating to see people in distress or need.

Robbie saw a lot more of the children than if he had still been a bookmaker and shared the responsibilities with Gai.

He even thought there could be a life without bookmaking, having always been short of money while chasing bad debts as a bookie. Bookmaking had become such a hard game at the time of his warning off that his and Bill Waterhouse's success depended on their ability to claim bad debts.

But he needed to get back to the racetrack to try to restore some of the damage done to his name.

Robbie also needed to keep on backing winners to support his family and pay for various legal actions. For several years his assets in the Waterhouse family business had been frozen along with those belonging to the rest of his family, due to the Waterhouse family equity dispute, and he had to rely on his own means.

His perjury case was going through various interlocutory stages and there were regular legal bills to pay there.

In addition, at the time Gai was gearing up for her Court of Appeal battle with the AJC, she felt insecure over their home, fearing they would lose it because of a complicated issue involving Robbie's brother.

In order to settle a taxation debt, his brother borrowed about $750,000 from a finance company against the security of a John Glover painting he owned, *The Bath of Diana*. Later he wanted to borrow from a bank to pay out the finance company and asked Robbie to help him with security for the loan.

Bill Waterhouse, whose assets were frozen at the time, told Robbie, 'You must help your brother, he needs you.'

So Robbie went guarantor for him and put his and Gai's

house on the line as security, allowing the bank to take out a second mortgage on the house on the promise his brother would sell his painting at a Sotheby's auction within a few weeks.

The painting was knocked down to an American for $1.7 million, but the Federal Government refused to allow it to leave Australia under the Movable Cultural Heritage Act. It was not sold to Australian underbidders. The bank then tried to take possession of Gai and Robbie's home in pursuit of debt.

It finished up with Bill and Robbie having to pay the bank a large sum in settlement of the debt by Robbie's brother, a situation which set the scene for bad blood later and a further round of litigation in the ongoing courts saga of the Battling Waterhouses.

Usually proceedings in the Court of Appeal are conducted in a polite and genteel manner.

Voices are rarely raised. Points of law are discussed in a detached, academic way. The three senior judges exchange views with the periwigged barristers at the Bar table in an atmosphere of civility.

Sharp legal opinions are examined and points scored, but usually there is an absence of emotion and the clashing of personalities which are common in other courts.

As Gai and her legal advisers filed into the Court of Appeal in the Supreme Court building in Sydney on 10 July, 1991 to challenge the ruling of the Equal Opportunity Tribunal, they wondered if this would be any different. Would the AJC again play it rough and tough in this more sedate atmosphere?

Barrister Bret Walker had prepared a meticulous case.

As soon as the Tribunal had dismissed Gai's application, he and Bruce Stracey set to work on the appeal. A junior barrister, Ian Jackman, was brought in to help Walker prepare all the authorities and documents needed and they managed to expedite the hearing.

In its formal dismissal the Tribunal said it was satisfied Gai had been denied her licence 'either because she was believed to be susceptible to the corrupting influence of her husband, or because of a fear that the public perception would be to that effect'.

It made the point the AJC's concern that there was a risk of her being manipulated by her husband had not been put to her at any stage.

But to succeed, said the Tribunal, she would have to establish that 'marital status' went beyond the mere fact of being married or not, extending to the identity or position of her husband.

That was the very issue involved in Reddrop. Mrs Reddrop was successful before the Tribunal, which held that 'marital status' extended to and embraced the identity and situation of the spouse. But that view was rejected by all three judges of the Court of Appeal.

Walker could go only one of two ways—say the Reddrop decision in the Court of Appeal was wrong, or the circumstances of Gai's case were different and should be distinguished from it.

He intended arguing that Gai's case was different, claiming Reddrop was not about marriage at all but the possible leakage of confidential information between two married people.

They had hung their case on the marriage and Walker intended arguing there was a clear distinction between the two cases, and consequently they should not be compared.

All the evidence necessary from the Tribunal was placed before the court in two thick appeal books. It was a matter of walking through it and picking out the points to build his argument.

The case opened quietly before Justices Kirby, Clarke and Hope but from Gai's point of view quickly became negative when Walker mentioned the previous references to Typhoid Mary. He needed to put that odious comparison with Robbie Waterhouse out of the way first if he was to succeed.

In the Reddrop case Mr Justice Mahoney had commented extensively on the Typhoid Mary example.

Walker said that if a man who had been cohabiting with

Typhoid Mary applied for a job as a live-in cook and was refused the job because the employer said 'but you are married to Typhoid Mary', he would not be breaching the Anti-Discrimination Act.

Such a refusal would not be based on the marriage but on the characteristics of his spouse—you could not have a person living in those conditions with Typhoid Mary and handling food.

Walker argued that if Typhoid Mary's brother had been living with her and shared the bathroom and kitchen facilities in a close relationship, the result would surely have been the same.

Mr Justice Kirby said, 'I see someone says your client was the Typhoid.'

Walker replied, 'My client never had her infectious state examined at all.'

Walker said the Typhoid Mary case was an example of correct reasoning on discrimination against somebody who, at the most superficial first glance, was thought to be discriminated against because of marriage.

'It is the classical example of discrimination, not on the ground of marital status but something else, namely cohabitation,' he said.

Mr Justice Kirby seemed to accept the point and said, 'The fundamental premise of the Act and of all discrimination laws is that people should be judged on their own qualities and not on relationships or perceived attributes which form stereotypes in the community and which might be quite unfair to them.'

Walker put forward a cogent argument for discrimination against Gai.

He explained Gai was not trying to overrule Reddrop, but distinguish it. In Reddrop it was not a matter of the marriage but the fact a chemist was living with a person who could make use of confidential information. Living together in the same house could allow an inadvertent leak of information.

He said the AJC did not make any inquiry when Gai applied for her licence. She had been discriminated against on the ground of marriage and that was the only reason on which they based their decision. Bell had made that clear.

Obviously the AJC did not think TJ Smith would be corrupted by Robbie Waterhouse. Yet they came to a different conclusion about Gai not because of her strength of personality compared to her father but only because she was married to Waterhouse.

The AJC did not ask about the relationship or Gai's character, deciding simply on the fact that she was married to him.

The AJC had never said they refused the licence because of her relationship with Waterhouse, only the marriage. They were stuck with that and could not change it now.

The subtlety of the legal argument on what one could call social values disappeared the moment Robert Stitt began replying for the AJC.

He spoke in his usual loud clear tones and tension rose in the court as he began banging the drum against Robbie Waterhouse in much the same way as he had before the Tribunal.

He was not about to change the tradition of the Sydney Bar, where usually no favours are asked and no quarter is given.

In those surroundings the atmosphere became almost tangibly brutal as the AJC's counsel repeated in vehement terms the arguments against Waterhouse's allegedly corrupting influence.

But Stitt quickly ran into trouble with the judges.

He opened by saying this appeal was not on the ground of natural justice. It was not concerned with the fairness or unfairness of the Tribunal's decision or whether it was correct or incorrect, but whether there had been a breach of the Act.

The Tribunal's findings, he said, involved concepts 'such as her characteristics, her personality and the characteristics and morality which relate to her husband'.

As soon as he said that, he began to run off the rails.

The judges challenged him, reading from the remarks made by the chairman at the end of the Tribunal hearing, to clearly show their decision was not based on the personality and characteristics of Mrs Waterhouse. Indeed, the Tribunal had said that was the kind of stereotyping it sought to eliminate.

Stitt argued that this was merely a statement made by the Tribunal and did not form part of their reasons, but Judge Hope said, 'I think you're wrong.'

The AJC reply was putting a completely different perspective on the proceedings before the Tribunal than was apparent from the transcript and the recollections of those events by Gai's lawyers.

Stitt then made a serious blunder by claiming Mrs Waterhouse had refused to give evidence.

That was simply not true. Gai nudged her solicitor unnecessarily to let him know.

The atmosphere became quite heated as the judges began interjecting and questioning the conclusions drawn by the AJC which were inconsistent with previous transcripts, and Bret Walker leapt up and down trying to make objections.

But the AJC doggedly went on with their approach.

Stitt: With respect, the factual basis before the Tribunal was a very limited one.

There was not any full investigation of the merits of Mrs Waterhouse's application. It was dealt with on the basis of agreed facts. Mrs Waterhouse got into the witness box and declined to be cross examined.

And the matter proceeded on the basis of assumed facts. In the transcript she got into the witness box. The matter was adjourned. We had discussions and the matter proceeded on a different basis.

Justice Kirby: Where does it say she declined to be cross examined?

Stitt: Page 109. I do not think it is in relation to the Tribunal. That was in relation to the Fine Cotton inquiry. Page 39 I think is where she was in the witness box and an attempt was made to tender the statement by Mrs Waterhouse. Then at page 50 . . .

Justice Kirby: Mr Walker came back and said there was

an agreement. Where is the refusal to answer questions?
Stitt: What happened was that a procedure was adopted whereby it was necessary . . .
Justice Hope: There was an attempt to cover matters by tendering a statement and you objected to it. There was a discussion and that is where her evidence ended. On the face of it, her evidence in chief had not been finished.
Stitt: She was not cross examined. There was never a full hearing on the question of the merits.
Justice Clarke: What you say is this—it is a finding made on incomplete evidence on a matter that was not litigated.
Stitt: Yes.
Justice Clarke: And also (reads from Tribunal findings), the distinction is that the Tribunal did not find she was corruptible, but it did find that the committee of the club believed that she was susceptible to the corrupting influence of her husband, and that is the finding in our submission which the Tribunal has made.
Justice Hope: Isn't it because she was married to him?
Stitt: It was the characteristics of Robert Waterhouse.
Justice Hope: He has characteristics, she is married to him, therefore she is liable to be affected by those characteristics?
Stitt: No, it depends on her personality. There is evidence at page 81 (the birdcage incident).

The legal exchanges followed rapidly in this tense, searching way. Several times the judges came back to the point that the evidence seemed to show it was because of the marriage that the decision had been made.

Justice Hope, taking up the reference to the birdcage incident, quoted the Tribunal as saying that it did not prove corruptibility.

Stitt's argument was forceful, but obviously the judges were looking at it with clear, penetrating eyes and open minds.

At one stage he said the employer in the Reddrop case thought there was an industrial security risk, therefore this was a similar case because the AJC considered there was a risk to the integrity of racing or the public perception of integrity.

Mr Justice Clarke interrupted and said that according to Stitt, the committee had decided on the basis of Robert Waterhouse's characteristics and Gai's personal susceptibility to influence.

When Stitt argued that both Bell and Capelin had said they thought Mrs Waterhouse was susceptible, Justice Hope said, 'At page 62 Mr Bell said that is why we didn't give it to her because she was married to him. There seems to be an assumption a married woman is influenced.'

The hearing went for two days with never a dull moment.

An observer in the court could well have gained the impression that it was a mistake for Robert Stitt to clash the cymbals so hard and often about Robbie Waterhouse.

It may have been this heavy approach which alerted the judges to the fact that the argument put forward by Bret Walker was correct—this case had nothing to do with Gai, it had everything to do with Robbie and the AJC.

Where a discussion on changing social values seemed appropriate, the AJC offered much in the way of red-blooded argument. The AJC in an attempt to justify their stand threw in too many points that could not be defended, such as Gai's alleged vulnerability.

This made it easier for Walker, thinking carefully on his feet, to suggest the whole of the case was suspect.

Piece by piece he pulled the AJC's arguments apart in the following way:

'In Robbie Waterhouse's orbit of influence the individual merits of various people including TJ Smith are examined, but for his wife there is no investigation . . . there was nothing said about her individuality to withstand the temptation.

'. . . The reasoning of the AJC is quite simple. If she is married to Robbie Waterhouse, that alone justifies one or both of the following propositions—because of marriage she is susceptible, or racing people think she would be susceptible . . . there was no evidence at all of any particular or peculiar susceptibility of Mrs Waterhouse.

'. . . My learned friend's answers to requests from the Bench show plainly that the concentration is on a perceived power of Mr Waterhouse to influence. What the AJC knew, and they say it on oath, she is not corrupt. In other words she has not yet been influenced. At the same time they say her deemed susceptibility is due to one thing only, marriage.

'. . . The carefully chosen word "susceptibility" masks what my learned friend is advancing under its cover. The real meaning is that here is some defect of character which describes someone as worse than the ordinary run of people. So something about my client is being slurred in this fashion, notwithstanding the evidence "she is not a crook, not a bit of it."

'. . . As to Robbie being a domineering, conniving sort of person likely to affect anyone who comes within his realm of interest unless they have the perceived merits of Tommy Smith to resist this magnetic effect, this is exceedingly crude, pseudo psychology being applied by the AJC.

'. . . In any event this is applied in a somewhat insulting fashion by imputing this to the racing public. It may be questioned whether the racing public or any part of the public would proceed in that sort of fashion. That is the very vice of stereotyped assumptions.

'. . . Mr Capelin's evidence that it was his own approach to investigate the circumstances in each case, was the very point he was denying Gai.

'. . . Tommy Smith's merits can speak for themselves, but his daughter's can't . . . Mr Bell and Mr Capelin's

evidence showed that nothing came between sub-
committee and committee to prevent the licence . . . that
is the hallmark of a stereotyped decision.'

At the end of the second day the court reserved its decision.

Gai was pleased because she thought her lawyers had seen
the best of the argument. But they all crossed their fingers hoping the court had taken the points on board. Nobody could be
sure.

The newspapers said, 'Gai Must Wait for Decision.'

Two and a half months later Gai and her legal advisers filed
into the Court of Appeal to hear the verdict.

After the traditional knock on the Bench door the judges
entered and took their seats. A hush fell as Justice Clarke picked
up his papers and read out the judgment in brief.

Gai felt a thrill surge through her when she heard His
Honour say the appeal was upheld—by the terrific margin of
three nil.

She felt like leaping in the air. All the months of pressure
and frustration had been worthwhile. Now she might get her
licence.

The judgment was a model of logic and common sense, just
as she and her advisers had hoped.

The Court of Appeal said she had been rejected because she
was liable to be corrupted by her husband who was a 'rogue'.
When one inquired why, the answer from the AJC was 'because
she is married to him'.

That prompted another question: 'Why did the fact that she
was married to a rogue mean that she was liable to be corrupted
by him?'

In circumstances where there was no suggestion that Gai had
a relevant character deficiency, the answer must be 'because all
wives are liable to be corrupted by their husbands'.

The Court said this meant corruptibility at the hands of one's
husband was a characteristic imputed to all married women,
which breached section 39 (1)(c) of the Anti Discrimination Act.

There was no evidence Gai had a character deficiency. In fact the AJC said she was of good character. Consequently the AJC lost.

The Court said that in Reddrop the potential employer was concerned about security risks and rejected the applicant because of the chance of company secrets being communicated to the applicant's husband.

This, it said, should be seen as a decision granted on a characteristic particular to Mrs Reddrop (and not generally imputed to married women), that is, she had a close relationship with an employee of a competitor.

No matter what influence was brought to bear by a husband on an incorruptible wife, he would not succeed in corrupting her.

He would only be able to achieve that if she had a particular characteristic—that she was corruptible.

The Court ruled that the AJC's decision was not based on Gai's close relationship with Robbie Waterhouse. He had close relationships with other people including TJ Smith, whom the evidence suggested would never be corrupted by him.

The AJC had rejected Gai's application because she was married to Waterhouse and being his wife was corruptible at his hands.

The relevant characteristic was that she was liable to be corrupted by him and if this was solely because she was married to him, it followed that Reddrop did not compel or even support the Tribunal's decision.

The Court made several orders including that the Equal Opportunity Tribunal relist her hearing to be decided in accordance with the law. As it was no longer bound by Reddrop, it could find in her favour, and indeed had no choice.

The Court also ordered that the AJC pay Gai's costs.

Outside the Court Gai told reporters she was elated. 'You know that car ad on TV?—that's me,' she said.

'This decision is for the women of Australia, not just for me. You should not just be seen as an appendage of your husband.

You should be able to be seen on your own merits. I'm glad at last to be treated as an individual. Hopefully now I should be able to get on with the task I have been trained to do, which is to be a horse trainer.'

One Sydney paper ran the story under the heading 'Gai out from under Robbie's shadow.'

After such a long ordeal the victory called for a celebration.

That night a few close friends gathered at Gai's home to drink pink champagne and dine on home-delivered pizzas. One or two irreverent types drank a toast to absent friends, in this case the AJC.

For once Gai did not ask her guests to leave early so she could rise at three to go to the track. But she was still on time at Randwick before dawn next morning.

The first thing Gai did was write again to the AJC asking for her licence in the light of the Court of Appeal decision.

In her popular weekly racing column in the *Sydney Morning Herald* Gai wrote happily about the judges' unanimous decision under the heading of 'Hear me roar: here's a giant leap for women's rights.'

In the course of it she said she had felt the AJC Committee's knockback as a public humiliation. She said:

> 'The disgrace of my husband's disqualification has been a hard and long ordeal for me.
>
> 'He was found, by the same AJC Committee, to have bet on the ring-in Fine Cotton with prior knowledge and was banned for "their pleasure". It has never been alleged that he was involved in the actual ring-in itself.
>
> 'I know the remorse and contrition he has expressed privately to the Committee, and publicly in this newspaper, are real and sincere. In the time since his banning his behaviour has been exemplary.
>
> 'We just live in the hope that "their pleasure" will not go on too much longer than the seven years we have already paid.

'I'd like to record my gratitude to the staff of the Anti-Discrimination Board for their many efforts at conciliation with the AJC.

'I'm profoundly grateful for the extraordinary and overwhelming support of people generally. Thank you.'

It seemed only a matter of limited time before she would be able to claim her inheritance.

CHAPTER EIGHTEEN

GAI IN HER OWN RIGHT

Just after the Court of Appeal gave its resounding victory for Gai Waterhouse, Tommy Smith made what he considered an important announcement. When Gai obtained her licence, she would take over the Tulloch Lodge stables.

At last he had recognised there was a dynasty. His statement meant that when Gai broke through the litigation, he would hand over the business that had been his life's work.

In the historic stables where the ghosts of Tulloch, Redcraze, Gunsynd, Kingston Town and other great thoroughbreds danced playfully in the champion trainer's memory, he had set records that would never be broken.

Many of the early details had not been kept but he had won about 7,000 races in all, including 35 Derbies. About 5,000 of the wins were in metropolitan Sydney, and prizemoney for his clients amounted to $40 million. Group One wins totalled 278.

In theoretically handing over to Gai at this stage, Tommy's words were tinged not with joy but with sadness.

He told the press, 'I'm only sorry it couldn't have happened under different circumstances.'

Those few words masked a personal tragedy for the man who revolutionised thoroughbred training methods in Australia:

Once again, the trail blazing Tulloch Lodge Ltd was not looking good.

As a public company it had still worked well for almost two years following its close call with the liquidators after the Spedley crash.

John Kluge and his money had saved the day and TJ had enjoyed his ride at the top again, training a big team of thoroughbreds.

The tycoon even came to Sydney to look over his bloodstock investment, attending the races at Rosehill where he was squired around by Smith and Gai, proclaiming his satisfaction at the way things were going.

Gai had kept her eye on the ball as a substitute director for her father at Tulloch Lodge Ltd, attending all the board meetings and watching Tommy's interests by scooting off to find out whatever information was needed to answer any problem raised by the other directors.

Suddenly the symphony was over for Tommy. It came in an entirely unexpected way.

Kluge's divorce from his totally unblushing bride of nine years severely dented the multi-billionaire's piggy bank. It reportedly cost Kluge $2 billion to leave the holy state of matrimony.

The former nude model obviously had a smart lawyer because up to that time, 1991, their parting was the biggest known divorce settlement in history.

Patricia Kluge's outlandish social climbing by throwing herself at upper-crust British society was described by friends of Kluge's as the reason for their differences.

He was particularly embarrassed on one occasion when the Fleet Street tabloids splashed the story of Patricia's porno past just as the Kluges were about to host a Royal evening, which had to be cancelled at the last minute when Prince Charles and Di dropped out.

That, of course, was long before the Charles and Di Show revealed to a fascinated world their extra-curricular sexual exploits as titillated in the Squidgey tapes and in Chilla romping with Camilla in the Royal undergrowth, where for once he found more to commune with than the plants.

A pity that pesky palace protocol prevented them from meeting: Charlie might have found Porno Pat a real live hit. Then again, with her towering social ambitions, she might have proved more of a prickly pear in the garden of life than Camilla, who although desiring a bed of roses remained a shrinking violet for a long time when it came to climbing the Royal social vine.

All that may well have been by the by as far as TJ and Gai were concerned except that when the former Soho stripper and brunette belly dancer left the tycoon's embrace, so did all his horses.

Apparently to keep peregrinating Patricia in the luxurious jetset style to which she had become accustomed, Kluge decided he would sell his newly-acquired bloodstock interests around the world.

That included all his horses being trained in Tulloch Lodge.

The sales had already begun before the Court of Appeal decision was handed down and now more were planned until every Kluge horse was gone from Tulloch Lodge Ltd.

Tommy had little alternative but to resign from the public company, pull down its sign from his stables which had been leased to the company, and prepare to start out again in a small way. The Tulloch Lodge company, a shadow of its former self, would train its remaining horses elsewhere.

A bright dream that should have succeeded brilliantly had ended abruptly in spite of Gai's superb efforts to keep it afloat with her daring rescue plan earlier, and in circumstances that were beyond Tommy Smith's control. It knocked the stuffing out of the normally cocky trainer.

The good old days were gone when he had 60 horses in training and 40 or so backing up with owners knocking on his door.

Winding down in a highly competitive field, he no longer had the zest to go out and find the new owners to maintain a big team.

He was left with only 15 or 20 horses of his own to train but made it plain he would not be retiring. 'I'll be buying, training and selling horses until the day I die,' he said.

When Gai obtained her licence he would let her train out of Tulloch Lodge and he would move around the corner to Bounding Away Lodge, where Gai had been 'managing' a small number of horses.

In making his announcement Tommy took an oblique shot at the AJC for not updating their rules and for keeping Robbie on the outer for so long.

'The rules of racing haven't been changed since Ned Kelly's day,' he said. 'They hanged Kelly but today he would only get three years.'

Gai felt sad for Tommy that his outstanding career should be fizzling out on such a note but she was buoyed up by the feeling that her moment of destiny had arrived.

Indeed, it was almost within her grasp and seemed a mere formality in the light of the Court of Appeal coming down on her side.

One week after she thanked everyone in her column the AJC, on 1 October, 1991, donned the gloves again.

Realising now they had a flaw in their rules, they changed them.

They knew now they should not have used the marriage as a reason. They should have used 'association' instead.

The AJC changed its rule 182(2)(a) by taking out 'spouse' and replacing it with a reference to 'close associate'.

That would be much harder to get around. It meant that if Gai's solicitors did not get her licence this time around, she may never get it. The new rule could shut her out for as long as Robbie was warned off, which could be a long time.

Then, almost immediately after, the AJC dealt another body blow. In a shock move it showed it had not changed its belligerent attitude one iota.

It decided to seek special leave to appeal to the High Court against the decision of the New South Wales Court of Appeal.

They would not give Gai her licence and intended to stick it out to the bitter legal end at further emotional and financial cost to all concerned.

The Equal Opportunity Tribunal then decided in December to put its cue back in the rack. Gai's hearing before them would be put on hold until the High Court Appeal was settled.

With a heavy sigh Gai rang her solicitors to be told it could be a year away before that appeal was heard.

'I just can't believe it,' she said. In spite of public opinion being heavily against them, the AJC were still full of fight.

Even at this late stage Gai wondered if it was worthwhile going on.

With all that she had been through, the prospect of obtaining her licence—which now seemed a long way off still—was not such a glittering prize. Indeed, it hardly seemed a prize at all.

Her name and Robbie's name had been dragged through the mud, she had been the butt of insults and jokes, it had churned her up emotionally, and the frustration of being on a high one day and a low the next and the pressure of living in a goldfish bowl under the lurid glare of media concentration all the time had proved a gut-wrenching experience. The struggle had taken over her life.

Apart from the long drawn-out nature of it all and the draining effect on her personal and family life, Gai was worried by the financial cost involved.

Against the might of the AJC with their host of legal advisers and unlimited resources, plus a Queen's Counsel to argue their case in court, Gai could afford only a junior barrister rather than a senior counsel.

Even then, with her solicitor Bruce Stracey charging reduced rates due to their personal friendship, it had already been a highly expensive exercise.

Tommy would not help financially because his advice right from the beginning had been not to fight the AJC, in spite of the justice of her cause. Several times since the case began he had expressed alarm at the costs being incurred.

It had been a battle for Gai and Robbie to pay her ongoing legal costs and if the AJC won its appeal to the High Court, the legal bill would be even more daunting because she would have to pay the AJC's costs as well as her own.

Until now Gai had the pleasure of having to pay the costs for a case which had not always been fought along lines she had agreed. Although the Court of Appeal had sided with her, many of Gai's friends and outside legal contacts had felt the damage to her and Robbie had been far too great.

Many felt there should have been tough cross-examination of both Jim Bell and Peter Capelin before the Equal Opportunity Tribunal to minimise the damage they caused in the public mind.

They believed Gai's lawyers should have gone on the attack, asking questions such as whether they approved of race stewards having affairs with jockeys' wives.

Some people were anxious to see them put under the microscope in the witness box, but it didn't happen.

Personal questions would probably have been ruled out on the ground of relevance, but it might have had the effect of reducing the holier-than-thou attitude of these witnesses.

Why, for instance, was the AJC so violently committed against Robbie Waterhouse when it had done nothing to stop George Freeman, a big SP operator and man with a criminal record, from secretly owning horses in other people's names?

Some time previously in a conversation with AJC Chief Steward John Schreck, I asked him that question. He said, 'You can't go about persecuting people.'

The same attitude was not extended by the AJC towards Robbie Waterhouse, even after he was punished for the only offence they charged him with, having prior knowledge.

Although the High Court would not be hearing any evidence and would decide the issue on points of law, another airing of the matter would still have the effect of dragging out all the past again when the media reported the court's decision, no matter which way it went.

Gai had no doubt her lawyers were technically correct in the way they had so far conducted the case, concentrating on the main issue of her licence and ignoring all the side defamatory remarks and character assassinations. But now it was a question of whether it was worth going through it all again.

Each day after she appeared in court she knew from reading the newspapers and listening to television that the media was interested only in taking the most sensational approach to attract more viewers or sell more newspapers, even if many reporters were personally sympathetic to her situation.

Gai weighed up all the pros and cons and discussed them with Robbie and the children. She was encouraged by the enormous pile of letters from ordinary members of the public who urged her to fight on.

After considering it and conferring with her lawyers, Gai decided, 'I've gone this far and it's cost so much money, I might as well take it a step further to see what happens.'

The AJC produced their application book seeking special leave to appeal to the High Court.

A lengthy document, it set out various exhibits and included the decisions of the Equal Opportunity Tribunal, the 33-page judgment of the Court of Appeal, a long affidavit setting out various legal points and questions of law and a draft notice of appeal alleging that the Court of Appeal erred on various points in its judgment.

The issue seemed simple enough, but the AJC lawyers came up with eight hair-splitting points on which they based their appeal, including 'the Court of Appeal erred in holding that there was no evidence to support a finding that the appellant believed that the first respondent had personal character deficiencies which rendered her vulnerable to the corrupting influence of her spouse.'

Obviously they wanted to rerun the whole thing over again. Hang the expense! The punters were paying for it.

The AJC asked that its appeal be allowed with costs against Gai and for the orders of the Court of Appeal to be set aside.

Gai didn't hold back in her press interviews.

'It's totally frustrating to say the least,' she told one newspaper. 'The AJC is just wasting time. I think they're terribly, terribly old fashioned.

'I'm sure most of the racing public support my case, but a few people in power want to deny me what the courts have said is just.

'At the moment I'm just trying to get on with the job of training racehorses with Dad. Hopefully this matter can be settled by early next year. I think I've earned the right to train racehorses in my own name.'

The AJC's pig-headed stand was all the more remarkable because of the hostile press they were receiving on the issue.

Reporters kept hammering them but they seemed completely out of touch with reality. In particular Max Presnell of the *Sydney Morning Herald* kept the spotlight on their unrealistic attitude.

He reported directors of the Sydney Turf Club were seething because they had discovered that under a special funding arrangement they were responsible for paying half the AJC's legal fees for the case against Gai—and they didn't agree with the AJC's stand!

Presnell also wrote that Gai's matter was one of the thorniest issues confronting the AJC, and it alone was costing them $50,000 in legal fees as their share (the figure was obviously conservative even if it represented only half the cost).

Nothing seemed to make any impression on this feudal, male chauvinist body still living in the past.

Gai's solicitor Bruce Stracey and his assistants began work with Bret Walker preparing their response to the appeal points, settling in for the long haul.

Friday 3 January, 1992, dawned much the same for Gai as any other morning.

She rose at 3 am, laid out the breakfast for Tom and Kate, checked on them in their beds, gave Robbie his lemon juice and hot water, jumped in her Holden and drove off soon after 3.30 to cross the Sydney Harbour Bridge and head for Randwick.

On the way she gazed in the rear vision mirror while she gave her hair a brisk brushing and applied her lipstick, always a vivid shade of red.

Although there was not another car on the road, she was careful to observe the speed limit, having recently been booked for speeding in similar circumstances by an over-zealous cop who had his eyes on the Commissioner's job.

At Tulloch Lodge stables where it was still dark she met Tommy, made a cup of tea for each of them, did a little office work, scanned the newspapers and checked in the stables before telling the strappers to move the horses out.

The sound of their hooves rang out sharply in the clear early morning air as they walked or jogged along deserted Bowral Street, Kensington, and into Doncaster Avenue before entering the dewy arena of Randwick racecourse.

Just before dawn Gai and Tommy climbed into his Rolls and drove the short distance to the track, walking out to the tower in the centre of the racecourse from where Tommy had traditionally given instructions for more than 40 years to the jockeys galloping his horses around.

Gai clocked them as usual, commented on their performances to her father and gave some instructions of her own. Tommy had only about 15 in training and it was over in less than an hour.

Back in the Tulloch Lodge office Gai did some more paper work, hit the phones about 7 am to discuss the horses with some of Tommy's owners, and was home about 8 am just after the children left for school but before Robbie left for the Waterhouse offices at North Sydney.

After a normally light breakfast of orange juice, fruit and muesli, she made a few more phone calls, pulled out the phones and put her head down for her morning rest.

She rose at 11 am and had just put the receivers back on when the phone rang.

'Ray Alexander here, Gai. What are you doing?'

Gai knew the Secretary/General manager of the AJC wasn't ringing just to find out how she was going, but he was polite, she knew him well and liked him and thought she'd answer him in the spirit of the moment.

'Just getting ready to go to the stables.'

'Can you be here in 20 minutes?'

'Yes. Why, what's happening?'

'We want to talk to you.'

That was all. Gai pondered on the call for a moment. Then she rang Robbie at his office and told him.

'Gai, this could be about your licence,' he said.

'I don't think so.'

'Well, be careful.'

As a precaution Gai rang Bruce Stracey and was lucky to catch him right away. 'I've just had a call from the AJC. They want to talk to me. Right away. What do you think I should do.'

Stracey thought about it briefly, wondering if it was appropriate for her to go to AJC headquarters on her own while the courts and lawyers were involved. There was no guarantee it was about her licence and indeed it could be about anything concerning the stables. Then again, it might not be.

'All right,' he said, after thinking out aloud. 'Go along and see what they want. But just don't say anything.'

'And whatever you do don't make a new application or sign anything until they give you your licence.'

Gai was already dressed in her gear for the stables, a pair of slacks and a T-shirt, best described as smart working clothes. She jumped in her car and pushed through the traffic to Randwick.

She was shown into Ray Alexander's office where he greeted her cordially and sat her down. Then came the shock.

'Gai,' he said, 'we're going to give you your licence.'

'Don't pull my leg, Ray,' she said in her direct, forthright way when she wanted it known she was not about to take any non-sense. 'You pulled it two and a half years ago and I'm not impressed.'

'I'm not pulling your leg, Gai—I'm being honest.'

Gai looked him right in the eye. 'These people lied to me before. How do I know they're not lying to me now?'

'Fill in a form and you can have your licence.'

'I'm not filling in any form. We're fighting on the form that has already been lodged. If I fill in another one, you can take me to court all over again.'

'No, no,' he began, trying to explain.

'How do I know you're not telling me a lie, Ray? How can I believe this group of men after what's happened?'

Alexander was clearly embarrassed. For a moment he didn't know what to do. Then he said he would prove it and called in the head of Licensed Persons and asked him to verify what he had told Gai.

'No, no, Ray is not telling a lie, Gai,' he said. 'It's true. It really is true.'

Gai was still sitting on the edge of the chair, having not moved since she sat down. She thought she should ring Stracey and ask his advice. She would have liked to have rung Robbie to seek his opinion but quickly gave up that idea. TJ, perhaps she should ring him.

She sat stock still, looking down, her brow furrowed in thought.

Finally she told herself she had to make this decision alone. She felt she had to take the bit between her teeth.

Suddenly she looked at Alexander.

'Give me the form.'

The secretary's office was silent as she filled it in.

She smiled grimly at the first few words that caught her eye:

To enable your application to be considered without delay . . .
Initials of Husband in case of Married Woman . . . R.W.
Type of Licence for which you wish to Apply . . . No 1 Trainers.

Please give Names and Addresses of at least three licensed Trainers who could be approached... TJ Smith, Bart Cummings, N C Begg, Pat Murray, Mal Barnes.

Experience... 1977–1989 full employment as assistant and foreperson to TJ Smith, horse trainer.

Please give Names and Addresses of at least three persons who are well-known in racing circles, or alternatively two persons holding professional qualifications or of professional standing who could be approached... TJ Smith, WM Ritchie, PE Sykes.

Alexander wasted no time.

As soon as she finished writing, he picked up the application form, checked that she'd signed and dated it and immediately ushered her into the Committee Room next door.

Unprepared, caught off guard and a little confused by the sudden turn of events, she found herself before the full Committee.

They were seated in high-backed chairs at a solid table with traditional fashioned legs, a comfortable old world atmosphere heightened by dark timbers, with dignitaries of the past gazing rather sternly down on the scene from gold-framed pictures amid photos and paintings of great horses from other eras.

She wasn't dressed for this kind of occasion. They sat her down and Chairman Bell began talking in his slow, folksy way.

'We have decided to give you your licence,' he said. 'But there are a few things we are concerned about.'

He paused for effect and went on, 'Firstly, we don't want Robbie in the stables.'

Gai said, 'I fully understand that I have been married to a warned off person for nearly seven years, and I know they are not allowed near stables, so that is not a problem.'

'Secondly,' said Bell, 'we don't want you writing your newspaper column any more because if we let you, everyone else might want to write columns.'

Gai tried to hang on to the column.

'I think that is very unfair and very unjust,' she protested. 'But if it stands in the way of my licence I will stop writing it.

'However, I will have to speak to my editor, and also I am committed to one more column.'

Peter Capelin then chipped in with two more conditions. 'And you won't be suing us for damages or following through for any legal fees,' he said.

In other words, she would have to give up her right to damages for the $40,000 she was claiming under the Equal Opportunity Tribunal and she would forfeit her right to the AJC paying her fees which the Court of Appeal had ordered them to pay.

She thought the matter of the fees particularly unfair because she was entitled to them. She knew they were denying her natural justice in taking away her legitimate rights but she wanted the licence!

'If you give me my licence in my hand now,' she told them, 'I won't hold you to legal fees or anything further.

'That is on the understanding that you give me my licence now. All I want to do is be a trainer.'

A few more words and the interview ended. No pleasantries or congratulations, just a matter of fact situation, as if they had carried a resolution to routinely name a new race after a well-known horse, certainly giving no sense of the drama that the issue had fuelled throughout Australia.

She agreed to the conditions and walked out with her licence. It didn't matter that it was a number two licence.

Two and a half years of tension, worry, character blackguarding and legal manoeuvring, all dissipated in less than five minutes.

But hallelujah. The AJC had caved in!

Gai drove back to the stables, gradually letting it sink in.

She said to TJ's longtime secretary Pauline Blanche, 'Talk about a let-down. All those years of fighting and I get my licence that easily.'

First up she rang TJ, saying, 'Guess what, Dad. They've given me my licence.'

'That's good,' he said, cautiously. But when she told him she had agreed to the conditions that the AJC would not pay her fees and she would have to give up writing her column, he reacted strongly.

'If you'd rung me first you wouldn't be paying your own fees—that was crook,' he said.

She tried Robbie but couldn't locate him. Then she rang her friend Lea Stracey. 'I've got it,' she said simply.

'Got what?'

'My licence.'

'You're joking. You're kidding. What . . . '

'Must fly. We've got to have champagne tonight.'

She was ecstatic, making call after call. Euphoria was taking over after two and a half years of an incredibly damaging battle against a Neanderthal body determined to keep her out, a battle which caused her enormous personal anguish and stress from having her affairs dealt with so publicly.

The brawl had made her feel desperately concerned that she was damaging her father's reputation and his friendship with the AJC, also that she was risking her husband's chance of ever having his warning off lifted so he could one day return to the racing industry.

Gai rang Bruce Stracey and briefed him. At first he was delighted but as all the details came out he was horrified.

'Don't you realise what you've done by signing a new application form?' he asked. 'We've all worked so hard and now you've signed away all your rights. They've amended the rules and now if they want to they can stop you from getting your licence because you're *associated* with Robbie. Marriage isn't important any more.'

'Oh well,' said Gai, 'they seemed to be on the level. We'll just have to keep our fingers crossed.'

'By signing a new application you come under the new rule and it could be a different fight,' said Stracey.

He was already forming a defence in his mind if this happened. They would argue the AJC had acted improperly by causing her to sign under duress.

The solicitor's concern took some of the gloss off Gai's happiness but she refused to be anything but thrilled.

The AJC's action in compelling Gai to sign a new application was intriguing. If they didn't use the new form, they were breaking their own latest rule, that someone *associated* with a warned off person could not obtain a licence.

An AJC member, Mr LP Alidenes, of Darling Point, had written to the AJC Committee protesting about the rule change.

In his letter he said, 'You cannot continue to punch after the bell. You cannot seek to legally ambush the intended victim by changing the rules, and you cannot tackle the player without the ball on speculation.'

The AJC would never invoke the new rule on Gai. Perhaps they were just as confused on the day as everyone else!

That issue was taken up by the *Herald-Sun* in Melbourne which pointed out that in granting Gai her licence the AJC had disregarded a new Australian Rule of Racing that no person who, in the opinion of the committee or the stewards, is a close associate of a disqualified person shall be permitted to train or race any horse.

Having said that, the newspaper quoted the Victoria Racing Club as saying that Gai was all right by them—she could train in Victoria if she wished.

That night after the AJC's stunning turnaround Gai and Robbie and a few friends including the Straceys drank champagne at their Clifton Gardens home, toasting a victory out of the blue.

Gazing down appropriately on the scene from the lounge room wall was the 'tonsil' shot or 'Gai having a baby' shot as she celebrated Star Watch, the horse she picked out at the sales, winning the 1988 STC Golden Slipper.

That's how she looked all night, radiating a dazzling, fixed smile as she showed all her exuberance and emotion in victory.

In spite of the special occasion, the guests didn't stay late.

Next morning the *Telegraph* front page headline said it all: 'Gai Wins'.

Displaying all her common sense, Gai said, 'Never at any stage did I hold a grudge against the AJC because of their stand.

'Really, I have always maintained a good relationship with the AJC and I believed it was only a matter of time before I would get my licence.

'I must say I feel wonderful and look forward to the future with great expectations.

'The only thing is now I have 10 boxes out at Randwick and no horses and no owners.'

Under the heading 'After two years of chaff, Gai can train,' the *Weekend Australian* carried a big picture of her sporting a silly grin and celebrating by spurting a bottle of champagne.

Typifying her positive attitude, she said, 'I think the AJC realises that public opinion was behind me and they weren't in step with the 1990s. But all that is past now. I am fully batting to be a credit to the training ranks and making a go of my opportunity.'

She thanked all those who had stood by her in battling the 'system', adding, 'A lot of wonderful people supported me and without them I couldn't have kept going.'

The *Sydney Morning Herald* ran her story under the heading 'AJC buckles and Gai the stayer gets to be a trainer at last.'

'I was caught unawares by the decision,' she said. 'I only wish it had come years ago when there were plenty of horses and owners, and when the economy was buoyant.'

In that report Tommy indicated he wasn't handing over the reins after all, or at least not just yet.

'It's more than likely Gai will train out of Bounding Away but if she ends up with plenty of horses then I'll give her Tulloch Lodge,' he said. 'Had she been granted a licence two years ago she would have had 90 horses to train.'

He compared her situation with that of the former champion

trainer Colin Hayes and his son David, who had become the leading trainer in Melbourne and Adelaide.

'David Hayes walked into his father's empire and Gai would have done the same two years ago,' he said.

In her last column Gai played it cool, saying nothing to draw the crabs in just a few paragraphs on the issue, warmly thanking her legion of supporters including other female trainers. The heading read: 'A dream comes true: I'm following in my father's footsteps.'

The press was suspicious on why the AJC had suddenly backed down. The AJC administration manager Tony King was quoted in one newspaper as saying Mrs Waterhouse's call-up to the office was not on the committee meeting's agenda. 'It certainly wasn't expected and she was only called at the last minute,' he said.

Gai felt sure the AJC caved in because Jim Bell could no longer stand the pressure from the press. Also, Queen Elizabeth was due to visit Randwick within a month or so and the Committee did not want to face adverse criticism from the press during her visit.

Inquiries by this writer confirmed that Bell decided it was time to end the whole affair. Bell kept the reason close to his chest but he took great pride in bringing about the solution.

He gave a few reasons to his colleagues that the time had come to end it, that the press had grown tired of it and he judged that it was time to move.

I have my own theory on that. I believe he was given the message by George Souris, the New South Wales Minister for Sport and Minister Assisting the Premier, that the AJC was out of line on the issue.

That view is supported by the fact that a network of people believed so strongly an injustice was being done to Gai that they banded together after the AJC took the final step of appealing to the High Court. Their purpose was to let the AJC know it was behaving ridiculously.

These people, who formed a loose association, included

politicians from both sides of the New South Wales Parliament, women interested in the feminist movement, members of the AJC and ordinary members of the public.

One of the persons involved in that action told me, 'We decided to put pressure on the AJC, covertly, to embarrass them for persisting with this injustice. Our aim was to suggest to Chairman Bell that it was political suicide to continue with their stand.

'I can't tell you who spoke to whom but that pressure was applied and one of the persons approached was the Minister in charge of racing at the time.'

Bell wasn't the only one who had been convinced Gai should not be given her licence. Insider reports said that when Bell told the Committee it was time to bring things to a close, another committeeman argued with him and Bell brought his authority and persuasion to bear.

Indeed, several other committeemen had supported their views. Even allowing for a ruling clique, it took more than two committeemen to maintain such a head-in-the-sand attitude and trench warfare to keep out a well qualified woman.

The weakness of some committeemen was shown when several claimed after the event that they really wanted to see Gai gain her licence all along—they claimed in private conversations it was really only Bell and Capelin who were responsible for the opposition.

No event in memory demonstrated more plainly that the AJC was a feudal anachronism than the way in which it treated Gai, first in refusing her licence and then in the manner of granting it.

To call someone in while they were locked in litigation and to deal with them outside their legal advisers was an extremely unfair thing to do. Only an autocratic group operating as a law unto themselves under their own act of Parliament could expect to behave in such a manner.

This wasn't your local tennis club or squabbling parents and citizens' association. It was the Australian Jockey Club with 150 years of tradition behind it.

And to deny her the legal expenses to which she was entitled—after they had lost the case in the Court of Appeal and had been ordered to pay them—was nothing short of outrageous.

It cost Gai and Robbie $120,000, which proved a burden to raise.

Robbie's life since he bet carelessly on Fine Cotton and failed to own up to it had been one long ordeal of finding money to pay for legal fees.

George Souris, the Sports Minister, made no bones about whose side he was on. He wrote a personal letter to Gai on Saturday, the day the newspapers ran the story of her win, in these terms:

> Dear Gai,
> What a great pleasure to learn from today's Press that the AJC has at last granted you your rightful trainer's licence. Your stoic and tenacious battle with the AJC was an inspiration to us all.
> I know your proud father would be thoroughly delighted as will the entire racing industry.
> Warmest personal best wishes—see you soon.
> (Signed) George.

Of course, legal experts would say that Gai accepted what was a classical compromise and as such she did not give up too much to get what she wanted.

In effect, she had to buy her licence by giving away rights.

But it meant she was able to begin training a year earlier than if the case had dragged on to the High Court. And who can tell what view that court might have taken?

The drollery of legal points might have triumphed over the argument for sensible social values, but the odds are that Gai would have eventually won the day.

It was unfortunate so much character damage was done in the way the AJC fought the case but Gai's legal advisers could think of no other way of obtaining her licence in difficult circumstances than to draw up the plan they did and stick to it in spite of extreme provocation from the AJC and anguish caused to Gai.

It must be said her lawyers were highly effective in executing a winning strategy and keeping emotion out of it.

The capitulation of the AJC enhanced the reputations of both Bruce Stracey and Bret Walker, who soon afterwards was appointed a senior counsel.

Perhaps Gai would have been mad to have refused the conditions imposed by the AJC, but the conclusion was inescapable that they took advantage of her in the manner in which they gave her what she rightfully deserved.

Their intransigence in stopping her from writing her column was put in perspective by the normally mild-mannered *Sydney Morning Herald* writer Alan Kennedy who had this to say under the heading 'Feudal racing system baulks at the idea of free speech':

> 'The feudal nature of racing became obvious a few weeks ago when Gai Waterhouse was finally granted a trainer's licence.
>
> 'The AJC's refusal to grant her one was based on a spurious argument over to whom she was married.
>
> 'The obvious question is: would they have applied the same test to a man? But Waterhouse is a determined woman and she kept up the fight against the AJC and finally won.
>
> 'In the process, unfortunately, she had to give away her right to free speech. Until she received her licence, Waterhouse was writing a column for the *Herald*.
>
> 'The response to the column was good but the AJC didn't like it and so it had to stop. Waterhouse agreed, albeit reluctantly, but she wanted that licence.
>
> 'She will not thank us for this column but the number of people ringing up and wanting to know why it isn't running has prompted me to tell them why.

'It was not our decision. We wanted it to stay. The AJC said it couldn't allow Waterhouse to continue her column because everyone else might want to write one. Can't have that, can we?

'Can't have people who make their living in racing and who have to live under its feudal system having a view. They might suggest changes that could improve the sport. The AJC decision is a blow against free speech and against Waterhouse's rights.

'We will be keeping up the pressure on the AJC to broaden its very narrow view of the world.'

Gai's victory was a significant turning point for her as a person.

It was also the making of Gai Waterhouse, the person the public came to know in the future.

CHAPTER NINETEEN

THE WATERHOUSE LEGACY FOR WOMEN

Oddly, in terms of strict legal significance, the Waterhouse case was not what you would call a leading case.

It would not even go into the law books on its own as Waterhouse v. AJC because it merely distinguished an existing case that was the barrier to her being considered on her own merits.

But in real terms it is destined to become one of the great mythical stories of Australian women's rights, one that will be told and retold down the years.

True, it was no earth-shattering legal decision to litter the law books, but in the simplest possible way it was vitally important for women throughout Australia.

Barrister Bret Walker's view was that it put paid to what is regarded as pillow talk or bed relations which justify discrimination against a woman.

'I think the importance of Waterhouse is it ended the notion that you can say wives are likely to be overruled by their husbands inherently because of their gender or marital status—

therefore they are to be treated differently because they are a woman or are married,' he says.

'Waterhouse has real significance in putting paid to justifying discrimination against a wife on the vice of her husband.'

Clearly the hidden issue of erotic sex is involved in people's attitudes about the susceptibility of a woman's feelings that she must knuckle under metaphorically to her husband, because of economic dependence, the need for emotional support and so on.

People generally feel this is so but don't articulate it very comfortably. Walker subtly dared the AJC to bring this out into the open with Gai and Robbie.

'They went close to the wind on this issue but did not spell it out,' he says.

In the eyes of Bruce Stracey the big factor arising from Gai's victory is that it made it unlawful for corruptibility to be imputed to all married women. 'And that is a very significant thing,' he says.

The decision at common law in her case made that the law in relation to all married women.

It led to Federal law being amended under what is generally known as the Waterhouse Amendment to prevent this type of discrimination occurring anywhere in Australia again.

But to see the real impact of Gai's win one needed to go out in the streets and to the races and observe people's reaction in the months following her victory.

It was seen as a victory for all women, releasing them from the shackles of prejudice and entrenched social attitudes which in many cases denied them self-respect and individuality.

The big unchartered change was that it reformed women's attitudes about themselves.

Gai herself felt as if someone had unlocked the gates of a prison and let her out. She knew of no other way to gain her emotional and career freedom than to obtain her licence.

Suddenly she was someone in her own right, no longer just Tommy's daughter or Robbie's wife or constrained by her father or her uncle Ernie but Gai Waterhouse her own person.

Victory was sweet but it was far more than obtaining a licence.

To be doing something recognisably on her own, although it was the same as she had done for her father for years, gave her a feeling of exhilaration that was unbelievable.

It was as though at last she had removed the leg irons, mentally and emotionally.

Gai was no feminist, no flag waver for the cause. She simply believed that an individual, male or female, had the right to succeed. She didn't set out to be a role model but became one all the same for the women who could not stand up and fight for themselves.

When she spoke she spoke for all the women who like to think that because they are married to someone they are not subordinate, that a woman is not an automatic attachment to a man.

Millions of Australian women thought like that, but could not express themselves publicly.

Gai brought it to the surface for all women of like mind, but unfortunately for her it had to be done in the public domain.

And they admired her for the way she did it, with her head held high in spite of her world caving in around her, remaining loyal to her husband and holding her marriage and family together, still managing to do her work successfully.

Only a person of exceptional character could have achieved all those things in the circumstances. Many women faced with such a challenge would give up. And how many young men put to the test in a similar fashion would look for an easy way out?

In showing women they could be independent and stand alone, recognised for their own personal qualities, Gai remained feminine in all respects.

Nobody could say she was aggressive, only tenacious.

She proved women can achieve their goals by being graceful and quietly persistent, that they don't have to go out marching in the streets. Forceful perhaps, but feminine too.

Once and for all she showed women in the workplace,

especially in the corporate world, that they *can* break through the glass ceiling.

Dr Meredith Burgmann, a member of the New South Wales Legislative Council and specialist in industrial relations, is one high profile woman who welcomed the Waterhouse breakthrough.

She closely followed the case as it unfolded, observing it was trying to impute that married women had no existence other than as the wives of their husbands.

To her mind it was about the AJC not conceding that Gai could have a successful career unless she was just a prop of her husband.

'I also think,' Dr Burgmann told this writer, 'that the AJC has always been seen as a very male-centred, stuffy and conservative organisation, and that Gai was seen to have taken them on and won, which was very exciting.

'Another point is that she was seen as a very gutsy woman who obviously enjoys what she's doing and does it very well—taking on the blokes and winning.

'It took enormous courage to do that. First she took on the establishment in a male-dominated environment and was prepared to take the battle on to the next stage. That was really terrific.

'Until this happened, women have generally had their traditional stereotyped roles in racing. Basically they were strappers and as wives of wealthy owners they placed sashes on the winning horses. These were the boundaries.

'The strappers did the menial tasks and the wives of rich men were there to sash the winners or as fashion plates at the various carnivals to enhance the glamour side of racing.

'To have women as jockeys was very exciting, but to have a successful woman trainer was just outstanding.

'Gai's success means that women have to be taken seriously instead of just playing a frivolous role.'

Dr Burgmann believes that to have a role model like Gai means young women interested in racing can now lift their aspirations. Her inspiration can extend to other fields.

'The AJC attitude in trying to keep her out of what she had every right to do displayed their very sexist view of the world,' says Dr Burgmann.

'The case is very important in showing up this sexist view that women cannot have an existence outside their husbands. In that sense, the case is important for any woman who wants to have a separate professional existence but is discriminated against because of who or what her husband might be.

'The wonderful thing now is that if a woman is discriminated against because of her husband, she can just say remember the Gai Waterhouse case.

'People remember it because it was a precedent and high profile. Publicity has made people conscious of this new law.

'This case is a watershed in women's rights, but women still have a long way to go for equal opportunities in the workforce.

'I applaud Gai Waterhouse for being a fighter and showing so much courage.'

But until Gai turned up at the races after her win the significance was not fully realised in the public arena.

Women of all backgrounds surrounded her to offer their congratulations, showing her appeal across the board.

They came from the members' stand too but mainly from the outer areas where the battlers and the ordinary people gathered. They ranged from kids to elderly grandmothers.

A boy of about 10 produced the packet from which he'd

just eaten a pie and asked, 'Mrs Waterhouse, will you please sign this?'

Young mothers with children, blokes in shorts clutching cans of beer, all converged on her and told her how much they admired her.

Racegoers queued to get her autograph. Although she loves the limelight, she was slightly embarrassed by the attention.

Lea and Bruce Stracey went to a Brisbane Cup meeting hoping to spend time with her and finished up as minders helping her move from one spot to another so she could saddle her horses and get them out on the track in time.

Bruce found it extraordinary. 'The crowd didn't do this to anyone else,' he said. 'She found time and a cheerful word for everyone and they all regarded her as a hero. I was amazed to see the effect she'd had on people.'

Nobody among her army of supporters looked upon Gai as a privileged person who had received a leg-up in life.

They regarded her as a worthwhile human being who had worked as hard as the next person to achieve her ambition, making many sacrifices along the way.

Many could equate with the fact that she had graduated from the University of New South Wales, regarded as the university of the strugglers, battlers and larrikins which produced many outstanding people who tried harder than Sydney University counterparts, achievers like Oz magazine publisher Richard Neville and playwright Alec Buzo.

Gai epitomised a lot of NSW University graduates who had a dash of derring-do about them and were prepared to give it a go rather than follow the traditional path.

Almost from the start as a trainer in her own right Gai was besieged with requests to address schools, women's meetings and specialist groups as a motivational speaker.

She took on many of these responsibilities but simply didn't have time to oblige all groups.

This disappointed some in the feminist movement but to make the most of her opportunity, Gai focused on one thing only—being a good trainer to prove them wrong for keeping her out.

Understandably, school girls and women wanted her to tell her story so they too could succeed.

Carmel Niland thought it unimportant that Gai did not become an active member of the feminist movement.

She says most women who make considerable achievements do not do so for altruistic reasons but because they want to, risking their public reputations and the ridicule of their friends. All women benefit from their example, anyway.

Men, she says, value action but women value relationships. Mrs Niland explains:

'Valuing relationships is a web that often holds women back because they say well, I will do it but what effect will it have on my family, how is my husband going to feel about this?

'A husband in the same circumstances might not even think of asking his wife how she feels about it.

'He will think I've been wronged and I have to take action over this, otherwise I'll be seen as weak and unmanly.

'Women don't think that way. They say gosh, I know I've been wronged but will this harm my kids or my husband, how is my father going to feel about it?

'And women don't get up on a soap box when they succeed and say, look I've won. Like Gai, they just get on with the job.'

With Gai, her action was personally, not politically, motivated. And after winning, she wanted to continue in the personal domain rather than the political.

As Mrs Niland read it, the fascination with Gai was that she won the private as well as the public war.

'I think Gai's achievement is remarkable,' she says, 'because she juggled a career, motherhood and a successful marriage and risked all the financial and emotional costs while going through a public process.

'Any woman who tests her courage publicly, protects her family, defends her husband, her talent and livelihood against friends and people she's known all her life, any woman who does that and wins is absolutely marvellous.

'If these people you stand up to are your friends, how do you demonise them? As soon as you stand up to them on a point of principle, the friendship itself starts to fall apart. They are the enemy within.

'Look, I have spoken to many women who are members of golf clubs like Royal Sydney. They can't play off at the same time as men and I say why don't you take action?

'They say it wouldn't be worth it, it would ruin my life and destroy my whole social circle. I couldn't put up with the stress so I won't rock the boat.'

Mrs Niland, who has her own consultancy and would like to enter Federal politics to pursue the cause of women's rights, believes Gai has helped not only in the public battle for women but also in the private struggle that has yet to be won for Australian women.

The battles of the 1980s took women into men's jobs like steel working, into bowling clubs and pubs, winning against sexual harassment and after that they moved into politics, leisure and sport, challenging sexism in the media.

Now, says Mrs Niland, the daughters of those front runners have the really tough job in front of them—to work out and improve in private the relationships between men and women and how this relates to the new emerging status of women.

'It's about how the men and women relate to one another as people, in the home, in marriage and various other kinds of relationships, the differences between us and how we negotiate those differences,' she says.

'It's not a matter of them or us but of partnership. It's also a matter now of women helping men who are under-performing in a whole lot of aspects of public life.

'Women are now saying, OK fellas, how about playing this game differently? Let's see it not as you and me but as us, and let us negotiate that. It's not a battlefield, it's a shift.

'It requires more than discussion because a lot of change is very painful. It's about, for example, men sharing housework and parenthood, and it's difficult.

'It's all very well doing it on the soapbox but when you try to negotiate it in the home, it's difficult. That's the challenge to women in Australia today.'

Mrs Niland says Gai helped point the way in this private transition because of the public example of how she held her marriage together, combining it with motherhood and career in the most trying circumstances.

In the year 2050, she predicts, women will look back on Gai Waterhouse and say there was a great front runner for women.

But right now Gai had to find some horses to train.

CHAPTER TWENTY

THE 'LADY' TRAINER

Impatient for success and feeling the obstacles were behind her at last, Gai turned up at the Summer Yearling Sales at Newmarket in Sydney just two days after being licensed.

She needed some young horses to fill those 10 empty boxes at Bounding Away stables.

But the usual bouncy, irrepressible confidence exuded by Gai was not in evidence. She should have been over the moon and said she was, but her demeanour was restrained.

In a rare moment of self-revelation she had said to Pauline at the stables after returning from the AJC, 'It's a strange feeling. 'I've fought so hard for this licence. Now I've got it, I don't know what to do with it.'

Pauline felt so taken aback, as if eavesdropping on a private conversation, she could not think of anything suitable to say, so said nothing.

Gai also had a sobering conversation with TJ in the Tulloch Lodge office the day before the sales. He was pleased for her but she knew from his quiet mood that he had reservations.

She knew instinctively what the problem was. Even when she tried to draw him out he didn't say what troubled him, but she talked to him as if she understood anyway.

'Dad,' she said, 'if I fail, who cares? It's no skin off your nose. Your records will still go down unblemished.'

'It's just such a tough game to do any good in,' he replied, skirting around his true feelings.

'If I can't make a success of it in a year, I'll be quite happy to retire from it. I really do believe that.'

He didn't say it to Gai but his big worry was she would fail. The thought was anathema to him. It would be two years before he confided to a few people that he had feared Gai might not succeed. Judged against *his* background, of course, success was relative.

In her heart she knew she would do well because she had served a long apprenticeship. And it was crystal clear to her how she wanted to train her horses. She had been under the microscope of Tommy's direct tutelage for 15 years, around horses with him from the age of six and attended sales with him from that time.

She had bought horses in her own right since she was 21, including those she and Robbie raced before being forced to sell them because of his troubles.

Ever since returning from her time abroad she had done the hack work for Tommy at the various sales, bringing the horses out of the stalls for him to inspect, being his eyes and ears and learning to judge them through his experience. She always told him what she didn't like about a horse and listened to his comments.

Usually she picked one or two and nominated them as her own. Tommy bought and trained them but to share in the benefits she had to find the owners.

Among those she selected without input from Tommy were STC Golden Slipper winner Star Watch and Combat, a Canberra Cup winner.

Gai loved the sales, was stimulated by them and regarded them as a natural part of her life. She had received a sound, professional grounding over a long period in this vital part of a successful trainer's role.

From the time she was a child she had sat around the dinner table listening to her father talk about horses and their qualities and the fascinating, intriguing and treacherous business of horse racing. Some of his knowledge had rubbed off on her over the years—how much she would soon learn.

Her first formal outing at the Newmarket sales ring as an individual trainer was a family affair. Both her parents were there beside her, so was Robbie and their children, Tom, nine, and Kate, eight, and the family's French poodle, Koinu.

Tommy listened to her thoughts as usual but this time she was on her own, which was how she wanted it.

Buying horses in Australia is something of a gamble because trainers have to choose the horses and put up their own money, then go out and find the owners to whom they retail the horses.

In Europe and America trainers rarely move unless the owners give their consent first and payment is assured.

Gai's first purchase proved an ironic false start.

She liked a chestnut colt sired by Papal Power and bid the top price of $32,000 for it. To her amazement auctioneer Reg Inglis knocked the yearling down to another bidder, a young Warwick Farm-based trainer.

'Sold to Guy Walter,' he said, banging his gavel. 'Thank you Guy—a great judge of horseflesh.'

'Hang on, I thought I bought that horse,' Gai called out.

'A sheila!' exclaimed a man in the crowd.

Mr Inglis realised his mistake at once, said he was sorry, the horse was hers and the same compliment applied to her.

Papal Power had a strong family connection. His grand-dam was Analie, one of TJ's best mares who won 16 races including the Doncaster and Metropolitan Handicaps and was Australian three-year old of the year in 1972.

Gai also bought two other yearlings, spending $60,000 in all. On the second day of the sales she bought another one for $40,000—the top amount she was prepared to pay.

Spotting a mystery buyer in the ring, she arranged an

introduction through the sales complex chairman John Inglis, and slipping straight into her promotional role the three-day-old licence holder said to him, 'I'd love to train your horses for you.'

The bidder was non-committal but later asked John Inglis if 'this woman' would look after his horses. Inglis replied, 'Go and see for yourself. Look at her stables and see how spotless they are.'

She went home and told herself, 'I've got four horses and no owners. What am I going to do? Dad will help me with the finance for a while, but if I can't find owners for them I'll be in trouble.'

It didn't take long for her to work out her strategy, 'Damn it, I'll come out and go on the attack and let the racing public know I'm around.'

She decided she would advertise for clients—something that had never been done before by a trainer in Australia.

A successful stable operation cannot be based on having one runner every now and then. Regular prizemoney is needed.

Gai wanted to be more accessible to potential new owners but would have to search for them. Already the new broom with innovative ideas for the industry was taking shape.

A week later she turned up at the Magic Millions Yearling Sales on the Queensland Gold Coast and bought two yearlings—a brown filly by Marscay out of a winning Noble Bijou mare formerly owned and raced by her father, and a colt by the American-based stallion Tejano, a multiple Group 1 winner as a two-year-old in the US.

Next, 10 days later, she and Tommy raided the National Yearling Sales at Trentham in New Zealand, where she bought eight horses. On a spree there five years before, they had bought 13 horses, all of which had won races in Australia.

While waiting for the yearlings to develop, she concentrated on the only three current runners in her stable.

The three were all promising—Silver Flyer, a yearling which she had selected for clients a year earlier and had just been transferred into her care from her father's stables after finishing second at his only start, Gifted Poet and a young New Zealand stayer, Te Akau Nick. Already she was boosting the stayer as a strong chance in the AJC Derby.

Silver Flyer was to be her first starter at Randwick. She knew plenty of people would be bagging her, saying she couldn't train if the horse didn't win. Her excitement was forestalled when the horse was injured in trackwork two days before the race and was scratched.

But in keeping with the Smith tradition, Gai made a flying start soon after in the winner's circle. Early in March 1992, less than two months after she was licensed, Gai saddled up her first winner, Gifted Poet, at provincial Hawkesbury races. 'I'm thrilled,' she said with that big smile.

She followed this up with her first win at headquarters, now officially known as Royal Randwick following Queen Elizabeth's visit just ended, on the State's first Sunday race meeting.

Gifted Poet wrote the lines for her again, giving her the distinction of winning at her first attempts in the country and city.

It felt like a soothing draught of the finest chilled champagne.

'The most fantastic feeling,' she enthused. Sydney was where the wins counted, where trainers were judged.

Press photographers snapped Gai and Tommy together in front of the old Randwick grandstand, scene of many of his triumphs.

The win was significant to Gai because 50 years ago to the day Tommy had achieved his first metropolitan winner here with his old bush horse, Bragger. He'd waited two years, a lot longer than Gai, for his elusive first winner.

Her unique idea of advertising her yearlings and services as a horse trainer in national publications and on radio was already creating interest—and causing a stir.

One ad said, 'No one can explain the thrill of owning a winner—let me introduce you to the fun of racing. Ring Gai Waterhouse.'

Traditionalists openly knocked her, saying it was touting for business. Gai just saw it as good business sense.

'If you waited for people to give you horses to train, you'd have empty stables,' she told the newspapers. 'I don't want to steal my father's or anyone else's horses, so I'm advertising and promoting myself.'

She could not afford to buy the more expensive horses for big established owners and had to make sure the ones she bought were saleable to ordinary people whom she planned to introduce to racing. To help her she called on the services of Harry Lawton, bloodstock agent and racehorse syndicator.

Gai knew many people would not dream of approaching a big trainer and offering $5,000 for a share in a racehorse, thinking they would be laughed at.

But if she had six owners each offering that amount as a sixth share she knew she could buy what she described as a nice horse with potential. But she had to buy well at that price to succeed.

Complaints were made to the AJC and STC when Gai advertised in official race books, but as it didn't break any rule they were powerless to stop her.

Some people made fun of her when an aggressive brochure she produced went out to the industry saying, 'With my style and TJ's secrets, let me introduce you to the winner's circle.'

Gai was determined to build up a strong stable like her father before her. In recent months she had been so embarrassed by the small string of horses TJ had at Tulloch Lodge that she felt sick in the stomach at times.

On Sunday mornings when owners came to see their runners and discuss them over a glass or two of champagne, Gai moved horses from the back and filled all the front stalls in order to create a better impression.

In spite of her good start and her excellent bloodlines which indicated she had the form to one day go to the top, as a woman Gai remained in the 'gee whiz' category.

Women as horse trainers still represented a strong novelty

value in the male racing scene. They were commonly referred to as 'lady' trainers as if they were an oddity or some rare breed apart.

Much to Gai's annoyance, she was being generally referred to as the Rookie Female Trainer.

She joined a small band of women who, although successful trainers in Sydney, were finding the going tough against the male dominance of the industry and chauvinist attitudes generally.

Against the trend, this small group had trained more than 500 winners in Sydney in the previous two years.

Betty Lane was one of the Sydney pioneers who broke into the field as a trainer and had a number one licence to train at Randwick.

Originally a Randwick girl, she went to live in Guyra, one of the coldest spots in New South Wales, where she obtained a country licence before returning to Sydney.

Betty went close to winning the Golden Slipper Stakes in 1978 with Smokey Jack who ran second to the fluent-striding Manikato.

Gai's entry to the ranks spurred comments in magazines and newspapers on the growing band of horsewomen on Australian tracks.

They included Helen Page, Kim Moore, Margaret de Gonneville, Lesley Pickin, Barbara Joseph, Sally Rowe and Gay Gauchi, a former Melbourne jockey-turned-trainer.

Fresh from her AJC battle, Gai contributed to the issue of how tough it was for women to succeed.

'It's worse for jockeys than trainers,' she told interviewers, 'and at the moment their chances of making it as jockeys are zilch. It's not that the girls aren't tough enough—owners are very reluctant to give them a go.'

All of them had nicknames which they considered derogatory to women. Kim Moore was 'Our Glamorous Rosehill Trainer', Helen Page was 'Wonder Woman from Warwick Farm', Margaret de Gonneville was 'Veteran Woman Trainer', Lesley

Pickin had the soubriquet 'That Canterbury Woman' and Gay Gauchi was called 'Gucci Gauchi'. The jockey Jodi Ridge had to tolerate 'Jockette Jodi'.

In the early 1980s South Australian jockey Lee Custance was described in newspapers as 'the attractive 25-year-old' when she was fined for showing red knickers through her silks—owing to the crude dressing facilities (a darkened caravan), she didn't realise her sartorial imperfection.

Women were not allowed to ride against men in Australia until 1979. New Zealander Linda Jones rode the first winner against the blokes in Australia, but had to threaten legal action before the AJC allowed female jockeys to compete on equal terms. Women had a tough time establishing themselves in Kiwiland too.

Like Gai, none of the early women trainers started out to train. Helen Page, married to leading trainer John Page, was a teacher, Margaret de Gonneville was a librarian in New Zealand and Kim Moore began her working life as a secretary.

Their parents were all opposed to them jumping into the macho world of racing. All of them made it against the odds, but none without sacrifice and struggle.

Some of them told the *Women's Weekly* of their experiences in the 'tricky' world of racing, revealing how difficult it was for women to compete when owners took a horse away from them if they lost, or even if they won, and how male trainers poached their horses as a matter of course if they found a good one.

Lesley Pickin described how her late father advised her not to go into racing because she would be 'bludgeoned' by men.

Nevertheless, on his death she inherited a stable of 20 horses. But most of them were quickly poached by male trainers.

Kim Moore had to be constantly on guard against the males who thought it would be easier to 'put one over' on a woman.

Helen described the dilemma facing a woman, 'I started off trusting everybody. Now I don't trust anybody, although to survive you have to delegate.'

Margaret said she could spend months training a horse to stay, and if she won she had to look out for a great deal of interest from males trying to poach the horse.

She often found herself at a disadvantage because she had to choose between checking out a horse in the stall after a race or trying to keep up with the horse dealing that went on in the members' bar where 'the old boys' network comes into play'.

Lesley picked up on the theme, 'You'll find that usually after a race the women go back to see how the horse is and talk to the jockey. But nearly all the men have to go straight into the bar. They either have to celebrate or cry on someone's shoulder.

'If you've won it's odds on there'll be a trainer in the bar with wonderful ideas on what he could do with your winning horse if only he had the chance. You've won but next morning it turns out you've lost—the horse has gone to a male trainer.'

Women in their experience were just more vulnerable than men.

When approached with propositions that were at best borderline, it was wise to smile and pretend that you hadn't quite heard.

And to make it all that little bit harder, the men's language was worse when they were in the company of women trainers than if only men were present.

In spite of the glass ceiling in racing, a few women had broken through to train winners of major Group One races.

Among them Mrs Deidre Stein of Bathurst trained Rising Prince to win the MVRC WS Cox Plate in 1985 and a number of other significant races including the AJC Queen Elizabeth Stakes.

Margaret Bull, a New Zealand trainer, won the AJC Epsom Handicap in 1985 with Magnitude.

Barbara Joseph from the New South Wales South Coast was the trainer of another major winner at Randwick. She brought a horse called Merimbula Bay from her stables in Bombala to win the 1989 AJC Doncaster Handicap.

Fifty years ago racing in Australia was almost completely a

man's game. Women could be owners, but not trainers or strappers, although even the women owners were thin on the ground then.

One of the leading owners of the 1930s in Victoria was Mrs LR Buxton. A widow with pots of the folding stuff, she was chief patron of one of Melbourne's leading trainers of the time, Jack Holt, whom scandalous rumour said was her lover.

Whether that was right or not this writer has no idea. The fact is reported to show that the same stereotyped sexual assumptions operated 60 years ago in racing as when Gai fought the AJC— behind every successful woman stood, or rather, lay, a man.

Another leading owner in Victoria was Mrs D Reddan, whose bay gelding Hoyle ran second to Foxami in the 1949 Melbourne Cup.

One of the trailblazers who like Gai helped break down the barriers has been Melbourne's Shelley Hancox, who became the first woman racing writer in Australia, on *The Age* in 1968.

Two years later she became the first female racing writer in Britain on *The Sun*. After that she bred, raced, trained and syndicated racehorses, with about 600 owners on her books.

Without women in racing in the 1990s, the industry would be financially poor, apart from being a social and cultural desert. Indeed, it would not be economically viable without them.

Half the strappers are girls who love horses and nearly half the owners or part-owners are women. Women feature in syndicates everywhere. Race books tell the story of the transition from 50 or 60 years ago.

The archaic rules of those days prevented women from being licensed persons and combined to cause one of the greatest injustices to a woman ever seen in Australian racing.

That was the celebrated case of Granny McDonald, who actually trained a Melbourne Cup winner but was robbed of the honour because she was a woman.

A New Zealander and wife of Allan McDonald of Palmerston North, Mrs McDonald trained Catalogue and set the eight-year-old bay gelding for the 1938 Melbourne Cup.

The owner, Mrs Tui Jamieson, a widely travelled racing enthusiast, was desperate to own a Melbourne Cup winner after seeing Wotan win it for New Zealand in 1936.

Catalogue was only a moderate performer but she and Granny McDonald, who had trained the horse for five years, were encouraged to think it could win after it ran a strong second in the Wellington Cup.

Mrs McDonald prepared the horse to be at its peak for The Cup, but was thwarted at the last minute by the Victoria Racing Club's oppressive rules. No woman could hold a trainer's licence, act as a strapper or even ride track work, although they happily took women's money at the turnstiles.

Mrs Jamieson almost scratched Catalogue when she learned the only thing against her trainer friend was her womanhood.

The only way out was for Mrs McDonald's husband to apply for a trainer's permit, which was granted by hypocritical racing officials who were fully aware of the farcical situation.

Allan McDonald became the official trainer although Granny was still the force behind the scenes, insisting the horse needed a run in the Coongy Handicap at Caulfield first to ensure its fitness.

He went into the record books when Catalogue won The Cup by three lengths at 25/1.

Mrs Jamieson became only the second woman to own a Melbourne Cup winner. The distinction of being first went to Mrs EA Widdis, a pioneer land holder from Gippsland in Victoria, when her colt Patrobas won the Victoria Derby–Melbourne Cup double in 1915.

An angry Mrs Jamieson spoke out at the presentation ceremony in the mounting yard at Flemington when Governor-General Lord Gowrie handed her the trophy.

After Lord Gowrie made small talk about the fact that she was only the second woman to own a Cup winner, Mrs Jamieson told him plainly that Mrs Allan McDonald should be standing there with her as the first woman trainer.

The Governor-General reportedly made the stuffy reply, 'Really?'

Wheeeeeee. After a struggle lasting nearly three years with racing authorities, Gai whips out the bubbly and lets fly when hearing the news that the AJC has finally caved in and granted her a licence to train. (*Telegraph Mirror*)

Right: A trainer at last in her own right, Gai is off to a flying start with her first provincial winner, Silver Flyer. She bought him for $25,000 at the Inglis sales in Sydney. (*Telegraph Mirror*)

Below: Gifted Poet, ridden by Darren Beadman, became the new trainer's first winner on a metropolitan track. Thrilled owners help lap up the heady moment. (*Bradley Photo*)

Above: Just three months after gaining her trainer's licence, Gai takes out the Group 3 Gosford Gold Cup with Moods, sticking his head in here between the winning trainer and TJ.
(*Bradley Photo*)

Right: The astute track watcher, checking the early morning gallops.

Left: The winning
Waterhouse style in
cheering home the
1988 Golden Slipper
winner Star Watch,
picked out in the sales
ring by Gai and bought
and trained by her
father for the publicly-
floated Tulloch Lodge
Ltd stable. Her sheer
exuberance and
emotion would be
repeated many times in
the future. *Come on!*

Centre: Oh no. Don't let
me down now...

Below: You'll make,
you're there...

Left: Beauty!

Centre: Gai reaches for Brian Yuill, boss of Tulloch Lodge Ltd.

Right: The agony over, Gai and Yuill embrace ecstatically. (*Star Watch series by Fairfax*)

Above: A pose at Tulloch Lodge stables? Yes, but she'll hop in and help, too.

Right: The working girl at Randwick's early morning trackwork.

Right: Why this big grin? Why indeed! Gai has just proved the knockers and racing officials wrong by showing she's a genuine Group One trainer. Still regarded by many race-goers as a novice, she has just snatched the $400,000 AJC Metropolitan with Te Akau Nick—the first woman to do so and the culmination of her long battle for recognition. Mick 'The Enforcer' Dittman shares her joy.

Below: Yeah, I guess it was a pretty good win, confides Nick in a post-race natter. (*Telegraph Mirror*)

Left: Never was there a more bubbly winning trainer, making her presentation speech at Randwick for Te Akau Nick's Metropolitan victory.

Below: Te Akau Nick showing how he did it in the Metrop. (*Martin King Sportpix*)

Left: Nick and Gai, good mates and a winning combination.

Below: Another winning duo— Gai and jockey Shane Dye, after Te Akau Nick wins the AJC St Leger Stakes. Also, Nick almost created history for Gai with his game second in the 1993 Melbourne Cup, surrendering only to Irish stayer Vintage Crop.

Left: Ooh la la. It pays to look the part as well as do the hard work. (*Bradley Photo*)

Centre: Oh my gosh. Praying was never as serious as this. Gai holds her breath awaiting the photo finish as her charge, Pharaoh, flashes over the line in a heart-stopping blur with two other horses in the 1994 $1 million Doncaster Handicap. (*Mirror Australian*)

Below: Glory, glory, hallelujah. Pharaoh's number goes up and Gai is the winning Group One Doncaster trainer by a nose. Remarkable scenes follow as Gai and winning Melbourne jockey Gavin Eades, accepting the trophy with her, jig and dance and the big crowd gives her a hero's ovation. (*Mirror Australian*)

Above: Gai continues her winning ways as Protara's Bay is led in by the
Neou family after taking out the listed Quick Eze Handicap at Rosehill on
Golden Slipper Day, 1994. (*Bradley Photo*)

Below: Who better to train brilliant Light Up the World to win the Queen
of the Turf Stakes at Rosehill for owners Valerie and TJ Smith than the gal
on the right? (*Bradley Photo*)

Left: This has to be something extra special. You're right, Pharaoh wins his second $1 million Doncaster in a row. Gai showed her exceptional training skills by getting the old crock to the line after the vets gave up on him. (*Fairfax*)

Below: Owners including wives crowd in to get a presentation buzz from Pharaoh's 1995 Doncaster. AJC chairman Bob Charley wants to be in it too.

Left: Who's in charge
around here?
One guess.
(*Queensland Newspapers*)

Centre: Some of the
new owners in Gai's
Asian connection.
Tony Huang is on
her right. At rear, the
odd ones out are
Denise Martin and
Robbie Waterhouse.

Below: You can *feel* the tension as part owners John Hodge, Helen Dalton
and Valerie Smith ride Nothin' Leica Dane to the line in the 1995 Victoria
Derby. (*Queensland Newspapers*)

Above: Nothin' Leica Dane cleans up the Victoria Derby field.

Below left: Gai Waterhouse, first woman to train a Victoria Derby winner, lights up the presentation.

Below right: Master and 'pupil' after Gai's Victoria Derby win. (*Fairfax*)

Above: Stony Bay, trained by Gai, hits out in Japan with Shane Dye preparing for the Japan Cup.

Below: What a smile! Gai accepts the award for 1995 Personality of the Year from the Victorian Racing Writers' Association.

Left: Yet another award, this time from the Thoroughbred Racehorse Owners' Association for the greatest contribution to racing in 1995.

Below: Couple in the limelight, share Gai's award success for her contribution to racing. Their marriage survived the most severe strains and pressures because of the Fine Cotton fallout.

Did they think of changing the rules after that flesh-crawling embarrassment? No. And not for a long time after that.

It was an absolute disgrace down the track that even several years after Gai's celebrated victory for women had shown the AJC Committee to be a bunch of troglodytes, no woman had served on the AJC Committee.

Three women had tried, including Angela McSweeney, without success against the overwhelming leaden weight of male members' votes.

Gai had no time to dwell on female issues or any other extraneous matters.

She was trying to focus on only one thing—how to find winners.

For her next success, four months into being licensed, she had a little bit of help from TJ.

He was a part-owner of Moods, a four-year-old horse which had been bought from its New Zealand owners for a six-figure sum in the previous year, and he persuaded the other owners to transfer the horse to Gai to train. Without a tried horse, she could do little until her yearlings matured and raced.

Gai entered Moods in the $200,000 Gosford Gold Cup, a Group Three feature race. She took full responsibility for training Moods for the 2100 metre event.

On Monday morning, 27 April, 1992, two days before the race, she was having a nap at home after her early trackwork when she saw the race being run in a dream. She saw Moods dash clear and win by five lengths. Rather than feel excited she was disappointed, believing that dreams never come true.

On the day with Kevin Moses up, Moods scored by not five but four lengths to give Gai her first major success.

Bouncing around dressed in a brilliantly-hued skirt and matching shoes with a crazy outsize hat, she declared in her customary jubilant fashion as she led the horse back to scale, 'This is just unbelievable. Sensational.'

At the presentation speech she warmly thanked her beaming

parents for her upbringing and for the opportunity of training Moods.

Then she gave the crowd a glimpse into the passion she felt over her work, 'Today has been the most exciting day of my life. I thought my wedding day was, but this might just creep past it. I am just so proud and overwhelmed. I love training and hopefully this will be the start of many big race wins.'

Tears oozed from Tommy. He had trained five Gosford Cup winners and knew what this meant to her.

'She's going to make a racehorse trainer, don't you worry about that,' he told sceptical racing writers.

Gai went home to Robbie that night and told him she could not describe her exquisite feeling of exhilaration at training a horse on her own to win a Group event.

He had often found her difficult to live with in the days when Ernie and her father kept the thumbscrews on her at the stables. She was cranky and complained nearly every night of her frustration at being held back. Now it was a joy again to be in her company.

Tommy, too, was beginning to gain pleasure from Gai's efforts, receiving the third boost to his career in the last few years since changing fortunes almost ended his remarkable days as a trainer.

The first was seeing Tulloch Lodge take off as a public company, the second John Kluge buying all the company's horses for TJ to train and retrieve a desperate situation, and the third was basking in the burgeoning success of his daughter as Old Father Time stifled the dynamism that his opponents could not match.

After she led in Seabid as a winner at Sydney's Canterbury track in June, he went public in an unabashed display of parental pride and confidence in her future.

There were sneers and bitchy comments from many sides when he said he wasn't kidding in stating she had the ability to become Sydney's leading trainer in three years.

She had the gift for training racehorses and if she could fill the stable she would train plenty of winners.

Hard work alone didn't make a trainer, said Tommy. They needed the gift and the eye. Gai had both. And she knew how to make horses fit.

Publicly the once all-conquering Tommy was seen to be right behind his daughter's every move, the doting father who could see no fault in his successor.

The reality was far different.

Gai still had some hurdles to overcome in that area before she could be completely her own person as a trainer.

And in the midst of her elation at her promising start, she was troubled by personal problems.

Robbie, the man she loved, had been spending a lot of time in courts lately.

A serious matter was about to come to a head and she was worried by it.

CHAPTER TWENTY-ONE

THE LAST HURDLE

Loyalty was a strong feature of Gai Waterhouse's character. It was one of the bonds that helped unite the Smith family in her father's struggling early days in the Australian bush.

And it made the Waterhouses generally stick together against outsiders and occasional mavericks within their own ranks.

Gai's father-in-law Bill Waterhouse and his brothers knew the meaning of family loyalty and so did Bill's children, Robbie and Louise. They both respected the characteristic in the best traditions of the family.

Loyalty as a quality in human relationships was generally under pressure around the world at the time of Gai's licence problems. It was seen to be less important as values changed and people became more sophisticated and cosmopolitan—the global village syndrome.

Where it stood out and endured in a public way it was appreciated all the more by people who regretted to see such a solid old-fashioned virtue become a victim of changing morality standards in the community.

Gai and Robbie in all their troubles remained intensely loyal to each other. And in particular Gai, who innocently had the sins of her husband visited upon her and paid an unwarranted penalty, remained affectionate and supportive throughout.

Australians admired her for standing by her man, not in some blind unthinking way but because she believed in him and was prepared to stand up and be counted in spite of the personal ordeal she was forced to suffer as a result.

It was the sheer character and guts of the slightly-built, positive, feminine woman that they came to respect in all of this.

Ever since her husband was charged with perjury—amazingly, five years after Fine Cotton and on the same day as the AJC considered her licence application—Gai knew her loyalty to him would be put to the test publicly.

At first she felt embarrassed and humiliated that he had put his family under such a glare of publicity. Then she decided she would just have to live with it and try to cope with it.

But like a festering sore, it never went away.

She knew all along that Robbie's crime was not that he had organised the ring-in but had bet on it and not admitted it. But right from the beginning things had gone out of control. She believed that even if he had owned up at the beginning, the repercussions of warning off would hardly have been any different.

Knowing someone as intimately as Robbie and seeing the situation surrounding him snowball so much, she could only react by saying to him, 'I can't believe this is happening to us.'

Nearly three years had passed since the perjury charge alleged he gave false evidence to the Racing Appeals Tribunal in that he said he was not involved in the betting on Fine Cotton in 1984.

In those three years the matter had passed through various courts and costly procedures leading up to a trial.

The bare bones of the situation were that after he was committed for trial for perjury, his counsel, Mr Cliff Papayanni, sought to have the charge set aside on the basis that there was no common law charge of perjury in New South Wales in 1984 when the alleged offence occurred.

In 1969 a number of old English imperial Acts were repealed in New South Wales, leaving a vacuum with no common law offence for perjury. This was not rectified until 1985 when a new section 327 of the State Crimes Act was introduced.

But Judge Ducker of the District Court ruled against Mr Papayanni's submissions on that and also refused a certificate to have it argued before the Court of Appeal.

If the judge was right, why was it necessary to cover the situation with a new section in the Act in 1985, one year after Fine Cotton?

The Director of Public Prosecutions (DPP) kept changing his indictment against Robbie after Mr Papayanni showed deficiencies in the charge. He proved the original charge showed no offence under the law! Back it went for amendment.

Eventually, because the DPP obviously thought the perjury charge may not stick, it amended the indictment to add a second charge under a different section of the Crimes Act, this time for false swearing.

Attempts to have both these charges quashed, then permanently stayed, failed.

The main points of law argued by Robbie's lawyers were that the proceedings in 1984 before the Racing Appeals Tribunal were not judicial proceedings, and the Tribunal had no power to administer an oath.

Judge Ducker was tough all the way through on the various legal points which he conceded Robbie had a perfect right to raise. He seemed determined not to let the high profile case, eight years old by the time it finally came before him in 1992 for sentence, go unresolved.

He ruled against all the arguments.

If Mr Papayanni was right in his interpretation of the law, Robbie should not have been charged with perjury because there was no common law charge in existence in 1984. It was only a statutory offence under the Racing Tribunal Act.

And under the statutory powers of the Racing Appeals

Tribunal, perjury or false swearing had to be brought within six months. The maximum penalty was a fine of $500.

They didn't charge him under that statute and time ran out.

When the former Judge Goran in the Tribunal confirmed Robbie's warning off at the end of 1984, Waterhouse lost all his business which caused large financial losses, suffered the personal shame and humiliation of that public rejection and the destruction of his good name, all of which, many people seemed to think, was punishment enough.

Then, five years later he was charged under a new section of the Crimes Act which was not introduced into common law in his counsel's opinion until after the offence occurred.

In the end, all the legal objections didn't matter.

After his challenge to the indictment was overruled, Robbie decided to forgo the trial. That saved the State time and expense. Although pleading not guilty to perjury, he pleaded guilty to false swearing and this was accepted in full discharge of the indictment.

All of this mattered to Gai, though. Under the perjury charge Robbie faced a maximum prison sentence of seven years. It was still five years for false swearing.

Six weeks after Moods won the Gosford Gold Cup for Gai, her husband was due to appear before Judge Ducker for sentencing. Gai elected to give evidence for him.

It was bad luck she found herself in this position. From a commentator's point of view, it is a fair assessment to say that Bill and Robbie Waterhouse were plainly unlucky to have elected to go before the Tribunal. A strong argument existed to show it had no jurisdiction to hear their appeal.

The whole Fine Cotton matter was a legal mess right from the start, with mistake piled on mistake.

First, as set out in *The Gambling Man*, the AJC could not find any offence under the rules of racing to deal with them in the normal way through the stewards, but proceeded against them outside the rules of racing by letter on behalf of the committee, calling on them to show cause why they should not be warned off. For this the new offence of 'prior knowledge' was devised.

There was no evidence to prove they had prior knowledge, but the committee suspected they were involved in organising or financing the ring-in.

The big mistake the Waterhouses made was in hastily appealing to the Tribunal without giving sufficient thought to the new Act which had established the Tribunal a year before Fine Cotton occurred.

The AJC in adopting an unusual procedure and going outside the rules of racing of the club did not have the clear power to warn them off, but it was assumed they did due to the 'AJC law' granted to them under their own Act of Parliament. This point was not challenged before the Tribunal, and the AJC got away with it.

To his credit for legal judgment, Peter Capelin QC opposed the move in Committee to deal with the Waterhouses through the Committee by letter rather than through the stewards as normal, but the decision went through when he was absent.

As a result of what happened to the Waterhouses, the *Australian Jockey Club Act 1873* is ripe for challenge in a number of areas.

Under section 15 of the *Racing Appeals Tribunal Act 1983*, a person could only appeal to the Tribunal based on an earlier appeal to the AJC Committee.

But the hearing before the Committee which warned off the Waterhouses was not an appeal—it was an original proceedings.

Anxious to use the newly-introduced appeal avenue, the Waterhouses went ahead and appealed, not realising the Tribunal had no proper jurisdiction to hear their appeal and they did not raise the point at that stage.

Once the appeal was lost, it was virtually impossible then to turn it around and use this point to their advantage.

To add insult to injury, section 13 of the *Racing Appeals Tribunal Act* said no appeal could be made to the Tribunal except in respect of a decision to *disqualify* any person.

Well, the Waterhouses were *warned off*. Legally the two were different, although the penalty was the same.

So what happened? Judge Goran wasn't about to let this celebrity case slip from his grasp. No sir!

He went to the Government and they gazetted an amendment to include 'warning off' in the Act as well as 'disqualify'— and they applied it retrospectively! That closed off any chance the Waterhouses and their lawyers had of nullifying the AJC action.

Clearly the Waterhouses should have gone to the Supreme Court first, not the Tribunal, and sought a declaration that the AJC action had no validity and had denied them natural justice.

Even the way the Tribunal went about hearing the appeals of the nine people warned off was extraordinary.

Four of those concerned had not been licensed and were obviously not covered by the rules of racing, yet all the evidence was taken at one hearing and lumped in together.

Each witness gave evidence for himself, yet it was used against all the others. For a fair go, the appeals should have been heard separately.

Nothing in the Act said that Judge Goran was empowered to take evidence on oath and Robbie did not know he would be sworn in until proceedings began. Then he took the oath without challenging it. (The AJC stewards and committee had not sworn in the witnesses at their earlier hearings.)

Although the Tribunal rejected Robbie's appeal and confirmed his warning off, it did not proceed against him for lying before it, nor did it recommend any action in that regard. Judge Goran obviously felt his decision to let the warning off stand was penalty enough for any misdemeanour arising out of the ring-in.

In those circumstances it is a travesty that a person should have been pursued under the Crimes Act later for perjury and further penalised eight years after the event.

It has been one of the wisest and most respected tenets laid down in the convention of law that justice delayed is justice denied. Good reason exists for such a principle. Put simply, the recollection of witnesses can become deficient after long delays and evidence can be presented out of focus.

Cases in the New South Wales Supreme Court have referred to this problem as serious and judges have roundly criticised solicitors for causing delays to criminal trials.

What caused the DPP to finally take action after such a long delay is a mystery and something that bears proper examination.

But it appears that when the perjury move against Waterhouse finally started rolling, there was keen competition within the DPP to take the case which promised a rich lode of publicity.

Nobody would normally pay any attention to the DPP for convicting an unknown person. But to send a prominent or famous person down the chute can be a notch in the belt.

On Monday, 22 June, 1992, Gai waited inside Sydney's bustling Downing Street court complex to give evidence on the character of Robbie Waterhouse before Judge Ducker passed sentence.

It had been a tense time for both of them in the events leading up to this day and both felt highly nervous for each other.

Gai had just obtained her licence and the implications of the judge's pending sentence were horrendous for both of them.

People had been saying Robbie would go to prison and he was appearing before a judge with a tough reputation.

The first witness was Justice Marcus Einfeld, of the Federal Court. He described Robbie as an impeccable father, a first class husband, an excellent son and a very good friend.

He said he had discussed the perjury charge with Robbie,

'particularly in the context as it seemed to me, he was being tried by the community and the media for an offence for which he was never charged, organising and being the mastermind behind this whole operation.

'I thought that was very unfair, a tendency the community has to exaggerate the nature of the matter and to make assumptions which are completely unsupported by the evidence.

'This has been a levelling experience for him . . . It's one thing to face a particular charge, but the self-protective mechanism seems to me to become very much more pronounced when you are protecting yourself against an offence with which you haven't been charged.

'My impression is that he has had a very arresting and very difficult experience in which a great deal has been at stake and he has lost a great deal.

'He has had to fight a real assault on his reputation and integrity.

'That's very difficult for people to do especially in public life because almost anything they say is reported, and often reported inaccurately or unfairly or out of context.

'I think he has lost a great deal of respect in his own profession, which again is very difficult to fight because you never really get the opportunity to confront your accusers and answer what they are saying about you.'

Justice Einfeld said it had been a devastating blow to Gai that she had had to wait for her licence because of the concept of what her husband might have done.

This in turn had affected Robbie, having to watch his wife wait seemingly endlessly on his account for what was her due.

'It's hard to think of anything that would be a more savage intrusion into your peace and serenity and the happiness of your family than that,' he said.

Next was Keith Moremon, well-known Sydney businessman and former Tattersalls Club chairman, and after him, Roger Nebauer, chairman of stewards of the Harness Racing Authority of New South Wales. They gave strong character evidence. A pile of written references were also placed on record.

Gai was next, the fourth of seven witnesses to be called. She began her evidence in a clear voice, although looking ill at ease.

She said she had been married 12 years, her children were aged eight and 10, Robbie was not just a good husband but an outstanding husband and a very good person in the community. She could trust him impeccably.

After the Fine Cotton affair she had discussed the subject with him and he had assured her he was not involved in the ring-in.

Since then she had also discussed with Robbie the untruths he had told which had brought him before this court. She had formed the view he was extremely remorseful.

'I noticed a great change in people's attitudes to him after the affair became public and allegations were made against him,' she said. 'I experienced tremendous slights and innuendoes. This put enormous pressure on both of us.'

At that point Gai became upset, broke down and cried in the crowded courtroom.

Nobody said anything. The judge, court staff and solicitors all waited patiently. It was a poignant moment, treated with respect as if everyone could understand her feelings.

She took out a handkerchief, dabbed at her eyes, drew in a deep breath and regained her composure.

She went on, 'He has been extremely supportive by marriage, and this has been reciprocated. I received great support from him in my application for a trainer's licence.'

Gai agreed with Robbie's counsel, Mr P Hidden QC, that because of remarks made to her by racing people she often came home quite upset and would sometimes burst into tears.

'And,' she said, 'many times when I was at the races, clients of my father's and supposedly so-called friends would make it extremely difficult and slight me and speak about my husband in front of me, and that has made our life very difficult.

'It's affected both of us, and enormously with Robert because he was so sorry he caused such enormous strain on our relationship and such hardship on us.'

She agreed that in spite of the strain and hardship, the relationship had endured and become even stronger as a result.

Robbie had expressed remorse to her many, many times for lying to the Tribunal. 'He has begged my forgiveness that he has caused such shame on our family,' she said.

She thought he had matured since 1984 and grown from a silly young man to a very mature one. He had realised his mistake and come out of it a much stronger and better person.

After Father Ernest Phibbs, journalist and political consultant Richard Farmer and professional punter Murray Dwyer gave evidence, Robbie was called.

Explaining why he had lied to the stewards, the Committee and the Tribunal, he said Ian Murray had insisted he not reveal that the money Murray bet on Fine Cotton belonged to him (Robbie), because Murray wanted to say the money was his own in order to distance himself from the ring-in.

From that point he felt trapped and on a roller coaster and could not turn back, even after Murray later changed his story which he'd told to the stewards and Committee and then revealed to the Tribunal the money he bet belonged to Robbie and had been bet for a friend of Robbie's.

Robbie agreed he had taken the easy way out to some extent, but said also he had lied to protect others who had put money on the horse for him and did not want to be identified.

He said a total of $60,000 to $65,000 was bet on Fine Cotton, and he stood to win $20,000 or $30,000. Garry Clarke had given him the money to bet on the horse 10 days or so before the race.

In preparing for his fate Robbie had previously sat in Judge Ducker's court to see him in action handing down sentences.

The judge had dealt with two prisoners who could be described as unfortunate persons with long records.

Robbie expected him to jail them both because they appeared to be a threat to the community. But the judge showed great understanding and consideration and did not send them to prison.

At his sentencing Robbie expected no more penalty than having to do community service—Crown officials had indicated this would be the outcome—by virtue of him pleading guilty, his previous good character and his many references and the fact that he had already suffered a great deal.

As soon as the judge began handing down his written

sentence, Robbie knew he'd made a mistake in thinking he was a kindly soul. Sitting next to Gai and hearing a stern judge rip him apart morally was the hardest thing Robbie ever had to do.

In these circumstances, the woman he loved beside him, he felt stripped bare in the court.

After preliminary remarks Judge Ducker quickly came to the nub of things:

> 'In the course of proceedings before the Tribunal the prisoner gave, what he now admits, was deliberately false evidence.
>
> 'He now admits that despite his denials to the Tribunal, he was in fact involved in betting on a horse racing under the name of Fine Cotton. That was a bald lie, and one, I regret to say, that was committed with a great deal of premeditation.'

Judge Ducker said it was not his duty to punish Robbie for the ring-in itself. Indeed, he said, the Crown elsewhere in the proceedings had conceded that it had no evidence to prove any connection between him and the substitution itself.

He accepted that Waterhouse had suffered the ignominy of being warned off all racecourses. That humiliation unjustly, but inevitably, would have rubbed off on members of his family.

> 'So much is obvious here,' said Judge Ducker. 'His wife, who appears to be a greatly respected identity in the racing industry, has been one of the persons who has had to suffer the brunt of many of the unpleasant things that have arisen as a result of this prisoner's behaviour.
>
> 'She said quite frankly that these events had placed a great strain on their relationship.
>
> 'Fortunately, I suspect due in no little measure to her strength in character, the relationship has managed to survive. I do take into account the considerable suffering that he and his family have undergone.

'Of course, the people involved here are more high profile than most, but it is the unhappy fact that in most
criminal matters where some person faces the court, faces
imprisonment, that great tribulation is caused to others as
well.'

He said Waterhouse had also suffered the humiliation of
being unmasked publicly, but he was entitled to credit for having the courage to get into the witness box and publicly confess
to having told lies. That helped to add credence to the evidence
of character witnesses who furnished written testimonials for
him that he was a changed man who had made great attempts to
redeem himself.

The judge said he was satisfied Waterhouse had demonstrated a measure of contrition. His plea of guilty had saved the
State the cost of a lengthy trial and for other persons to give evidence. He had taken this into account in his favour.

But he regarded it as a serious case of false swearing and said
he was satisfied Waterhouse's primary motive for lying was not
to protect others although his self-interest and their interests
were really in common.

*I believe the judge was wrong in forming that view. There is no
doubt Waterhouse at that stage was also trying to protect others who did
not wish to become involved. If he had only self-interest in mind, he
would have owned up to his betting at once, mentioned those who had
bet for him and those who had approached him with the betting commission. But once he had made denials, he was committed to that path.*

*In racing an informer is the lowest form of life. If he had changed
his mind and become an informer, he would have been regarded in racing circles as the lowest individual in the world.*

Judge Ducker said he believed a custodial sentence was necessary. But he was persuaded by the delay in the case, the character evidence and the immense anguish suffered by his family,
to sentence him by way of periodic detention.

He sentenced Robbie to eight months periodic detention, telling him if he felt aggrieved by that he could always dwell on what might have been the most likely alternative.

Gai and members of the Waterhouse family were grim faced and silent as they left the court. It was one of the worst things that had ever happened to either family. An episode on which more insults would be based.

Gai felt to some extent he was being punished for his celebrity status. The legal system saw him as a fortunate and privileged member of the community and it had to be seen that he should be taught a lesson, yet every day blatant lies were told in the courts.

He appealed to the Court of Criminal Appeal on the severity of sentence, but lost that; he sought leave to appeal to the High Court but before that was refused he wanted to get it over with and served his detention, spending weekends at Sydney's Malabar Detention Centre.

The other weekend inmates laughed heartily in disbelief that he was sentenced just for telling lies. They were all there for serious crimes like drug dealing, some with lengthy criminal records.

Gai's last great hurdle was ironically TJ Smith, one of the greatest trainers the world had seen and the reason why she was a horse trainer in the first place.

He'd given her a splendid start with Bounding Away Lodge as her own stables and the inspiration to become a trainer.

But, as well as helping her, he would remain a rival for about the first year after she was licensed.

In the beginning Tommy could not understand why some people preferred Gai to him.

As she began to build up the number of horses in her stables, he would say to her, 'Why do they want to give a horse to you and not to me?'

To others he would remark, 'Why are they giving these horses to Gai? Why not me?'

It was really common sense. Tommy, although slowed down, was still the master trainer with his outstanding record intact.

The business of training horses was expensive and even if there had not been any prejudice against Gai because she was a woman, she was still untried in the eyes of most owners.

The big difference, of course, was that Gai had a completely different approach to owners than Tommy. Once the horses passed through his portals at Tulloch Lodge, you could forget about receiving any information on them.

Gai could hardly wait to pick up the phone and tell owners, even the smallest shareholders, everything about their horses.

In addition, she was more patient than him. If a horse was slow to develop or had a problem, Tommy was likely to get rid of it, whereas she would spend more time to nurture it.

If for example a horse was a barrier rogue, Gai would go to inordinate lengths to train it by putting it into the stalls—a laudable quality, but more expensive.

For some time after Gai obtained her licence, Tommy would want to train all the horses, including hers.

He always kept a couple of his in her stables so he could go and look at them all and the rivalry was intense.

Tommy often used to be first at the track of a morning and when Gai arrived she would find her horses had already been worked or they were already around the track and Tommy had given instructions for them to be worked.

So then she would try to work his horses in reprisal.

They competed to see who could get out on the track first.

Blazing rows ensued out on the track and it appeared to onlookers they almost came to blows at times.

Gai prided herself on being able to get through her work around the stables without swearing, and would not tolerate swearing by anyone in her stables. But when she and Tommy had a row, bystanders said the procreative word flowed freely on both sides.

Tommy simply couldn't help himself or see any difference in which one of them did the training, as long as he did.

When she found he was already working her horses, she always tackled him straight away. At first it would be just a lively discussion.

'Dad,' Gai would say, 'in respect to you I would no more fly than train your horses while waiting for you to come out.'

Tommy would give a curt reply and Gai would say something like, 'How dare you do this to me. What do you think I've had to put up with for the last two and a half years . . .'

Then it would be heated. Tommy even said he would give up training if Gai spoke to him like that again.

At one point Tommy shouted at Gai, 'You stay in your backyard and I'll stay in mine,' and she replied, 'That suits me fine.'

Gai was gradually taking over all the administrative details in the Tulloch Lodge office including her own Bounding Away Lodge work. Basically she still carried out all her Tulloch Lodge foreman's duties for TJ such as doing the nominations and lining up the jockeys for his saddles as well as hers, and increasing her control.

She described him as her most difficult owner.

He had different ideas to her, and as a horseman would always see some things nobody else could. Obviously at times he was right and at others she was right.

But while always listening to his advice Gai was prepared to go it alone and was incredibly determined to establish herself firmly in her own right and for everyone to know that.

Gai knew she could not capitulate to Tommy because if she did she would never be able to stand on her own.

She felt grateful to him and fortunate that he had laid out the blueprint for success and established the structure for a successful stables.

She knew she was fortunate also to have been trained to do things properly. She would not have had the knowledge otherwise, and may never have learned it on her own.

She was lucky to have been born into a household that breathed racing, storing away knowledge that would come to the surface later, lucky to have lived in a racing atmosphere all her life and could see and feel things that were obvious to her while perhaps not to others.

But there were also pitfalls in entering an established stable.

The good part was that Tommy's advice was based on his greater experience over five decades of being a successful trainer.

The negative side was that being the boss's daughter, having been pigeon-holed as just a PR girl, there was a great deal of bias against her within the stable. Nobody wanted to take orders from her. What would she know?

There might have been abundant boxes in the two stables, but to a large extent they were empty. She could not take advantage of the established stables until she overcame the prejudice against her, and then she had to build up the clientele.

Tommy's loyal secretary Pauline Blanche had no objection to Gai taking over the office and operation. She knew it was Gai's heritage, that it was inevitable and she was happy to help Gai do it.

But Pauline had installed the office system about 30 years before and Gai wanted to make sweeping changes. Just as Gai had rights and was fighting for them, Pauline had to fight for hers.

Knowing TJ would be bowing out and she would become responsible to Gai, she was still his secretary looking after his personal and private interests. While helping Gai establish herself, she still met TJ's needs, but after a difficult and tiring adjustment period, it worked well.

Gai had the boxes, the land, the staff, but unless she could attract the owners and buy the horses, she would have nothing.

Hardly anyone wanted to give her a horse to train, except a few close friends and good contacts.

Gai had always been more than a PR girl, but she would have to prove herself every step of the way before she could break out of that mould. Being the daughter of a famous trainer meant nothing unless she demonstrated that she had the innate ability. The failure of some sons of trainers proved that point.

Many people still found cynical humour in the situation that Gai was trying to follow in her father's footsteps. And being a woman added to the fun.

The difficulty she found in trying to persuade people to give her a horse to train proved the prejudice against her.

She was looking to charge people about $20,000 a year to train a horse and nobody would part with their money just because they thought she was a good PR girl. Most people are astute and discerning when asked to part with their money, and racing people are no exception.

Some of the jockeys tried to treat Gai as a joke in the beginning. Normally if they expect to be given race rides they must ride trackwork in the mornings, but Gai could hardly find a jockey who would turn up to offer themselves for trackwork. When they did it was only on fast mornings, Tuesdays and Thursdays.

She took a tough stance with them, insisting that if they didn't ride trackwork they would not be put on hers or Tommy's horses on race days. So she used apprentices in races. It often created a difficult situation but she gradually wore them down, having to win races before they came around to her way of thinking.

Her arguments with TJ were never on the administrative side, only with the horses. And with horses it was always the result that mattered to both of them, not the argument.

It was difficult for him to relinquish the reins, having been the big boss for so long, but some thought he actually did so gradually with a fair amount of grace.

Gai always had to run the gauntlet of his gimlet eye on everything she did. When she bought horses he could be very critical, often finding fault or saying she had paid too much.

Sometimes at a sale Tommy would ask Robbie, 'How much has she spent?' And Robbie would hedge and not say. When he found out at the end of the day he would make some explosive comment.

Gai would always turn the master's grumble aside with a

bright and breezy air, like 'Oh well, Dad, I think they're nice horses and I wouldn't have bought them if I didn't think so.'

She had to constantly prove herself to him, under the microscope on everything she did. But Gai, always wanting to improve herself and put her best foot forward in every way, looked on this as being to her advantage. It meant she was just not allowed to drop the standard of her game, even if inclined to do so, which she wasn't.

She never baulked at having to do an unpleasant job in the stable and would not ask anyone at the stables to do anything she wasn't prepared to do herself.

Even those who knew her well for some reason found it remarkable that there was nothing of the snob about Gai in the slightest way.

Perhaps because she looked so glamorous and feminine and was educated, displaying flair and style, they expected her to show airs and graces while working with horses, but that never had any part in Gai's persona.

She was practical and pragmatic, qualities she needed to face up to the resentment in the industry from men who couldn't accept that she could succeed, either because she was a woman, a Smith or a Waterhouse.

Trainers still laughed at her and she knew they were joking about her as she walked on or off the track. She heard them sniggering after she passed by. It only made her more determined to do well.

They thought Tommy was bullshitting too as the indulgent father bowing out with stars in his eyes for his daughter, when he proudly declared to anyone who cared to listen that she had 'the eye' for it.

But he knew better.

CHAPTER TWENTY-TWO

THE EYE HAS IT

When Gai first started buying horses on her own, the famous vet Percy Sykes thought her eye was 'terrible'.

But, he noted, she was a quick learner.

By the time she was moving to take over Tulloch Lodge and forced to buy horses that could run or else face failure as a trainer, she could simply look at a horse in the chancy sales ring and tell at a glance if it could gallop.

Having a good eye is winning half the battle. It enables a trainer to walk into the stable and see things immediately, to know at a glance when the horse is trotted out if it has a problem, whether it is relishing its work or needs more work to reach fitness.

Gai is the first to admit her eye is not infallible but her ability to simply look at an animal and perceive its qualities and faults can probably be likened roughly to the judgment of a lusty young man who looks at a pretty girl in an attempt to assess her sexual appeal at a glance.

I remember having this demonstrated to me once by a licentious Athens taxi driver in what was probably the ultimate sexual stereotype assumption.

Pushing his way vigorously through the city's congested streets, he worried me a little because he kept leering lasciviously at almost every passing woman on both sides of the street, even back over his shoulder at times, paying little attention to the traffic.

A glimpse of the Parthenon on the Acropolis high above the city from one of the cab's back windows was not enough to soothe my nerves.

With a view to coaxing him to cast his eyes on the road ahead instead of the curves at the side I said to him, 'Are you looking for somebody?'

'No. You've read Henry Miller?'

'The bohemian American novelist?'

'Yes.'

'Yes, I have.'

'Henry Miller said you can always tell a woman by the movement of her arse. I think he was right.'

If this keen but chauvinistic physiological researcher from Plato's old town was correct in his judgment of kerbside kinetics and their relationship to heavenly bodies, then it must also be possible to look at a horse and divine how it might be able to perform.

Gai certainly had developed a talent for picking a good horse and making it fit.

Picking horses is very much a business of managing to miss out on buying the bad ones and obtaining the good ones. A trainer who can exclude the horses with adverse qualities is a long way along the track in buying the good ones.

The trainer who can buy a sound athletic looking individual has a good chance of developing a racehorse that can gallop.

Buyers of yearlings largely fall into two categories: Those who are adept at spotting athletic types but are not aware of the potential problems; and the others who, like vets, are sharp at spotting problems but can't see the good qualities.

Gai, like her father, is aware of both sides.

Gai knows from experience that when you have a horse with some sort of problem, like a weakened or malformed sesamoid, you begin to hate it when seeing the horse every day and you try to avoid that problem in the future. It costs money and you upset your clients and yourself.

She is aware that the ability to buy horses is one of the

factors which distinguishes successful from unsuccessful trainers.

It is like a football team—no amount of effort can make them into a top side unless the players have ability.

Women, because of the prejudice against them, have difficulty in convincing men to buy horses from them. When a woman trainer asks someone to spend $50,000 or $100,000 on a horse, she is really saying I'm a very smart person with horses and if you pay this money and follow my advice, you'll do well.

At the time Gai began making her run it was a hard thing for men to accept that a woman can be so skilled at this mysterious art that she can return value for money.

But unless Gai had been able to convince men to buy her horses, she would have remained with a string of only three or four. In fact, that is one of the areas in which Gai has shone.

The first thing noticeable about Gai when she attended the sales was that she did what very few others did—she literally looked at every lot beforehand. She wanted to be prepared in case someone asked her about any horse.

It might well be that the last horse she saw was an outstanding athlete and nobody else would have seen it. After studying them all she was in a position to tell a potential owner, 'Look, this horse is one I really want to train. I've looked at them all and picked out this one. If you want a good horse, this is the one to buy.'

It took a lot of time and effort but it was just part of Gai's methodical and professional approach. She also visited studs to inspect horses and probably saw 150 horses there before they went to the sales, flying and driving to the studs and fitting the time into her busy schedule in what was always a nightmare to arrange.

To save time she sometimes flew to the studs by helicopter, providing her only rest from the telephone.

She filled the void on board by catching up on paper work. In a year she would inspect about 3,000 horses.

Where most other trainers merely went through the motions, Gai put in the hours and the detailed work.

At sales the most that can be looked at are about 20 lots an hour. That alone meant 25 hours work at a normal sale of 500 lots.

Not even Tommy did that in his heyday.

He would go through the catalogue and look only at selected drafts. On the Australian thoroughbred sales scene, not more than three or four other people have looked at every horse.

Among others who did so was a vet, Ross Teitzel, who made comments for various clients, trainer Kevin Connolly who operated for Chinese buyers, and Richard Galpin, a British bloodstock agent.

In the obscure and somewhat esoteric world of bloodstock sales, there is not a great depth of expert opinion available, in spite of what the connoisseurs would have you believe.

Any eavesdropper at the sales is apt to hear trainers say, 'I'm good in looking at older horses but gee, it's hard to tell how a yearling will turn out.'

These people do not have trained eyes. Gai was trained in all aspects of yearling spotting. She believes it is a gift as in the case of Tommy, but she also believes it can be developed. To the extent it was born in Gai, her gift was fostered and encouraged by Tommy over many years at sales in Australia, New Zealand, America, England and Ireland.

When Gai looks at a yearling, she does exactly what the great Irish trainer Vincent O'Brien did—in her mind's eye she envisages how it will look as a fully mature animal. How will it look in one, two or three years' time?

Before going to a sale Gai has a sales book or yearling catalogue rebound with blank pages inserted. She uses these pages for making copious notes on her observations.

The note might simply read, 'Strong colt. Great shoulder.' And she also writes down what the stock sold for in the past few years to give her an idea of the previous prices.

Nobody else in Australasia goes to sales as well prepared and backgrounded as Gai.

If she likes a horse but is concerned over a potential problem and whether it will stand up to racing, she always asks the vets for their input, but in nearly every case her purchase is based entirely on her own opinion.

As Tommy wound down, he and Gai actually competed sometimes for the same horses. She bought her own and only when he said to her I like this horse and think you should buy it, would she accept his opinion and do so.

In her buying Gai follows the technique established by her father, who in his career picked out not one but two champions from the ring of hope and glorious uncertainty, Tulloch and Kingston Town.

She, too, is looking for a steal out of the sale ring, a horse that will develop with work, one that will extend but still be quite tight, not one that will become top heavy and be too hard to train—hence, the picture in her mind of its future shape.

Among the first qualities she looks for is a loose horse, one that is free and relaxed in his movements when he walks.

From this she can tell if he will grow into his frame. She likes an animal with an intelligent eye because it denotes the horse's intelligence. She dislikes a horse with small ears and those 'piggy' eyes Tommy had always been so much against.

The prejudice against horses with piggy eyes goes back to the days of Tommy's father when running his horse teams out on the black soil plains of south-western New South Wales, transporting wool and timber. Neil Smith would never buy a draught horse with a pig-eye, believing it showed dishonesty in an animal.

Tommy was convinced this truism ran to racehorses too, and Gai has had enough experience to go along with the idea that a horse's intelligence, alertness and will to win can be detected in the eyes.

Gai likes a horse with a good square jaw when viewed head on, a nice length of rein, she loves and demands a good shoulder and girth where all the 'apparatus' is housed, and insists on what she terms a good hind leg and hind quarters. A well proportioned head is a must.

In assessing breathing capacity she doesn't go to the bizarre lengths of TJ in surprising the poor animal by sudden movement in a 'grunting' test. She lets her eyes do the work here, a square-jaw indicating good eating capacity and room to breathe freely.

She doesn't worry too much about breeding, although keeping in mind bloodlines that have been successful or not.

Her main requirements are all incorporated in the build of a horse, which means it has to be proportioned well from head to hoof, to indicate good balance.

Often she can gauge if a horse is smart or not by the way it looks around and shows awareness of what is happening.

Gai looks for a good walk but as Tommy always said, you're not buying a horse for a walking race. But it gives an indication of what the horse's gait might be.

She can assess these co-ordinated qualities just by looking.

Few people can. She isn't sure if she was born with this natural horseman's gift or not, but she knows she has developed an 'eye' with her father's help over the years.

Her cleverness with her eyes extends to spotting quickly if a horse is not quite right. She can pick out faults and treat symptoms before they became problems, sometimes when Tommy could not do so.

Tommy was prepared to pay for her horses up to a point. He would sign the cheques and carry her until she sold the horses, but it meant she had limited time and had to move the horses quickly.

Her unusual step of advertising, although causing unfavourable comments, helped recruit owners. What else could she do? She was not backed by any major stud, syndicate, major owners or groups of wealthy people and had to go out and catch her own.

Her selection of yearlings had to be good because she could afford only the cheaper animals. Occasionally she would lash out and buy the more expensive horses, but mostly she was restricted to those in the $20,000–$30,000 price range.

On that basis she was competing at a disadvantage with people like the Inghams, Jack and Bob, whose average yearling purchase was in the range of $150,000 or more. They could afford the most expensive horses, the best brood mares and stallions.

And they had several times more horses in work at their Crown Lodge stables, able to draw on more runners interstate.

In effect, she was competing with Holden handbills against Maserati money.

It meant that the big owners and trainers outgunned her in quality and quantity. Her methods and fine tuning had to be excellent to compete.

Like an artist painting a picture, she made up the difference with meticulous attention to fine detail.

The first factor was her ability to buy good athletic horses that came through later as winners.

Next, she insisted on her horses being broken in and educated by professional, efficient breakers. Some trainers do not understand that rough and ready breakers can ruin a horse for life.

The third factor was she made sure her horses had the best possible feed, the highest quality oats, corn and other feed.

Where some might give their horses one and a half dippers, Gai gave them up to three. They were the most expensively-fed horses in racing. Even when her horses went for a spell, she saw to it that they had the best quality.

Gai is such a person that when some of her horses were staying in rented boxes in Melbourne, she noticed that the horses nearby were being given inferior feed. Although they were racing against hers, she gave them extra feed from her own bins.

In the old days the good trainers bedded their horses down on straw to make sure they had a nice soft bed and slept well. But it became so expensive that hardly any trainers do it any more, using instead sawdust, sand or even newspaper shavings.

However, Gai insists on straw. The difference is that in most other stables the horses stand while sleeping. In Bounding Away and Tulloch Lodge they lie down when sleeping, ensuring a good rest.

Another difference and a key factor in Gai's training methods is that she strongly believes in walking her horses.

The story goes in racing folklore that Bayley Payten, the leading Randwick trainer of the 1940s, used to train near William Inglis's saleyards and complained that to work his horses he had to walk them a long way to the racecourse and back again.

That's when he was successful. When he became richer he bought stables right at the course, no longer walked his horses and soon deteriorated as a trainer.

Gai walks her horses for three quarters of an hour every morning and afternoon to limber them up before and after track-work. Like an athlete limbering up it enables her horses to stretch out in trackwork and gives her a low breakdown rate.

But it has been expensive, adding about $10 a day to the fees for each horse, and requiring a big staff. Because she does not penny pinch in any way, Gai has had to win numerous races to run a profitable stable.

If Tommy taught Gai one thing well it was that she must run her stable as a tight ship, leaving nothing to chance.

In her first year as a trainer she took a five-day holiday when she would have liked to have gone away for two weeks. One of her owners said to her, 'Gai, you have a good staff, why didn't you go away for a longer break?'

'Yes, I know I have a good staff,' she said. 'But the reason they are good is because I am constantly pushing them and asking them to do this and that and making them perform as I expect myself to perform and my horses to perform.'

Gai has strict views on the running of her stable which some people might consider come under the heading of idiosyncratic. But they are her rules and they have to be followed.

Smoking and swearing in the stables are out. So is long hair. No male strappers are allowed on the premises if wearing earrings.

'Either take it off or leave now,' she tells transgressors.

It doesn't matter that some young males consider it

fashionable to wear earrings. She doesn't think it appropriate in the stables and that's that.

Also, they are not allowed to listen to the radio while mucking out the boxes and doing other menial work. To anyone who complains, Gai says, 'You're here to work, not listen to the radio.'

These things haven't mattered much in days gone by at Tulloch Lodge (except the long hair), but Gai is fastidious in the way she wants things run.

A strict disciplinarian, she has a more hands-on approach than Tommy ever had but gives 100 per cent of herself in every way.

Quick to anger, she does not hesitate to tear strips off employees for doing the wrong thing, but she doesn't hold grudges and is quick to recover from any outburst. She never fails to tick somebody off if they let her down but moves quickly on to the next item.

She doesn't shrink from confrontation, whereas Tommy would try to avoid it. There is nothing furtive about the way Gai operates. She tells 'em straight, on the spot.

To offending workers who deserve it she is likely to say, 'If you think I'm going to put up with fools like you, you've got another think coming. Go and tell them to make up your pay.'

When industrial relations legislation made it difficult to fire people on the spot, Gai began handing out warnings in writing, along the lines of, 'Dear Ezra, this is your first warning . . .'

Some employees were lucky if they didn't receive one or two warnings a month. Gai handed them out fairly freely. But if a fired person apologised and asked to be taken back, she always gave them another chance.

In one example Gai gave a former employee a job telling him he must turn up every morning. One morning he didn't and she said to him, 'This is no good. If you don't turn up we have to get someone else to handle your three horses. It's a real headache. We're paying you to be permanent and if you're not coming in you must ring up early and tell us.'

A short time later he didn't arrive and didn't ring, but turned up the following day with a doctor's certificate. A few days later he did the same thing and came next day with a certificate. 'Are you sure you're not sleeping with this doctor?' she asked.

Some time later at the morning trackwork she saw this person push his girlfriend from a horse galloping around the track and over the inside running rail. She stormed across and said, 'You're fired. I never want to see you again.'

He took her to the Anti-Discrimination Board, alleging among other things that she had accused him of sleeping with a doctor, who happened to be male. Her solicitors wanted her to compromise but she refused. The matter later lapsed.

Gai showed she was not frightened to take on any situation. But her staff soon respected her for her no-nonsense approach and for her willingness to do any job herself.

If a strapper doesn't know what to do in any area or isn't doing a task properly, Gai will pitch in and show him. She knows exactly what has to be done and is prepared to demonstrate.

A strapper was making heavy weather of cleaning a stallion's sheath one day and Gai took control. Horses have a sheath around their penises and each week it has to be cleaned with a cloth and soapy water.

'Here,' said Gai, grabbing hold of the sheath, 'let me show you.'

Still wearing her expensive diamond engagement ring, she reached in and gave it a good wash.

It is not known how the horse reacted with a valuable diamond ring whisking around his penis but the anecdote shows Gai's direct approach and how she is prepared to lead by example.

Many women would be too embarrassed to show a male strapper what to do in those circumstances, especially as the stallion is likely to get a monstrous hard-on.

That night Gai noticed that her diamond ring was discoloured and needed a good, if delicate, cleaning.

The touch of glamour the new-broom trainer brought to

racing was proving to be a bonus for her. The dash of colour to
leaven the hard work and dedication she was putting into her
operation was beginning to attract people.

Gai had the eye, the training method, the stables and the
financial backup, and she was beginning to draw new owners
and make headway with her horses.

But many still could or would not accept her as a trainer.

The attitude was best exemplified by a wealthy owner who
admired a horse Gai had bought at the sales.

'I'll buy that from you, Gai,' he said.

'Well, you can buy it on the understanding I train the horse.'

'That's fine,' he said.

A few months went by and Gai said to the owner, 'This horse
is outstanding.'

'Outstanding, eh? You think it's outstanding?'

'Definitely,' said Gai.

Almost immediately the owner switched the horse to
another trainer. She was bitterly disappointed but could do
nothing but accept the situation. Unfortunately for the owner,
the horse broke down under the new trainer and its racing days
were over.

If Gai had retained the horse, with her patience and understanding, it would almost certainly have gone on to win races.

People like that who entertained negative thoughts about
Gai would soon be forced to eat their words in big, indigestible
chunks.

CHAPTER TWENTY-THREE

THE
BREAKTHROUGH

Group One races are the Everest of the thoroughbred racing industry, the ones trainers dream of winning.

They are the Big Ones with huge prizemoney which allow stables to get out of the red, they establish reputations, set standards, bring out the champion horses, excite the punters, fire the imagination and ambitions of wealthy owners and wasting jockeys and create the excellence for which thousands of people strive in the industry.

Some established trainers never win a Group One event, others win only one or two in their entire careers. Many of the best jockeys fare poorly in this field.

Group One races cannot be won unless horse and rider are as perfect as possible.

Competition is so fierce that victory is impossible at this level if a horse has had any setback in its preparation. Peak fitness on the day is paramount.

Gai Waterhouse knew this well, fortunate to have seen Group One races around the world in her actress days and studied her father prepare his record number of big winners.

The Group system to stratify racing was adopted around the world after the English Jockey Club introduced it in the mid-1970s. Robert Sangster was one of the movers and shakers behind it and it was no accident his bloodstock interests benefited from the better prizemoney.

Broadly, under the stratified system there are restricted races for horses that have never won a race or a set number of races, then handicaps for horses that have won any number of races but are weighted right out once they have won two handicaps.

Then come the more valuable listed races, winners and placegetters of which are entitled to have their names recorded in light black type in the sales catalogues.

Above these are the Group Three, Two and One races, whose winners have their names listed in thick black type in sales catalogues.

Australia has about 60 races a year in each of the three Groups, and about 180 listed races. Prizemoney in each Group One race like the Melbourne Cup, Derbies, Doncaster and Golden Slipper is worth $2 million.

Six weeks after obtaining her licence Gai was 'lucky enough' to have promising New Zealand stayer Te Akau Nick arrive in her Bounding Away stable to train.

But luck had nothing to do with it as David Ellis, Kiwi businessman and managing partner of the syndicate that owned the horse, explained.

Ellis bought Te Akau Nick for $NZ40,000 at the Magic Millions sale at Trentham in 1990. He thought Nick would make a genuine racehorse and syndicated him to 20 people from New Zealand, Hong Kong and Japan.

By Grosvenor, the classic winning son of champion sire Sir Tristram, out of Antoinette, he was a typical big strong New Zealander who in racing parlance was expected, like an uninvited relative, to 'stay all day'.

The name Te Akau in the Maori language means 'success.'

The horse hadn't set the world on fire with three wins and two places from eight starts. But he finished third in the New Zealand Derby in 1991 behind Cavallieri and Veandercross, the best of their age in that country. It convinced his owners he'd have a future in Australia.

David Ellis was a Smith stable client and when he mentioned his plans, naturally Tommy put in a bid for Gai to be the trainer. Ellis took little persuading. He'd known Gai for some years, was impressed by her horsemanship and admired her as a communicator.

Gai set the bay gelding for the AJC Derby. He was responding well to her methods when back problems halted his preparation and he had to be spelled.

On his return in late August of 1992 Gai set to work again, this time planning to run him in the Metropolitan Handicap in October.

Te Akau Nick was the best horse she had trained and she decided to fine-tune her technique with him. As he improved, so did Gai.

TJ had taught her that a horse must be rock-hard fit on the day. She planned his program so he would be at his best for the big race in early October.

At his first start a young apprentice rode him but the horse was so powerful he needed a stronger rider so Gai engaged Mick 'The Enforcer' Dittman for his Sydney campaign, including two leadup races to prime him for the Metropolitan.

It was her first test in preparing a stayer for a particular event.

She knew she had to be extremely observant to gauge when Te Akau Nick needed more work and when she should slacken off.

Without enough work Te Akau Nick, like any other horse, could become gross and physically go out of control. With too much work, he would taper off early.

She was dealing with a living, moving animal and had to react sensitively to his development if she was to learn the finer points of conditioning, knowing exactly when to strike the right balance.

She closely watched Nick trot, walk and gallop, trying to 'talk' to him through the way he responded.

As with her other horses, she always chatted to the jockey after he worked the horse, trying to pick up a snippet of information which might help her put the puzzle together.

Gai believed there had to be an affinity between trainer and animal. She went into their boxes and developed a rapport. Horses like Silver Flyer recognised her voice and pricked their ears when she came near them. She had a similar affinity with Te Akau Nick.

She handled Nick and other horses but didn't physically strap or dress them in their boxes. If necessary she didn't mind showing a strapper how a horse should be dressed, but if it was a big strong stallion she might ask someone to hold him because she was not a strong person physically.

Gai saw herself as a trainer first, and a teacher of thoroughbreds second. She loved seeing the horses respond to her exercises and gradually improve.

To her the work was not monotonous in the slightest. She gained enormous enjoyment from it, obsessed with every detail, no matter how small.

Unlike most other trainers, she regularly communicated her feelings to trackmen—'Isn't Nick enjoying his work? He's improved since last week.'

She did the same to her staff and the owners of other horses she trained, constantly saying out aloud what she saw on the track and what she thought about the horses. Gradually she generated an air of enthusiasm around her.

Gai was absolutely explicit with her jockeys on what she expected of them in trackwork. It was not a case of telling Te Akau Nick's rider 'Oh, let him go 15 to the furlong' as many trainers did with their track riders.

It was clear and definite: 'I want you as soon as you get on the track to go at three-quarter pace over a good mile and a quarter, and I want you to start working him on the way home doing your best on the post.'

In the yard she was a perfectionist, perhaps picking up a horse's hoof to make sure the staff had tarred underneath.

Every day she walked twice around the yards at Bounding Away and Tulloch Lodge, asking herself questions about the various horses, checking whether something was done or if she should have a second look at a horse.

Dressed in her best, most expensive Gucci suit, Gai felt a surge of excitement as Te Akau Nick and the 14 other runners were led around the saddling enclosure at Randwick on Monday, 5 October, for the running of the Metropolitan Handicap.

She had a gut feeling she might win. Nick was at his peak.

Many others also thought the horse had a good chance. Trackmen had observed his gallops and the word was out around the traps that Te Akau Nick was the horse to beat.

That information on the grapevine didn't bother Gai. She wasn't a punter except to have a small interest. All she was concerned with was achieving the best for her owners, their horses and herself.

'Just keep him close to the pace,' was all Gai said to jockey Dittman as she legged him up.

Punters had backed the horse heavily from the time betting opened and when they trotted out on to the track he was 2-1 favourite. Doubles bookies faced huge payouts if he won.

This was Gai's chance to prove she could train, to show them how rotten they'd been to her.

Leaving the saddling enclosure to go into the members' stand, she heard a familiar voice in the crowd call out 'Gai, Gai.'

She went across and leaned over the fence to where the Bag Lady was standing at her usual spot on concrete steps near the enclosure, her worldly possessions in plastic bags beside her.

The Bag Lady had seen better days, but she was one of the less privileged folk who enjoyed a day at the races seeing the big punters put their money on with the Rails bookies, and catching a glimpse of the celebrities in the hope some might speak to her. Mostly they didn't.

But Gai always had a smile and a few friendly words for her. 'Te Akau Nick is a good two dollar bet today,' she said.

'Thank you, dear,' she responded.

A few minutes later the starter's gates flew open and they were off on the 2600 metre journey.

Sir Winston set the pace and led right from the barrier and Te Akau Nick trailed him into the straight where he tackled the leader to fight out an epic finish.

Dittman, who had wasted to make the weight, suffered stomach cramps in the tough finish as he drove his mount on under the whip. Rival jockey Kevin Moses received welts on his arms and shoulder after getting in the way of 'The Enforcer's' flailing whip.

Nick outstayed Sir Winston in the torrid struggle to win by three quarters of a length. Beachside, trained by Tommy Smith, was third. Gai's smiles just about lit up the stand as a buzz went through the crowd acknowledging her victory.

Winning a big race. She had never felt anything like it before. The way the adrenalin pumped through her was fantastic.

After just nine months as a trainer she had won her first Group One, becoming the first woman to train a Metropolitan winner.

As racegoers shook her hands, kissed and hugged her offering their congratulations, all Gai could think of was now I can attract those owners, now I can sell my horses.

From the attitude of well-wishers she could tell her battle with the AJC was on everyone's lips or in their minds. She'd shown the AJC up as fools for keeping her out for so long.

She'd signalled to the racing public, the punters, owners and breeders that she was a force to be reckoned with, that she had the patience and skill to train a stayer and was someone who could remain at Group One level.

Gai Waterhouse had arrived.

She felt certain this would be her most satisfying win ever.

At the presentation ceremony AJC committeemen, the men who had rejected her, clustered around to congratulate her and she became highly emotional.

As she went to the microphone she looked up at the smiling

faces, thrilled to the applause and the crowd's happy mood and thought fleetingly of London.

'This is what I wanted in the theatre, but I never had a starring role,' she told herself.

Not knowing what she was saying and without a trace of rancour, she reminded them of her struggle with officialdom by paying a tribute to her family.

'I couldn't have done it if it wasn't for my husband, Robbie and the children,' she said, without preamble.

'At times I was disillusioned but Rob, my son Tom and daughter Kate kept saying don't give up. Had they said "it's not worth it", I probably would have quit.'

She politely thanked the AJC committee for granting her licence.

Gai couldn't hold back the tears of joy and Tommy was misty eyed too, happier for her than if his own horse had won.

He knew the effort it had taken and what it meant to her future. In his time he'd won seven Metrops with Redcraze, Wiedersehen, Oncidon, Analie, Passatreul, Bon Teint and Sir Serene.

At that moment 'Svengali' Robbie was sitting at home listening on the radio, wishing he was there to share it with her.

Gai already had Te Akau Nick booked on a flight that afternoon to fly south for the Melbourne Cup.

The newspapers all picked up on her AJC battle, treating readers to a re-run of it under the headings 'Gai's Triumph' and 'Gai's Joy'.

Hundreds of faxes and letters poured in from ordinary people who admired her for beating the AJC and proving her merit.

A few days later she celebrated by spending her hard-earned percentage on replacing her Holden with a new BMW wagon, which became her new mobile office, complete with an array of hats, caps and clothes items to meet weather changes.

Nick, not a natural mud runner, didn't shine in the heavy going for the rain-affected Cup, but he would be back another day.

The win gave her enormous confidence and set her on the path to building up her business and winning more feature races.

Suddenly more people began to take her seriously, making it a little easier for her to find clients for the horses she was buying.

But there was still a vast sea of prejudice against her. She felt it so strongly she persuaded Tommy to retain one-sixth ownership of the horses she bought and sold to prevent the owners taking them away from her and giving them to other trainers.

Some people talked about her as being 'too pushy', without realising the battle she had to compete with men on their terms. If she was a man, most people would have regarded her as forthright and dynamic, with leadership qualities.

Soon afterwards, at the end of her first year, she applied to the AJC for a number one trainer's licence.

She had to go before the committee to justify her application. One of the committeemen asked, 'Why do you think you're worthy of a number one? You've only been training a year.'

Gai replied, 'The reason is I've already trained my first Group One winner, Te Akau Nick, and I'm sixth on the trainers' premiership, although I only have a handful of horses.

'I have also trained a listed winner, Moods, in the Gosford Gold Cup, and most importantly I have brought more people into racing than all six of the leading trainers at Randwick. On those grounds alone I think I should be granted a number one licence.

'And I also think it's a very important thing from a prestige point of view that owners realise their trainer has a number one licence.'

With that, John Schreck, the Chief Steward, leaned forward and in what could only have been an attempt to put her down said, 'But you have only been training for five minutes.'

Gai was equal to the occasion. 'I don't care if I've been training for 55 years,' she said, 'it's what I've done in the time that matters.'

Tony Allport, a solicitor on the committee, still had a reservation.

'What happens,' he asked, 'if I go to the races and one of the members says to me, you fool for giving her that licence?'

She gave that one short shrift, too, 'I'll tell you what to say, Mr Allport. You say, mind your own business, we are the committee, we know what we're doing and we don't need to be told by you.'

He accepted that and she was granted her number one licence.

In Gai's first year if punters had put one dollar on every horse started by every other trainer in Sydney, they would have lost.

They would lose every year. The reason is there are so many outsiders with little chance of winning that the races are mostly won by favourites at short prices.

But if a punter had put one dollar on every one of Gai's runners in that first year, they would have been $21 in front. If they had invested $100, they would have been $8,000 to the good.

Those figures, assessed by a keen punter, were based on Gai's strike rate, a rate that would continue to be excellent.

In her first year, a short one, she finished seventh in the Sydney trainers' premiership but third in the prizemoney stakes.

Just as Gai was beginning to make an impact on racing through new promotional and communication methods, she also made her presence felt in the way the Tulloch Lodge stables operated.

Training conditions varied greatly in the industry. Some trainers operated from open yards with limited resources. In the old days TJ had set the pattern in running a large horse factory and had the field almost to himself. But now there was real competition to anyone with a big stable operation.

In some ways, it is a crazy business. In racing as in any business that is glamorous, where clients are offered similar services in a competitive atmosphere, it is hard to make money.

After the struggle to be licensed, Gai had the job of operating a business made doubly difficult because she had to build it up first. It was a costly exercise, especially as she would not compromise on quality.

To be successful she had to be a businesswoman as well as a good trainer of horses, a communicator, marketer, publicist and probably a few other things as well.

Business trends had changed and so had racing. The single owner was no longer the backstop of a stable. Increasingly now stables were based on syndicates of owners.

Suddenly it was tough for the battling trainer to succeed. No longer could he still do it merely by training a horse in the mornings and saddling it at the races.

Society had changed and Gai was smart enough to know that to bring new people in she needed to establish a relationship with them, to talk about business, travel, general affairs, to be regarded as a worldly business partner and not just a trainer of horses.

With good communications in mind and to sound more approachable, she had asked the AJC soon after receiving her licence if she could go in the racebooks as Gai Waterhouse instead of GM Waterhouse. A minor point, but typical of her meticulous methods. She wanted everyone to call her Gai.

As a PR person in the stable she had always spent time putting out brushfires among the staff or with complaining owners. She could be diplomatic but was usually firm and direct.

Some men of long experience in the racing game found it hard to take instructions from a woman, but with her they would just have to get used to it.

Gai didn't mess around and always came to the point. An onlooker might wince slightly on hearing her say to an owner, 'Surely you're not going to let Shane Dye sit in the grandstand while you put a second class jockey on your horse, are you?'

She was going through an acceptance period, and winning.

The famous Tulloch Lodge sign, which had been taken down when the stable was leased to the public company, went up again.

A new plaque out the front in Bowral Street read 'Gai Waterhouse and TJ Smith'.

Tommy remained managing director of the company that owned the two stables, but Gai was now running the operations. Soon they would buy the stables two doors away owned by Peter Myers and add them to their complex.

Gai went right through the office at Tulloch Lodge, which was the administrative side of Bounding Away Lodge as well. She did not consider the computer system good enough and upgraded it, obtaining new machines, copiers and so on.

More office staff were employed to do the computer work and accounts and prepare regular reports for owners and do the other extra administrative work that Gai introduced. Some of the manual methods begun by Pauline 30 years before were retained as an alternative.

Gai quickly proved herself a good administrator, conscious of all facets of the business, including the financial side.

She made technology work for her in every way including faxes, mobiles and pagers. She lived on her mobile, writing in her diary while driving, talking to whoever was in her car at the same time. Not a second was wasted.

As soon as the office received the various fields, they were faxed to every owner who had a horse racing. With races at provincial centres and in the city and with up to six owners for each horse, this created a great deal of work. Her personal secretary Jane Abercrombie and other office staff were kept on their toes.

Gai had her staff turn out colourful glossy brochures in her quest to find new owners and syndicate her horses. These carried the message 'words cannot describe the thrill of winning' and offered the tempting prospect 'let me put you in the winner's circle'.

They also produced regular newsletters for the industry.

Gai hauled a secretary off to the track at dawn once a week to take notes on performances and faxed these to owners in 'Track Flash'.

She also innovated a system of faxes to newspapers and racing writers outlining her runners and their prospects. It let everyone know she meant business.

In writing to her cross-section of owners, she related well to each person, showing a good sense of humour with an old-fashioned quote here, a joke there, a more formal attitude with others. The spelling, though, wasn't always perfect.

The stables were made more attractive.

She looked at the old benches in Tulloch Lodge where racing identities had sat over the years and said, 'Out they go. New ones.'

She thought the hanging baskets looked grotty and replaced them with serviced flowers and plants once a month.

Gai couldn't stand gazing at anything in the office that looked seedy or worn. Chairs were refurbished. Everything had to be as fresh and attractive as possible.

Although she could be abrasive, staff regarded her as being fair dinkum in her dealings and considerate.

The birthdays of lads in the stables were remembered, various kindnesses were observed in a natural and uncalculating way, like financially helping an employee with dental problems.

If owners wanted something done and it was reasonable, Gai always tried to oblige. Close observers said it wasn't because she was young and fresh and wanted to be liked and acknowledged that she tried to accommodate people. It was the way she wanted to run her business.

In the same way her facility for associating easily with people was not contrived but sprang naturally from within her. When she talked to anyone she showed genuine interest. If strappers had something to say, they had her attention.

One of the great skills she brought to racing was the refreshing habit of communicating quickly with owners, especially if their horses had a problem.

Injuries or worries could develop quickly and the last thing she wanted was her owners hearing about it from someone else.

Nothing was seen through rose-coloured glasses and everything she did was based on common sense and experience.

Gai was so honest and fair minded towards her owners that some of the things she did were unheard of in racing.

For instance, if a horse could not be worked for some reason at the track, she reduced the fees by half for the days involved. Yet it still cost as much to walk the horse and have the box mucked out.

No other trainer did that. The concession was great for the owners but not for the economic running of her stable.

Above all, Gai wanted her owners to enjoy their racing. No carnival-day girl only with delusions of grandeur about the sport of kings, she was passionate about it the whole time.

She was practical and patient, believing in maximising the most number of wins for her owners. As a result she took her horses through the classes and soon demonstrated she was skilled at placing them in the right races.

Tommy would put a good horse straight into an open company race, believing it was better to run his horses in the city. But Gai was more orthodox. Conscious of the needs of her owners, she looked for the best prizemoney for them.

Gai was likely to place a horse in a maiden at a provincial race, win that and perhaps run it in the country again before taking it to the city as a restricted horse.

Racegoers in the bush came to adore her because she took her horses to their cup meetings. Among her early country wins was the Queanbeyan Cup, Tamworth Cup and Wellington Boot.

By operating this way it showed that Gai didn't have any tickets on herself as a big-time trainer and was prepared to work hard at being successful, progressing through country meetings as well.

She had set out to make it on the force of her own character, effort and personality.

But she would need to win more Group One races to stay on the right side of the ledger.

CHAPTER TWENTY-FOUR

THOSE HATS, THAT GEAR

P ulp fiction writers would probably call it a vivid red slash.

The lipstick rimming the perpetual smile. That and the Audrey Hepburn scarf wrapped around her head were as near a trademark as anything else about the lady.

And the nearest thing to making a fashion statement. The rest was just fun, expressing how she felt at the time.

As for the smile, well, anyone with a perpetual grin like that certainly couldn't run a mortuary chapel—the customers couldn't take it.

Just as well she found herself in the theatre business after all, out there at the track parading and performing, dancing, waving, chatting, cheering, dressing up to look pretty.

The lipstick came in various shades of rich red. And always the same brand, Yves St Laurent. Lipstick, she once said, was the most important thing in her life. Well . . .

'I couldn't train racehorses without it,' she declared on another occasion, showing a penchant for bright phrases as well as bright lips.

It was nonetheless an essential part of her lifestyle, if not of her actual credo. When she walked into Tulloch Lodge at 4 am six days a week while the rest of the city slept, the lipstick was in place, retouched often during the day from an array of lipsticks in her handbag.

Later in the morning when she returned to the stables after going home for breakfast, to work the phones and take a brief nap, her face of faultless porcelain would be fully made up and remain like that all day.

She had the knack of looking glamorous by putting on her face in literally under five minutes with a flick of the powder puff and a quick touch up here and there.

Gai's business was horses but she was at her office like any other business person and wanted to look bright and attractive.

She had as many lipsticks as hats, and that was considerable. A charity group exhibiting hats on the Gold Coast asked her to help out and she loaned them 36, with still more in reserve.

Gai loved dressing up just as much as in the fanciful moments of her childhood, but now her attire was a constant source of comment, ranging from awful to elegant. One critical observer went on record saying she attended the races with glasses by Dame Edna, clothes by St Vinnies and shoes by Imelda Marcos.

None of that worried Gai in the slightest. Although, she did feel a little annoyed at times when reporters rang her at home to ask what hat or outfit she would be wearing.

She wanted to be taken seriously as a trainer and would rather they asked about her horses. She was a trainer first and a woman second. It smacked still of the old stereotype that as a woman she could not be regarded seriously around horses.

When journalists continued to write about her appearance, her hats and suits, it signalled to her that they were still having trouble coming to grips with the fact that she was a trainer, not a fashion plate. Here was the old frivolous syndrome still being applied. They couldn't cope with a glamorous, charismatic female being a trainer.

But if that was their attitude, let it be.

Gai had never sought publicity through her clothes sense. She had always dressed well and shown flair, style and variety as a natural part of her personality, and if the scribes wanted to write about it and it gave them something to do, that was OK by her.

The more they wrote about her appearing in a riot of colour topped off with a flowered hat, the better known she became to the public, although she preferred to be known for her ability.

Gai wasn't alone in noticing the effect this had on the public. When she appeared in the saddling enclosure, men as well as women in the stands trained their binoculars on her, and others followed the glasses with the naked eye to gaze at her.

Gai could see this going on and knew instinctively they were talking about the dress or hat she was wearing.

The race callers also made comments on her appearance.

She looked upon this as fun and it made her keener to dress differently each time, in something eye-catching and fetching.

It was a little tiring, though, to keep reading that she was making a fashion statement.

All her friends knew the observation was wrong. She was just being Gai, dressing as she felt.

Beryl Jents, prominent Sydney couturier, felt offended that anyone should criticise Gai for the way she dressed. Beryl believed Gai's clothes expressed her mood, always being happy, bright and bubbling. She told this writer:

'Gai may have her knockers but how dare a woman criticise another woman for the way she dresses. There is no snobbery about her and she has never tried to make the social scene.

'The love of her life is horses, not clothes.

'She doesn't just want people to look at her. She does wear a variety of styles, but they all suit her. I've known her since she was a little girl and I can tell you she's a bright, happy soul who doesn't really care what people think because she's not trying to set a fashion scene.

'She dresses correctly and sensibly for what she does.

'See her at the track of a morning and she's dressed for

the job, jodhpurs, boots, tweed hat pulled down over her eyes and at the races she's completely different and lovely.

'The thing I like about her is she doesn't try to make fashion statements with her clothes but just dresses for Gai, colourful, but classical and tailored. The hats are different, though. I think on reflection her chapeaux makes a bit of a statement.'

When Gai goes to the races she feels she's going to a show, a performance, a big colourful pageant. She loves the glamorous side of it, dressing up and wearing extravagant hats.

But, as always, there's a practical side to her approach.

She wants her owners to delight in looking at her because they are paying anything from a few thousand up to hundreds of thousands of dollars for the horses, and she wants them to be pleased with her and to recognise her easily.

She feels the theatre helped prepare her for the drama of racing, the long rehearsal in conditioning the horses leading up to opening night with the race-day punters as the audience. If she plays her part well, she can earn the plaudits she craved before the footlights.

She wears something bright because racing is a colourful scene with the jockeys in their bright silks and the beautiful horseflesh on centre stage, the tradition of the clerk of the course decked out in his red coat on a white charger leading the performers in and out.

Gai enjoys the whole moving panoply of racing. To her it is not just a spectacle but a theatrical experience. What can be more theatrical than the players parading in their multifarious colours and costumes before going out on stage, with the bookmakers, punters, stewards, trainers and booth attendants all playing a role?

She is not putting on the show, merely acting out her role.

Even the headlines kept this imagery alive: 'Gai on centre stage in Sydney training scene,' said *Bloodhorse* magazine.

And to obtain the right 'costumes', she goes to some pains, putting her own stamp on the garments. It is all part of Gai doing her own thing, not allowing anyone else to dress or categorise her.

That means trying to avoid buying off the rack, although she wears the famous German Bognor line in slacks, skirts and sports jackets because they suit her lifestyle, and she also sometimes wears creations of the French label, Courettes.

And if she walks past a shop anywhere and sees something that suits her and it fits, she will buy it on the spot. She has a quick eye for clothes and makes her mind up without fuss.

Normally though, Gai thumbs through magazines to choose designs and buys fabrics while on her two annual holidays abroad, then has her dressmakers run them up. She likes buying scarves of famous labels and having dresses made from them. Two dressmakers she often uses in Sydney are Helen Esdaile of Cremorne and Sue Bookallil of Darlinghurst.

Her outfits are not cheap but she doesn't consider them expensive at the end of the day for the number of times they are worn.

Gai doesn't have an unlimited budget, and makes the most of her wardrobe by imaginatively swapping them around, mixing and matching or even renovating them from a few years before to produce something that looks new and fresh.

She is always confident with whatever she wears, ignoring snide comments as coming from people with nothing better to do.

One of her girlfriends said, 'Gai has had many disappointments along the way and realises life and work are not all rosy.

'But in the 14 years I've known her she's never changed, retaining a positive attitude about everything.'

Away from the racecourse in private, she dresses more conservatively.

Her hair colour changes took some keeping up with, including an auburn red. When friends rang to speak to her after a colour change, Robbie would answer by saying 'Gai who?'

Friends told her they didn't like the platinum blonde look. It made her too severe, too much the Sergeant Major when deep down they knew she was just a big softie. But she kept it until she felt she needed another change.

Her hats were the eye catchers in this movable feast, from sombreros to what were unkindly called upturned chamber pots.

Indeed, they were chosen with great care to reflect her exuberant, effervescent character. Most women at the races admired her style in this department.

Gai had definite ideas on what she wanted designed by her milliners, Jane Lambert of Double Bay and Isabella Klompe of Bronte.

She didn't set out to shock and above all the design had to be practical—her face was small and had to be seen clearly while the hat stayed on, and it had to be versatile enough to enable her to use her binoculars freely.

This often presented a fashion challenge, but without fail the innovative style of her lids caused heads to turn.

After the hats had two or three airings, Gai often changed the flower trimmings to make them look like new creations.

All this was part of the show. But Gai knew that unless she could produce another big performance or two, she would never star but would be destined to remain among the extras.

Gai was building up the number and quality of horses in her stables and scoring some creditable wins.

She nearly took out the feature double at Randwick in the autumn carnival of 1993 when Te Akau Nick finished a gallant second to Azaam on a dead track in the Sydney Cup.

Gifted Poet, the horse Gai trained from scratch to win for her at his first country and city starts, almost snatched the Group One Doncaster Handicap with a brilliant third to Skating.

Nick also showed his class by winning the Group Two AJC St Leger Stakes and the Group Three AJC Chairman's Handicap.

Among her promising new young horses was Protara's Bay which she had to teach to race, putting him through the classes. He won three of his four races for her and in the spring of 1993 she entered him in the $60,000 City Tattersalls Club Cup at Randwick.

The lightly-raced Protara's Bay easily won the event in strong company. Racing writers described her as an emerging star because of her skills in training the horse to handle a big step up in distance to 2400m. Only a trainer with the right method could do that.

It required getting inside the horse's head and teaching him to think that he could perform over the longer distance.

She thought he might make a likely starter for the Melbourne Cup a few months away.

But Te Akau Nick was still her best horse, although he suffered a serious setback preparing for the Brisbane Cup by wrenching a foreleg joint on the Eagle Farm woodfibre track. Gai hoped to have him ready for the spring campaign of that year.

Both horses were among the small string she took to Melbourne for the spring carnival, but Protara's Bay didn't make it for The Cup. She set her sights on getting Te Akau Nick to the post in the big race, although his preparation was indifferent.

After a long spell Nick was still beset by nagging problems, soreness in the near foreleg and an abscess on the hind leg. And although she pounded quite a few kilometres into him he would have only three lead-up races for Australia's most gruelling race.

That was the year, 1993, when the Melbourne Cup went international with two northern hemisphere starters, the English champion Drum Taps and the Irish stayer, Vintage Crop.

With Australia's strict quarantine laws, as well as being on the other side of the world, the race had failed to draw European horses in the past, in spite of racing becoming a more global sport.

The VRC in a special gesture had reduced the quarantine time to a month and provided special facilities to attract them.

A controversy broke out because the European horses were lightly weighted by the handicapper.

Dermot Weld, the Irish trainer of Vintage Crop, had dreamed of winning the Melbourne Cup from the time he was a youth when his imagination was fired after reading Banjo Paterson's *Man From Snowy River*. Someone had given it to his father, who was a trainer.

Gai gave Nick a 'quick draw McGraw' preparation owing to his problems, but he'd trained well in recent weeks and she was confident he would justify being a final acceptor in the race.

He improved in each of his leadup races and was due to run in the Dalgety on the Saturday before The Cup.

In her new column in the Sydney *Telegraph* (yes, she had started up again without trouble from the AJC), she urged punters not to sack Te Akau Nick, declaring him to be good value in The Cup at his then odds of 40/1.

But Nick disappointed in the Dalgety at Flemington, running sixth.

Gai still wanted to start him in The Cup, believing he was just beginning to come good. Tommy was dead against it. 'Don't be ridiculous, don't waste your money,' he told her.

'Well,' said Gai, 'I'm going to pay the acceptance fee. I think he's just hit a patch where he's going as well as he ever did. He'll run the two miles all right.'

The owners also took some convincing but she persuaded them the $8,000 acceptance fee should be paid.

On Monday the day before the race who should turn up on the front page of the Melbourne *Herald Sun* but Gai, in full colour. She said she hoped to join her father on the honour roll with Te Akau Nick.

On Tuesday when the horses lined up at the barrier, Te Akau Nick was a despised 160/1 outsider. Gai couldn't believe it, nipping back to the bookies to have a few more dollars on him.

The day was wet and windy and rain still fell lightly. Gai was among the beautiful people in the Prince of Wales Stand, sitting right behind trainer David Hayes and his wife.

With yellow boutonnieres in their lapels, privileged punters who had left their run too late to squeeze into a seat, stood in front of the stand sharing their umbrellas.

Gai, adding a dash of colour in a pink silk blouse, just before the start blew a kiss to Andrew Peacock, former Federal minister and former husband of Susan Peacock-Sangster-Renouf. He waved back as he brushed mud off his dapper grey morning suit.

She could hardly contain her excitement as the field jumped in Australia's most famous race before packed stands, crowded outer areas and car parks with millions watching on television.

As the runners worked their way around the Flemington course over the 3200m journey, Te Akau Nick was well placed but as usual it was still anyone's race. At the turn into the long Flemington straight the leaders were bunched up with Te Akau Nick right in the running. Something could happen here!

Then, half way down the strip of turf where Australasia's best horses had been cruelly tested over the years, Te Akau Nick was summoned to produce every last ounce of his strength, every skerrick of courage in the punishing muddy last furlong.

Now it was all or nothing.

Two slashes of the whip, the jockey driving him on, and Nick answered the challenge, kicking away slightly from the pack, heading gamely for the post and fighting off all contenders.

Fifty metres out he had it won.

Gai was screaming her lungs out. David Hayes and his wife would probably be stone deaf for hours.

Suddenly Vintage Crop, the big chestnut from Ireland whom the local experts had scoffed at and said couldn't win because of his light preparation, lengthened his stride after a trouble-free run and showing the class that had won him the Irish St Leger, gathered in Te Akau Nick to win by three lengths.

Three lengths away from immortality.

Had it not been for the Irish invader Gai would have become the first woman in 132 years to officially train a Melbourne Cup winner—Nick had clearly outrun the rest of the field.

Granny McDonald might well have raised a cheer from her grave.

Down in the saddling enclosure, Gai's pink blouse was speckled with mud after receiving a celebratory bear hug from her jockey, Bob Vance.

As she stood in the second placegetter's stall, spots of rain trickling down her face, she trembled all over from excitement. Even her legs were shaking.

'Isn't it fantastic,' she told the owners. They were $400,000 better off.

She might as well have won it judging by the kisses, hugs and tears all round as Gai celebrated with her friends. TJ was on the scene quickly to kiss her. Vintage Crop was a forgotten animal.

Already the talk was in full flight about The Cup leaving Australia for the first time after Dermot Weld told the crowd on accepting the trophy in bleak and gusty conditions he hoped it would be a two-way street and Australian horses could start competing in Europe.

Gai was telling reporters she had mixed feelings about The Cup going international.

'I think it's wonderful in some ways, but it's sad that they pitched the visiting horses into the race at not correct weights, and I'm not saying that as the second place winner,' she said. 'I also don't think Australian and New Zealand horses can compete in Europe as stayers.'

Gai knew the European scene well. Australian horses were of a high standard but they were bred for speed and trained that way. European horses were generally more refined in their breeding, they were bigger, developed more slowly and trained to race over middle or staying distances. They raced less frequently than in Australia and due to their classic breeding brought higher prices as yearlings and in syndications.

351

Surprisingly, the immediate significance of Gai's achievement seemed to be largely lost. She received little publicity, less than her individual hats and bright gear normally attracted.

Could it be the racing hierarchy and pundits had difficulty in accepting that a woman had almost pulled off the impossible, like Bond winning the America's Cup? Surely not. Perhaps it was just lost in the brouhaha over a foreigner pinching Our Cup.

Whatever the reason, it was not mentioned by the Cup TV commentators except in a routine way, it wasn't featured in the TV news that night and it had scant mention in the papers next day.

Only two or three media outlets realised its importance in equine and feminine folklore.

The Sydney *Telegraph* ran a page one pointer ('Gai's Cup elation') to a page three story under the heading 'Gai's sweet defeat. Battling trainer has winning ways.'

The paper made the point that she still had a tough task convincing racing people that she had what it took to follow the path set by her famous father.

Only one other paper gave it a swish. The *Sportsman* ran a big picture of Gai looking like a plot from Flemington's gardens, but the editor's heart was in the right place even if he was a frustrated botanist.

His heading read 'Waterhouse on road to the top' and the story noted that she had shrugged off the legacy of a tumultuous past in which bookmaker-husband Robbie was warned off.

Gai told the paper she hadn't hit her peak yet and although it was difficult to compete with big stables that had 100 or so horses, she still aspired to win a Derby, a Golden Slipper—and The Cup.

She remained in Melbourne for the races on Thursday and instead of staying to enjoy the parties still going on in the city's hotels, clubs and Toorak mansions, she flew back to Sydney that afternoon to celebrate over dinner with Robbie and Tom and Kate.

Amazingly, there still seemed reluctance on the part of racing administrators and the big names of the industry to accept her as a serious trainer. Their silence was ear splitting.

But the ordinary people, the little punters, the ones who kept the turnstiles clicking, didn't overlook her achievement.

They wrote to her in their hundreds, and she received congratulatory faxes from New Zealand, France, Ireland and America. In her meticulous way she wrote back to every one of them.

Gai knew where she was heading.

Her newsletter appeared under a new logo in which the legendary name TJ Smith was relegated to minor status.

It featured 'GW' in large white letters on a black background, surrounded with the words 'Gai Waterhouse Horse Training Stables'.

And in small print underneath, 'in conjunction with TJ Smith'.

That should have told the racing world something.

The *Sportsman* reference to Gai having shrugged off the past was spot on.

It took her at least 18 months to work the battle with the AJC out of her system and put it behind her.

From the time she almost stole the Melbourne Cup, it was as if she was Gai for Gai's sake. She was no longer living life because she'd had the fight with the AJC or was a party to a popular cause, having it raised all the time due to her marriage to a person whose name was constantly in the papers.

The deep effect it had on her psyche was one of the reasons why she plunged into work so quickly and fully on receiving her licence, wanting to leave the bad memories behind.

In a way she was saying hey, I'm me, not one of my *alter egos*, please judge me for what I am.

The Melbourne Cup result meant more than running second in one of the world's great horse races. It gave her the confidence to feel that finally she was her own person.

*

353

To increase her circle of owners Gai had to look increasingly outside Australia to Malaysia, Taiwan, China, Hong Kong and Singapore.

At first she had to seek them out or make contact through chance meetings. Later, as her reputation increased, they would come looking for her.

Reputations in the racing game are hard won but can easily and quickly be destroyed. Racing runs on rumour and gossip to a surprising degree and reputations are often ruptured or torn apart for all the wrong reasons.

But when a trainer makes a serious mistake with a horse, or does a bad deal, reputations are ruined probably forever.

It doesn't have to be deliberate. It can just be due to the luck of the game.

Gai was conscious of her integrity and her professionalism and tried to rule out the luck side of the equation in all her dealings.

While on the lookout for a top quality horse for groups of Australian and Asian owners, Gai heard that the New Zealand miler Golden Sword was for sale. The prospect attracted her at once.

Golden Sword was a budding champion. Originally bought at Auckland's Karaka yearling sales for $80,000 for a Singapore-based syndicate, the New Zealander was a son of the Sir Tristram sire Kaapstead out of the Vain mare Lovenvain.

The stunning chestnut hit his straps by overcoming a wide run to power home and take out the 1993 Group One Epsom Handicap at Randwick, a week later showing his authority to seize the Group One Toorak Handicap at Caulfield.

He was then four years old, having won eight races from 20 starts. The feeling was he would be a truly great miler with further maturity.

Gai negotiated a price of $420,000 with the owners. But before completing the deal she insisted on having Golden Sword sent to her so she could work him for several days, just cantering and trotting him. She found he was constantly lame.

She called in her vet, Dr James Whitfield, and they examined him closely. She could see the horse had problems, but could not put her finger on the cause. She said to her vet, 'If I was familiar with his background, I might be able to cope with his lameness.'

She had already paid a deposit and had the cheque for the remainder, nearly $400,000, in her hand from a group of Australians. This was to be one of the biggest investments her potential owners intended making in Australian racing.

The proposition was tempting. Many trainers would have wasted no time in having the horse in their yard. But after thinking about it she was not prepared to take the risk for her willing investors.

She gave them their cheque back and said 'the horse is lame', and sent it back to its home.

Golden Sword then went to stud, but was infertile. He served 28 mares but did not put one in foal. An insurance company had to pay out on that, something like $1.5 million.

After that the horse had a few more runs but eventually broke down at Warwick Farm and was finished. A second large insurance payment was made.

Her caution, her desire to do the best for her owners and act with integrity, had saved her from making what would have been regarded in the industry as a serious error of judgment.

The luck of the game.

She could see bigger and better things to come for her owners.

Gai could now see the way ahead to buy horses that didn't have problems and could be Derby, Cox Plate or even Golden Slipper winners.

CHAPTER TWENTY-FIVE

PHARAOH'S PURSE AND OTHER RICHES

Fate has an odd way of asserting itself in the racing game.

A likely scenario can evaporate quickly and after the event which sparked it has receded into the past and perhaps left the memory, it can suddenly remind us that it was destiny after all.

Gai was always pragmatic and never superstitious in her decisions. But sometimes she developed a feeling over a horse.

It was her 'eye' or sixth sense, something innate but balanced or tempered by the yardstick of experience.

At the Karaka sales in New Zealand in 1988 with Tommy, Gai picked out a little brown yearling that took her fancy. His breeding wasn't all that flash, from the unfashionable American sire Sackford, but his grandam was the brilliant Leica Show who had been trained 15 or so years before by Bart Cummings.

He was little more than a foal, and plain looking. But Gai saw he was nicely proportioned, intelligent with an alert head. Although never likely to grow very big, he was seen by Gai in her mind's eye as a future tough little horse who was likely to be a winner.

'I'd love to train him, Dad,' she told Tommy.

TJ liked the colt too and decided to bid for him.

But Bart Cummings also had set his heart on the yearling. Bidding between the pair was keen but TJ dropped out at $500,000.

Gai was disappointed but she put the little colt temporarily out of her mind, expecting to see him appear in the winner's circle some time in the near future trained by Cummings.

But a year later when a major syndication scheme of Bart Cummings collapsed, the little horse was suddenly on the market again. TJ thought he'd pick up the colt, still unraced, for a song at the Cummings firesale but he had to go to $75,000 to obtain him, sharing ownership with two others.

TJ's secretary Pauline Blanche, who named most of his horses, came up with Pharaoh, hoping the title of Egypt's ancient kings might yield some riches.

Tommy trained Pharaoh but although showing plenty of ability, he was injury-prone with knee problems and had to be nursed along. He was coaxed through some Listed wins but the Big Ones eluded him.

Tommy was losing patience with Pharaoh due to his constant lameness from arthritic joints and sesamoid troubles and early in 1994 Gai began taking over his preparation, although the horse was still officially under Tommy's care.

Then Tommy had to go into hospital for an operation. He, too, had knee problems. Gai strolled into the Tulloch Lodge office and Pauline said to her, 'You know your father has given you Pharaoh to train?'

'Is that right?' she replied. 'Typical of Dad, he didn't even mention it to me.'

'He's already signed the horse over to you. From hospital.'

A leading vet associated with Tommy said to Gai, 'You've got to put this horse out to spell. He'll never race again.'

'Oh,' said Gai, 'I don't think so. I want to keep him in the stables. I'm exercising him differently, with lots of swimming. He hasn't broken down yet.'

The vet couldn't believe it, especially when she said she was starting him in the Doncaster, a few weeks away.

The Doncaster Handicap over a mile, with prizemoney of more than $1 million, was one of the toughest Group One races to win.

To everyone but Gai, Pharaoh seemed a dim prospect, although lightly weighted for the race. TJ had already put in some patient work on him in the hope of having him fit for the race and he agreed Gai should go right ahead.

He said to her, 'If I won another Doncaster they would all say ho hum. But if you win it, they'll sit up and take notice. You've virtually trained the horse for the last few months anyway. So if you can do any good, why shouldn't you get the credit?'

Other Randwick trainers took their horses to the fresh water pool at Randwick. Not Gai. She took hers to Botany Bay where they could swim further and fight against the salt water current. They had to try harder but Gai saw it as a tonic which kept up their spirits while they swam for miles.

It toned up Gai's runners even if it was more expensive, requiring strappers with wet suits and transport to and from the stables.

Her great patience in swimming and working Pharaoh slowly, building on Tommy's previous work on the track, improved his condition without risking a breakdown.

It took confidence, courage and insight for Gai to do it her way.

Pharaoh was a classic example of Gai changing the whole routine of a horse. Where TJ believed in keeping the pressure on them, Gai was more lenient. She believed in working the horses strongly to keep them fit, but she was also willing to ease off or change their work routine to suit an individual horse. Pharaoh was one such case.

As Doncaster day neared, drama occurred over who would ride Pharaoh. The list of suitable jockeys was shrinking fast. Gai had just patched up an early morning argument she'd had at the track with Gavin Eades. He was something of a larrikin but she thought he could do the job and put his name forward.

TJ left it to Gai but the other two part owners objected, saying he was not a big-race rider. Gai had to telephone them repeatedly before wearing them down. Even then they almost scratched the horse at the last minute.

Doncaster Day, 2 April, 1994. Royal Randwick was thronged by 38,142 Easter racegoers, the biggest Doncaster crowd for 15 years.

The racetrack is not a venue where miracles should safely be entertained. Devotees of the supernatural are soon relieved of their lettuce at the track.

But allowing for even a slight suspicion that some agency above the force of nature is sometimes at work on the turf—what punter can deny it?—it must be said it took a minor miracle to line Pharaoh up at the barrier on the day.

At least Gai's foreman, Irishman Eddie Dunn, was convinced of it, as were the vets.

Months before, Eddie had returned to Ireland and on his way home had called in at Lourdes where he bought a statuette filled with Holy Water. He'd been waiting for the right moment when he felt divine guidance might be needed.

Before Pharaoh left the stables this day Eddie took it upon himself to sprinkle a few drops on the nuggety little horse's head and back.

The big crowd settled into position and a hush fell as they awaited the start. The gates banged open and the field was off in the hotly contested race.

Pharaoh seemed to love the spacious running at Randwick and set about his work with a will. He was well placed coming around the turn when suddenly he met severe interference.

Mistador almost fell right in front of him, forcing jockey Eades to ease Pharaoh back in case Mistador fell on top of him.

Sections of the crowd groaned in dismay, thinking Pharaoh was out of the race. When the field straightened up Pharaoh was

10th and front runners Kingston Bay and Telesto looked to have the race to themselves.

Through her binoculars Gai saw Eades kick for home in what was the moment of truth. Could the plucky little Pharaoh fight back, or was it too late?

Pharaoh put his head down and desperately set out for the leaders.

The crowd roared as he narrowed the gap. With the finishing post looming up Kingston Bay and Telesto were fighting it out for the lead.

Eades used the whip with merciless rhythm in a final desperate bid and Pharaoh, running on heart-stopping courage, his feet pounding furiously into the turf, made a last-gasp effort to flash over the line with the leaders.

The winner was impossible to pick.

The judge called for a three-way photo. The connections of the three horses all thought they had it won, excitedly anticipating the result. But the judge couldn't separate it.

He asked for another print. The seconds ticked over agonisingly as the crowd, thrilled by the stirring finish, speculated on the result.

Gavin Eades sat on Pharaoh, stiff as a sentinel.

Gai, wearing a big hat that looked fresh out of the Botanic Gardens, waited with her hands clasped in front, prayer-like. Praying had never been as urgent as this at Rose Bay Convent or in church.

She had glamorised herself for the occasion, too. The tortoiseshell glasses were gone, replaced with contact lenses.

Finally the semaphore board flashed number nine.

Pharaoh! By an eyebrow.

'Oh my God, we've won the Doncaster,' yelled Gai, evoking the team spirit of her stable.

Eades the maverick from Melbourne reached over and kissed the surprised clerk of the course Mick Stanley, who almost fell off his white charger. Then the jockey repeatedly punched the air.

Gai was squealing with delight, all set to kiss everybody in sight, when she found herself being bustled out to bring the horse in.

As she started running across the turf, with Eades soft-shoe-shuffling towards the weigh-in, Gai was suddenly caught up in the heady emotion of it all.

She started jigging and dancing, throwing her arms around in a spontaneous burst of joy.

The whole crowd, many of whom were already applauding her victory, joined in to make it a universal celebration around the track.

They rose to their feet in the stands, cheering and clapping in a heartfelt burst of pleasure and admiration.

Gai stood on the turf below, smiling and waving back, her arms held high.

It was one of the most popular wins ever seen on a racecourse, although Pharaoh at 12/1 had not been favourite.

This was a moment when the sport rose above itself, a moment long to be savoured. It lifted racing beyond the banal, the ordinary, the predictable speeches of wealthy winning owners.

But the immediate drama of the closest finish since three horses fought out the Hotham Handicap in 1956, wasn't over yet.

While the crowd and Gai were still emoting, jockeys Grant Cooksley and Brian York on second and third placegetters Kingston Bay and Telesto, asked Chief Steward Schreck to look at the official film to see if a protest against Pharaoh was justified.

Eades waited outside the stewards' room with his arms folded.

When Cooksley walked out Eades asked him what was happening and he replied, 'You've won the Doncaster.'

Eades grabbed Cooksley and vigorously bear-hugged him. It was his first Group One win.

The official photo showed Kingston Bay had actually hit the

line first—his front leg was ahead of Pharaoh's nose, but it is a horse's nose that is adjudicated in a finish. The judge, Damian Foley, had seen this happen only twice in five years.

At the presentation Gai's first thoughts were for her father.

Tommy, out of hospital and recuperating at home, had missed his first Doncaster for 60 years. He saw the running on television.

Gai told the crowd, 'This has been the most wonderful day, but most importantly, thanks Dad.'

She was still waving to the crowd 20 minutes later.

The AJC Chairman Bob Charley was moved to tell the media, 'This is the greatest reception I've ever seen after a big race. The crowd really became involved with Gai's win. She is obviously very popular with everyone and this is just a fantastic scene.'

One newsman led off his story: 'It was racing theatre at its very best.' The idea was catching.

Another reporter noted that Pharaoh needed a miracle to win after striking the trouble at the home turn. The stable foreman was right!

But the *Sun-Herald* in Sydney had the best headline. It said a mouthful in two simple words: 'Payback time'.

Robbie wasn't there to share in the thrill. He still sat at home, feeling deprived.

But present for the first time in almost 10 years had been Ian Murray, the man who like Robbie had lied over his role in the Fine Cotton affair, changing his story several times. Indeed, he was a self-confessed liar who had turned informer, a 'dobber' in the ordinary Australian parlance.

He was among those warned off over Fine Cotton at the end of 1984. But the AJC had shown leniency and let him back.

The situation had a sequel a few weeks later when the AJC Committee once again refused Robbie Waterhouse's application to have his ban lifted.

Next day, a Saturday, the *Sydney Morning Herald* in reporting their decision carried a quote from Gai calling for a 'fair go' for Robbie and describing the Committee as 'pig-headed'.

At the Randwick races that day Gai was called to the stewards' room and censured by Chief Steward Schreck.

She ran from the room choking back tears. When waiting reporters asked her what had happened, she said, 'It's A-OK. You'll have to see them.'

Gai raced to the birdcage where jockey Larry Cassidy had already mounted her runner, Over The Top, favourite in the next race. Cassidy said later she seemed flustered because she told him not to lead.

But Over The Top led all the way to win, giving Gai the first leg of a winning double with Pops Dream winning a later race.

The press took Schreck and the AJC apart for their tactics in grilling Gai behind closed doors.

Max Presnell in the *Herald* described how Schreck had said it was a 'licensing matter' which Presnell said was 'his reason for holding the hearing in Star-Chamber conditions: no media allowed'.

Presnell commented:

'Schreck advocates open government in racing until a delicate subject comes to the fore, and he then puts the "licensing" tag on it to prevent details from becoming known.

'But it was a very frustrated lady who came out of the stewards' room on Saturday. Being under the licensing banner, perhaps the stewards threatened to take her training ticket away because she is being so uppity? The same licence over which she had to take the AJC to the anti-discrimination court to get.

'That's what is wrong with closed hearing—the guesswork.

'Which is also the case with Robbie Waterhouse. Why doesn't the AJC come out of the closet and disclose why he isn't allowed back?

'Tommy Smith remembers when the AJC Committee had inquisition-like power; the time when sour old men walked around with the authority to take away a livelihood at whim.

'We like to think this is a more enlightened racing control.

'Surely a wife is entitled to ask for justice for "Rob" if she thinks he has been wronged—without having to front like a truant schoolgirl.'

Ken Callander in the *Telegraph* expressed a widely-held view among the public under the heading 'AJC way out of line'.

'You have to wonder whether you are in good old democratic Australia when Gai Waterhouse gets carpeted behind closed doors for sticking up for her husband,' he began.

'Remember it is only racing we are talking about, not nuclear war or international espionage.

'Why the drama? Just because you are a licensed person, surely you are still allowed to speak your mind?

'We are not living in Nazi Germany.

'Does the AJC think that gagging everybody fools the public?

'Surely in 1994 we do not have to put up with a feudal system of adult people not being able to speak out?

'It is totally undemocratic. It might have been acceptable in wartime Germany or Communist China, but it is not acceptable today in Sydney, Australia.'

Callander described how Gai, carpeted over comments calling for a fair go, was asked by chief steward John Schreck if she'd been correctly quoted in the papers and,

'like the quality person she is, she said that she had been.

'Personally I don't know one racing person who has

given racing better value than Gai, of one person any more aware of any so-called obligation to racing.

'Like her dad before her, she is continually telling all sections of the media what a great sport racing is and she is forever giving her time and energy to promote the sport through all possible avenues.

'In gagging her, racing will be the loser.'

You would think the AJC might learn something from such strong views expressed by respected media commentators.

Also from the views of an overwhelming section of the community and the battle the AJC had fought against Gai, which was so much against public opinion a clam with both hands over its mouth could have told them they would lose in the long run.

They would soon have the opportunity to show if a shaft of sunlight in the form of public opinion and fair play was about to reflect on their faces with dazzling brilliance from the dark-panelled walls of the Committee Room when matters of moment were discussed.

Robbie was about to apply once again for his licence.

Never one to give up, Gai approached a friendly Committeeman at the races at the end of 1994 and said, 'I need your support with Rob putting this application in.

'I'm not asking you to do anything you don't believe in, but as a very reasonable person you must think that Rob has served long enough.'

The Committeeman said, 'One of our terrors in letting him back is the influence he would have over you.'

'Hang on,' protested Gai, 'we've been in these waters before.

'We've fought these complaints before, and you lost. Rob has no influence over me when it comes to training horses. That's something you don't have to worry about.'

She couldn't believe it.

Ten years after Fine Cotton, three years after she had fought them in the courts and beaten the socks off them, they were still using the same old argument.

The wrong reasoning was obviously etched on their minds. They had learned nothing.

Their difficulty was they were not moving with the times and could not see that each case should be dealt with on its merits—which is what they professed to do.

Robbie Waterhouse had a letter delivered to the AJC on Wednesday, 30 November, 1994, asking for his warning-off to be lifted so he could return to the races. He also asked to speak to the Committee, a vain request made several times.

That night the AJC Secretary, John 'The Admiral' Rouse rang him at home and told him he'd be called about 10 am on Friday.

About 9.30 next morning, Thursday, Gai rang him at his office to say he would be getting a call from the AJC. Robbie, who hadn't yet mentioned the possibility to Gai, asked how she knew.

She'd heard it from two people, the wife of a bloodstock agent she knew and a motor dealer who said he had been told by a journalist who said he had been told by an AJC steward.

Once more someone at the AJC was leaking like a drover's dog at a bush picnic.

John Rouse, angry that the press had been tipped off, rang Waterhouse about 11.30 on Friday and asked him to come in at 3 pm. He gave him details on how as a warned off person he could enter the AJC premises.

He was to go to the carpark where a racecourse detective would hand him a letter inviting him to attend before the committee and he would have to agree to be escorted to the Committee Room.

The detective escorted him up the back stairs where he waited under escort on a bench-style seat.

Summoned, he entered the inner sanctum where Committee members were sitting around a horseshoe shaped table.

The first question by Chairman Bob Charley was why he thought his application should be considered when he was refused the previous February?

Waterhouse said he believed he'd served a very harsh penalty being out for more than 10 years. One or two committeemen, especially Peter Capelin, seemed to bridle at that suggestion.

The questions kept coming. They wanted to know all about Fine Cotton, how it came about, whose money it was he bet and so on.

Waterhouse was humble, apologising for his actions which he said he regretted, and basically saying he was now a more mature person who had tried to lead an exemplary life since Fine Cotton and he would not offend again.

The Committee, understandably, gave him a torrid time.

One member, Tony Allport, told him how difficult it was to sit in the same room with him where he had lied previously and he wanted to be sure he was telling the truth this time.

Much of what Waterhouse said to the Committee had already appeared in *The Gambling Man*.

This included that Garry Clarke had come to him with the scheme, Clarke had given him $40,000 as a commission to bet on Fine Cotton but had not told him whose money it was, that he did not know it was a ring-in until after the event, although he had a fair idea the horse had plenty going for it and he had not told the truth about the money he had arranged to put on for himself.

All that was old hat. He'd been out for more than 10 years for officially having prior knowledge.

By their questions it appeared some members suspected he was guilty of more than having prior knowledge, that he might have financed the fiasco, or worse, organised it. If some Committeemen were thinking that, it posed the obvious question: Was he being punished now for something for which there was no evidence?

They wanted to know how he had been making his living and he told them about his factoring business, and volunteered the information that he was sending females to the racecourse to bet on the tote for him. That was how he supported his family. The Committee did not raise any complaint on that.

He couldn't enter the racecourse but apparently the AJC was happy to accept his money there.

Waterhouse appeared to have made two mistakes.

Asked if he would want to own horses if they allowed him back, he tried to crack a joke by saying it would be no hardship if they denied him the right. But nobody laughed.

Again, asked if he would want to become an AJC member, Waterhouse said he would not apply if the Committee didn't wish it but he had taken heart from Ian Murray's return.

Capelin took the mickey out of him on that, saying Murray was a man who had helped the Committee.

They then introduced Gai's name.

The Chairman asked the leading question, 'One of the things we have to weigh up in your application is that your wife is a very successful horse trainer and is highly regarded in the industry, and your presence on the racecourse may well be seen as a hindrance to her career?'

He answered by saying he would never do anything that would threaten Gai in any shape or form.

Gai, he said, if she was present would tell them that her career had been hindered by him not being on the course, having the slur of this against her. And she would prefer him to be on the course.

He stressed he was not asking to come back as a bookmaker but as an ordinary racegoer.

Bill Rutledge asked about the long running family court case and if there was any other court case pending that might affect their thinking on him.

The AJC had been told, falsely, that defamation proceedings concerning The Gambling Man *would seriously embarrass them. This was one of the ploys used by enemies of Robbie Waterhouse to try to prevent him being allowed back.*

In his answer Waterhouse said there was a problem with his brother, who was suing his father as a trustee.

'Unfortunately,' said Robbie, 'my father and I had to pay a debt on his behalf, and I have joined my father in counter-suing him. I believe this matter will be resolved.

'We have also been joined in a defamation action in which we say we have absolutely no case to answer . . . So the answer to your question is, no there is not.'

Dr Treve Williams, saying he hoped Gai would be a first class trainer for many years, asked if he thought it would be a conflict of interest if he became a bookmaker.

Waterhouse said that when a bookmaker he had not been interested in Gai's opinions on a horse, had treated her runners like any other in the market and repeated he would never do anything to harm her.

The Committee adjourned to consider its decision. Waterhouse and the various AJC officers waited outside for 45 minutes.

He was recalled at 4.45 pm when the chairman announced, 'Mr Waterhouse, your application to have your warning off ban lifted has been denied.'

The result was reported in the press next day.

But a bombshell concerning the decision hit the Sunday papers.

The Committee had originally voted six to three to allow him back. But one member in particular argued to get his way— and the Committee had then reversed its decision!

To reach a decision after due deliberation, then do an about face, was unbelievable.

These were the men responsible for running the multi-billion-dollar racing industry.

Pshaw!

The fabulous tale of Pharaoh was still full of running.

One week after winning the 1994 Doncaster, Pharaoh had fractured a sesamoid bone in his left fore fetlock, apparently from the stress of sprinting on the hard ground in the race of his life.

Percy Sykes, the famous veterinary surgeon who had been associated with Tommy Smith since his early days more than 40 years before, thought he had only about one chance in 50 of coming back and racing successfully. Two other vets agreed.

Tommy decided to bail out, thinking the horse was finished. He sold his one-third share for a measly $500.

But Gai said to the owners, 'I want to continue training him. Let's turn him out for six months. If he comes back and he can't stand, well, he's already won everything you've dreamed about.'

Pharaoh was sent to Woodburn at Cootamundra. When he returned to the stables, Gai persisted with him, working him differently to how Tommy had.

She knew his problem was wear and tear, and if she kept wearing him away, something would tear for good.

She swam him more than she worked him slowly on the track, a technique that called for a lot of belief in her ability. She knew it was the right preparation for the horse, but it was so unorthodox most other trainers laughed at it.

But Gai knew the old crock was responding.

In her mind's eye Gai could see in what direction and to what level she wanted to take Pharaoh. Anyone wanting to be a top trainer needs to have that kind of vision, not allowing themselves to be carried along by the horse, the owners or outside influences.

Veterinary surgeon Dr James Whitfield, who worked with Gai on Pharaoh, said he was literally a day-to-day proposition during this preparation. His pain threshold amazed the vet.

Pharaoh's improvement and ability to keep going when all advice was against it defied veterinary science.

'I always loved Pharaoh because with all his problems he was a courageous little horse,' Dr Whitfield said. 'He wasn't cranky and had a personality all his own. Gai showed great patience in persevering with him.'

Gai set him for several major races early in 1995 but as soon as she put him through pace work, his joints inflamed and he went sore on her again.

The tragedy was he showed such heart and zest for work.

He had an easy run in the Group Two Challenge Stakes at Randwick in January, finishing ninth. Trackmen and clockers, knowing his problems, just about wrote him off.

But while all the glamour gallopers were out on the track getting fit, Gai was planning her own assault on the autumn riches by having Pharaoh clock up the nautical miles in Botany Bay.

Gavin Eades became so attached to the horse he visited the stables every day and Gai broke her rule to use only strappers for exercise by allowing Gavin to take him for long walks. Pharaoh was spared the risk of strain by not being galloped at the track.

After finishing a strong third in the Expressway Stakes at Randwick, Pharaoh thrashed the field in the Group Two Apollo Stakes at Warwick Farm, his last leadup race for the Big Ones.

Next in line was the Group One Chipping Norton Stakes at Randwick on 11 March. Pharaoh led all the way to win on a soft track, downing Caulfield Cup placegetter Air Seattle.

The win astounded Tommy Smith, who deputised for Gai that day in saddling him up.

Gai was in Melbourne, continuing her winning ways.

She was in the midst of a purple patch, the result of her careful planning and preparation as a trainer over the past three years.

At that moment she was fresh from hailing her flying filly, Light Up the World, as a potential new champion in smashing a long-standing course record for 1200m at Rosehill. The filly ran the distance in an astonishing 1:08.62sec.

On the day that Pharaoh cleaned up the Chipping Norton field in Sydney, she sent out her horse All Our Mob at Flemington to defeat Melbourne sprint champion Hareeba in the VRC Newmarket Handicap, the prestige sprint race of Australia.

It was her first interstate Group One win.

A Flemington win had been elusive but Gai did it in style, Hareeba being the shortest-priced favourite in Newmarket history.

All Our Mob, a tried horse from Brisbane and a Stradbroke winner, had been bought by Hong-Kong-based Tony Huang, who transferred the chestnut to Gai's stable—a tribute to her growing status in the industry.

[Gai would prove her ability again later by turning All Our Mob, a sprinter who had never run more than 1400m, into a relaxed stayer to win over 2400m. This was a difficult training feat with an older horse, who was set in its ways.]

Gai sizzled next with Stony Bay, a moderately performed little beauty she discovered in New Zealand after poring through form printouts and studying race videos. He had won only two from 10 starts.

Sired by Dahar, an American stallion owned by Texan oil billionaire Nelson Bunker Hunt which stood at his stud in New Zealand, Stony Bay was bought by Gai for what would be a bargain price $120,000. She chased up new owners and the horse made its Australian debut for her in the spring of 1994.

After three conditioning races Stony Bay also lit up the scene, scoring two back-to-back Group One races in the autumn period of 1995 when Gai hit the winner's circle like a thunderclap.

Both times Stony Bay left Horse of the Year and Melbourne Cup winner Jeune in his wake.

The first was the $300,000 Ranvet Stakes at Rosehill on 25 March coming in at 15/1. 'You beauty, wasn't he good odds?' Gai shouted to the crowd.

Stony Bay followed up by winning the $1 million BMW on April 8, fighting off Jeune half way down the Rosehill straight.

That gave Gai her fifth Group One win since she began training only two seasons earlier after rushing out and hastily buying four horses.

But the autumn *pièce de résistance* was yet to come.

Pharaoh, after running third in the Group One George Ryder Stakes, trotted out on to a soft track at Randwick on 15 April in the Doncaster with his mate Gavin Eades again in the saddle.

This time the horse carried Gai's colours, purple with white stars, but under those silks for good luck Eades wore former part-owner Tommy Smith's colours of blue and green which he carried to victory the year before.

Eades was so moved to see his injury-plagued friend still running that before the race he ceremoniously kissed Pharaoh's forehead.

In the week before the race Gai worked Pharaoh only once on the track—on the Tuesday morning, and then only at three-quarter pace. She feared anything else might break him down.

At seven years, the oldest horse in the race, Pharaoh jumped from the same barrier as the previous year, number nine, and didn't look like losing at any stage.

After topping the Randwick rise Pharaoh shot clear with the race in his grasp, bringing the crowd to its feet in thrilling anticipation.

Pharaoh won easing up this time, although fast-finishing Aunty Mary reduced the winning margin to three quarters of a length, with Brave Warrior third.

In 129 years, only five other horses had won successive Doncasters. The win brought the old crock's earnings to $2 million.

As Pharaoh ruled again, it was a case of the same barrier, same jockey, same trainer, same celebrations. Only the fashions had changed.

Gai, in a stunning red Santa Claus suit with gold shoes, gold bag and white pillbox hat, once again raced across the Randwick sad-dling enclosure lawn to greet the horse, its ears pricked, and the emotional jockey, who punched the air and called out to the crowd.

Some wags yelled 'Give us a dance, Group One Gav,' and he twisted and gyrated in reckless fashion.

Steward Schreck called him aside after the weigh-in and told him to 'be sensible'.

Gai's followers, now referred to as Gai's Army, cheered themselves hoarse. The big crowd rose to its feet once more and clapped and clapped. The ovation was even greater than in the previous year.

They weren't cheering for the horse, although he was all part of the euphoria. They were cheering for Gai.

It was one of those rare moments in sport, the kind of ovation that brought the crowds to their feet for champions like Kingston Town and Super Impose.

The Doncaster was Gai's third Randwick win of the day, after scoring earlier with Sprint By and Juggler.

The enthusiastic trainer's method of celebrating a big win was now well known. At first she tended to throw her hands high in the air. She always sat next to the owners and usually hugged them first. If TJ and Valerie were nearby, they were next.

Then she found someone to hold her handbag and binoculars.

Group hugging followed, lots of hugging and kissing of her supporters, people who worked in the stable, those who followed her success and sometimes people she didn't know but who were thrilled with her success.

Excitement filled the air. Her pleasure was spontaneous, her face alive, the enthusiasm infectious. The feeling was pure exhilaration.

Her whole support team and those around her, especially the owners, felt the elation of her wins. The feeling remained until the next race.

Her friend Denise Martin says, 'When she walks away, you can see people smiling, a smile that lingers, thinking to themselves what a warm and caring nice lady.'

When she won, the crowd was overwhelmingly behind her.

Theatrical her reaction undoubtedly was, but calculated or posed, never. It was impossible to feign such excitement.

Behind that unrestrained joy was a commitment to hard work, long hours and a desire for excellence.

Nobody ever enjoyed winning as much as Gai Waterhouse.

CHAPTER TWENTY-SIX

GAI TIME

The racing year 1994–95 was a vintage time for Gai Waterhouse.

At the end of the season in July 1995, she finished a remarkable second just behind John Hawkes in the New South Wales trainer's premiership, with 74½ wins.

She had almost 500 owners on her books, most of them small investors. All of them she had to find herself.

John Hawkes had only two owners to think about—Jack and Bob Ingham, the wealthy 'Chicken Kings' who operated the ultra-modern Crown Lodge training empire at Warwick Farm.

The Inghams had considerably more brass to play with than Gai, who had to rely on her father for financial support to buy new horses until she could find the owners to take them over.

Gai had 60 horses in Tulloch Lodge and Bounding Away Lodge, and the Inghams had several times as many.

Yet Gai, who was not licensed until January 1992, dominated in almost every sense.

Even in the trainer's premiership, if for argument's sake two-year-olds were excluded, Gai trained more winners than Hawkes. While Hawkes was overall winner, she was the leading trainer at Randwick.

Ironically, before John Hawkes took the job with Crown Lodge after the Inghams' trainer Vic Thompson retired, Gai wrote to Jack Ingham offering to train some of his horses.

The reply must still be in the mail. She never received one.

Not one Committeeman of any race club in Australia had given Gai any horse to train. The establishment of racing left her hanging.

No doubt the Robbie factor had something to do with that, but it might also have had to do with her being a woman.

For all that, she showed 'em. Showed 'em what she could do.

This little woman weighing a touch over eight stone, with the big smile, incredible energy and enormous courage, had done what no other individual had ever done.

In only her third full season as a trainer—to use a perfectly good cliché—she had taken racing by storm.

She didn't always walk softly as she carried the big stick.

She dominated the 1995 Sydney autumn carnival and for the first time in the world out-performed male trainers at a major carnival. And she dominated at the sales.

Gai scorched the rest of the field in races and prizemoney won.

On feature-race days only in that carnival, Gai trained 13 winners. Her closest rivals, John Hawkes and Bart Cummings, had only six each.

She led in more Group One winners than anyone else at the carnival and had more stakeswinners. Her horses earned $2,139,482 in prizemoney. By comparison, Lee Freedman earned $1.5 million and Bart Cummings, just under $1 million.

Racing observers believed her performance to have been the best of any woman trainer in the world at a major carnival.

Europe had some outstanding women trainers in Criquette Head of France and Jenny Pitman of Lambourn, England. Some of the best trainers in America too were women, and in the north of England quite a few of the successful trainers were women.

Gai could be likened to Pitman, hailed as a heroine in the women's movement, the first to train a Grand National winner and a pathfinder for women trying to break into the male preserve of racing in England.

376

Criquette was a 'lady' in a man's world but Jenny was somewhat more aggressive and outspoken than Gai, usually in rampant form like her horses. She made English Jockey Club officials dive for cover and spoke plainly to journalists.

'Listen,' she told one pressman, 'I don't want people to think I've got a great stubbly beard and legs like a shire horse.' She loved being involved in the men versus women confrontation.

Gai would not be drawn into a battle-of-the-sexes argument after her outstanding performance. 'I'm just another horse trainer and that's how I want to be treated,' she said. Gai just concentrated her efforts on the job at hand.

But in terms of winners at a carnival, neither Criquette nor Jenny could approach Gai's effort.

She was the dominant buyer at the Newmarket Easter Yearling Sales in 1995, buying 34 horses for $3.105 million. That's how much her confidence had soared, and how much Tommy now believed in her. Gai's purchases included the top price of $575,000 for a Danehill colt.

At the end of April, before the premiership was finished in July, John Hawkes had 73 city winners compared with Gai's tally of 61.5. But he had 480 runners to her 258.

It gave Gai the remarkable strike rate of a winner for every 4.1 runners. She finished the season with a winner every 4.6 runners, the highest strike rate of any metropolitan trainer in the land, earning more than $5 million in prizemoney for her owners.

She had built up such a following with punters that her number of runners affected holdings on the NSW TAB. Off-course punters were simply going to TAB centres and backing her horses.

The TAB boss Ken Page acknowledged that if she had only one runner, TAB revenue fell.

At the races punters were not willing the horses home so much as backing Gai, calling out 'Go Gai, go Gai!'

In Fiji, the betting shops owned by the Waterhouse family in conjunction with Francis Grant had a bad result when one of Gai's horses came in anywhere in Australia.

By the sheer quality and extent of her success, Gai became the darling of the media.

The scribes reached deep into their cliché books to come up with suitable descriptions. She was Queen of the Turf, Australia's Queen of the Turf, First Lady of Racing, Pinup Trainer for Sydney Punters, Best Advertisement for Racing, Trainer of the Moment, Punters' Pet.

Headline writers worked themselves into a lather as they competed to produce the brightest headings for the constant flow of upbeat stories on her.

Among the offerings: Golden Gai Time; Dawning of a new Gai; Queen of the turf bounding away in dazzling times for Australian racing; Golden girl Gai sales to glory . . .

Feature writers, always looking for something fresh and interesting to focus on, turned their attention to her, striving to produce the most original and arresting tale of her battle with officialdom, having to live in the shadow of her husband but still gaining remarkable success.

These usually cynical wordsmiths, who love to knock the stuffing out of prominent people and wear this attitude as a kind of badge of honour, recognised her professionalism and essential decency and gave her a very fair go.

Even Jeff Wells, a columnist on the *Sydney Morning Herald* who normally ate gravel and nails for breakfast and washed them down with sulphuric acid before facing up to the day's writing task, hopped on the Gai bandwagon and said nice things about her under the heading 'Perfect 10 as Glorious Gai saves the AJC's bacon'.

Jeff went to the Doncaster meeting the day Pharaoh won for the second time and reported in his colourful style that he hadn't seen such excitement among jaded newspaper types since the Happy Hooker, Xaviera Hollander, arrived in Melbourne in 1978 and offered to demonstrate some of her routines to the press.

He gave Xaviera only 8½ out of 10.

But he gave Gai 10, for different reasons.

'Has there ever been anyone,' wrote a usually trenchant Jeff, 'anywhere, better for horse racing than Gai? I doubt it.

'Or has Australia finally been irreversibly feminised?

'When hordes of male mugs line the fence of the mounting yard, and the members stand to a man, to worship a lady trainer, it makes you wonder.

'Is it finally time for all bronzed, or unbronzed, Aussie males to undertake compulsory detestosteronisation, hand over our daks, and struggle through the carpark in stilettos on the arms of sugar mommies?

'Or is this really the triumph of the devalued Australian male ideas of mateship and a fair go? Of course it is. Hand me back those daks.

'We love Gai because she copped a rotten deal from the silvertails at the AJC. Now she has bored it right up them with winner after winner.

'And she celebrates like any third-grade rugby league player who wins a grand final, or a Test bowler who takes a wicket.

'We of the weaker sex who, unlike dour females, are prone to exhibitions of unashamed emotion, appreciate this.

'And she is the punters' mate because her horses are fit and reliable. Fair dinkum, Gai's the sort of good scout you'd want in the public bar even if it wasn't compulsory.

'With Gai and jockey "Group One" Gavin Eades doing their thing, it was better than Barnum and Bailey.'

Or as one anonymous jockey remarked, 'Gai is the most exciting thing in racing without taking your clothes off.'

Gai could suddenly see, through her success and the influence of public opinion, how she was gaining respect in the industry.

The jockeys, who at first refused to ride track work for her and expected to just throw a leg over her horses on race days, were now coming around every morning and offering to work her horses.

Usually 10 or 12 turned up. Some complained there was too much competition!

All the Committeemen's wives were pleasant to her and some went so far as to genuinely commiserate with her on the fact that her husband could not be at the track to share in her glory.

In all this changing scene, Gai remained true to herself.

One AJC Committeeman's wife, Mrs Margaret Allport, stopped Gai at the races one day while showing some overseas visitors around and said to her friends, 'I'd like you to meet Gai Waterhouse, one of our Randwick lady trainers.'

Gai politely said, 'No, Mrs Allport—your *leading* Randwick trainer.'

The only child was always in good voice.

Even hardheads among the racing writers like Keith Robbins came around to accepting her ability. Robbins, who would walk barefoot over broken glass and back again to get a meaty story, wrote demurely of her in terms of admiration.

Her popularity was such that she was replacing Princess Di as a celebrity to sell newspapers and magazines. Writers and editors were saying a front page picture of Gai meant a lift in sales.

When one of her yearlings died of suspected botulism, a picture of Gai and the story ran over two full columns on the front page of the *Sun-Herald*. Thousands of horses died each year—the story had value only because of Gai's celebrity status.

Knowledgeable racing people can always tell when a trainer is successful—the trainer is rumoured to use drugs.

It had happened to every good trainer down the years—if they're winning, they must be doing something sneaky like having the 'good juice'.

The fact that Gai had the best strike rate of any leading trainer in Australia was enough to set the rumour mill grinding away. Ray Thomas had the story in the Sydney *Telegraph* with a big picture of Gai under the heading 'I'm no cheat'.

Gossip had it that Gai was treating her horses with steroids. She took it head on, giving a frank interview and explaining that a Queensland conman had been offering his services with steroids and claiming to have treated her horses. His name was known to officials.

Gai made the obvious response, 'I fought for my trainer's licence too long to do anything stupid.'

That one was a fizzer.

But with those rumours flying around, Gai was upset to be fined $5,000 by the AJC when the drug clenbuterol was found in one of her horses. She was distressed because it was a genuine mistake and she hated anyone thinking that she might be cheating.

The drug was not a performance-enhancing substance but the rules of racing said a horse could not have a drug of any description in their system when they ran.

With the assistance of her vet, Dr Whitfield, Gai was able to show that the mistake occurred when two food bins were not changed over after the horses changed boxes.

The drug, commonly used by trainers and in veterinary practice, was intended for one of her horses with respiratory problems and not one which was racing.

Gai stopped using the drug as a medication in feeds after that to prevent such a mistake recurring. No action was taken against the stable hand responsible.

Some of the trainers gossiped about Gai because they were jealous of her. She was successful and they weren't.

The jealous ones, always cracking jokes behind her back, were calling her Super League.

Her success was due to a careful, well disciplined approach and hard work.

She also had good horses. In her first year she had only one good horse in Te Akau Nick, but she now had at least a dozen top flight horses with many promising two-year-olds, and she was challenging the major stables like Freedman and Hayes.

But the real secret was she concentrated on her own horses and clients and ignored her competitors. Many of the other trainers tended to spend time worrying about their rivals.

It didn't occur to Gai to think about what other trainers were doing. She thought only about her own business.

Many of the attempts to put her down sprang from the way she operated out in the centre of the track in the mornings. With her big team she dominated the scene of controlled chaos, shouting her orders like an Army drill sergeant, ignoring the others.

But she had become the role model for women in a good year for women in racing, when their significance improved dramatically.

Moira Murdoch, the hobby trainer from New Zealand who ran a small string of horses on a farm outside Auckland, made a hit and run raid with Solvit to capture Australia's greatest weight-for-age race, the $1.5 million Moonee Valley W.S. Cox Plate, beating all the men like Lee Freedman, John Hawkes, Bart Cummings, David Hayes and countrymen John Wheeler and Dave O'Sullivan.

She paid only $NZ4,500 for Solvit as a yearling, proving the dream that kept racing alive was still open to the small operator and the best prizes were not the exclusive province of rich men.

Kay Miller was another who walloped the men when Starstruck won the Group One Australian Cup.

Gai was the woman who set the landscape alight with her strike rate and extraordinary following with punters. Not even Tommy Smith at his peak could match her there.

One of the problems of living a frenetic lifestyle was that Gai could never find enough time for relaxation.

She was constantly tired from working and travelling, always on the move either going to the races or to the bush, interstate or other countries to inspect and buy horses or recruit new owners.

Apart from two attempted holidays a year when she and Robbie took the children skiing, her visits to other countries were always rushed affairs on business. There was never time to sniff the flowers.

But she departed from her usual punishing regimen just before the Easter sales of 1995 after her new client, Tony Huang, invited her and Robbie to be his guests in China.

She had made his acquaintance at the Magic Millions Sale on the Gold Coast when she wanted to buy All Our Mob but could not arouse any interest in potential buyers before the sale. Tony Huang bought the horse, she went up to him and congratulated him, and through an interpreter he offered her the horse to train.

He had bought other horses since and would soon buy the Danehill colt in Sydney from Gai for $575,000.

A former journalist, Tony was a wealthy exporter from Shanghai whose main business was in Beijing with an operation in Hong Kong.

He was a gracious host, overcoming the language difficulties, and Gai and Robbie spent a wonderful 10 days taking it easy as they visited Beijing and Shanghai, the Great Wall, the Forbidden City and the Ming Tombs.

It had been a long time since Gai was an ordinary tourist. At first, with the daily pressure off, she suffered work withdrawal symptoms and had to consciously wind down to enjoy the fascination of being in this ancient land.

From her hotel in Shanghai on the famous road known as The Bund alongside the mighty Yangtse, Gai imagined she could be looking out over Paris.

The beautiful mini skyscrapers and gardens here reflected the hub of life in pre-liberation days when the British, French and Germans lived and played in lingering colonial splendour. The architecture expressed in stone the wealth of Shanghai in the 1920s and 30s.

A small park on The Bund, laid out by a Scottish gardener, once excluded Chinese, except those accompanied by their foreign employers—which allowed the Chinese amah or nanny to be on hand. Foreigners and Chinese had lived separate lives there, although cheek by jowl.

All around this area was once a luxury shopping paradise where the finest silks and embroidery were found. Opium could be smoked in the best company, served on silver trays like afternoon tea and tired, lustful businessmen were catered for in every way. Now the banks and Municipal Government were very much in evidence.

Beijing was nothing like the big city Gai had imagined. It seemed more rural than cosmopolitan but she enjoyed the Imperial Palace, its ceremonial halls and gardens, marvelling at the antiquity and history of it all.

The 13 Ming emperors' tombs built at the foot of the Tianshou Mountains to the north of Beijing proved an eye opener, going back to the year 1368 and giving an insight into how the emperors of the Ming Dynasty lived for almost 300 years.

Huge human stone figures at the Big Red Gate, the entrance to the tombs, were 500 years old but still in good condition.

Gai couldn't help noticing the imperial cemetery had only one tomb for the princes but six for concubines.

Gai's host laid on a splendid banquet in the dining room of an old hotel near the Great Wall for his visitors and an entourage of about 12. They were the only ones there. The waitresses were paid a wage of about $3 a week and on receiving a tip of $30, were delighted.

The only dampener on the feast was when the chef brought out a tortoise and in looking around the table, it rested its doleful eyes on Gai. Later when the chef served his culinary masterpiece, the tortoise in little pieces, Gai felt quite unwell. It did nothing to settle her squeamishness when the attentive concierge later offered her an even greater delicacy—first crack at drinking the tortoise's blood.

It said something for Gai's determination and capacity for work that she was prepared to visit China to spend time with a potential owner.

But she had no choice. She had to work as hard as that in order to consolidate. Unfortunately Australia as a country was not becoming richer but poorer. She saw Asia as part of her future and was prepared to go there to find investors.

Playtime in China over, she spent three days in Hong Kong on the way home making contacts for new owners over numerous cups of coffee, morning and afternoon teas, lunches and dinners, pounding the phone, working the whole time.

She knew it could take years to develop these contacts but she was pleased to see that she was more recognised there among racing people this time. Some of her press releases had made the Hong Kong papers.

The Hong Kong trip had an unusual sidelight which showed the alarming effect Gai was having on her rival Sydney trainers.

A Hong Kong man who kept horses with a Sydney trainer had asked Gai to contact him on her visit. The Sydney trainer was so concerned on learning this that he jumped on a plane and turned up there to see what was happening.

In his absence a Sydney owner went to his stables to give him a new horse to train. Finding him away, he gave the horse to another trainer. It turned out to be a Group One winner.

Gai's style in bringing new owners into the game was seen at the beginning of the new racing season in the late winter of 1995 when she posted her first winner.

She ushered seven bubbling, novice owners into the mounting yard at Canterbury Park to see the 2/1 favourite Colmerino contest the Rothmans Handicap.

Colmerino, the daughter of Balmerino who finished second in the Prix de l'Arc de Triomphe, was a maiden and green but came home a winner after racing three wide.

Gai wasn't a bit concerned when the siren sounded and jockey Darren Beadman protested on behalf of the runner-up, Kaaptree.

'Come on down to the stewards' room,' she told her brood of seven, mustering them like a mother hen, 'isn't this fascinating? Have you ever been to a protest hearing before?'

Inside the stewards' room she put her case concisely and firmly: Kaaptree had missed the start, got into difficulty and that caused the interference. Protest dismissed.

The Waterhouse bandwagon moved on for drinks after more kisses, handshakes and photographs. 'This is what racing's all about,' Gai told a passing journalist. 'Seven people who've never previously raced a horse, now own a city winner and it hasn't cost them an arm and a leg. Isn't it wonderful?'

She made it look easy but behind the enthusiasm and her small army of new owners was a massive amount of work.

To help her manage her business and bring in new clients, Gai had linked up with Denise Martin of Star Thoroughbreds, an expert in marketing and syndication.

Denise came from a racing background in Tasmania and had wide marketing experience in hotels. She moved from Melbourne to join Gai to help her syndicate horses and manage her diary—a task in itself.

She joined Gai at the time of the Easter sales and autumn carnival and had never seen a person work so hard in her life. In that one week races were held on Saturday, Monday and Wednesday and the sales on Tuesday, Wednesday and Thursday.

'In that week,' said Denise, 'Gai didn't sleep more than three or four hours on any night working out which horses would be owned by which stable, and what new clients she could introduce based on their needs and financial capacity to pay.'

On a Thursday soon after that, Gai had horses to train, a speaking engagement at Loreto Convent in Sydney at lunchtime and a debate in Melbourne that night at the Victorian Bloodhorse Breeders' Association.

Gai rose as usual at five minutes to three in the morning, went to the stables, sent Denise a message on her pager at 3.45 am, worked all that morning, made her lunchtime address at Loreto, was on the plane to Melbourne at 3 pm, did paper work on the flight and napped for five minutes only.

After checking into her hotel, Gai worked on the phone to

potential clients trying to sell a new colt she had bought, rang Denise in her room and said simply, 'sold'. And left for the function without sleeping.

It was a long night, the debate not starting until 9.45 pm. Gai had been awake 19 hours. 'I looked at her and thought, she won't make it,' said Denise.

'But when introduced, she suddenly sat upright, raised herself three or four inches, and without notes gave a brilliant presentation on why racing should make changes. She looked fantastic in the red pants outfit she wore to the Doncaster.'

Denise found that Gai was a good marketer who would send off hundreds of advance brochures to luncheon groups, never missing an opportunity to promote her stable, realising that racing was no longer a sport but a business.

'She has developed such camaraderie in the stable that everybody embraces her success—a win is a win for all,' said Denise. 'Her communication skill is phenomenal.

'At the Sunday functions in the stable, she still shares in the washing up. If she brings a horse out of a box to show the owners and it has been standing in let's say something other than hay, she will bend down and clean it, wash her hands and when the owners leave, say "I won't shake your hand."

'Her problem is everyone wants a slice of her time, and there's so little of it.'

The media can be a double-edged sword. Those who live by publicity can also suffer from it when the focus turns the other way.

Gai had to pay for her high profile in more ways than one. When the Australian Workers Union was campaigning to improve conditions for stable hands, Gai was singled out so the union could drain the last ounce from the issue.

Complaints from the industry applied more to other stables than Gai's but she was chosen as the bunny.

It arose after one or two strappers on her staff of 25 complained about having to work seven mornings a week. Several had to come in for three hours on Sunday mornings to look after the horses, for which they were paid double time.

Gai already paid over the award wage and her stable was one of the few in Australia that paid a bonus for stable wins.

A roster system was worked but the dissidents didn't want to work on any Sundays. The AWU wrote to Gai asking to see time sheets and wage books and inspection was arranged for the following Monday.

On Saturday morning Gai called a meeting of her staff to see what it was about. She was angry because it had embarrassed the stables and could have been rectified if somebody had referred it to her.

While the meeting was in progress at Tulloch Lodge a female union delegate arrived and asked to attend. Gai refused, saying it was an in-house meeting and she wanted to hear what the problems were first from her staff.

The delegate showed her a card and demanded entry. Undiplomatically, Gai tore it up, handed the pieces back and asked the delegate to leave.

Blood pressures rose and on Monday a protest was held outside the stables and the TV cameras rolled. In a burst of unfavourable publicity, Gai was made to look like a Dickensian employer.

It went to arbitration and was eventually resolved.

Percy Sykes, master veterinarian and superdoc of the equine world, is among the professionals of the industry who pays tribute to Gai.

He told this writer that among the racing fraternity the reaction to Gai varied from antagonism to grudging admiration and respect for her ability.

After Gai had produced four Sydney winners on one day on top of three winners on a previous day, he heard two trainers talking about it.

Percy says, 'One said fancy getting four winners, and the other turned his back and said, wouldn't you if you had Tommy Smith as your fucking foreman?'

But Percy gives her enormous credit for achieving her success through her own ability.

'Very definitely,' he says, 'I must say it has surprised the living daylights out of me. I really thought things would collapse when Ernie left Tommy. They were such a duo I thought the dynasty would end.

'In a way Gai was lucky to have Tommy as the pathfinder, with the stable and staff. But the cupboard was bare when she came in and she had to develop her own string of horses and clientele.

'While her success has surprised me, I must say she's an avid learner, who doesn't have to be told twice. She listens to everyone's advice and forms her own decision.'

Percy Sykes declares that Gai is unquestionably a person in her own right. He recalled times when Gai and Tommy argued over horses and Tommy would say 'I part-own the bloody horse' and Gai would say 'and I bloody train it.'

They usually ended up doing it Gai's way. She is an individual, says Percy, not a daughter talking to her father.

He says, 'She is a great networker and her public relations is exceptional. She's a tireless worker with incredible enthusiasm and stamina.

'She likes people and can relate to everybody.

'I've never heard her make one critical comment about any other trainer or anybody else, which is very unusual in this business.

'Her most exceptional quality is loyalty. Her loyalty to Robbie is unbelievable.

'The difference between Gai and TJ? She has a nicer personality, is far more reasonable to deal with and is more lenient on her horses, and far more patient.

'You can't knock results. You can fluke a few things but you can't fluke repeated success.'

Dr James Whitfield, who has worked closely with Gai, describes her as a top professional for the way she runs her stable and handles her staff.

'Within the stable everyone respects her enormously for what she has done in a short time,' he says.

'Women trainers are in the minority and she set out to prove what a lot of people thought was beyond her.

'By working hard she sets an example and I believe a lot of the staff enjoy working for her. She does have set rules—clean shaven, punctuality, no shirts off in the stable, no earrings, swearing or smoking, will not tolerate people failing to turn up in the morning.

'She insists on the boxes being cleaned, the horses groomed and properly looked after. If a strapper misses something, she's right on to him. She can be very sharp but is frank and up front.

'Every horse that is galloped is trotted up before me twice a week for checking to prevent injury developing. In most other stables you are shown a horse only when the lameness is there. She never leaves a stone unturned and keeps her eye on everything.

'She alternates her horses from box to yard and walks them a lot.

'She swims them more than other trainers. The classic case was Pharaoh—I really think it was a fantastic feat of training to get the horse to the second Doncaster, let alone win it.'

Dr Whitfield says he knows for certain Gai is a trainer in her own right and no longer in the shadow of TJ.

'People may not fully realise it yet but Gai is no flash in the pan with TJ looking over her shoulder,' he says.

'She's a professional with the right background and I can see that she can do nothing but improve from here.'

John Inglis, managing director of the famous Sydney firm of thoroughbred auctioneers, describes Gai as an amazing person.

'There's not much of her and she doesn't look physically strong, but she has a lovely personality and untold energy and just keeps going. I think she's a tremendous person in the industry.

'I don't know anyone who informs her clients and looks after them better than Gai. I've known Tommy from the time he started.

'We used to think he was a one-off type, but she's just the same. Only being a girl, she sparkles and bubbles more.'

Jockeys who ride for various trainers are in a privileged position to form an opinion. Leading jockey Shane Dye describes Gai as an outstanding trainer who has the ability to relax horses.

'She's different because she listens and values your judgment,' he says.

'You can tell some trainers there's something wrong with a horse, and they take no notice. Gai does, regardless of whether it's the best or worst horse in the stable. She's sharp, a workaholic and a good talker—you have to be in this business.

'Gai is good at reading a race, too. But she had a good teacher in Tommy. Everybody rides a bad race and you know when you do. Gai is similar to Tommy in that she doesn't blow up when this happens or when things don't work out as planned—they both take the view that the race is over and nothing can be done about it.

'A lot of trainers don't keep their jockeys for long. Tommy kept them for years—George Moore, Malcolm Johnstone, Kevin Langby, Mick Dittman and me. Gai sticks to you too.

'She knows how to get her horses fit. Does a lot of

three-quarter pace which is why she has developed so many good stayers. It doesn't burn them out.

'Gai certainly knows what it's all about, no doubt helped by a good teacher. I think she is the equal of Tommy now, and in one sense has gone a step further through her publicity and marketing.

'For all I know she may still be learning from him, but at the track every morning she's the boss.'

Leading jockey Glen Boss says he believes Gai is so good it is a pleasure to ride for her.

'She's young, exciting and has brought an outstanding quality to racing,' he says.

'She knows exactly what she's doing. If you ring her on Saturday night after a race, she'll tell you when and where the horse is nominated for next.

'Her work load is amazing. I've said to her, if ever you write a book you'll have to call it "How to Work Eight Days a Week and 25 Hours a Day without Sleep".

'Gai can train a sprinter to stay, and not many can do that.

'She doesn't do this bang crash in one preparation but gives it a good patient grounding. She knows a horse's body may be willing, but the horse will not stay unless the mind is attuned that way. To do this with a horse gives owners more value for their money.

'Gai reminds me of the old cliché—it's taken her 15 years to become an overnight success. People look at the Gai Waterhouse of today but they don't realise all the hard work that has gone into the end result. She had one of the best educations any trainer could get from The Master himself.

'Her instructions for a race are usually spot on. She knows how races are run and if things don't go right, she can be very understanding. She has been very firm with me at times but she's pulled me aside to do that, not blown up in front of everybody.

'Some trainers fly off the handle and blow you up in front of the owners, but Gai might catch you next morning. She's professional.

'I think she is the up and coming trainer of Australia. She's not telling others how to do their job but others will have to do the same as her if they want to better themselves.

'I know she was in tears soon after she started when the owners took away one of the first horses she obtained. Now they're trying to get back into the stable.

'Sure, she got a lot of help from Tommy along the way. But in the end she's had to do it herself.'

CHAPTER TWENTY-SEVEN

HER CUP
RUNNETH OVER
. . . ALMOST

Soon after the new racing season began in August 1995, Gai experienced the bitter-sweet emotions of the sport.

With a strong team of horses behind her it promised to be her most successful year. Then at Randwick this day some of the punters for the first time demonstrated against one of her winners.

The horse, Licence Renewed, had been beaten by 10 lengths at its previous start at Canterbury when 3/1 favourite. But when it won easily next start in what punters considered a form reversal, they yelled abuse retrospectively through their pockets.

Gai was called upon by stewards and the press to explain. She pointed out it had been announced over the PA before the first race that Licence Renewed's work had improved since his previous outing and the horse was expected to run well. And on radio 2KY that morning she'd said he would be very hard to beat.

She told new Chief Steward Ray Murrihy the horse had not hit peak fitness as quickly in this preparation, perhaps due to a niggling sore back.

It showed the fickle nature of the sport. Some followers would settle for nothing less than perfection—a tough call.

Later in the day she accepted her trophy for being the most successful Randwick-based trainer for the season.

While responding to the presentation, she became emotional. Whether still upset from the earlier demonstration or whether the name Licence Renewed touched off a feeling, she did not know.

But while thanking the AJC she suddenly launched into a passionate plea to the Committee to allow Robbie back on the track.

She was seen on television throughout Australia and her words were reported in every metropolitan newspaper when she said, choked with tears, 'Please, please, if you have any compassion you will let my husband come back to the races after 11 years.'

Reaction was mixed. John Tapp, Channel Nine race commentator, said the timing was not appropriate but most people were moved by her emotion. It indicated the depth of her feeling and the strain she had lived under for so long because her husband remained a barred man, unable to join her in that part of society where she excelled.

It was the one joy still missing from a life that was otherwise fulfilled to overflowing.

Gai then sent out seven runners in the Metropolitan, thought at first to be a world record number of qualifiers for a Group One race.

But Tommy had done that before, saddling seven runners for the 1973 Epsom Handicap which he won with Lord Nelson.

It showed the strength of her stable.

In the big race her stayer, the favourite Stony Bay, tried to lead all the way, but was kept under pressure by Western Approaches, another of her runners. There was no team riding by Gai's jockeys.

Electronic, a fully exposed mare she bought in New Zealand

for $90,000 although it had won only one race there, put up a gutsy showing to win the $500,000 Metropolitan, giving Gai her second win in the race. She also trained the third and fifth placegetters.

The victory prompted her mother to say at the presentation, 'I never thought any trainer could be compared with Tommy Smith, but Gai is getting there.'

The scribes produced a new line: 'Sydney's darling of the turf.'

Gai next set her runners for the rich spring carnival in Melbourne hoping to culminate with The Cup, the race that stops the nation, where the full tapestry of Australian life parades and flaunts itself in one great cultural pageant. A horse race? Not at all.

Her colt Nothin' Leica Dane went out and thrashed the field in the $800,000 Victoria Derby, one of the most taxing of all races, giving her the eighth Group One of her short career.

The brilliant colt, in only his first preparation and ridden by Shane Dye, outclassed AJC Committeeman Jack Ingham's boom colt, the equal favourite Octagonal.

Part-owner Tommy had spotted the Danehill colt in a Magic Millions sale in Queensland and bought him with two others, Helen Dalton and John Hodge, for $165,000.

Gai was mobbed in the mounting yard by photographers and television crews. 'It's unbelievable, it's every trainer's dream,' she shouted above the melee. She became the first woman to train the Derby winner.

She had reservations about starting the young colt in The Cup.

He was due to be spelled and it had always been felt the two-mile Cup was too demanding for a three-year-old. But TJ said, 'We'll start him—we're having too much fun down here.'

One of the great regrets of his life had been giving in to pressure and scratching Tulloch from The Cup as a three-year-old in 1957, when most judges thought he would win.

The connections paid the $40,000 late entry fee for The Cup

and in a sensational performance Nothin' Leica Dane, badly checked by a clod of dirt in one eye, was desperately ridden by Shane Dye to finish second to the Lee Freedman-trained Doriemus.

In just three months the horse had gone from a maiden to almost winning one of the toughest staying events in the world.

Once more Gai had gone close to that 'impossible' dream.

The Melbourne press hailed her as Australia's leading trainer with Lee Freedman. Newspapers, magazines and TV gave her the celebrity status of a Hollywood star. Some commentators even attributed the resurgence in racing largely to her influence and popularity. Autograph seekers surrounded her in Melbourne streets.

To prove her selling power, the *Bulletin* ran a Cup special with her smiling picture in colour on the cover with an overlaid heading: 'GAI POWER. When she whispers, horses listen'.

Inside, her name was mentioned in only one paragraph. Her photo was used simply to sell the magazine.

When one of the Freedman brothers branded her a 'publicity seeker', respected Melbourne columnist Patrick Smith of *The Age* urged him to 'keep his mouth shut'.

'Waterhouse is the best thing that has happened to racing since Phar Lap,' he wrote. 'She gives it humour, expertise, glamour, dreadful hats and accessibility. We should all sing her praises.'

In Sydney the experienced turf writer Bill Whittaker predicted Gai would carry all the records before her.

'Provided she remains in good health, in the next few years she will win the Melbourne Cup, the Cox Plate, Golden Slipper and the other Derbies,' he declared.

At the time of the Melbourne Cup, Gai had another victory, this time nursing home a slow runner in the defamation stakes.

Her action against the *Daily Mirror* and *New Idea* six years before when they used Ernie Smith's comments about her, finally lined up at the starting barrier.

But her rival runners decided to scratch before going out on the track and settled, forfeiting the race. The prizemoney was said to be a large amount, including costs.

The legal luminaries who steered this listed runner home were the redoubtable and experienced Clive Evatt, appropriately a former member of the betting syndicate known as the Legal Eagles, assisted by barrister Judith Gibson.

Among the imputations raised in the articles were that Gai Waterhouse was incompetent as a racehorse trainer.

Ernie had said, 'I don't think a woman can run a racing stable.'

Gai's work load and insistence on personally supervising everything meant she had little quality time, or time out for herself.

No longer was there a game of golf or tennis or a night at the movies. Even reading novels was now rare.

Most people on coming home at night sat over a cup of coffee and turned on the television, but Gai's idea of relaxation due to her hyperactivity was to dust the furniture and clean the bathroom and kitchen. Although she had help in the house she did it every night before retiring and setting the alarm for just before three.

As a result Gai was often tired and sometimes exhausted.

Time was the killer. Any time at home, beyond the demands of her career, was spent on motherhood and marriage.

But if there was one part of her that was defensive, it concerned her children. Whenever the often-asked question arose on how she combined career, marriage and bringing up her children, her friends wished they could answer for her because they believed they could do it better.

She usually said things like, 'Oh, I get their cereal ready before I leave for the stables at 3.30 am, and I try to be home to see them off to school. I don't see as much of them as I'd like.'

Privately she complained about young Tom, saying he was inclined to fall asleep over dinner at restaurants, spent too much time on the telephone ('disgraceful'), was always running late and didn't listen when spoken to at home.

All her own characteristics!

Catherine Hale says of her:

'In fact, she does a fantastic job. And as well as looking after her own children, nobody mothers my children better than Gai. She mothers Lea Stracey's children too.

'She's always taking the brush to the hair of my eight-year-old, Sophie. She has taught my Amy to ride. And when I was having a difficult time with my 10-year-old Nick, she said he must come and stay the night. When her friends are frazzled with their children, she speaks to them with tolerance and understanding.

'Her children are well balanced and respectful, have good manners and love her dearly.

'I have often heard the implied criticism that if Gai is so good at horse training, how can she be a good mother too? Well, as a mother, she sets an excellent example.'

Gai was extremely upset when Tom, aged 12, went to the races one day with her during school holidays and was quoted in a newspaper, 'I enjoy the races and at least this way I can get to spend some time with mum. Kate and I see more of mum in the newspapers and on television than we do at home.'

Gai explained to him how this was untrue and hurtful. Every night, although her children would like to have eaten their dinner in front of the TV, she insisted on them sitting around the table as a family and discussing the day's events.

That was the quality time Gai looked forward to every day.

Regrettably, as her available time lessened, friends did not see as much of her and had to use the pager like everyone else to make contact.

Her job came first. As her friend Lea said, quoting an American writer, 'The only thing to do is hug one's friend and get on with the job.'

Gai's Rotorua friend, Liz Wells, said Gai was a caring person who had always encouraged her friends to achieve more in their lives.

'We don't see so much of her these days but we're happy to see her achieve so much,' said Liz.

In achieving her ambitions against all odds, Gai had inevitably made many personal sacrifices.

But when she walks into Tulloch Lodge in Bowral Street, Kensington, the place is now alive with laughter, excitement, industry and promise.

If Gai had not seized her destiny, the famous stable where the likes of Gunsynd, Redcraze and Kingston Town held sway would now be bulldozed to the ground by Tommy Smith in his transition from champion trainer to just being an owner.

In its place would be an impersonal block of units.

Who knows what champions of the future might have been forsaken?

On Monday, 22 January, 1996, Gai left her home in Clifton Gardens to drive to the offices of the Australian Jockey Club at Randwick.

She had been at the stables since before dawn and had rushed home to dress, hoping to reach the AJC by the nominated time of midday. She wanted to be by Robbie's side when the decision affecting them both was handed down.

Frustratingly she was delayed by traffic.

In previous weeks her husband and former glamour bookmaker had faced a public inquiry into yet another application to walk on to a racecourse in the distant wake of the Fine Cotton affair.

He had already spent 11 years on the outer after being warned off for allegedly having prior knowledge that Fine Cotton's race at Eagle Farm on 18 August, 1984, was a ring-in.

To make it easier Waterhouse said he would not apply for a bookmaker's licence for five years, only seeking the right to walk on to the track the same as any other member of the community.

Gai had sat beside him to give emotional and moral support as the hearing, spread over three weeks, developed into an outpouring of hatred in what was a private dispute in the Waterhouse clan.

Never before had the media feasted on a Roman holiday with an Australian family the subject of such juicy gossip and lurid headlines.

Newspapers, TV and radio played up what was billed as a Cain and Abel feud as Robbie's brother gave evidence against him, saying he was there to prevent him from returning to the races.

Sydney's best-followed soap opera, some papers called it. Others described it as Bad Blood, the Waterhouse War.

Gai gave evidence on the first day, describing the effect the ban on her husband had on the family.

'This has been a cause of enormous sadness because my husband has been denied what I call justice,' she said, looking directly at the committee.

'It's put a strain on our marriage over the past decade. It was the cause of me not being able to get a trainer's licence for two and a half years.

'I've tried to explain the situation to our children, Tom and Kate. I've told them to hold their heads high, not to be embarrassed or humiliated and to be proud of their father.

'They have learnt over their lives to cope with the situation. I'm not saying they cope well but they cope with it.'

Asked if she'd discussed Fine Cotton with her husband, she said yes, but only the fact that he wasn't involved in the ring-in. She wasn't concerned about the betting.

With patience, endurance and a heavy heart Gai faced up to legal barbs and innuendoes against her husband as she listened to what she knew much of the time were lies coming from the witness box.

She sat with Robbie near the united members of his family, his mother Suzanne, sister Mrs Louise Raedler, and when he was there, the patriarch of the family, Big Bill Waterhouse.

Suzanne Waterhouse told a TV reporter who asked her whose side she was on, 'I'm here to support my son, Robbie. That decision was made a long time ago.'

Gai missed attending on only one day, while still on her Christmas holiday with her children and parents in Austria.

She and Robbie had cut short their pre-paid Austrian skiing break by delaying their departure from Sydney for one week to suit the convenience of the AJC because its counsel was not available and as a result the hearing was held over to the following week.

But even after that delayed start Waterhouse missed out at the other end of his holiday as well by having to return early to be at the resumed hearing. The AJC knew the full details of his holiday situation but resumed for only one day in the week's break between Christmas and New Year.

To make it in time, he had to drive almost 100 kms through a snow storm along treacherous Austrian mountain roads due to the famous Arlberg Pass suddenly closing, scrambling on board his flight in Zurich with minutes to spare.

As things turned out, it really wasn't worth the effort.

Some witnesses the AJC relied on against Waterhouse had been shown in other hearings to be untruthful.

One aspect of the hearing was farcical to even the most casual observer. Many spectators and most witnesses bowed to the Committee on entering and leaving the hearing as if they were appearing before Supreme Court judges!

The tribunal members were not judges and it was not a court of law. This was 'AJC law' at work.

Sunlight streamed in from large windows behind the committeemen, reduced to six because of perceived conflicts of interest, sometimes diffusing the outline of their faces.

The 'witness box' was a table placed not in some neutral location but right next to the AJC's counsel.

The unsatisfactory nature of the hearing was apparent right from the opening addresses of the AJC's counsel, Robert Stitt QC, and Frank McAlary QC, counsel for Waterhouse.

Stitt, who had acted so aggressively against Gai in her discrimination case, said Waterhouse must satisfy the committee that although he was unfit when warned off, he was now fit. Present fitness was the ultimate question.

He said if Waterhouse wanted his warning off lifted, he should satisfy the committee he had given a full and truthful account of his involvement in the Fine Cotton substitution and the substantial betting that lay behind it. Each party was to outline the evidence on which they intended to rely.

McAlary took a different view. He said procedural fairness and natural justice had to be available to Waterhouse. A large number of findings had already been made and a problem he faced was to know which findings the committee would rely on.

'I have no difficulty with the findings already made but one of the problems is the underlying sleeper-type findings which are being run surreptitiously and without being openly stated,' he said.

'What I don't want is to simply discover as the case drags on that matters which I have never appreciated as being involved will suddenly raise their ugly head, and I will be told that has always been involved.

'I would ask in the orders you make to reflect the tradition of the English system of justice, where the person against whom a finding is sought has the opportunity of hearing the evidence and meeting it, not some form of Star Chamber or inquisitorial inquiry, in which the accused has first to go into the witness box and confess all, and then be cross-examined as in the Star Chamber about why he did not confess more.'

Asking for due notice of any additional findings Stitt might seek, McAlary said:

'I put it bluntly. If my friend wants to run the case that
Mr Waterhouse organised the whole thing, then he
should say so, and he should provide evidence about it.
What I don't want to do is to have him run that case
surreptitiously, under the table, never coming into the
opening and saying it.'

When the proceedings came on for mention again, Stitt said
it was wrong for McAlary to say by their approach the committee was regurgitating the Fine Cotton affair. 'Nothing could be
further from the truth. We are not re-running the Fine Cotton
affair,' he said.

McAlary replied that 'to hunt round and look at everything
that has ever been said about it and try to put a crowbar in and
lever that up to see if you can expose another little piece of
material is really to engage in a selective re-run of it.'

Later Stitt said to the Committee 'This is, I think, the third
time I have made this submission and my friend seems to be
incapable of picking it up. We are not re-running the Fine
Cotton substitution case. It is no part of my case to re-run the
Fine Cotton substitution scandal.'

But McAlary did not see it that way. At the next hearing,
referring to the evidence to be called, he said 'What we are getting here is a re-run of it and nothing else.' And he made similar remarks at other times.

McAlary accused the Committee of holding a kangaroo court
for breaking assurances to give reasonable notice of evidence
and allowing a long statutory declaration from Robbie's brother
to be admitted as evidence at the last minute.

When the AJC refused to allow an adjournment to give
McAlary time to investigate the statutory declaration, he and
Waterhouse walked out saying they would seek justice from the
Supreme Court. McAlary said he was not going to be ambushed.

Waterhouse, who had 'no commented' on his case for years,
took the unusual course of issuing a press release.

He said the Committee's original directions had ensured

fairness to everybody, giving him time to answer the case against him.

'Now,' he said, 'an extraordinary 65-page statement has surfaced at the last moment from my brother who is motivated by his personal animosity to me. This requires a thorough investigation.

'The AJC attempted to prevent the appropriate examination and investigation of this evidence by my counsel.'

The AJC then adjourned to a date which gave McAlary time.

McAlary told the resumed hearing it should not be a retrial of Waterhouse's involvement in the Fine Cotton affair—he had already been punished for that in his 11-year banishment.

The issue was whether he was a fit and proper person *now* to be allowed to walk back on to a racecourse.

He pointed out it would be 'double jeopardy' to punish someone twice for the same crime. It would be a denial of his civil rights if he were not allowed on to a racetrack now.

One of the main witnesses for Waterhouse's readmission was racing enthusiast Alan Jones, Australia's top-rating breakfast broadcaster.

He said that considering Waterhouse had been in racing exile for 11 years, he 'would have been better shooting a horse and killing a trainer' than having simply bet on Fine Cotton.

'There are murderers, rapists and burglars here at Randwick every Saturday—but no Robbie Waterhouse,' said Jones.

Then he touched on a raw nerve.

He challenged the Committee to look to its own record in regard to the licensing of Gai Waterhouse as a trainer.

'It is germane to this argument,' he said. 'She's gone from not being able to get a licence to become Mrs Racing. If you'd had your way and she had not fought so hard, your industry would have been much the poorer.'

In his summing up Stitt made much of the fact that Waterhouse had elected not to give evidence.

He claimed the unique feature of Waterhouse's warning off was that the 'true facts' of his involvement had never been disclosed.

'This is not a case where it is known with precision what really happened,' he said.

Stitt said the Committee had to decide whether Waterhouse had given a full and truthful account of his involvement in Fine Cotton and the substantial betting.

McAlary summed up by saying the hearing had been 'bastardised' as a re-run of the Fine Cotton affair, although his client could not be tried again for his Fine Cotton involvement.

He said he did not accept one word of what Robbie Waterhouse's brother had said in evidence. 'He is a total fabricator, amoral, a prevaricator and driven by nothing more than a desire to get money out of his family.' McAlary said the brother made his statutory declaration thinking it could never be contradicted by the discovery of records which luckily had turned up later.

In cross-examination McAlary had accused the brother of blackmail in demanding more than $1 million from a family trust, which the brother denied, and McAlary gave instances where two judges had attacked the brother's credibility as a witness, one judge describing him as a 'devious and unreliable witness'.

McAlary said Bill Waterhouse, who had been called as a witness, had given evidence on affidavit that he and Robbie were not involved in organising the ring-in. This, he said, was effectively accepted by Stitt who did not ask him one question on that.

He pointed out that John Gillespie and others had been convicted of organising the Fine Cotton substitution.

The hearing adjourned. On resuming, a large scrummage of media people gathered at Randwick to hear the AJC's finding.

As Gai neared the AJC in her royal blue BMW she half expected the decision to be unfavourable following an obviously-leaked report the day before in a Sunday newspaper.

After reading the report she had said to Robbie 'I don't think they're going to let you back in.'

'I'm sure I'll be getting back,' he said.

'As always, you're the supreme optimist.'

Right on midday Gai drove speedily into the AJC carpark.

Seconds later, Chairman Bob Charley began reading out the Committee's finding.

After preliminary remarks he came to the crunch:

'The Committee was denied its best opportunity to determine the applicant's present fitness by his failure to give evidence and submit himself to questioning by the Committee and/or counsel assisting the Committee.

'This has left uncontradicted a body of evidence not to his advantage.

'The onus rests with Mr Waterhouse to satisfy the Committee on the balance of probability he is now a person of character sufficient to establish a fitness to return to racing.

'On the whole of the evidence, that onus has not been discharged and consequently his application is refused.'

At that moment, at 12.03 pm, Gai burst into the Committee room and looked around for her husband.

He was sitting alone in the crowded room in the front row of chairs, a seat reserved alongside him.

Smiling brightly, she hurried across. The atmosphere was strained.

Before she could slide into the vacant seat he turned towards her and said without a flicker of emotion, 'We've lost.'

'What!' exclaimed Gai.

'They've turned me down,' he said, gazing towards the Committeemen once more.

Gai reached for his right hand and held it.

It was another kick in the guts for Australia's first lady of racing on an issue that had already dragged on beyond reason.

Most eyes were fixed on her. But her expression barely changed, defying the sense of outrage, sadness and disappointment she felt.

Gai was not about to show her true feelings to this audience.

She felt that as the hearing was largely a re-run of Fine Cotton, it had been pointless and a waste of time and money.

She believed the AJC had used her husband's failure to give evidence as an excuse not to let him back.

It was assumed he did not go in the box owing to an alleged conflict in evidence previously given over the origin of the money he placed on Fine Cotton. His counsel was confident he could answer the question.

McAlary did not want his client to go in the box and have the whole Fine Cotton affair opened up again. In his opinion it was irrelevant, he had been punished for that, and it was not the basis on which the hearing should have been conducted. If the AJC refused Waterhouse's application, he believed he would have grounds for seeking relief in the Supreme Court. But he considered the evidence against Waterhouse had been sufficiently discredited to give him the verdict.

McAlary also took the view that the AJC had had the right to call Waterhouse as a witness if it wished.

Gai's attitude was why should he subject himself to further interrogation when he had already told them all he knew?

She knew it was untrue to suggest he had not explained to the Committee his role in Fine Cotton.

Previously he had given them written evidence, with corroboration, and he had already subjected himself to lengthy interrogation on that evidence before members of the Committee, who included two QCs and two solicitors.

He had already denied he had anything to do with organising or financing the ring-in—that was already an integral part of his evidence.

So why the untrue suggestions by the AJC now that he had not yet given a full account of his Fine Cotton role?

And what was the 'uncontradicted body of evidence' against him? They did not say.

If the AJC meant the claim made at the inquiry that he and

his father had placed almost $1 million on Fine Cotton with SP bookmakers, McAlary showed that to be false.

The cheques representing money which Bill and Robbie Waterhouse had allegedly paid to SP bookmakers over Fine Cotton were produced by them to prove that this money had nothing to do with Fine Cotton but had been paid legitimately to other people.

Despite her disappointment, Gai's loyalty to her husband was as strong as ever.

He looked punch drunk and grateful for her support.

There was nothing left for them to do except walk outside and face the media, waiting in droves for comments and photos.

Before emerging, Gai said quietly to Robbie, 'The leaky ship that is the AJC leaked it all out yesterday in the Sunday paper.

'It just shows how incredibly ordinary are the people who sit on the AJC Committee when someone at the AJC can get away with this.'

Outside, he could only tell the press he was devastated.

Arm in arm with him, Gai said to reporters, 'I've never known a case where the punishment so outweighs the crime.'

Asked what he intended doing now, Waterhouse simply said, 'I'll consider my position.'

There was a limit to how much strain could be put on Gai and the children.

As Gai reflected on the scene, it occurred to her that the proceedings and all the hype and headlines surrounding the case were more like theatre than justice.

The audience had demanded that he step up to the footlights to deny the allegations to satisfy the craving for drama, conflict and sensation that the case had created.

From the public viewpoint, it was probably a mistake not to give evidence, although Waterhouse's legal advisers considered it to be a correct decision.

Clearly the AJC must bear responsibility for leaving the Fine Cotton issue still unresolved. It really wasn't a fair go to re-run the old Fine Cotton plot based on 'new' allegations 11 years old.

As McAlary said, the penalty for the crime was already adequate.

By their decision, they ensured the malady would linger on and come back another day to strike a further discordant note.

And what of the decision leaked beforehand to a national mass-selling newspaper?

The newspaper announced without qualification on its front page the day before the AJC decision was given that Waterhouse's application would be turned down. On two pages inside, it ran the story in great detail under the heading 'Robbie bid fails'.

Someone within the AJC pre-released that. Imagine the furore if a Supreme Court judge leaked his judgment to a newspaper on a public issue before handing it down?

The trouble with most statutory bodies is that when they are handed quasi or semi-judicial powers, the rule of law and the presumption of innocence often suffer.

It's unfair to the public to delegate these powers to statutory bodies which are not answerable to the public.

The AJC has not been answerable to anyone except itself for more than 150 years.

Unfortunately for Gai Waterhouse who longed for a favourable result, the AJC committee at the time was looking over its shoulder facing the first-ever challenge to its power when it considered her husband's case.

This may have led them to be more cautious than usual, leaving the issue up in the air and perpetuating an aura of mystery over the affair.

Their failure to resolve it would probably be taken into account by the New South Wales Government in deciding whether to remove control of racing from the AJC.

If the AJC is still concerned over the damage to racing from Fine Cotton, there is only one way now for the public to be assured of the truth.

There should be a public inquiry into the ring-in, either parliamentary or judicial, with broad terms of reference and vested with full powers to call witnesses and get at the facts.

I'd like to see that, and be a witness. The alternative is to accept the facts as they are known and put an end to the matter.

Three hours after the hearing Gai and Robbie were on a flight to New Zealand to attend more yearling sales, leaving the flaring publicity behind.

Gai had more important things to think about. With her positive approach to life and exciting challenges in her career, she would quickly recover from the hurt.

As soon as they were airborne Robbie apologised for the negative result after putting her through yet another ordeal.

'Look, Rob,' she said, cutting him short, 'we're so lucky. Things could be far worse. We have two beautiful, healthy children. They could be sick or seriously ill, some member of our families could be stricken down. We have a lot to be grateful for.

'Let's concentrate on productive things rather than waste our time worrying about the injustice just meted out by the AJC. They made a fiasco of it, we know that.

'There's my work and yours to take our minds off it, so let's just get on with our futures.'

Robbie had lost ground. He wanted to appear on national television to explain his position and minimise the damage.

But Gai said no. He had to think of the children.

They were both in exclusive Sydney private schools and television was a powerful medium.

The hearing was over and the children had to be protected from snide comments that would inevitably follow interviews with him.

Robbie still thought he should appear. Gai said with deadly emphasis, 'I won't stop you, but you know my feelings.'

He knew when not to push his luck.

He compromised with a radio and newspaper interview in which he said he'd needed all his strength of character to cope with the onslaught on his name and reputation and the effect on his family.

In the interviews he paid a handsome tribute to Gai, saying how grateful he was for her extraordinary support.

'I don't know how she keeps going at times because she's the one who keeps getting kicked in the teeth,' he said.

Gai was looking forward to a brighter future.

She had so many ambitious plans to embrace there was no time to dwell on negative things, past or present.

Of immediate interest was the current NSW trainers' premiership. With a few months left of the 1996 season, Gai was having an exciting tussle with John Hawkes.

If she succeeded she would not only be the first woman to do so and become Australia's leading trainer but she would also be the first woman in the world to achieve a major premiership.

Winning it was not a priority but she felt it would be nice to return the championship mantle in the near future to famous Tulloch Lodge where it had remained for so long with her father.

More than anything she wanted to win big races like the Cox Plate.

Gai's reputation had spread beyond Australia to Japan, Dubai, Hong Kong and Europe.

She was invited to enter her horse Stony Bay in the Japan Cup, placing her in the big league of international trainers. A trainer for the powerful Maktoum family of Dubai gave her one of his horses to train.

Perhaps she would take Nothin' Leica Dane to Japan next.

And she would hope one day to have a horse good enough to win the Prix de l'Arc de Triomphe, which she regarded as the greatest race in the world for quality horses.

Nothin' Leica Dane might be the one to do it next year.

Among her ambitions was to race horses in the Breeders Cup series in America, and in the King George and Queen Elizabeth Stakes in England.

And she would like to enter a horse some time in an annual novelty race in St Moritz, Switzerland, where she and Robbie and the children skied.

Wearing special spiked shoes the horses gallop on a frozen lake beside the Palace Hotel. It just appealed to her sense of fun, a grand social occasion for the jetset crowd.

In a new milestone to her popularity she was presented with the award of Racing Personality of the Year at the Australian Cup ball at the Regent Hotel in Melbourne. The first woman to win it, she joined the ranks of other winning personalities like Bart Cummings, Lee Freedman, Colin Hayes, Dermot Weld, the late Geoff Murphy and TJ Smith.

Gai's rise to championship class in only four years was meteoric.

To break through so quickly was akin almost to achieving the impossible.

Nobody expected her to outshine the new crop of trainers who began at approximately the same time—people like Alan Denham, Anthony Cummings, Sterling Smith, Alan Bell and Mark Connors—let alone blitz the big established trainers.

Gai was showing similar qualities, ability and determination as TJ Smith which enabled him to leave the bush as a penniless urchin in the depression and become a legend in his lifetime.

In the same way she had already shown the knockers and critics and old boy networkers what she could do.

If ever anyone answered her critics, Gai did.

Tommy did it his way, Gai was doing it her way.

His record in Australia could never be beaten but Gai hoped to carve out her own individual niche by making an impression in the highly competitive and expensive international racing scene.

Meanwhile, is there an AJC committeeman in the house?

One who has eaten enough crow to give the lady a horse to train?

Racing history was created in New South Wales on Tuesday, May 14, 1996.

The Minister for Gaming and Racing, The Hon. Mr Richard Face, announced he was stripping the Australian Jockey Club of its power to control the State's racing after an unbroken term of 153 years.

The new body taking over control and management of the thoroughbred racing industry from the AJC would be called the AJC Principal Club, with 10 voting members, four from the AJC, two each from the Sydney Turf Club and the Country Racing Council and one from the provincial sector.

One member would be from a new advisory committee representing owners, breeders, trainers, bookmakers, jockeys, industry employees including stable hands, and punters.

Punters!

In other words, a much broader cross section of those involved in the multi-billion dollar industry would now have a say in its operation.

Announcing this momentous shakeup, Mr Face said these reforms had come about in response to recommendations by Mr Ian Temby, QC in his 1995 Report on the industry, and following extensive consultations with the AJC, other race clubs and industry associations. Legislation would be introduced with a view to seeing the new body operating early in 1997.

Mr Face did not offer any criticism of the AJC. Indeed he paid tribute to it for its work over the past 150 years. But, he said, he believed even the AJC recognised the industry must move with the times and Governments throughout Australia were realising that participants in racing, and not just the race clubs, should have a say in their industry.

In the months leading up to Mr Face's decision being approved by State Cabinet, the AJC lobbied other NSW State Ministers, gaining an increase in membership on the new body from three to four and amending some other recommendations of Mr Temby. But the AJC failed to stave off major change.

The AJC will become an ordinary race club, like the Sydney Turf Club, responsible for just two racecourses, Randwick and Warwick Farm.

It will still wield a good deal of influence through its large membership on the new controlling body, but its trappings of power are gone. No longer will it control the Stud Book, the stewards, the drug testing laboratory. And a new appeal panel will be appointed to hear appeals that have always been the hallowed preserve of the AJC.

If it is found that the AJC influence on the new body is too strong, obviously the way is clear, now that the AJC's absolute power has been broken, for fresh rules to be introduced to maintain industry balance.

The new body will also be required to report on its activities each year in a public document, including independently audited financial accounts.

It took a Minister from the industrial, working class city of Newcastle to end the AJC's long reign. Richard Face earned the plaudits of bemused punters for giving them their first official, if minor, voice in the sport they alone keep alive. For without them, racing would not exist.

'Racing today,' said the late Phil Bull, publisher of the *Timeform* rating bible for punters when campaigning for change in the English Jockey Club, 'is a branch of the entertainment industry, subsidised not by direct grants from the Treasury but by punters' money, lifted out of their pockets.

'Don't let anyone kid you that racing is about improving the breed or the supremacy of the thoroughbred. Racing is about betting. In a modern democratic society an entertainment industry like this, heavily subsidised at the punters' expense, should at least be controlled and administered by a body answerable and responsible to the people involved in the industry . . .'

Racing is now completely divorced from its original concept when a group of amateurs under their own Royal Charter or Act of Parliament had the right to control their own sport, and spectators, dressed in their Sunday best, gathered to watch a match race between horses. In the context that racing is now a huge industry based on betting, autocratic control by an amateur body is no longer appropriate.

Introducing similar reforms to those imposed on the English Jockey Club in 1993, Richard Face was careful not to spell out specific reasons, saying only that it was time for change.

No doubt Gai Waterhouse, the courageous young mother who succeeded so brilliantly as a trainer after her heroic struggle with the AJC, played a significant role in fanning the winds of change. The episode proved a turning point in public attitude.

As a result of her victory and the example she set, more young women in a whole range of capacities can now look forward in the new era ahead to finding rewarding careers in the traditional male field of horse racing.

Due to her inspiration, they too can 'move with the times'.

GAI
WATERHOUSE'S
STATISTICS
AS TRAINER

1992
FEATURE RACES WON:
Group 1 Metropolitan (2600m)	Te Akau Nick
Group 3 Gosford Gold Cup	Moods

1993
Awarded the Sarah Kennedy Award for contribution to racing.

FEATURE RACES WON:
Group 1 Fosters Melbourne Cup (2nd place)	Te Akau Nick
Group 2 AJC St Leger Stakes	Te Akau Nick
Group 3 AJC Chairman's Hcp	Te Akau Nick
City Tattersalls Hcp	Protara's Bay
Prime TV Handicap (1400m)	Silver Flyer
Carlton Mona Lisa Plate	Pops Dream

TOTAL WINS FOR THE 1992–1993 SEASON: 25

1994
FEATURE RACES WON:
Group 1 $1 million Doncaster Hcp (Group 1)	Pharaoh
Group 1 VRC Derby (3rd place)	Stony Bay
Group 3 Liverpool City Cup	Silver Flyer
Derby Trial Stakes (Listed)	Stony Bay
Christmas Cup (Listed)	Pops Dream
Frank Underwood Cup (Listed)	Red for Go
Quick Eze Handicap	Protara's Bay

TOTAL WINS FOR THE 1993–94 SEASON: 40

1995

Awarded the Telecom Silver Horseshoe Award for Trainer. Awarded the VRC and Thoroughbred Racehorse Owners Association Archer Award for outstanding achievement and contribution to the racing industry.

FEATURE RACES WON:

Paramatta Cup (Listed)	Balmeressa
Prime TV Handicap	Persian Flyer
Triscay Plate	Light Up The World
Queanbeyan Cup	Beloako
Light Finger Stakes (Group 2)	Flight to Fantasy
Newmarket Handicap (Group 1)	All Our Mob
Chipping Norton Stakes (Group 1)	Pharaoh
Carlton Wellington Boot (Open 2YO)	Iron Horse
Birthday Card Quality Hcp (Listed)	Light Up The World
Ranvet Stakes (Group 1)	Stony Bay
Sky High Stakes (Listed)	Balmeressa
$1 million BMW (Group 1)	Stony Bay
Ajax Stakes (Group 3)	Protara's Bay
Queen of the Turf Stakes (Group 3)	Light Up The World
$1 million BMW Doncaster	Pharaoh
Carbine Club Stakes (Listed)	Juggler
Frank Packer Plate (Group 3)	Juggler
Ajax Stakes (Group 3)	Protara's Bay
Japan Racing Association Plate	Protara's Bay
West End Draught Stakes (Group 3)	Balmeressa
Gosford Gold Cup	Sprint By
Rough Habit Plate	Juggler
Australia Remembrance Cup (Listed)	Grand Connection
Ansett Aust. Premiere Stakes (Group 3)	Light Up The World
Warwick Farm Spring Cup (Listed)	Electronic

Carlton Wyong Cup (Listed)	Sea Captain
Tattersalls Plate (Listed)	Electronic
Kingston Town Stakes (Group 3)	Balmeressa
AWA Hills Stakes (Group 2)	Stony Bay
AWA Shannon Quality Handicap (Group 3)	Sprint By
Dulficy Quality Handicap (Listed)	Nothin' Leica Dane
Japan Trophy Race (Group 3)	Western Approaches
Spring Champion Stakes (Group 1)	Nothin' Leica Dane
Craven Plate (Group 3)	Stony Bay
Nissan Metropolitan (Group 1)	Electronic
Turnbull Stakes (Group 2)	All Our Mob
Canberra Cup (Listed)	Jay Bee Cee
Tattersalls Club Cup (Listed)	Pops Dream
Waterford Crystal Mile	Juggler
Norman Robinson (Listed)	Nothin' Leica Dane
Victoria Derby (Group 1)	Nothin' Leica Dane

1996

Awarded the VRC racing writer's personality of the year.

FEATURE RACES WON:

Challenge Stakes (Group 2)	Light Up The World
Hobartville Stakes (Group 2)	Nothin' Leica Dane
Chipping Norton	Juggler
Apollo Stakes (Group 2)	Juggler
Caulfield Autumn Classic (Group 2)	Iron Horse
Canterbury Stakes (Listed)	Sprint By
Canterbury Cup	Electronic

Ranvet (Group 1)	Electronic
Stanley Wootten Stakes	All Our Mob
Global Sky High Stakes	Darbaas
$1 Million BMW Doncaster (Group 1)	Sprint By
Japan Racing Assoc Plate	Darbaas
NEC St Leger Stakes (Group 2)	Linesman
Chairman's Handicap	Juggler
Gosford Gold Cup	Darbaas
Prime Minister's Cup	Electronic
Doomben Cup	Juggler